Postcolonial Netherlands

Dear Joan,

Thank you so much for your
inspiring keynote at our
emancipation-conference!

Kees-Jan

Bram

10-14-2011

Linda

GERT OOSTINDIE

Postcolonial Netherlands

Sixty-five years of forgetting,
commemorating, silencing

AMSTERDAM UNIVERSITY PRESS

The publication of this book is made possible by a grant from Netherlands Organisation for Scientific Research (NWO).

Original title: *Postkoloniaal Nederland. Vijfenzestig jaar vergeten, herdenken, verdringen,* Uitgeverij Bert Bakker, 2010

Translation: Annabel Howland

Cover illustration: Netherlands East Indies Memorial, Amstelveen; photograph Eveline Kooijman
Design: Suzan Beijer, Amersfoort

ISBN   978 90 8964 353 7
e-ISBN   978 90 4851 402 1
NUR   697

TABLE OF CONTENTS

Introduction   7

1 Decolonization, migration and the postcolonial bonus   23
    From the Indies/Indonesia   26
    From Suriname   33
    From the Antilles   36
    Migration and integration in the Netherlands   39
    The disappearance of the postcolonial community and bonus   44

2 Citizenship: rights, participation, identification   48
    The right to remain Dutch   50
    Postcolonial organizations: profiles and meaning   55
    Political participation   66
    Ambivalent identities   70

3 The struggle for recognition: war and the silent migration   73
    From war to exodus   75
    War and *bersiap*   76
    The 'cold' reception   81
    The uprooting of the Moluccans   85
    Veterans and the Indisch community   88
    Memorial culture   91
    West Indian and Dutch stories and silences around war and exodus   97

4 The individualization of identity   101
    Identity: individual perception, public significance   102
    Indisch identity, from Tjalie to Indo4Life   106
    Moluccan identity around and after the RMS   114
    Diversity without unity: Caribbean identity   117
    Recognition and erosion   125

5 Imagining colonialism   130
  The Companies   131
  'Something magnificent was done there!'   135
  The West Indies: without pride   144
  Colonial slavery, postcolonial settlement   148
  Unfamiliar discourses and new silences   155
  Pleasing everyone, all of the time?   159

6 Transnationalism: a turning tide?   163
  Decolonization, migration circuits and generations   165
  Citizens and their transnational orientations   168
  Postcolonial organizations and transnational politics   172
  Cultural transnationalism, 'diaspora' and community   184

7 An international perspective   188
  Migrations in post-war Europe   189
  France: republican dilemmas   192
  The United Kingdom: Britishness and multiculturalism   197
  Portugal: reluctant re-migrants   201
  A typical case: slavery in European memorial culture   203
  Colonial past and postcolonial migrations: a broad comparison   208
  Typically Dutch?   212

8 'Postcolonial' (in the) Netherlands   215
  Postcolonial migrants: integration, identification, community   217
  New ideas about the 'Netherlands'   223
  Intermezzo: international heritage policy   228
  Postcolonial studies in the Netherlands, a missed opportunity?   234
  The future of the colonial past   238

Notes   243
Bibliography   262
Acknowledgements   281
Index of people, organizations and memorial sites   282

INTRODUCTION

The Netherlands is a small, but densely populated Western European country, a large part of which was reclaimed from the sea. Once a prominent player in world history, it is now a middle-sized partner in the European Union. There have been times when the Dutch were proud of their accomplishments and their position in the world, other times when they were self-effacing or frustrated, and often all of these at the same time. This Dutch ambivalence has also caught the eye of foreign commentators. The British historian Simon Schama observed that even at the zenith of their power and wealth in the seventeenth century the Dutch were constricted by an 'embarrassment of riches'.[1]

The image of the Netherlands in the Golden Age is of a country of industrious workers, adroit merchants, ruthless colonialists, and God-fearing Protestants who took pleasure in their wealth with mixed emotions. This society was reputed to be exceptionally tolerant of religious diversity, to have a flourishing cultural and scientific life, to be a magnet for migrants, and a state that rejected the notion of a hereditary monarchy. The Republic liked to see itself as setting an example. But over the next few centuries it was increasingly cut down to size until it became a modest player on the world stage, significant in world politics largely because it managed to maintain its position as a colonial power, with the Indonesian archipelago as the pearl in its crown. And thus it remained, even after it became a monarchy following the Napoleonic Wars and, in 1848, a parliamentary democracy – albeit initially a strongly elitist one.

The Second World War brought the German occupation of the Netherlands, the Japanese invasion of the Netherlands East Indies, and American and British protection of the Dutch Caribbean colonies of Suriname and the Netherlands Antilles. It was not until later that the extent to which the Netherlands had suffered from its imperial overstretch became clear; the way in which the political elite stubbornly tried to avert Indonesian independence revealed a provincial mentality that did anything but tally with the domestically, widely-held conviction that the Dutch could teach the world, not just its colonies, about selfless development and gradual emancipation.

Indonesia refused to be appeased, let alone repressed any longer; only the two small Caribbean colonies voted to remain Dutch. 'Indië verloren, rampspoed geboren' (The East Indies lost, a disaster born) is how the colonial lobby presented the change to the Dutch, but this pessimism turned out to be unfounded. Even without its colonial wealth, the Netherlands showed robust economic growth in the post-war years, growth that was partly translated into a gradually expanding system of generous collective provisions. Decades of almost uninterrupted development once again turned the Netherlands into one of the most prosperous countries on the planet. The Netherlands also became a consumer society. In this it differed little from other countries in the Western world, but it was often experienced as a more profound rupture with the past, because the archetypical image of the Dutch had long revolved around a strong work ethic and great thrift.

Decolonization and increased prosperity brought great demographic changes. Just as in the Golden Age, the Netherlands once again became a land of immigration. In 1945, the population numbered around nine million inhabitants; today over 16.5 million. In 1945 the Dutch population was almost entirely white, today there are around three million 'migrants', first and second generation, most of whom come from the global South. The number of Dutch people with roots in the colonies is estimated to be around one million – colonial history has, literally, come home.

At the same time a radical shift occurred in the realm of religion and ideology. The image of the Netherlands as a Calvinist country may have remained unduly strong for centuries, as Catholicism continued to dominate regions outside the urban agglomeration of Amsterdam-Rotterdam-Utrecht, the Randstad. However, more decisive was the way in which religious and ideological differences had been pacified since the late nineteenth century. Verzuiling or 'pillarization' was key to this. Catholics and Protestants, but also socialists and liberals, organized themselves into their own 'pillars', presenting their members with a broad spectrum of duties, mores and services. Education, from primary school to university, was segregated into Catholic, Protestant and 'public' (non-confessional) institutions and each pillar had its own political parties, press, unions, and broadcasting corporations. Even the leisure sphere was subject to verzuiling, right down to the ideological persuasion of women's magazines and sports clubs.

In the post-war Netherlands, which had emerged destitute from the Second World War, this system – which has been termed 'consociational democracy' by the political scientist Arend Lijphart – had a stabilizing effect initially.[2] As the pillars' leaders kept their grassroots in line, trying to keep them away from other pillars, they increasingly found themselves having to reach compromises at a political and labour-relations level, where each pillar had something to gain. The post-war reconstruction of the country owed much to this policy of compromise. The turbulence of 1960s and '70s brought the first cracks in this pattern. The Netherlands launched into a rapid process of secularization and a strong wave of individualization pulled the rug from under *verzuiling*, which was increasingly experienced as claustrophobic. Within a matter of decades the Netherlands had changed from a sober and prudent country to one that was overwhelmingly secular, in which citizens took less and less notice of the traditional authorities. As sociologist Frank J. Lechner puts it, 'Once a stodgy backwater, the Netherlands earned a reputation as part of the international liberal vanguard'.[3]

The loss of the traditional socio-political compartmentalization of society and the arrival of large numbers of migrants from the global South were two unrelated phenomena. In retrospect we can establish that the way the issues of migration and multiculturalism were addressed by politicians and society as a whole was strongly influenced by the removal of traditional religious and socio-political divisions. On the one hand this was expressed in a drastic underestimation of the continuing significance of religion for newcomers, especially Muslims – the naïve notion was that they, as the Dutch had earlier, would soon lay aside their religion or at least come to regard it as a strictly private issue. On the other hand, and entirely within the spirit of the old *verzuiling*, there was an acceptance of religious and cultural diversity in the opinion that newcomers could easily retain their own culture while simultaneously integrating in the Netherlands.

The change, when it came at the end of the twentieth century, was dramatic. Whereas the post-war Netherlands had previously been praised for being a tolerant nation, which did not begrudge newcomers a safe place to live and where there was no room for racism, the social climate suddenly and dramatically hardened. Globalization brought enormous pressure to bear on the welfare state, giving rise to ever more open discussion, followed by ever harsher judgements, of the cost of immigration – despite continuing low unemployment, the levels of participation of certain groups of migrants in the labour market were perpetually low, while take-up of social provisions and levels of representation on the wrong lists of statistics (school drop-outs, crime etc.) was correspondingly high and therefore expensive. The theme of national identity was latched on to and far more parochially defined than it had been before. The bone of contention was the supposed unwillingness of Muslims – almost a million citizens – to identify them-selves with the Netherlands and to regard their religion merely as a private issue.

This was the Netherlands that around 2000 brought forth the phenome-non Pim Fortuyn, a flamboyant anti-politician who turned increasingly more fiercely against what he called 'backward' Islam and a political estab-lishment which, in his view, had condemned the Netherlands to a pathetic and counterproductive multiculturalism. Fortuyn was murdered in 2002, not by a Muslim – to the relief of many – but by a radical, white, animal rights' activist. Yet, his party enjoyed considerable success at the general election shortly afterwards, the effects of which echo down to the present day. In 2004, commentator, writer and filmmaker Theo van Gogh, famous for his tirades against Muslims ('goat shaggers') was slaughtered, his throat cut, in an Amsterdam street. In *Murder in Amsterdam*, Ian Buruma presents a penetrating picture of a new Netherlands in which praise of multicultur-alism was silenced and replaced by enormous doubts about whether Mus-lims could or, especially, wanted to integrate into the Netherlands.

This sentiment remained and in the 2010 general election the party of Fortuyn's political epigone, Geert Wilders, became the third largest party. A laborious cabinet formation process resulted in a right-wing, minority cab-inet of the conservative liberal party, the VVD, and the Christian democratic party, CDA. The cabinet had to agree its policies in advance with Wilders' PVV (Freedom Party), to guarantee PVV support in parliament, and it will have to continue to do so. And so the Netherlands, which in the past had a progressive and open reputation is now jointly governed from behind the scenes by a politician whose trademarks are a frontal attack on Islam, on migrants from the global South and on what he calls 'left-wing hobbies', such as multiculturalism and the arts.

Of course, no more than fifteen per cent of the population voted for the populist PVV and, of course, the VVD and CDA were heavily criticized for putting themselves in a position that made them so dependent on Wilders. The Netherlands is still a comparatively open society without hard, formal ethnic divisions and is still a land where open racism is not socially accept-able. But this does not diminish the fact that the social debate has incontro-vertibly hardened. In the early 1970s, British scholar Christopher Bagley praised the Netherlands for being 'one Western country which can claim a measure of success in its race relations' – that type of tribute is certainly not the first thing that comes to mind today.[4]

In the many debates about the problems and petulance of the contempo-rary Netherlands, it often appears as if migration, especially from the global

South, almost by definition leads to higher economic costs and an attack on social cohesion. The issue of migrants over the last few decades, in part influenced by the 9/11 attacks, has implicitly narrowed down to the Muslim population. *Postcolonial Netherlands* focuses on migration from the former colonies, which was largely an earlier and predominantly non-Muslim postwar migration from the South, and on the formation and relatively successful integration of the postcolonial migrant communities – one million, mainly non-white Dutch citizens. It is, moreover, a study of the national identity of a country that has come to realize – only in the last few decades and after the fact – that it has fundamentally changed; beyond its traditional *verzuiling*, secular, more firmly integrated into Europe, postcolonial and, whether it likes it or not, multicultural.

Let me continue this Dutch story from a personal perspective. In August 1961, just six years old, I set foot for the first time into my primary school. The German occupation was still recent history. My Johannes Post primary school, in the Amsterdam suburb of Amstelveen, had been named after a resistance fighter who had been executed by the Nazis. He had belonged to the Dutch Reformed Church and my school was a Dutch Reformed Church School; that is how things were organized in the *verzuilde*, compartmentalized, Netherlands of the day. *Verzuiling* was a matter of course and the war was still fresh in the memories of my parents and the stories of my teachers.

The Netherlands at that time was still almost entirely white. And yet, in my class, there was a Chinese-East Indian boy, a Moluccan boy and an Afro-Surinamese boy. These specifics did not occur to me until later. I played with them; the Chinese boy was later even best man at my wedding. I cannot remember having learned at school about where they came from or why their parents had come to the Netherlands. I do not think we ever talked about it amongst ourselves, even though they looked different and I may have thought, well what?... that they were just a bit different.

The school supported Protestant missionaries in Suriname – the Netherlands East Indies had been 'lost' and most Antilleans were Roman Catholics and consequently, I understand now, none of our business. We collected for the Evangelical Brotherhood, an offshoot of the Moravian Protestant mission. We sold boxes of glasses house to house, six in a box representing the 'types' that lived in Suriname. I remember an Amerindian, an Afro-Caribbean Creole, a Maroon and a Javanese, but there must have been an Hindustani and a Chinese too, or perhaps a *boeroe* (descended from poor Dutch immigrant peasants). In geography we probably also learned about the Antilles and Suriname, perhaps Indonesia as well, but I cannot remember having any idea why so many different 'types' lived in Suriname.

The decolonization of the East Indies was over and I associated wartime suffering only with the German occupation. At secondary school in Amsterdam we learned a bit about colonial history; the 'West Indies' were a footnote. When, in 1975, I saw TV news images of Surinamese in Amsterdam celebrating the transfer of sovereignty on the night of 25 November, I asked myself with casual amazement why they had come to live here in the first place. By that time I had begun to study social sciences and history at university and would ultimately specialize in Latin America. I did not learn about colonial history until late in my studies and then only as an optional subject. I learned nothing about that migration. I could quite easily have graduated in history without knowing a thing about colonial history or postcolonial migrations.

Since I graduated, the focus of my academic research for the last quarter of a century has been the colonial and postcolonial history of the Netherlands. The Netherlands has changed dramatically in this time, in part due to migration. I never imagined that I would end up married to the daughter of a postcolonial migrant. At primary school I sometimes harboured vague worries about what would happen if I were to fall in love with a Catholic, but I never dreamed that she might also be a different colour and come from a different background.

What is striking about the postcolonial Netherlands is that the religious difference that was so significant in our youth seemed to be irrelevant two decades later and never provoked any comment. The process of secularization has been thorough. The churches have almost entirely disappeared from our own lives and little thought is given to this around us. 'When two religions lie on one pillow, the devil lies between' is a disqualification of differences within Christianity from a distant past. No less illustrative of the postcolonial Netherlands is that the differences in our colours has always been a theme, but that only one of these colours is always noted. This does not detract from the fact that today there is a level of familiarity, intimacy even, with ethnic differences that was inconceivable in my youth.[5]

Forty years after leaving the Johannes Post primary school, I attended and was involved in the organization of two commemorations of the colonial past, partly in my professional role as director of the Royal Netherlands Institute of Southeast Asian and Caribbean Studies, founded in 1851 as an integral part of the Dutch colonial enterprise and today one of the world's largest libraries and research centres for these areas. On 20 March, 2002, a solemn ceremony in the *Ridderzaal* (Knight's Hall) in The Hague marked the founding of the VOC (Dutch East India Company) on the very same spot four centuries earlier. Queen Beatrix and PvdA (Labour) Prime Minister Wim Kok, surrounded by prominent figures from all kinds of social bodies, added lustre to the occasion.

More than three months later, on 1 July, the day on which in 1863 slavery was abolished in Suriname and the Antilles, the National Monument to Dutch Slavery was unveiled in Amsterdam's Oosterpark. A more modest and select number of prominent figures attended here – the business community was not interested in this event – but once again Queen Beatrix and Prime Minister Kok were in the front row. By attending both events they indicated that while the history of the VOC was still something to be proud of, its counterpart in the West, the WIC (West India Company), whose core business had been the slave trade, should fill us with shame.

That is fine, but it raises a question of consistency. Historians are not keen on competitions about misdeeds and victimhood, but they do like comparisons. As it happens, the VOC was no less involved with slavery and the slave trade than the WIC, but this fact has apparently been forgotten. The broader question then arises as to why certain episodes in colonial history have been forgotten and others remembered, with pride or shame, but seldom neutral. There seems to be a pattern here. Our understanding of the past reflects, to a degree, 'how it really was', but also the inclination to meet half way those groups who feel strongly attached to certain themes. In the most favourable instances, this can lead to new insights and a more balanced view of the past. In the worst instances, history is rewritten according to the motto 'Please everyone all of the time'.

Postcolonial migrants have played an important part in this ongoing process of reviewing our history and hence our national identity. A million Dutch citizens were born in the Netherlands East Indies, Suriname or the Antilles, or have one or both parents who come from the former colonies. Their arrival and assimilation were linked to post-war decolonization and to a broader history in which the Netherlands became a rich country and a more or less multicultural society.[6]

Postcolonial Netherlands is about these migrants and the country they found when they arrived and which they helped to shape, not always in harmony with the indigenous Dutch and other migrants. My aim is not to present a complete history of the highly diverse experiences of these postcolonial migrants, and even less of post-war society in the Netherlands as a whole. What I have tried to do is present a broad picture of the way in which migration changed the country and how, in the postcolonial Netherlands, such notions as 'citizenship', 'identity', 'community' and 'nation' have shifted. This research seems to me to be essential to a better understanding of the debates that are raging today on the subject of Dutch identity.

This raises more than enough questions. What desires were fostered by postcolonial migrants regarding full citizenship? How and by whom were these desires articulated? What space was given or demanded for this and to what extent did it change Dutch views of national identity and citizenship? Is there any point to continuing to view migrants from the former colonies and their descendants as separate communities?

Each of these questions requires elucidation. Desires regarding full citizenship have a hard edge; this relates to unhindered rights to travel to and take up residence in the Netherlands, to enjoy all the same rights that established citizens have and to put these rights into practice. Citizenship also has a softer side, often articulated in terms of the possibility of such intangible notions as identity and the space granted to all citizens, regardless of their differences, to join together in the national community, to belong. Efforts were made to retain cultural specificity, while also recognizing that precisely this specificity is part of the national identity. Processes that are described as bonding and bridging run through one another continuously.

I argue that postcolonial migrants took part in identity politics. This term refers to a form of social and political organization which aims to represent the interests of a group that feels itself to be 'different' from the rest of society. Ethnicity and cultural specificity are often the markers of difference. Identity politics demands the right to be different from what is regarded as being the norm. *Postcolonial Netherlands* reviews significant organizations and leaders, their strategies and forms of action. I have gradually become convinced that, in recent Dutch history, the successful integration of postcolonial migrants was a condition rather than consequence of identity politics, although the articulation of 'ethnic' desires according to the laws of 'strategic essentialism' could strengthen the significance of bonding a 'community'.[7]

The space ('political opportunity structure') that was dedicated to postcolonial identity politics grew over the years. This corresponded with changes in Dutch society, in particular the declining importance of *verzuiling* and the development of a minorities policy and ideas on multiculturalism. Where gradually more space was allowed for identity politics, it stemmed from the attractive, but empirically elusive assumption that this would boost identification with Dutch society and hence, ultimately, integration too – perhaps an echo of the 'pacification policy' of *verzuiling*, or the subsequent policy of 'repressive tolerance'. I draw the conclusion that postcolonial migrants were given more room for identity politics than other newcomers from the South.

Views on national identity change all the time and did so in the post-war Netherlands too. The loss of the colonies, the Netherlands East Indies in particular, played an important part in this, but so too did such factors as *ontzuiling* (secularization and the declining importance of *verzuiling*), the large numbers of migrants who took up residence in the Netherlands, and European unification. Migrants from the East Indies were confronted by a far more provincial country than later arrivals – though it remains a puzzle to what extent the intensive pre-war relations with the colonies would linger in the collective mentality of the Netherlands.[8] Both the loss of the Netherlands East Indies and the establishment of an Indisch community forced a reappraisal of pre-war views of the Dutch nation. This process has continued ever since, with the first generation of postcolonial migrants paving the way for a broadening of minds. New conceptions of Dutch identity gradually emerged and the significance of the colonies within it. The rediscovery of colonial history also led to new and remarkable inconsistencies and silences.

One cannot think, as a matter of course, in terms of one general or more 'postcolonial' communities. First one needs to establish that there is virtually no point to describing Dutch people from Indisch or Indonesian, Surinamese or Antillean backgrounds as a single community. This is not how they see themselves, is not how they organize themselves, and they do not behave either individually or collectively within these terms. More interesting is the question of whether the separate 'national' groups can be regarded as individually having a special relation to and place within the Netherlands. This was only true to a limited degree when they first arrived and, it seems to me, to have become even less relevant over time. From the colonial perspective, the extent of the sense of community was linked to such factors as ethnic difference and class distinctions. In the Netherlands, the idea of community was undermined by the changing of the generations, exogamy (long-term relations outside one's own group) and the declining importance of transnational orientations – even though in these respects considerable differences still exist between the various segments of the postcolonial Dutch. In any case, strategic essentialism grew to be increasingly at odds with the evaporation of a firm 'community'.

In *Postcolonial Netherlands* I introduce the notion of the 'postcolonial bonus'. Migrants from the colonies had both individual and collective advantages over other non-Western migrants. This involved both 'hard' judicial civil rights, advantages in the realm of cultural capital (knowledge of and familiarity with the Dutch language and culture) and the space that could be demanded for cultural specificity. This postcolonial bonus generally eased their integration and extended the duration of the different postcolonial communities. It also explains why in debates about Dutch history and identity over the last few decades, a relatively large amount of room has been extracted for postcolonial perspectives on colonial history. However, this postcolonial bonus is, I argue, now evaporating, along with the notion of 'postcolonial community' and hence, one may also predict, the end of postcolonial identity politics.

The history of postcolonial migrants takes place within a broader context in which the Netherlands became multi-ethnic and more or less multicultural without, moreover, needing or wanting to give up what were felt to be fundamental values and norms. I interpret both postcolonial identity politics and the political responses to it as an element in the process of these groups' integration. 'Integration' is a gauge for the degree to which a community, in this case immigrants, conquer a space for themselves in a society. My premise is that integration is worth striving for and even inevitable, if marginalization is to be avoided. One-sided and complete cultural assimilation is, however, not at stake. Where most newcomers and their descendants, while retaining elements of their own culture, over time adopt the most dominant public conventions of the land in which they have settled, they also always contribute to the development of these conventions. There has never been a culturally homogeneous understanding of nationhood in this continuous process, although an urgent demand did arise for what the influential Dutch commentator Paul Scheffer called 'a defined idea of the Netherlands'.[9]

There are different dimensions to integration. 'Hard' socio-economic criteria, such as income, labour-market participation, levels of education and housing, are considered to be relevant to this book and are looked at in brief, but not discussed in detail. More attention is paid to socio-cultural participation (politics, societies, religion) and, above all, to the process of identification with Dutch culture – whether aspired to or not – and how this culture was changed in the process and became more clearly 'postcolonial'. I argue that the desires of postcolonial migrants seldom conflicted with the core values of Dutch society; this explains why so many were ultimately accepted, but also raises the question why this sometimes took such an excruciatingly long time.

I should also clarify my use of the term 'postcolonial'. It has a simple descriptive meaning, of course, in the sense of after the colonial period, after decolonization and after the end of the Dutch colonial empire. Furthermore, in the next chapter I argue that even this apparently simple, chronological explanation requires qualification. The 'repatriation' from the Dutch East Indies was indeed a direct consequence of decolonization and occurred primarily during the transition and shortly after independence. The exodus from Suriname was set in motion by the prospect of a rapid transfer of sovereignty and took place largely prior to this transfer. Permanent migration of Antilleans to the Netherlands was a consequence of the Antillean refusal to accept independence. The decision to choose a postcolonial arrangement of non-sovereignty implies the continuing right to free access to the metropole.

However, in this book I use 'postcolonial' more broadly than simply in a temporal or demographic sense. Here it also alludes to the ways in which the colonial past and decolonization have left their material and immaterial legacies, ranging from metropolitan demographics, politics and culture, to the ongoing ideological and, possibly, psychological impact on all the nations involved. On the other hand, I do not consider my work as belonging to the paradigmatic field of postcolonial studies and the related field of cultural studies. As I will discuss towards the end of the book, I have serious concerns about the use of what I consider to be idiosyncratic jargon and the moralizing, heavily politicized character of, and lack of empirical research inherent to, much of this branch of academia.

Postcolonial Netherlands opens with a chapter in which I examine the relation between decolonization and migration, the characteristics of the different groups of postcolonial migrants and the course of their integration.[10] I discuss how one group benefited more from the postcolonial bonus than another and what role class played in this. I argue that it is becoming ever less fitting to speak of postcolonial 'communities', particularly in the context of changing generations and the frequency of exogamy.

The next two chapters discuss how postcolonial migrants' organizations struggled for full citizenship against the background of the development of a Dutch migration and integration policy. Where this involved the 'hard' dimension, the right to unhindered access and full entitlement, this struggle was, on the whole, successful. Where it was about compensation for unsettled accounts associated with involuntary migration to the Netherlands – at least for the repatriates from the Dutch East Indies – and what they experienced as a cold reception when they got there, the outcome was less satisfactory. Partly as a consequence of this, there was a far from unambiguous identification with the receiving society. Nonetheless, the assumption that Dutch with colonial roots grew to become citizens more than other migrants from the global South would seem to be justified.

Speaking of postcolonial migrants as members of a separate community presumes there is a distinct identity and an associated unique cultural heritage. This presumption cannot be taken for granted. In the fourth chapter I first examine whether these migrants saw themselves as bearers of a separate identity and how they defined and disseminated this uniqueness, then and now. I also look at the (dis)continuities between characteristics and discourses in the colonial world and in the postcolonial Netherlands. With this I once again question the notions of 'community' and 'identity'.

The struggle for the recognition of colonial history, a preeminent element in identity politics, is addressed in Chapter 5. Bridging and bonding were intertwined in the call for recognition and public remembrance: drawing on the past united the migrants, while at the same time linking them to the wider society, compelling it to broaden the terms of the imagined national community. New canonical formulae for Dutch history were thus formulated. However, such new conventions were far from consistent and often created new silences.

Research into relations between postcolonial migrants and their descendants and the country of origin can provide insight into the extent to which they are still distinct from the broader society and internally bond. In the sixth chapter I conclude that the meaning of transnationalism has distinctly diminished with successive generations and that there are clear and explainable differences between the different segments. This too has implications for the usage of 'community'. After all, where the orientation to the country of origin declines, postcolonial singularity and communality become correspondingly less important.

Comparison is vital to this research: between the different groups of migrants from the colonies, between these groups and other migrants, but also between the Netherlands and other countries. The Netherlands is just one of a series of European countries confronted with mass migration after the Second World War, both from their own colonies and elsewhere. The Dutch case is placed in an international context in Chapter 7. The most relevant comparisons turned out to be with France and the United Kingdom, although I also draw comparisons with other former colonial powers, European and others. There are significant differences in the leeway that was granted to (postcolonial) migrant culture and to critical views of colonial history. These contrasts relate partly to national memorial culture and partly to the scale and nature of the postcolonial migration.

In the final chapter I look back briefly on the arrival and rise of postcolonial communities, how they have broadened or become diluted, the evaporation of the idea of ethnic uniqueness and the simultaneous widening of the symbolic boundaries of Dutch citizenship, as well as the controversial and often inconsistent expansion of the imagined community of the nation. To this I add a short tour around postcolonial heritage policy – domestic, but primarily foreign. Here too a picture emerges of change, of a broader acknowledgement of the significance of colonial history for the Netherlands today. Postcolonial migrants played a pioneering role in the broadening of the national horizon, but this phase appears to be reaching its end. This does not mean that there is no longer social deprivation among postcolonial migrants or their children, much less that every Dutch citizen has made the colonial baggage its own. The focus of policy and debate has shifted to other migrants, who have no (post)colonial relation with the Netherlands. This raises questions, I argue, about the doctrine at the heart of postcolonial studies, with its strong emphasis on historical continuity between colonialism and contemporary postcolonial societies.

A pile of excellent studies have been published over the last few years on the migration from the Netherlands East Indies; the history of Caribbean migration has been less thoroughly chronicled, but is certainly not a blank page. The literature on migration and integration in the Netherlands is overwhelming. I have tried to make good use of all this scholarship, but, in view of the framework of this book, I have had to limit myself considerably: maintaining distance, remaining incomplete. This has meant that I have rarely portrayed postcolonial migrants, their organizations and leaders in detail, although I have addressed specific questions through many conversations and recently through a questionnaire." The same applies to the institutions, leading players, and Dutch society at large. I have abstracted more than some readers would like. At the same time, I have incorporated many personal experiences, which on the whole are not named; experiences of an often surprised contemporary who has played his small part in the rediscovery of colonial history.

Over the last few decades I have, in a variety of roles, spent much time in close contact with Dutch citizens with postcolonial backgrounds. I have witnessed the emotional significance of colonial history as it is rooted in solidarity, including the outrage at things that were felt to be unjust, whether past or present. Emotions sometimes ran high and have not left me unmoved. But I have usually remained an outsider, by choice and/or ascription. My engagement has been founded on a more intellectual and critical premise, towards all the parties involved. This has sometimes led to incomprehension and impatience, back and forth. I have also commented on the absurdity that in every postcolonial community there is discontent about how little the average white Dutch person knows about *their* backgrounds, while their own interest in other migrant communities, even postcolonial, is equally limited. I have seldom seen a Moluccan attend the 1 July ceremony to commemorate Caribbean slavery, an Antillean at an Indisch event, a Hindustani on Aruba Day; and seldom a 'postcolonial Dutch' person at 4 May Remembrance Day ceremonies. People tend to celebrate and remember in their own social circles and complain about the lack of a widespread recognition that they themselves are unable to muster for others. Furthermore, it is striking that the modest numbers who do attend these events contrasts starkly with the size of the supposed grassroots.

I have discussed such observations at length with prominent members of all these groups. At times these were difficult conversations, especially when my observations were interpreted as a denial of emotions and justifiable desires. It was often difficult to convince them that this is not for me the issue. The final line of defence for some of my interlocutors was that even the Dutch commemorations on 4 May – the day of the German surrender in 1945 and since then the national war remembrance day – has become less and less a matter of course and less broadly attended: that is simply the way things go, over time. This objection, which in itself is correct, merely underlines that little can be taken for granted in Dutch memorial culture today. Yet, it is not incompatible with my position: that the time for postcolonial commemoration is drawing to a close.

In *Postcolonial Netherlands* I sketch a picture of political and intellectual processes around identity and community. How individual (post)colonial migrants and their descendants experienced their backgrounds in the past and how they do so today has largely been left out of this picture. This does not mean that I believe these experiences to be unimportant, that those involved have themselves forgotten or try to forget their own origins, nor that I think they should. The experience and celebration of ethnicity as a feeling of solidarity and security goes far deeper than passing nostalgia.[12] I am equally not suggesting that the wider society has come to accept the different postcolonial communities without any questions or doubts, and I am certainly not saying the Netherlands is free of racism. Rejection frequently pushes people precisely to identify more strongly with their own ethnic group. My argument is simply that a postcolonial background provides less and less grounds for political organization and that identity politics defined along 'ethnic' lines will only continue to lose its force. In my view, this shift was possible partly because the Netherlands, quite rightly, became postcolonial, also in how it grasped and tentatively accepted colonial history and its legacies.

Thus the Netherlands became more open than it had been before – certainly more open than when I, sitting on the school benches at Johannes Post primary school, could assume that 'we' were all born and brought up in the Netherlands and that brute violence was something that had been inflicted on our country long ago by Spanish Papists and recently by Nazi Germany.[13] Colonial history returned, came 'home', with the migrants from the colonies. Since then we have been trying to find a way to accommodate this past, sometimes refreshingly, perhaps all too predictably, often guiltily, frequently inconsistently; always looking for an elusive balance.

1

DECOLONIZATION, MIGRATION
AND THE POSTCOLONIAL BONUS

In retrospect, the story of postcolonial migrations to the Netherlands presents itself as three straight-forward series of cause and effect. The independence of Indonesia unavoidably led to the exodus of the groups which had been linked to the colonial regime. The hastily executed 'model decolonization' of Suriname inevitably led to the migration of half a nation. The decision to keep the Netherlands Antilles within the Kingdom of the Netherlands meant that Antilleans would continue to settle in the wealthier, European region of the Kingdom.

In reality, decolonization nowhere went according to predetermined planning and Dutch politics was, time and again, surprised by the unforeseen phenomenon of postcolonial migrations. Successive generations of Dutch politicians failed to shine in terms of vision or sense of realism. In this they differed little from their colleagues in neighbouring countries. As psychologically and strategically unprepared for decolonization as the colonial powers were on the eve of, and even following the Second World War, they equally failed to anticipate the scale of the migrations that would write the final chapter in their colonial histories.

This chapter discusses and compares the dominant themes of post-war migrations from the three former Dutch colonies and the patterns of integration that ensued. This history is then placed within the broader context of migration, integration and government policy in the post-war Netherlands. Migrants from the Dutch East Indies/Indonesia, Suriname and the Antilles all had the benefit of a 'postcolonial bonus' which, however, has become devalued, little by little, along with the notion of the 'postcolonial community'.[1]

The term 'postcolonial' requires some clarification. In the narrow sense of the word it simply means 'after the colonial era', in this case also post-war. Following this, postcolonial migrants came to the Netherlands, which was no longer a colonial metropole and hence now postcolonial itself. Reality was more complicated than that. The Netherlands decolonized in fits and starts and with surprising outcomes. The migrants from the Netherlands East Indies indeed arrived in the Netherlands shortly after decolonization, forced to leave Indonesia or at least convinced that there was no future for them there. The term 'postcolonial migrants' fits this otherwise heterogeneous group without further qualification.

However, most migrants from Suriname left for the Netherlands not after, but on the eve of independence. They voted more or less with their feet against the transfer of sovereignty. The link between their arrival and decolonization is, therefore, somewhat different, but can nonetheless be clearly defined as 'postcolonial'. The relation between the migration of large numbers of citizens from the six islands of the Netherlands Antilles and decolonization is different again. The explicit and consistent refusal of the islands to accept the 'gift' of independence gave rise to a complicated postcolonial arrangement which combines elements of autonomy and neocolonial subordination. One of these elements is the full citizenship of the Kingdom of the Netherlands and, consequently, the unrestricted access of Antilleans to the 'metropole'. Hence, the Antillean community in the Netherlands did not come about as a result of independence, but precisely because this step was not taken. For these reasons it will also continue to grow and a decision to choose independence later will be almost impossible. The 2010 dissolution of the constitutional entity of the Netherlands Antilles meant that the six islands seceded from one another, but remain within the fold of the Kingdom. The notion of 'postcolonial', therefore, only applies to the Antillean community if we qualify current kingdom relations as such. And there are valid arguments for doing so.

The Netherlands can also be described as 'postcolonial', at least in the sense of 'after decolonization', in that it took its leave of Indonesia and Suriname in succession and settled into permanent postcolonial political ties with the Antilles. However, more is contained within this term: the suggestion of a continuation of a colonial history, not only through the migrants, but also through contemporary legacies and obligations stemming from the colonial period, which somehow affect all Dutch citizens. Much of the postcolonial debate in the Netherlands, as will become clear later on, revolved around the interpretation and acknowledgement of the colonial past, including possible continuities into the present.

Speaking of 'postcolonial migrants' might suggest closed communities which feel a natural bond with one another. Neither of the two applies. There were strong internal divisions within each of the three postcolonial 'communities' when they arrived in the Netherlands, and since their arrival inte-

One of the last boats carrying 'repatriates' from Indonesia arriving in the Netherlands in about 1962. By far the largest number of migrants from the former colony disembarked between 1945 and the mid 1950s. The last, minor peak in 1962 was caused by the handover of New Guinea to the United Nations and hence, indirectly, to the Republic of Indonesia. (COLLECTION INTERNATIONAL INSTITUTE FOR SOCIAL HISTORY)

gration and exogamy have blurred the borders between them and the surrounding society. Equally, there was no natural sense of solidarity between migrants from different colonies: Dutch with colonial roots associated themselves with the Netherlands East Indies, Suriname or the Antilles, but rarely with the broader context of colonialism itself.[2]

The three postcolonial migrations more or less succeeded each other. This meant that the migrants arrived in a country that was becoming more clearly postcolonial over time. Immigration from Indonesia peaked in the first five years after the Second World War, coming to a halt by the early 1960s. At the beginning of this period the Netherlands was destitute, to the extent that many Dutch were themselves emigrating. Fifteen years later, by which time immigration from Indonesia had trickled to a standstill, the Netherlands found itself in the midst of a period of stupendous economic growth, yet the social structure was still firmly anchored in *verzuiling*. The Surinamese exodus dates from the 1970s. By this time the Netherlands had become a land of immigration, an initially painful transition to a postcolonial economy was taking place, and secularization and impatience with old socio-cultural models was leading to the breakdown of *verzuiling* and to social and political renewal. Antillean migration did not peak until the 1990s. The Netherlands by then had become wealthier, more European and more multicultural than ever before, but it was increasingly divided on the subject of the integration of minorities and questions of national identity.

FROM THE INDIES/INDONESIA

Post-war migration from Indonesia was the most voluminous of the three postcolonial migrations. The history that led up to it, the migration process itself, and the episodes of settling and integrating in the Netherlands have all been thoroughly described in recent studies, in far more depth than the later Surinamese and Antillean migrations. It is striking that these studies – in particular Ulbe Bosma and Remco Raben, *De oude Indische wereld*; Hans Meijer, *In Indië geworteld*; Wim Willems, *De uittocht uit Indië*; Bosma, Raben and Willems, *De geschiedenis van Indische Nederlanders*; and Henk Smeets and Fridus Steijlen, *In Nederland gebleven* – were government funded. They were commissioned not only in the hope that they would mark the end of an era, but also as a final gesture of respect for the first and second generation migrants, perhaps even a compensatory gesture.[3]

The migrants from Indonesia were ethnically diverse. In all cases they were minority groups which had had a direct relationship with the colonial regime. The colonial system distinguished in law between three ethnically defined groups. Europeans and 'foreign Orientals' (*vreemde oosterlingen*, primarily Chinese and Arabs) formed small minorities alongside the overwhelming 'native' majority. The juridical category Europeans included immigrants from the Netherlands and their offspring (*totoks*), as well as Indo-Europeans, or *Indos*. Later, this group, with its stronger cultural and ethnic ties to the East Indies than the *totoks*, became known as Indisch Dutch.[4] In 1942, during the Japanese occupation of the Netherlands East Indies, around 300,000 'Europeans' lived on the archipelago, 175,000 of whom were Indo-European, just under 100,000 *totoks*, and a few tens of thousands of other Europeans. Their share of the total population was marginal: on the eve of the Second World War there were 70 million inhabitants in the colony.

The Japanese interned the *totoks* in camps during the occupation, separating men from women and children. Many *Indo* men were interned as well; other men and most women and children from this group lived outside the camps, but also in perilous conditions. Indonesian independence was declared on 17 August, 1945, two days before the Japanese surrendered. This was followed by the anarchic *bersiap* period (named after the motto 'be prepared') and futile attempts by the Dutch to restore their authority – four years of the kinds of atrocities that are inherent to contested decolonization processes.[5] Between the end of the war and the final chapter of decolonization – the handover of New Guinea in 1962 – almost all who were European under colonial law opted for repatriation, often reluctantly.

The composition of the migrant community gradually became broader than it had been just after the war, when *totoks* had dominated. The majority of those designated as 'rooted in the East Indies', i.e. the *Indos*, also sought sanctuary in the Netherlands. Depending on their class, many had a degree of knowledge of the Dutch language and culture, but only a small minority had any firsthand experience of the Netherlands. Their more-or-less Asian appearance made them visibly 'different'. In the colony, class and colour distinctions had divided the 'Europeans' – the *totoks* versus those who were 'rooted in the East Indies', and had resulted in subtle subdivisions within the *Indo* group. In the Netherlands, such distinctions would over time become somewhat erased by the memory of a shared past and resentment about decolonization and the 'chilly' reception all had received in the Netherlands.

The 'repatriation' of the lion's share of those defined as European, totalling between 250,000 and 300,000 people, was no party.[6] In the Dutch East Indies, most *totoks* and at least some Indo-Europeans had enjoyed a good life and considerable status. During the war and the *bersiap* they had endured a wretched time. The hope of returning to their old lives afterwards turned out to be an illusion. Almost always disillusioned and often destitute they accepted the involuntary 'journey back', leaving behind a number of lost years. If only the Netherlands had protected them better from 'the Japs' and the 'collaborator' Sukarno, who in their view had misused the Japanese occupation to further his despicable nationalist programme...

In the Netherlands, as many were to experience, there was little and decreasing sympathy for the resentment they felt about the end of colonialism and their complaints about inadequate accommodation and the cold reception they had received. Requests for compensation for lost possessions and unpaid salaries were turned down. The Netherlands was too busy with its own reconstruction and with forgetting about the East Indies to pay much attention to the Dutch repatriates. Moreover, they increasingly came to be regarded as reactionaries who longed to return to a gilded colonial existence. The initially silent *Indos*, now designated Indisch Dutch, were still seen as outsiders, for the time being – difficult to place and not taken completely seriously in a country that was still almost entirely white. In most later studies of 'European' repatriates, the distinction between *totoks* and Indisch Dutch is more diffuse, more so than it had been in the Netherlands East Indies. Estimates of the total size of the Indisch population often include all the migrants who came from the former colony, although the picture was dominated by the largest group, the *Indos*. Crucial is how unrepresentative the migration from Indonesia was. The category that was defined as European under colonial law consisted of only a fraction of the colonial population, but dominated the migration. Almost no *totoks* remained behind in Indonesia and only very few Indisch Dutch; with the exodus their history in the archipelago came to an abrupt end.

This did not apply to the three groups of non-European migrants: Moluccans, Chinese and Papuans. The contemporary Moluccan community in the Netherlands descends mainly from a group of 12,500 immigrants who arrived in 1951, a vast majority of them soldiers in the Royal Dutch East-Indian Army (KNIL) and their families; almost all were Christians.[7] They were demobilized in the Netherlands against their will. Most of these Moluccans were poorly educated, spoke limited Dutch, had had modest social status under colonial rule, and were regarded as 'natives'. Their ties to the colonial authority and their post-war support for the struggle for an independent republic, Republik Maluku Selatan (RMS), made them pariahs in the new Indonesia – and in the meantime they had come to make up just a small part of the entire Moluccan population in Indonesia. In the Netherlands too, their post-war history would be marked by marginalization.

Measured in terms of command of the Dutch language, levels of education and social status, the cultural capital of the Moluccans was as weak as that of the ethnic Chinese who settled in the Netherlands was strong. There had been a large Chinese population in the colony for centuries. This *peranakan* Chinese population had developed an elite which, in the higher echelons of the late-colonial hierarchy, was put partially on an equal footing with the Europeans. Their children went to Dutch schools, some became Christian, a few hundred studied at Dutch universities. From this group, a small minority – less than 10,000 – ultimately decided to settle in the Netherlands; the ethnic Chinese population in Indonesia was well over a million. Their socio-economic integration in the Netherlands was highly successful, though in socio-cultural terms this group remained relatively closed for a long time. These Indisch or *peranakan* Chinese, in a recent study referred to as 'initiated outsiders', are only briefly touched upon in this book. This in part reflects their small number – estimates range from 20,000 to 40,000 – and the fact that this well-educated and socially successful group rarely features in debates about minorities. What is more important is that they have displayed remarkable internal cohesion, but have never contrived to translate this, either symbolically or politically, into identity politics – not in Dutch society and even less so towards Indonesia, where many familial and commercial ties are maintained to this day.[8]

Papuans are also not addressed in this publication. Their numbers in the Netherlands are small, in the order of a few thousand. In 1962, the Dutch government under severe international pressure handed the former New Guinea over to Jakarta 'for the time being', in anticipation of a free referendum that never came. From that moment on, a few isolated Papuans in the Netherlands agitated for independence. The struggle of these men – Nicolaas Jouwe, Marcus Kaisiepo, and later Saul Hindom and Victor Kaisiepo – was fruitless, as was the struggle that was fought in Papua itself. There were internal divisions and the militant Papuans in the Netherlands became increasingly less relevant to independence fighters in Papua. The Hague ignored them as much as possible and they went almost unnoticed in Dutch society.[9]

The Netherlands, we may safely assume, was not eager to accommodate all these newcomers. And there were many reasons for this. Initially there was the illusion that the Dutch East Indies could be retained and the migration consequently symbolized defeat. More consequential post-war factors were the desperate state of the Dutch economy; the housing shortage; the belief that, with nine million inhabitants, the country was already full; and pessimism about the future. Indeed, in the early post-war years, the government actively stimulated the emigration of around 350,000 Dutch, mostly to Canada and Australia.[10]

This is why it was possible for people to express their doubts in public, and even more so in private, about the wisdom of allowing into the Netherlands those who were 'rooted in the East Indies'. Certainly, their European status gave them the right to come. Moreover, their position in Indonesia became stickier by the day. But what were the chances of successful integration in the Netherlands and would they really want to assimilate? Members of government and top civil servants expressed their considerable reservations in private. Labour Prime Minister, Willem Drees (PvdA), felt that accepting a large group of Indisch Dutch was 'highly contestable'. However, in public he spoke of the Dutch 'duty' to 'welcome' them. In so doing, he acted from a conviction that would dominate for decades to come: that the political elite must not allow any room for xenophobia, it being hard enough as it is to accommodate newcomers."

What happened next is well known. By far the majority of 'repatriates' wanted to integrate as quickly as possible and were even prepared, if necessary, to become fully assimilated 'potato gobblers'." The government intervened wherever necessary, in particular through an active housing policy. The gradual improvement of economic conditions also facilitated their entry into the labour market. And so the integration of the Indisch Dutch ran smoothly in the end. A success story, judged the British sociologist Christopher Bagley in the late 1960s. His study *The Dutch Plural Society* states that the Dutch held few prejudices for people of a different skin colour, as long as they adapted. Respect for other cultures, Bagley claimed, was deeply anchored in Dutch society. The government helped a bit by investing massively in social areas where immigrants needed some initial help. A contemporary study published under the auspices of the Ministry of Culture, Recreation and Social Welfare, exuded the same optimistic, even self-satisfied air."

Different times! Few academics today would so unreservedly sing the praises of Dutch openness. The change is unsurprising. At the time Bagley carried out his research, the number of 'newcomers' in the Netherlands was in the order of 400,000, a vast majority of whom were 'Europeans' from Indonesia. A lot has changed since then. The number of immigrants has multiplied, far more problems have arisen, and the minorities debate has become focused on Islam. Bagley was able to paint such a rosy picture of Dutch tolerance around 1970 because it had barely been tested by the 'repatriates' from the Dutch East Indies. Tolerance, it seems in retrospect, was also a euphemism for indifference.

It is telling that once Dutch minorities policy got going in the 1970s, the Indisch experience played little more than a background role. In early studies, such as *Allochtonen in Nederland* (Verwey-Jonker, 1971) and *Immigratie en minderheidsvorming* (Van Amersfoort, 1974), some attention was still paid to the Indisch Dutch, but they later disappeared from view. They played no part in subsequent minorities policies, thanks to what was regarded as their 'silent' integration. They also did not feature in the increasingly more detailed documentation of 'problematic' migrants.

The profile of the largest postcolonial community in the Netherlands, labelled 'Western migrants' in contemporary statistics, can only be approximately determined (Table 1).

Table 1. Population figures of the Netherlands, proportion of postcolonial and non-Western groups, 1960-2008

	1960	1970	1980	1990	2000	2008
Total population	11.4 million	13.0 million	14.1 million	14.9 million	15.90 million	16.4 million
INDISCH DUTCH Total				404,200A	403,900A	458,000B
1st generation	203,000A	204,000A		140,000A	138,900A	179,000B
2nd generation				264,000A	265,000A	280,000B
MOLUCCAN Total		25,900C	35.200C			42,349
1st generation						ca. 10,000
2nd generation						32,349
SURINAMESE Total	12,900A	28,985D	157,091	232,776	302,514	335,799#
1st generation			126,107	158,772	183,249	185,284
2nd generation			30,974	74,004	119,265	150,515
ANTILLEAN* Total	approx. 2,500D	13,630	40,726	76,552	107,197	131,841#
1st generation			29,515	54,881	69,266	78,968
2nd generation			11,211	21,671	37,931	52,873
MOROCCAN Total	approx. 100 E	17,400E	69,464	163,458	262,221	335,127#
1st generation			57,502	112,562	152,540	167,063
2nd generation			11,962	50,896	109,681	168,064
TURKISH Total	ca. 100E	23,600E	112,774	203,647	308,890	372,714#
1st generation			92,568	138,089	177,754	194,556
2nd generation			20,206	65,558	131,136	178,158

Source: Statistics Netherlands (CBS), unless stated otherwise:

a. Nicolaas & Sprangers, 'Buitenlandse migratie', 38, 40, 44; including Moluccans.

b. Including Moluccans. Beets et al., Demografische geschiedenis, 79-82, Beets, Van Imhof & Huisman, 'Demografie', 58 (458.000 Indische Nederlanders, 2001), Nicolaas & Sprangers, 'Buitenlandse migratie', 38, 40, 44. The illusory growth between 2000 and 2008 stems from differences in definition.

c. Penninx, Schoorl & Van Praag, Impact, 19.

d. Oostindie & Klinkers, Knellende koninkrijksbanden, II, 225.

e. Blok, Bruggen bouwen, 61.

* From all six islands of the (former) Netherlands Antilles; the vast majority are from Curaçao.

Statistics Netherlands' estimates for the third generation: 22,000 of Surinamese origin; 9,300 of Antillean origin; 3,100 of Moroccan origin; and 5,000 of Turkish origin.

The number of the first and second generation of Indisch Dutch and repatriates is estimated to be more than half a million, if one includes the Moluccans and the almost 15,000 Chinese who came from the Dutch East Indies. The Moluccan community contains almost 45,000 souls. There are no representative socio-economic or cultural statistics available. It is clear that the Moluccans are still less integrated. They are, therefore, also the only community with Indisch roots that still falls under Dutch minorities policy, even though they have been registered as 'Western immigrants' since 2000.

Is it still relevant to speak of an 'Indisch' community and if so, who belongs to it? That depends. In *Ons Indisch erfgoed*, Lizzy van Leeuwen demonstrates that for *totoks* the emphasis placed on their Indisch experiences was a matter of choice, whereas for *Indos* it was unavoidable. In his biography of the Indisch protagonist Tjalie Robinson, Wim Willems makes clear the extent to which the notion of 'community' was reinvented in the Netherlands.

Arrival of Surinamese migrants at Schiphol airport c. 1975. Mass emigration followed the announcement by the Surinamese cabinet of Henck Arron in February 1974 that Suriname would become independent at the end of 1975. About a third of the population voted with their feet and chose the security of the former 'metropole' over the young republic. (COLLECTION INTERNATIONAL INSTITUTE FOR SOCIAL HISTORY)

identity' could be taken less and less for granted. [...]ally a community apart. Only in the last decade [...]egun to draw closer together, both in the cultural [...]government, where the main concern is publicly [...]e war. The Chinese Indisch community has not [...]ective part of the Indisch world. Insofar as one can [...]munity', this is manifested mainly in a socio-cul-[...]round questions of identity.'[14]

[...]raphically complicated too. The *totok* group has [...]solved into Dutch society; this is not the case with [...]However, the integration of these segments has [...]vel of interpersonal relations. As early as the 1950s, [...]sch Dutch started marrying indigenous Dutch, a [...]d ever since; the same applies to the Moluccans.'[15] It [...]half of all Dutch with 'Indisch roots' have parents and/or partners who are not, or are only partly Indisch or Moluccan. This not only makes every estimate of the scale of this postcolonial 'community' contestable, it also makes clear that the very existence of a distinct community has become highly debatable, especially now we are talking about a third or fourth generation.

FROM SURINAME

Shortly after the war, there were a few thousand Surinamese living in the Netherlands; in 1970 this was 30,000; in 1980 almost 160,000; today there are more than 335,000 (Table 1). This number is still way below the total population of Indisch origin, but, for Suriname, it reflects a far more dramatic history. Where the migration from Indonesia was by no means representative in ethnic terms and in demographic terms only of minor significance, the migration from Suriname took on the character of an exodus. More than a third of the population, a representative section of the population, left the country in the mid 1970s. Ever since, the Surinamese population has grown faster in the Netherlands than in Suriname; today around 40 per cent of all Surinamese live in the former metropole.[16]

Once again, decolonization provided the impetus for the migration, but the context for what Henk Wesseling says was 'the first true colonial hangover' was entirely different.'[17] Where post-war Dutch governments had tried to retain the Netherlands East Indies within the Kingdom, around 1970 it was the Netherlands that wanted to steer the former colonies towards independence. There were various reasons for this. The Hague was weary of its colonial image and wanted to avoid having to intervene in the policies of Suriname and the Dutch Antilles, which were autonomous countries within the kingdom. Alongside this, economic aid to both countries increased considerably, which provoked many questions back home. Finally, the migration issue began to play a role. The presence of more than 40,000 Surinamese and Antilleans in the Netherlands was felt to be undesirable; a transfer of sovereignty would also bring an end to Caribbean migration.

History ran a different course from the one planned by The Hague. Dutch politicians failed to convince the Antilles to accept independence, but they were able to do business with Suriname. In February 1974, the Surinamese government, under Prime Minister Arron, announced that Suriname would accept independence at the end of 1975 – news that struck most of Suriname like a bolt out of the blue. The announcement led to frantic negotiations, deep divisions within Suriname itself, ever more concessions from The Hague – intended to ensure the separation went ahead – and the beginnings of a veritable exodus. Independence, consequently, lost much of its gloss straight away and the Republic of Suriname got off to a seriously weak start. Economic and political problems in the years that followed led to more emigration, which was ironically eased by the generous terms for access to the Netherlands that the Surinamese government had negotiated prior to independence.

Doubts about whether the Surinamese could integrate successfully in the Netherlands were expressed more broadly and more loudly in administrative circles, the press, and socially than they had been in relation to the Indisch migration: 'Stop the Bijlmer express!' read the weekly *Elsevier*'s headline in 1974.[18] Suriname, so the argument ran, was much less socio-economically developed and levels of education and work experience among migrants were far lower; this could only cause problems for the Dutch job market and put too much demand on what by now was a sophisticated Dutch welfare state, but which had been under strain ever since the oil crisis. Racial arguments were rarely used openly. Concern about the ability of the new arrivals to adapt were expressed in veiled terms, just as the worries about those 'rooted in the Indies' had been previously. The fact that the Surinamese immigrants were ethnically and educationally highly heterogeneous played almost no part in the Dutch debate. The rights of the Surinamese to Dutch citizenship and, consequently, residence in the Netherlands, ultimately remained intact up until the transfer of sovereignty on 25 November, 1975 and, in actual fact, until 1980. Only then did the Surinamese become real 'foreigners'.

Despite the initial widespread pessimism, thirty-five years on Surinamese integration in the Netherlands is often praised for its success. There is good cause for this. The unemployment figures among Surinamese Dutch have gradually fallen and are now lower than any other non-Western minority group. The Surinamese are also relatively successful in the realms of education and income; only the figures for juvenile delinquency are unfavourable. However, this good news has to be qualified on two points. A gulf between the Surinamese and indigenous Dutch populations is still visible, even in the second generation and it is unclear whether this gap will close in the third generation. It is also doubtful whether all ethnic segments of the entire Surinamese-Dutch community integrate equally successfully.

This question brings us back to the ethnic composition of the Surinamese community. This seems to be a reasonable reflection of the Surinamese population around 1975.[19] At that time, Surinamese of African descent made up just under fifty per cent of the population and Surinamese of Asian descent just over. The Afro-Surinamese, also known as the Creoles, fell into 'urban Creoles' and Maroons. The Creole urban middle class was the most 'Dutch' in terms of religion, culture and language, the Maroons the least; culturally, most Afro-Surinamese fell somewhere between the two poles. The majority of the Asian population was of British Indian origin and a minority hailed from Java. The majority of the former group was Hindu, a significant minority was Muslim, as were most Javanese.

Suriname was not (and is still not) a melting pot, but a pluralist society in which ethnic difference continued to play a vital role. Nonetheless, the education system served nation-building in a paradoxical way. Through this system, Dutch, which was not the first language of any ethnic group, became the binding national language. This would ultimately facilitate integration in the Netherlands, but prior to that gave rise to an exclusive orientation towards the metropole, which would culminate in the exodus around independence that was so tragic for the republic.

How significant were ethnic differences for the integration of Surinamese in the Netherlands? There are remarkably few hard facts available on this subject, because it is a methodologically complex topic, but perhaps also because it is considered to be a thorny subject. The little comparative research there is suggests that inter-ethnic differences are not (yet) very large; the question is whether this research is representative and, above all, whether it is indicative of the future. After all, one cannot assume that all ethnic groups integrated equally easily. In Suriname, the Asian groups have managed to turn their initial disadvantage around and are now regarded as more successful than Afro-Surinamese; there are indications that a comparable process is taking shape in the Netherlands. In the United Kingdom ethnicity is an obvious indicator of social mobility, whereby Hindus are far more successful than 'Black Britons'.[20]

From this perspective it is risky to interpret general indicators of the social integration of Surinamese Dutch very optimistically. Relatively favourable statistics for the whole community may disguise ethnic differences and poor performance of the Afro-Surinamese segment. Indeed, concerns about this have been expressed in recent years by this very community. It is feasible that a number of negative indicators for social integration that apply to Antilleans in the Netherlands, but which are equally relevant to West Indians in the United Kingdom, or Afro-Surinamese in Suriname itself, also apply to a section of the Afro-Surinamese community in the Netherlands. This issue is only lightly touched upon in this book, namely, insofar as ethnic distinctions within the Surinamese community are thematized as such. This usually occurs, unsurprisingly, only furtively.

Surely, then, it is hard to speak of a single Surinamese community in the Netherlands. Just as with earlier migrants from the Netherlands East Indies, it is not simply a question of ethnicity, but also class – the higher the class, the more Western the education and orientation – and, again, generation. Soon the second generation of Surinamese Dutch will be larger than the first and the third generation is already estimated to be 22,000. But how 'Surinamese' are those later generations, even in demographic terms? Once again the estimates are extremely tentative, but, as with migrants from the Netherlands East Indies, they suggest a strong increase in the frequency of interethnic relations and, consequently, children of mixed descent. This means that the notion of 'community' also changes with the advance of the generations and refers more to a choice of identity than to origins. To make things even more complicated, interethnic relations with white Dutch are more frequent among the traditionally more Western-oriented and overwhelmingly Christian Afro-Surinamese (and Antilleans) than the culturally and religiously more closed communities of Asian Surinamese. Afro-Surinamese are therefore closer to the indigenous Dutch population in this respect.[21]

FROM THE ANTILLES

Of the three postcolonial migrations, the one from the Antilles was the last and the least voluminous, but has since become the most controversial. This can be explained by recent problems with Curaçaoan migrants and the fact that the Antillean migration continues uninterrupted. This again stems

from the consistent rejection of independence, which has enabled Antilleans to retain their citizenship of the Kingdom of the Netherlands and thereby unhindered access to the Netherlands. Once again there is a direct link
between the course of decolonization and the postcolonial migration, but
this time it is antithetical. Free access to the Netherlands even became Antillean citizens' most important argument against independence – and such
a large proportion of the Antillean population now lives in the Netherlands
that the perspective of political separation has, in fact, vanished.[22]

The Antillean migration can be called 'postcolonial' because the Charter
of the Kingdom (1954) marked the formal end of the colonial era. Over the
last few decades it is precisely Antillean politicians who have resisted pressure from The Hague to accept a transfer of sovereignty arguing that decolonization was completed in 1954. In this view, which is now considered nationalistic by the islands, the postcolonial phase began more than half a
century ago. But outsiders continue to describe the current political relationship, including the migration, as colonial or neocolonial – just as the
relations between France and her overseas *départements* or the United States
and Puerto Rico. As will become clear later on, there are several parallels
between these post- or neocolonial arrangements and the ensuing migration processes.[23]

Strictly speaking, it is inaccurate to speak of *the* Antilles or *the* migration. The six islands, which shortly after the war were given the collective
name 'the Netherlands Antilles', were previously referred to as 'the Colony of
Curaçao' or 'Curaçao and Dependencies'. The political construction of the
Netherlands Antilles-of-Six ended in 1986 when Aruba was allowed to step
out of the Antillean relationship, while still remaining within the Kingdom. The dismantling of the country of the Antilles-of-Five was completed
in 2010. The terms 'Antilles' and 'Antilleans' used in this book are, therefore,
conceptually imperfect, but still the most useful.

When speaking about Antillean migration, moreover, we need to specify
that by far the largest number of these migrants originated from Curaçao. If
we compare the scale of the 'Antillean' population in the Netherlands
(132,000) with that of the six islands (around 300,000), we have to speak of an
exodus. The comparison becomes even more telling when we realize that
more than 100,000 Curaçaoans live in the Netherlands and around 140,000
on the islands.

A majority of Antilleans is of African descent, the most important exception being the large mestizo population segment of Aruba. The official
language of the Leeward Islands is Papiamentu, on the Windward Islands
English. The level of education on the Antilles is low compared with Euro-

pean standards, which implies, among other things, that most Antilleans speak mediocre to poor Dutch. What are the other characteristics of the Antillean migration to the Netherlands, apart from the spectacular increase since the 1990s? First, there is the circularity, continuing problems with integration and, partly as a consequence of this, political controversy. The circularity, the character of the to-ing and fro-ing, is linked to the possibilities citizenship offers; unlike migrants from Indonesia or Suriname, Antilleans have the right to settle now here, then there, without having to worry about being refused entry into either the Netherlands or the Antilles.

The problems around integration are relatively large, at least in relation to a section of the Antillean population. In contrast to a well-educated and integrated middle class, there is a large group that is poorly integrated and which scores highly on all the wrong kinds of lists – from dropping out of school, through unemployment, to crime. The association of Antillean migration with social order issues explains why the 'Antillean dossier' has become politically highly controversial over the last decade for the first time in parliamentary history. Through the Dutch minorities debate, the islands of the Antilles became the subject of such substantial parliamentary controversy that, against The Hague's better judgement, a definitive split with the islands (imposed independence) became a topic of political debate once again.

The large scale of Antillean migration reflects a paradox that is no less characteristic of other non-sovereign islands in the Caribbean. Compared with the rest of the region, the standard of living is high, and civil rights and freedoms, the functioning of democracy and territorial integrity are all excellently protected. That much of this is thanks to the 'neocolonial' status of these islands is something the local population on all six islands understand all too well; this is why they consistently refuse to take the final step towards independence. At the same time Antilleans know that many things are even better organized in the metropole. And, precisely because they have the right as Dutch citizens, many choose to seek such opportunities across the ocean.

This is also the story of Antilleans in the Netherlands. That their migration at first generated few problems, but now more, is not illogical. Initially it was mainly the middle class that settled in the Netherlands, often temporarily, to study. This segment is still there, but the long-term deterioration of the situation on Curaçao has had drastic consequences. Over the last ten or fifteen years, unemployment has been consistently high on the island, education standards have dropped, including the command of the Dutch language, and the influence of international (drugs) criminals has grown.

These social problems have been translated to the Netherlands. A growing section of the Antillean – primarily Afro-Curaçaoan – migrants was underprivileged and poorly educated. They spoke inadequate Dutch, and often had no options open to them other than social security benefits, income from petty crime, or both. In addition, the majority came from single, young mothers, which is a well-known risk factor. In other cases, national borders would close in the face of such migrants, but not inside a political entity such as the Kingdom; chain migration did the rest.

Thus a picture formed that of all postcolonial migrants in the Netherlands, precisely the Antilles – the only collection of tropical (is)lands still constitutionally tied to the Netherlands – produced and, moreover, continue to produce the least successful migrants. This may be too sombre a picture. There is also a group of highly successful Antilleans in the Netherlands. Furthermore, the history of mass Curaçaoan migration is still relatively young; it is perhaps too easily forgotten that in the initial phases, the earlier migrations from Indonesia and Suriname were also accompanied by integration problems. However, these subtle distinctions do not necessarily lead to optimistic prognoses.

MIGRATION AND INTEGRATION IN THE NETHERLANDS

In 1945, the population of the Netherlands was just over nine million, today it is 16.5 million, more than three million of whom are post-war immigrants and their offspring. This demographic development alone is spectacular, certainly from the perspective of the early post-war years, when the Netherlands was said to be full and the government organized mass emigration. Add to this the changing ethnic composition of the Dutch population: more than a million postcolonial migrants; over 800,000 Muslims, mainly from Morocco and Turkey; and smaller groups of migrants from all over the world. The Netherlands as a whole is becoming multicultural, a condition that has characterized the big cities for quite some time.

A lot of social unease surrounds immigration and integration issues. One reaction to this, intended to be reassuring, is that the Netherlands already has a long history of immigration, the outcome of which in the past was, on the whole, positive. This is true, especially in the period when the Netherlands was a rich oasis in Europe, but the relevance of this nuance is disputed. Integration is never straightforward and takes time. Even so, the question remains whether the result is always positive. One question is whether cultural difference in the past was less important than it is today;

in earlier centuries migrants usually came from neighbouring, culturally more similar countries. A second consideration is that the labour market in the past was not 'disrupted' by government provisions: migrants who found no work or could not hold down a job had little opportunity to stay long in the Netherlands. Moreover, the correspondence between earlier migrants and the labour market was more favourable than it is today in a post-industrial economy. The weight of these respective factors is hotly debated among scholars and politicians alike.[24]

What is clear is that the Netherlands in 1945, unlike France and the United Kingdom, had only limited recent experience of foreigners settling permanently in the country and even less so of colonial migrants.[25] Equally, there was no geographical centre operating an active policy to bind separatist regions to the national culture. The *verzuilde*, 'pillarized', Netherlands had no strong tradition of directed nation-building and felt it could also do without; the *verzuilde* institutions would help willing newcomers to assimilate. The hesitation about whether to allow large numbers of Belgian refugees into the country during the First World War, or Jewish refugees from Nazi Germany during the interwar period, was prompted by economic or political motives, not by concern about national identity. The free access of migrants from the colonies to the pre-war Netherlands was not a serious topic of discussion, because their numbers were so small. It is therefore hardly surprising that the post-war arrival of people 'rooted in the East Indies' provoked many concerns, as the arrival of Surinamese and Antillean migrants was to later. It is more surprising that the initial agitation about the first wave of migrants of colour had no consequences for government policy and that in the recruitment of migrant labour from the Mediterranean region, little thought was given, by neither the left nor the right, to the possibility of these foreigners settling permanently in the Netherlands.

In the 1950s and '60s, the reception of repatriates from the Netherlands East Indies was arranged at a basic level – more targeted, but frugal and paternalistic. The government organized and financed things like (dispersed) housing, otherwise leaving as much as possible to private, primarily church, initiatives. Assimilation was the undisputed goal. In the 1970s, the Netherlands, now much wealthier, was taken more or less by surprise by the massive influx of Surinamese and Mediterranean migrants. National coordination was meagre, policies for the different minorities were fragmented across three ministries, and local councils had to concoct their own policies. The illusion of return, but also a more open social climate, led to a slackening of the goal of complete integration. Consequently, in the 1970s, space was created to accommodate 'the preservation of one's own identity' and migrants' organizations came to qualify for government funding.

The *Etnische minderheden* report (Ethnic minorities report, 1979) by the Scientific Council for Government Policy (WRR) articulated what was still a controversial realization at that time, that the migrants would stay in the Netherlands. By now there had been the Moluccan train hijacking and a few small 'race riots' and the rise of a small number of xenophobic politicians like Hans Janmaat had begun to take shape; something was brewing, it seemed. In 1983, outlines for a relatively systematic integration policy were laid down in the first Minorities Bill, this time from the Ministry of the Interior and Kingdom Affairs. A general policy (for the disadvantaged) became the norm, while policy aimed at specific minority groups was seen as second choice. Socio-economic integration was increasingly more explicitly endorsed as a top priority almost across the board in the House of Representatives. Nonetheless, the next Scientific Council for Government Policy report, *Allochtonenbeleid* (Immigration Policy, 1989), concluded that the policy had failed, that too much focus was still being placed on cultural issues, making minorities too dependent on government provision. Once again the Council was proved right. Work, education, and assimilation were the spearheads of the policy, including in the Purple Coalition's bill *Integratiebeleid etnische minderheden* (Policy for the integration of ethnic minorities, 1994). Half a decade later, anti-establishment political leader Pim Fortuyn would successfully argue that it had all been too lax – and ever since all parties have hardened their positions and multiculturalism and even prudent cultural relativism has become regarded with suspicion or quite simply as an anathema.[26]

Discontent about the multicultural Netherlands over the last few years has led to a caricature of the policy that was implemented; it is presented as if (left-wing) The Hague had thrown the borders wide open for immigrants, without placing any demands on them in terms of integration and assimilation, and, under the flag of multiculturalism, had discarded national culture. The reality was just a bit different. Like its European neighbours, the Netherlands had tried from the 1970s to execute a restrictive immigration policy; but this too had only a limited effect, until recently, because the instruments were inadequate and social resistance was, indeed, strong. The room to experience cultural specificity was considerable; however, this can sooner be attributed to avoidance and the absence of a policy, rather than the deliberate encouragement of diversity.

Integration, argue migration historians, takes time; only in the third generation can anything meaningful be established about whether a specific group of immigrants has integrated successfully or not. The disadvantages and problems experienced by the first two generations obscure other more favourable developments, which require more time to evolve. In this view, Dutch immigration policy suffers from counterproductive impatience. This optimistic view is not without its challengers. Sceptics stress that migration history also teaches us that not all groups of migrants integrate with the same ease. Certainly not if they take their problems with them to other – in terms of work and education – far more demanding worlds, where welfare provisions conceal rather than solve the problems. The more pessimistic view has, over the last decade, translated into ever broader criticism of what has been described as 'weak' or ineffective integration policy. The Blok parliamentary committee (2002-2004) seriously questioned whether this policy, which cost 1.6 billion euros between 1980 and 2003, had indeed had any impact on integration.[27]

Questioning the effectiveness of the policy is not the subject of this book. Yet, it must be said that the image of a naive, multiculturalist immigration policy is one sided. The decision at the end of the seventies to adopt a national minorities policy was prompted by significant concerns about the integration of Moluccans, Surinamese and 'guest workers' from Mediterranean countries. The glorification of diversity at that time was simply not an issue. The *Minderhedennota* (Minorities Bill, 1983) mentioned a 'multicultural society' and 'adjustment on both sides', but explicitly expected the immigrants largely to adapt.[28]

In line with the long tradition of *verzuiling*, a lot of room had already been created and subsidized for minority organizations from the 1960s, also on religious grounds; far more, unsurprisingly, than in centralist France with its republican tradition.[29] In the decades that followed, the government continued to attune its policies to the leaders of these organizations. This sometimes led to naive aims, making it possible for 'integration while retaining one's own identity' and 'education in one's own language and culture' to be looked back on in scorn. However, political and thus financial support for that policy rapidly evaporated.[30]

In the 1980s, the government settled on a policy in which the role of the 'categorial' welfare institutions for individual ethnic minority groups was limited. This policy has not altered since. The government finally set up the national minorities consultation platform LOM (*Landelijk Overleg Minderheden*, 1997) which included representatives from SIO (*Surinaams Inspraak Orgaan*), LOWM (*Landelijk Overlegorgaan Welzijn Molukkers*) and OCAN (*Overlegorgaan Caribische Nederlanders*). The government subsidized the cost of an office for each group and that was all. At a national level, at the time, the notion of a costly 'minorities circus' was not an issue. At the level of local government, foundations and associations were often more important; their role, however, has gradually been limited. Decisions about allocating funds to minority organizations have for years essentially been governed by the question of whether or not they build bridges to the wider society.[31]

In short, neither financing nor promotion, but rather the tolerance of cultural difference within the boundaries of gradually more defined norms has marked Dutch policy. Unlike the United Kingdom, multiculturalism has never formed the core of minorities policy, let alone been raised to the level of an ideal underlying policy, and the rhetorical celebration of cultural diversity has never been dominant. Public support for multiculturalism was limited from the start.[32] This was confirmed by the view popularized by Pim Fortuyn, that the glorification of multiculturalism was primarily a discourse of the indigenous Dutch (leftist) elite. But the policy had never been deliberately radical, rather it was a pragmatic and therefore more indulgent policy than in retrospect was deemed desirable. With its moderate multiculturalism, the Netherlands swung back and forth between the British and French models. The primacy of socio-economic integration was never abandoned, space for the cultural freedom of minorities was highlighted – sometimes more, sometimes less, but gradually more with words than funds. Multiculturalism was implicitly abandoned as early as the 1990s, thereafter, under the influence of the Fortuyn revolt, also explicitly.[33]

Over the last decade, the demands for 'full citizenship' in a cultural sense have tightened and the alleged incompatibility of a specific culture with peaceful integration – Islam, which is often presented as homogeneous – has been explicitly put on the agenda. Only a small minority of postcolonial migrants are Muslim. Consequently the Islam debate barely touches upon them and is perhaps positive when it does – they are seen as the opposite of the Muslims whom many believe find assimilation so difficult. The Dutch minorities debate has come overwhelmingly to focus on Islam. Historical survey works, from *Nieuwkomers* (Jan Lucassen and Rinus Penninx) to *Komen en gaan* (Herman Obdeijn and Marlou Schrover), still comprehensively address postcolonial migration. However, recent books on integration by such opinion makers as Paul Scheffer (*Het land van aankomst*, translated as *The land of arrival*) and Ian Buruma (*Dood van een gezonde roker*, previously *Murder in Amsterdam*), or the report *Bruggen bouwen* (*Building bridges*) by the Blok parliamentary committee, barely mention postcolonial migration, if at all.[34] This fits into a broader and perhaps somewhat overly optimistic view that postcolonial migrants will ultimately all integrate successfully. Revisiting Bagley, it might give some a sense of triumphant satisfaction that it is not Dutch aversions, but purely due to the Muslims themselves that they are less well integrated.

Meanwhile, all groups of postcolonial migrants over the last few decades have become more and more explicitly players in a broader social debate about national identity. In this debate, which came about through the influence of migration and advancing European unification, postcolonial migrants had a significant rhetorical advantage over all other migrants. After all, only they can trace their presence in the Netherlands back to centuries of colonial rule overseas and the associated, ambivalent affinities. They embody a history that has come home and are therefore, many argue, one up on other immigrants. This provided excellent, fertile ground for identity politics, for which The Hague developed a certain sensitivity and which held up even when the general minorities policy hardened.

This is also interesting in comparative terms. The Netherlands is one of four European countries which were confronted with mass migration from their former colonies in the post-war period. In France, the United Kingdom, and Portugal a majority of post-war immigrants came from the former colonies, whereas in the Netherlands there was a second wave of immigration, comparable in size to the first, from countries with which it had no existing historical ties. In view of the central role given to Islam in contemporary debates on minorities and integration, it is significant that, unlike in the United Kingdom and France, there is little overlap in the Netherlands (and Portugal) between the categories 'postcolonial migrants' and 'Muslims'. It seems therefore logical that these differences would have repercussions for the comparatively benevolent tone used in the Netherlands to speak of postcolonial 'communities' and their longing for the acknowledgement of (post)colonial injustices.

THE DISAPPEARANCE OF THE POSTCOLONIAL
COMMUNITY AND BONUS

Migrants rarely have an easy time. Whether they leave for economic, political or other reasons, they settle elsewhere in the hope of a better life for themselves and possibly their offspring. Sometimes they achieve this, though it usually takes time, sometimes they do not. They are often welcomed onto the labour market, but rarely are they welcomed with open arms as (potential) new citizens. Even less so if they are perceived by the population of the new country to be fundamentally different – culturally, ethnically, religiously, or racially.

This also applied to postcolonial migrants in the Netherlands. And yet their history is different from that of postcolonial migrants elsewhere in Europe or other migrants in the Netherlands. The course of decolonization determined the successive postcolonial migrations to the Netherlands. Unlike France or the United Kingdom, the needs of the Dutch labour market were not a decisive factor, on the contrary. The 'repatriates' from Indonesia arrived at a time when a larger number of Dutch, with government help, were emigrating in the belief that the country was full. The Surinamese exodus reached its conclusion just at the point when the Netherlands had already ended labour recruitment and hoped to minimize further immigration. Antillean immigration coincided with a boom period, but this group connected poorly with the labour market.[35]

In none of these cases did the demands of the Dutch labour market determine the arrival of the migrants, unlike in the case of guest workers. Other migrants would have been refused entry in similar circumstances. The fact that postcolonial migrants were admitted was a direct consequence of colonial history. By far the majority of migrants from the Dutch East Indies/Indonesia were Dutch nationals; those who were not were later allowed Dutch citizenship on political grounds. All Surinamese who chose to settle in the Netherlands in 1975, and even up to 1980, had the right to do so; many more Surinamese were granted Dutch citizenship after that on political grounds. Antilleans are citizens of the Kingdom of the Netherlands and therefore still have the right to settle and live in the former metropole.

This is a crucial postcolonial bonus. Most migrants from these three countries could claim citizenship on legal grounds, which migrants from elsewhere could not, or only with a great deal more difficulty. Of course, these rights were at times controversial and attempts were indeed made by The Hague to reign them in. However, more importantly, citizenship for postcolonial migrants remained intact and in many cases was extended on political grounds to citizens from the former colonies who had no (longer a) formal right to it.[36]

The postcolonial bonus was of broader significance. Whether we look at the reception in the Netherlands or at the characteristics of the migrants, the picture is none too rosy. Dutch society was no exception to the rule that the arrival of 'strange' newcomers was seldom rejoiced at. Many studies and innumerable memories of Indisch, Surinamese or Antillean migrants confirm this. But equally clear is that there was a particular sensitivity in political and intellectual circles for arguments in the realm of 'we are here because you were there' – arguments and deeply-felt emotions which were often translated into the demand for compensatory treatment, even if only to ease colonial suffering. Migrants from elsewhere could not play this privileged register.

Compared with other non-Western migrants, postcolonial migrants were able to pull other more direct advantages out of their colonial baggage. To differing degrees they had at their disposal social or cultural capital that advanced their integration into Dutch society. This capital included having been educated in a system that had been based on the Dutch system, a command of the Dutch language, and a familiarity and often affinity with Dutch culture. In this respect, successive generations of postcolonial migrants were in a better starting position than other newcomers. This was certainly the view of policy-makers in The Hague. Of all postcolonial minorities only the Moluccans, who were to remain isolated for a long time, were still deemed eligible for (modest) financial support for education in their own language and culture.[37]

Needless to say, this social and cultural capital was unevenly distributed. Class was a determining factor for all groups; the higher the class, the greater the familiarity with the Dutch language and Dutch culture, and the greater the chance of integrating successfully. The more laborious integration of the Moluccan and Antillean population is in part linked to the low levels of education and limited command of Dutch among the first generation. Class was also reflected in the degree of cultural proximity – where all postcolonial migrants to a certain extent were bearers of a colonial mixed culture, the strength of the Dutch component corresponded with their social and socio-economic position.

In the current Dutch minorities debate, a great deal of importance is attached to minorities' cultures, in particular Islam. This is seldom positive and often with an amazing underestimation of the importance of socio-economic factors. But be that as it may, this pessimistic culturalist perspective is fairly irrelevant in the case of postcolonial migrants. Almost all migrants from the Netherlands East Indies belonged to the Christian minority in an overwhelmingly Islamic country. Almost all Antilleans and Afro-Surinamese are also Christian. In terms of religion, the vast majority of postcolonial migrants therefore merged seamlessly with the Netherlands as it had been before it became secularized. The only segments that did not fit into this meanwhile diluted picture of a Christian nation, were the Surinamese of Asian descent. Most of them were Hindus; the total number of Muslims would not have been more than 50,000. This leads to the cynical conclusion that the postcolonial bonus may also be formulated in the negative: 'not Muslim' and hence not suspected of holding strongly differing values and norms.

The postcolonial 'community', however heterogeneous it may have been, therefore benefitted from the beginning from a bonus that went beyond strictly juridical aspects of citizenship. Measured against hard integration indicators, postcolonial migrants have been more successful than the other two large groups of migrants, the Turks and the Moroccans.[38] The postcolonial bonus is not the only explanation for this. The class structures of the postcolonial communities when they arrived was already more varied and favourable. Moreover, postcolonial migration got underway earlier, so the integration process has had more time to develop.

However, it is now becoming clear that the postcolonial bonus is not granted for eternity. The comparative advantages held by first-generation postcolonial migrants eventually decline. The advantage of free access is no longer relevant to the settled citizen. In the second and later generations, postcolonial Dutch have no more rights than any other citizen with roots in another country; everyone is equal before the law. In terms of government provisions or the labour market there is no formal preferential treatment for any group of 'migrants' or any ethnic minority. What remains of a possible advantage for postcolonial communities is merely the intergenerational transfer of social and cultural capital inherited from the colonial era. However, it is rapidly becoming apparent that other ethnic groups are making this Dutch cultural capital their own, especially through education, while on the other hand, intractable integration issues in parts of the Moluccan and Afro-Caribbean communities suggest that the bonus is less effective there.

It is not only the bonus that evaporates; so too does the notion of postcolonial 'community'. This is in part a question of demographics. High degrees of exogamy mean the second generation of postcolonial Dutch is already, to a large extent, mixed – a process that is both visibly and predictably continuing in subsequent generations. This demographical 'dilution' is amplified in cultural terms, because only a minority of citizens with postcolonial roots mix mainly with people from their own segment in public. This all contributes to making it less and less obvious to speak of an Indisch, Moluccan, Surinamese or Antillean 'community', or to link the identity of these citizens primarily to their postcolonial roots. This presents a dilemma to the spokespeople of each of these groups. As will become apparent in the next chapter, they grounded their struggle for recognition on references to the unique, but misunderstood or denigrated the background and identity of their grassroots. Over the years this struggle for recognition took on a surprising additional charge, namely, to defy the creeping evaporation of that self-same 'community' and 'identity'.

2

CITIZENSHIP: RIGHTS, PARTICIPATION, IDENTIFICATION

The photo of a Moluccan demonstration at the Dutch parliament square Binnenhof in The Hague in the 1950s tells a clear story of identity claims. The banner *'Christelijk Nederland doe ons recht!'* appositely expresses the mood of the demonstrators: you Dutch are Christians, so are we (because you colonized us), so be just to us! No favors were being asked, it was simply a demand for rights. The desire for those rights stemmed from a centuries-long colonial alliance and were further underlined in the appeal to a shared religion. The Netherlands should not shirk its Christian duty.

The Hague, and Dutch society as a whole, has shown itself sensitive to this appeal from kindred spirits over the last 65 years. A large majority of postcolonial migrants were able to settle in the Netherlands and become rightful citizens without having to undergo complicated procedures with uncertain outcomes. Their Dutch citizenship gave them legitimate entry into the mother country. Although there were strong objections in The Hague circles to the idea that judicial rights stemming from the colonial period should be translated into full citizenship of the Netherlands, what is more relevant is that these rights were ultimately accepted. The acceptance of the right to cultural difference, which Indisch community leader Tjalie Robinson defined forty years later as a 'civil right', was trickier.[1]

Citizenship has many dimensions, even if we ignore recent debates on transnational and postnational citizenship and look exclusively at citizenship within a single nation state that assigns rights and exacts duties. Besides the formal criterion of legal insider status, there are the dimensions of civil rights and participation in all spheres of society. Ideally, every citizen in a democratic society has equal access to these, but in practice this is often not the case. Finally, there is the dimension, even harder to quantify, of belonging, of affinity with the society and feeling at home within it. The degree to which migrants identify with their new society varies enormously.

Moluccan demonstration, parliament square Binnenhof, The Hague, 25 April 1953, in support of an independent Moluccan Republic. (COLLECTION MUSEUM MALUKU)

This has to do with their own history and culture, but also with the space the receiving society grants diversity.[2]

Three interlocking dimensions of citizenship are addressed in this chapter. First I will examine how discussions about the granting of Dutch citizenship invariably ended with the acceptance of postcolonial migrants' rights, but also raised questions about the meaning of their citizenship. I will then discuss the participation of this category of newcomers in Dutch society and subsequently the political field. The assumption here is that for postcolonial organizations and politicians with Indisch Dutch, Surinamese or Antillean backgrounds the bond with their country of origin remained important, but that participation within Dutch society gradually took higher priority. Finally, I will indicate how citizenship and identification related to each other – a step towards the struggle for recognition of a separate identity and thereby for a broadening of the meaning of 'Dutch' culture.

For centuries, two interpretations of citizenship have stood diametrically opposed to one another. On the one hand jus soli (related to birthplace) and on the other jus sanguinis (inherited and, therefore, ethnically determined). The first allowed more scope to acquire state citizenship, as long as the new citizens adapted to the dominant culture; the French republican model is the perfect example of this. In practice, the relevance of this polarized approach has been drastically devalued. Even a country like Germany, where citizenship was traditionally tied to jus sanguinis, has seen that this literally exclusive definition cannot be maintained in the face of large and diverse 'migrant' communities. It was no different in other countries in 'old' Europe. Almost everywhere, large and permanent immigrant communities prompted a more pragmatic approach to diversity and thereby a more open interpretation of citizenship and national identity. This again led to violent reactions against what was experienced as excessive multiculturalism; a 'return' to a romanticized, monocultural society is, however, inconceivable.

The Netherlands took a third way, in accordance with their tradition of verzuiling or 'pillarization', the compartmentalization of society around 'pillars' organized along religious and political lines. Under a policy of moderate multiculturalism, this allowed a great deal of room for diversity without requiring immigrants to distance themselves from their 'own' culture. Acquiring Dutch citizenship was, until recently, a strictly legal affair. The culturalization of citizenship did not become an explicit element in minorities policy until about 2000.[3] Theoretically, civic integration (*inburgering*), now also defined as identification with Dutch culture, is a precondition for acquiring citizenship for new immigrants. For earlier generations of immigrants who already hold citizenship, this identification has also increasingly come to be seen as a normative obligation.

Formally, this discussion has only limited relevance to the history of postcolonial migrants in the Netherlands. With the exception of the Moluccans, the majority of migrants from the former colonies were able to capitalize on their previous Dutch citizenship, a part of the postcolonial bonus. The prime question is what the response within these communities was to the defensive and dismissive reactions of the Dutch and whether, following the completion of decolonization, attempts were made to extend 'colonial' rights to those who stayed behind overseas. The question of the normative meaning of Dutch citizenship simmered in the background long before it came to the fore in the integration debate, as did the idea of obliging citizens of the Netherlands Antilles to take a civic integration course, despite being Dutch passport holders.

Studies by John Schuster and Guno Jones have shown that politicians in The Hague had serious doubts about maintaining or granting citizenship to citizens of the former colonies.⁴ Such doubts were not directed at Dutch repatriates, but against non-whites: the Eurasians 'rooted in the East Indies', the Moluccans, and the migrants from the Dutch Caribbean. Racist arguments were rarely used openly; this would have been an anathema to the post-war, postcolonial Netherlands. The scepticism surrounding the capacity of immigrants to conform to Dutch society was frequently articulated in cultural terms, often with complete disregard for the crucial factor of class.

For the majority of migrants from the Dutch East Indies (now Indonesia), retaining or formally acquiring Dutch citizenship was not difficult, even if people grumbled in the Netherlands about the arrival of Indisch Dutch. The metropole was now forced to live with the colonial logic of a judicial, tripartite division of the population into Europeans, alien Orientals, and natives. There was some confusion regarding the in-between categories. The question of which Chinese or natives could be considered as 'equal' to Europeans and their rights in a colonial context were not clearly arranged. For the Indisch Dutch, there was the formal criterion that the father had to be legally European and to have formally recognized the child as his own; the offspring of a European mother and a native father were not legal Europeans. This had led to confusion in the colonial period and continued to do so in the postcolonial migration process.

Objections from the Dutch to the immigration of Indisch Dutch were often expressed in sniggers; however, the fact that they were associated with Dutch colonial authority and held Dutch citizenship also carried moral obligations. Practical arguments were used to object to the migrants: the poor economic climate, the housing shortage and the fact that the Netherlands saw itself as a land of emigration rather than immigration. But what gave rise to the greatest number of concerns was the presumed inability of lower-middle class Eurasians to adapt; from 1945 on, members of administrative circles remarked constantly that their presence was both problematic for the Netherlands and not in their own interest. Although the word 'race' was never used, these 'Indies-rooted' migrants were presented as being so completely different, that Schuster speaks convincingly of 'racialization'.⁵

Their arrival was, therefore, discouraged. 'They would only be unhappy in the Netherlands and present the risk of forming an antisocial element', opined a civil service report. In 1953, Minister of Social Work, F.J. van Thiel expressed the conviction 'that the interests of the majority of those born and bred in Indonesia, who hold Dutch citizenship, would be best served by their remaining in Indonesia.' No one would be served by 'uprooting' these 'mixed-blooded' people, who in Jones' words were 'construed as being incompetent and alien citizens' who did not understand that they had no future in the Netherlands.[6] Yet by the mid-1950s, when it became clear that the Indo-Europeans who remained in Indonesia had little hope of a future in the new Republic of Indonesia, it was reluctantly accepted that most of them, known as *spijtoptanten* or 'regretters', should be allowed to come to the Netherlands after all.

Such dismissive reasoning among the highest echelons of society sheds a revealing light on the myth of a broadminded and tolerant land; it suggests too that colonial prejudices had found their way into the postcolonial Netherlands. Yet, in retrospect, it should be no less surprising that all these objections had so little effect. In the end, almost all Indisch Dutch migrated to the Netherlands, some before the transfer of sovereignty, some long after. In almost all cases, their rights as Dutch citizens were recognized and honoured, and their travel and residence were financially and organizationally facilitated. This was also the case after 1949 when, it could be argued, the formal rights of the colonial period no longer applied.

This grudgingly supportive policy stemmed from a sense of responsibility among Dutch politicians, a sense of commonality kept alive by an influential lobby of earlier repatriates and migrants from the East Indies who placed the responsibility for decolonization and forced repatriation firmly at the feet of the Netherlands.[7] Organizations arguing for a generous admittance policy for *spijtoptanten* enjoyed broad support in the Indisch community. The admittance of the leaders of this lobby to The Hague elite, including prominent, often right-of-centre Members of Parliament, was crucial. Crucial, but not surprising. An administrative elite of *totok* (an Indonesian/Malay word for full-blooded Europeans) repatriates and Indisch elites were able to make their own pre-war experiences and affinities with Indonesia resound powerfully through the administrative centre of post-war Netherlands, where many of them went on to pursue administrative careers.

More complicated was the question of nationality for the Moluccans. However Dutch-leaning and, above all, monarchist they were, the Moluccans who served in the Royal Dutch East-Indian Army (KNIL), were considered neither European, nor equal to Europeans. They and their families, consequently, had no natural right to Dutch citizenship. There were also serious doubts about their ability to assimilate into Dutch society. The same Van Thiel declared that they would not find 'happiness' in the cold Netherlands.[8] This played no part in their admittance to the Netherlands, which was intended as a pragmatic, temporary solution. On arrival in the Netherlands, the soldiers were forcibly demobilized and, with their families, jettisoned into a political vacuum. The Netherlands tried to repatriate them as soon as possible and would have preferred them to accept Indonesian citizenship. However, Indonesia was not prepared to do this as long as this group continued to support the movement for a Republic of the South Moluccas (Republik Moluku Selatan or RMS). The Moluccans were interested in neither Dutch nor Indonesian nationality, because they cherished the hope of returning to an independent Moluccan republic.

As a consequence, by the end of the 1960s, 80 per cent of the Moluccans lived in the Netherlands and were still stateless. This stalemate was broken much later. Today, almost all Moluccans have Dutch citizenship. The judicial chapter of the integration of the Moluccans contains little for any of the parties to be proud of; it was concluded in silence.[9] Meanwhile, so much time had passed that there was no hope of a political lobby on behalf of the *spijtoptanten* or those who had been refused transportation to the Netherlands fifty years earlier. The Moluccan community in the Netherlands now had other priorities, mainly in the Netherlands. It is striking that throughout the preceding decades, during all the negotiations between representatives of the Moluccan community and the Dutch government, The Hague silently presumed de facto Dutch citizenship. That this was not stated aloud reflects a characteristic reluctance to acknowledge that the RMS and remigration were illusions.

By the time of the Surinamese exodus, the Netherlands had already become a country of immigration, but was disinclined to admit it. The Hague had finished recruiting guest workers and was operating a policy of remigration and deterring family migrations. This policy was to fail, just as it did in neighbouring countries. The exodus that followed the 1974 announcement of a speedy independence for Suriname was precisely what The Hague had hoped to avoid by accelerating the transfer of sovereignty. In the 1960s and 1970s, administrative task forces secretly discussed the option of calling a halt to migration by making a legal distinction between Dutch as opposed to Surinamese and Antillean citizenship. The conclusion that was reached, time and again, was that although this approach might have been legally possible, it was politically undesirable.[10]

The first part of this conclusion is still disputed, but the second part is no less interesting. The argument was constantly put forward that rapid growth in migration from Suriname would not only be disastrous for the country itself, it would also be problematic for the Netherlands. Reference was made to the difficulties Afro-Surinamese from the lower classes were expected to have with adapting – there was no anticipation of an exodus of Indian or Javanese Surinamese. It was suggested that these problems were already evident in crime figures for Surinamese in the Netherlands. The option to follow the earlier British model of simply shutting the borders did not suit the political climate of the 1960s and 1970s and even less so the centre-left cabinet of the social democrat Prime Minister Joop den Uyl. During the independence negotiations, members of the government did nothing that would jeopardize the desired transfer of sovereignty or create an image of the Netherlands as an inhospitable, even racist country. By adopting this attitude, the cabinet ignored the majority of its own population, which supported immigration restrictions.[11]

The irony is that the concessions offered to the Indian opposition during the negotiations leading up to the transfer of sovereignty in Suriname included the prolongation of the right to retain Dutch citizenship. The Hague had commenced the negotiations with the idea that most of the 30,000 Surinamese in the Netherlands would adopt Surinamese nationality and go back. The final outcome was utterly different. Not only were all Surinamese able to choose Dutch citizenship by taking up residence in the Netherlands, this option was extended for five years after the transfer of sovereignty, up to 1980.

Surinamese already living in the Netherlands, supported by Henck Arron's cabinet in Suriname, were mainly interested in retaining their Dutch citizenship or, if possible, attaining dual citizenship; they were only successful in achieving the former.[12] Meanwhile, one-third of the entire Surinamese population moved to the metropole between 1974 and 1980. Following the military coup in 1980 and the December Murders of 1982, Surinamese organizations in the Netherlands contributed to The Hague's decision to allow thousands of *spijtoptanten* to settle in the Netherlands. But there were limits. This political lobby was not strong enough to ensure support for the reopening of Dutch borders.

Antillean immigration has not yet been subject to legal restrictions. Again, there were concerns and secret task forces, but the conclusion once more was that restrictive admittance policies were legally possible, but politically undesirable. It wasn't until the late 1990s that the Dutch parliament began to consider a tough line, particularly with respect to lower-class and potentially delinquent Antillean migrants.[13] To this day, these ideas have not been transformed into policy. Antillean migrants, therefore, continue to benefit from a juridical bonus that no longer exists for migrants from Indonesia and Suriname.

To summarize: in all cases there was social and political resistance in the Netherlands to large-scale postcolonial migration. These were sometimes articulated in racist-sounding expositions, but what is essential in all three instances is that, in the end, the right to take up residence in the Nether-lands as a citizen of the former colonies was not rescinded until the transfer of sovereignty and, indeed, for several years beyond. This meant that all postcolonial migrants retained the right of abode and the same civil rights and duties as any other Dutch citizen.

It has been claimed that Moroccan, Turkish and other migrants' dual citizenship symbolizes an ambivalent loyalty to the Netherlands which, it is claimed, impedes their ability to integrate. This has never been an issue in the debate about postcolonial migration; only in the case of the Moluccan minority was the question of nationality a burning and unresolved issue for many years. Among the first generation of Surinamese, a minority may still have dual citizenship, as do some people from the same generation in Suri-name. However, in the Netherlands this is never a matter for discussion and the question is irrelevant for Antilleans. In the Netherlands, an engagement with Indonesia or Suriname is praised and encouraged rather than problem-atized. This is in marked contrast with the suspicion that resounds in de-bates about the dual loyalties of other, usually Islamic migrants.

POSTCOLONIAL ORGANIZATIONS: PROFILES AND MEANING

Citizenship implies the right to self-organization for socially acceptable ends. What is deemed acceptable may vary from society to society. In open societies this can include anything that is not regarded as criminal. Ethnic forms of organization are facilitated and supported unevenly. The Nether-lands, with its tradition of *verzuiling* and, later, its moderate form of multi-culturalism, took a relatively positive stance on this subject for a long time. The underlying view was that religious and/or ethnic groups should have the right to maintain bonds with each other, while self-organization could also serve as a bridge to the broader society and thereby promote integra-tion.[14]

But a bridge cannot be built from one end. General provisions also need to be adapted to fit the changing composition of the population. This not only applies to political systems, but also, for instance, to the media. The Dutch government played a significant role here. Since the 1980s, the public broadcasting company has been obliged to dedicate a percentage of its pro-gramming to ethnic minorities. Such regulations cannot be imposed on other parts of the media. Although there is no doubt that the landscape of broadcast and print media today is less white than in the past, discussions today revolve around whether they adequately represent the diversity of

Dutch society. Meanwhile, ethnic minorities continue to support and use their own media as well.[15]

Postcolonial migrants' orientation to the media in their country of origin is modest compared with most other migrant groups. Satellite dishes are useless to them. Their easy use of the Dutch language plays a significant role as does the psychological distance that separates the Indisch community from contemporary Indonesia. Considering the small scale and more limited means of Suriname and the Antilles it is not surprising that media transfer is mainly one-directional: all the media in Suriname and the Antilles make extensive use of Dutch products.

Postcolonial societies and associations have a long and rich history in the Netherlands. Even before the Second World War, migrants and temporary residents from the colonies organized themselves into societies.[16] This tendency really took off once migrants were no longer counted in the thousands, but hundreds of thousands. Bosma and Alferink have been able to identify around 2,600 organizations that were founded by, with, or for postcolonial migrants. They indicate that this number may have been higher in reality, but that a number of these organizations only existed for a short time or were dormant.[17]

The development of postcolonial organizations is remarkable. Between 1945 and the end of the 1960s, no more than ten new organizations were set up annually across all the groups combined. In the subsequent two decades the picture was very different. There was an increase across all groups. The number of new Indisch organizations was just under ten on average, while for the far smaller Moluccan community it was higher. Spectacular growth characterized Surinamese organizations. The annual number of registered new organizations grew between 1973 and 1985 from ten to fifty, but dropped back after that. Even so, in the early years of the new millennium, the figure was still as high as twenty. Antillean organizations did not take off until the 1980s; in the next two decades about ten societies were started each year. Demographics only partly explain this growth. Another factor may have been the Dutch government's subsidy policy. However, Bosma and Alferink refute the view that there is a direct and consistent link between subsidies and the founding of societies and associations. A significant factor is that the migration process by this time had been closed off for all groups except the Antilleans; on the whole, the first generation of migrants dominates the founding of ethnic organizations. In absolute numbers, according to Bosma and Alferink's research, the highest number of ethnic organizations founded prior to 2007 were for Surinamese Dutch (1223), followed far behind by those for Moluccans (454), Antilleans (346) and Indisch Dutch and migrants

(338). Relative to the current size the ethnic grassroots, the number of Moluccan organizations is highest, while those with an Indisch character are the lowest in number. The ratio for Surinamese and Antillean organizations falls somewhere in between, and is of the same order as for Moroccans and Turks.[18]

But why did these different groups organize themselves and why are the differences in the ratios of migrants to organizations so great? We may outline a few broad tendencies, with reference to Bosma's thorough analysis *Terug uit de koloniën* (Back from the Colonies). The Indisch pattern of relatively few organizations does not necessarily reflect a low density of organizations, invisibility or a weak lobby. The opposite is more likely to be true. The first post-war generation founded a number of organizations with a broad range of paying members or subscribers. This was all about self-organizing in the interests of repatriates and *spijtoptanten* in the Netherlands and in Indonesia, and they were led mainly by men who had direct access to Dutch government circles. Then there were organizations that aimed to maintain an Indisch identity. In the 1980s, new organizations were founded, often with the same political aims. What is striking in all of this is the impressive membership of organizations like the *Nederlands-Indische Bond van ex-Krijgsgevangenen en -Geïnterneerden* (NIBEG 1945. The Netherlands-East Indies Union for Former Prisoners of War and Internees), the *Pelita* foundation (1947), a magazine like *Tong Tong* (1958), a festival such as *Pasar Malam Besar* (1959), or more recently, the umbrella organization *Indisch Platform* (1991).

The comparatively modest number of Indisch organizations cannot simply be explained by efficient concentration. The decision to organize themselves into separate clubs was not an obvious one for the first generation of migrants from Indonesia. Government policy in the first few decades after the war offered little room and even less money for private, let alone ethnic, organizations. Social welfare was still in its infancy and was left largely to church organizations. An umbrella organization was set up to coordinate the integration of Indonesian migrants, the *Centraal Comité van Kerkelijk en Particulier Initiatief voor Sociale Zorg ten behoeve van Gerepatrieerden* (CCKP 1950. Central Committee of Church and Private Initiatives for Social Care for the Repatriated) in which Indonesian organizations were well represented. The establishment of separate religious societies was unnecessary, since migrants from Indonesia were almost all Christians and could join existing churches. Here too, the social capital they brought with them linked in well with Dutch society. By the time the government began to operate an active integration policy two decades later, the Indisch 'community' was already as good as integrated.

It should therefore not come as a surprise that a large number of Indisch organizations focused on addressing the colonial past. One theme was the recognition of the suffering caused by the Japanese occupation, the violent *bersiap* period that followed, and finally the 'repatriations' caused by decolonization. The other theme was the defence and, consequently, celebration of Indisch culture. The first appealed strongly to the claim for full Dutch citizenship, the second stressed the right to cultural diversity.

The underlying argument was that the Indisch 'community' had a right to all of this, precisely because it had always been Dutch. Such Indisch claim-making was supported by Dutch repatriates, often in high places. The characteristic colonial differences between the *totoks* and Eurasian *Indos* also faded somewhat. Furthermore, the 120,000 soldiers who fought the last colonial war between 1945 and 1949 came increasingly to belong to the 'Indisch generation'. This is typified by former Minister for Foreign Affairs, Ben Bot, a *totok* in the Dutch East Indies, who in 2005 was given the task of reconciling repatriates and former military men with the new government line that the Netherlands had 'stood on the wrong side of history' in Indonesia. Bot was considered the best man to put the message across as he was regarded to be an 'Indisch chap'.[19]

In making amends, Bot was not referring to colonialism itself, but to the Dutch position in the decolonization process. It was, of course, the Indisch lobby, in which repatriates played a major role, that had kept The Hague captive in a dismissive attitude towards the Indonesian nationalists for so long. At the end of 1946, a 'petition' for the 'unity of the state' organized by this embittered group and sent to Queen Wilhelmina was signed by 300,000 Dutch citizens in the space of just two weeks.[20] Organizations in these circles continued to agitate strongly against compromising with Indonesian nationalists, right up to Indonesian independence in 1949 and even until 1962 when Irian Barat (formerly Dutch New Guinea) was temporarily placed under the administration of the United Nations. Although Dutch conservatives, *totoks* and *Indos* could all count on each other's support, it was ultimately in vain. Here there are clear parallels with agitation carried out by repatriated *pied noirs* in France against the decolonization of Algeria. However, opposition in the Netherlands never became violent, as it did in France.

The Indisch community was more successful in its struggle to gain Dutch citizenship for the *spijtoptanten*, Indisch Dutch who had initially remained in Indonesia, but who no longer saw a future for themselves there and wanted to move to the Netherlands after all. The *Nationale Actie Steunt Spijtoptanten in Indonesië* (NASSI. National Action Support 'Regretters' in Indonesia, 1960) was highly effective in the way it lobbied The Hague with no less than twenty local branches. As a result, ten thousand more Indisch Dutch were able to acquire Dutch citizenship and settle in the Netherlands.[21]

The history of Indisch organizations presents a picture of concentration, intense participation, good connections with administrators in the Netherlands, and a focus on rights and recognition. Acknowledgement was a key issue for the Moluccans too, but history took a completely different turn in their case. In the beginning, it was primarily the national organization *Door de Eeuwen Trouw* (DDET 1950. Faithful Down the Centuries) that articulated the ideal of returning to an independent Moluccan republic. The association's magazine *De Stem van Ambon* (The Voice of Ambon) was printed in unbelievably large editions of several tens of thousands.[22] The enormous number of organizations at a national and local level reflects a long tradition of an orientation towards the islands of origin, a long-held refusal to see the Netherlands as the final destination and, partly as a result of this, a continuing impediment to integration that persists to the present day. The *Badan Persatuan* association (1966) came to stand at the heart of this, behind DDET, and saw itself primarily as a government-in-exile of the future, free Moluccas.

This is how the overwhelmingly Protestant Moluccans came to form their own churches instead of joining existing churches, to organize themselves for transnational political aims for which there was next to no support in the Netherlands or elsewhere, and why the first generation, especially, preferred self-organization and collective housing in segregated camps, and later in neighbourhoods, to settling amidst the Dutch population. *Badan Persatuan*, which enjoyed the support of almost the entire community, initially resisted the Ministry of Culture, Recreation and Welfare's (CRM) cautiously implemented integration policy. *Badan Persatuan* insisted that 'maintaining our own identity' was a part of Moluccan welfare and was indeed successful in persuading the Dutch government to grant it a large number of seats on the government-initiated discussion platform *Inspraakorgaan Welzijn Molukkers* (1976. Moluccan Welfare Platform). It is striking to see how strong the ties remained between the Moluccan grassroots and its organizations throughout the rest of this history and how the Dutch government was unable to develop any policy without these organizations.[23]

Taking into account the weak socio-economic position of their grassroots, the leaders of the Moluccan organizations' persistent grip on an increasingly unrealistic political programme seems to have considerably delayed integration. Academics and administrators, of course, hotly debate the impact of ethnic organizations on integration.[24] If a single case supports the pessimistic vision of the link between self-organization, participation

Moluccans resisting being moved from a camp to a housing estate in 1963. The desire to keep their own community intact, as well as militant group coercion, extended the isolation of the first and second generation of Moluccans in the Netherlands by several decades. (COLLECTION INTERNATIONAL INSTITUTE FOR SOCIAL HISTORY)

and integration, then it is the early history of the Moluccan organizations. It was not until the 1990s that they and the Dutch government began to pursue a joint integration policy. By then, a large number of Moluccans had married outside their own community or had gone to live outside the Moluccan camps and neighbourhoods. Such individual choices may well have had a far more significant impact on Moluccan integration than all the policy efforts put together.

The landscape of Surinamese organizations in the Netherlands is marked by fragmentation along ethnic lines, which in part explains the different characters of the ethnic groups. While most Afro-Surinamese joined existing Christian churches, Hindus and Muslims needed to develop their own religious institutions. Yet even where joining forces for the benefit of socio-economic integration would have seemed an obvious strategy, and one also stimulated by the Dutch government, organizations soon crumbled into

Minister Brinkman of Welfare, Health and Culture visiting a Hindu prayer room, Bijlmer, Amsterdam, 7 March 1986. Indian and Javanese Surinamese organizations, unlike Afro-Surinamese ones, were mainly formed along ethnic and, especially, religious lines. (COLLECTION NATIONAL ARCHIVES)

Netherlands accepted several tens of thousands more Surinamese and granted them Dutch citizenship. The level of influence of Surinamese organizations on this policy is difficult to measure, but it is safe to assume that regular demonstrations and a constant lobby to keep Suriname on the political agenda contributed to this relatively open Dutch policy.

Just as most Antillean migrants came from Curaçao, the bulk of Antillean organizations were also dominated by migrants from this, the largest island. The organizations that represented the other islands specifically were in the minority. The pattern is familiar: the number of organizations increased strongly as the Antillean community grew, representing the members interests as well as offering a home way from home. There were few religious organizations; Antilleans usually joined existing churches.

Like the Surinamese migrants before them, the Antilleans who left prior to the exodus were more highly educated than those who came later. Consequently, the early organizations were firmly nationalistic, sometimes had an anti-colonial hue. More recent organizations are associations like the *Antilliaans Netwerk* (Antillean Network) and various student societies. What they all had in common with the early associations of better-educated Antilleans was precisely the same middle-class character. The difference lies in the way the anti-colonial rhetoric has faded into the background. Unlike three or four decades ago, a significant majority of students now remain in the Netherlands to live and work after they have graduated. And the younger generation also seems to take more distance from political life on the islands than was the case in the past.

In the meantime, problems arose around the integration of migrants from lower social classes. The Dutch government could no longer manage without newly-founded Antillean welfare organizations, in which language was a major factor: it was almost impossible to communicate with underprivileged Antilleans in Dutch. This continued to be the forte of Antillean welfare groups which went under the collective name *Forsa* (1991). Problems with integration did not improve and around the country municipal administrators in the 'Antillean municipalities' came to the table to talk with Antillean organizations for whom there was no longer space at the level of national policy. Such organizations worked under the national umbrella *Overlegorgaan Caraïbische Nederlanders* (OCAN 1985. Consultation platform for Caribbean Dutch, 1985).

Unlike other postcolonial groups, Antillean organizations in the Netherlands were rarely formed to influence Dutch policy on the country of origin, or to exercise direct influence on the governments there. This was logical as the islands and the country the Netherlands Antilles have their own governments which negotiate with the Dutch government all the time. They saw migrants, on the whole, as self-selecting outsiders and were able to maintain this view because conflicts with the Dutch government rarely became very serious and because the islands never had a crisis of the order of Indonesia or Suriname.

It is characteristic of Antilleans on both sides of the ocean, either jointly or separately, that they have only recently begun to develop a strong lobby to target precisely the subject that unites them literally and figuratively: the successful struggle, so far, against restrictions on the right to abode in the Netherlands and, hence, against any other infringement of their right to equal citizenship within the Kingdom of the Netherlands. Since the late 1990s, time and again, and supported by a majority in the Dutch parliament, legislation was prepared that would limit access to the Netherlands and make it possible to repatriate (potentially) criminal Antilleans and, in a milder version, to establish a registration system for high-risk Antillean youths. A long and hard struggle has been waged on the islands by politicians and in the Netherlands, led by *OCaN* and the organization *Movimentu Antiano i Arubano pa Promové Partisipashon* (MAAPP 2000. Antillean and Aruban Movemement to Stimulate Participation). This has culminated in The Hague not introducing restrictions or registration – as yet, one should probably add.[29]

This brief overview reveals a strong culture of societies and associations that varies from group to group. But what significance did these organizations ultimately have for the integration process? The Blok parliamentary commission in the Netherlands was not positive about the role of the migrant organizations, which it found were too preoccupied with identity politics and consequently promoted isolation rather than integration. Researchers have arrived at different views on the subject, just as they have on the question of whether the considerable amount of government funding for ethnic organizations played a significant part in this.[30]

Bosma and Alferink arrive at different conclusions in relation to postcolonial migrant organizations.[31] Based on their database, which contains 2,600 organizations, they counter the view of a direct and proportional link between government funding and the foundation of ethnic organizations. This link is weak in the case of Indisch organizations; for other groups of postcolonial migrants the link is stronger, but not decisive. Moreover, they make clear that a significant number of Surinamese organizations were religious in nature, namely Hindu; there are no indications that this hindered socio-economic integration or the level of identification with Dutch society. They are ambiguous about the extent to which the exceptionally closed and highly, explicitly ideological Moluccan organizations formed an obstacle to integration. There is good reason to be sceptical about this.

One feature of these organizations remained implicit. Over the past 65 years no organizations were founded jointly by all postcolonial groups. Fragmentation along colonial and ethnic lines was the norm. This was also true of the media. Leafing through Indisch magazines like *Tong Tong* or *Moesson* the complete lack of interest in Caribbean or even Moluccan affairs simply flies off the pages; Indian magazines like *Lalla Rookh* and *Aisa Samachar* are primarily aimed at their own group and general Surinamese news, as are the Afro-Surinamese magazines *Jere* or *Famiri*. This is once again evidence that a single postcolonial community never existed in the minds of the migrants and their offspring. 'The postcolonial migrant(s)' is an analytical abstraction without street value, as spokespeople explicitly state.[32]

Postcolonial Netherlands revolves around the way postcolonial migrants introduced their colonial backgrounds into debates about Dutch identity and what it means to be Dutch. Migrant organizations played an important part in this. After all, they lobbied on behalf of a community and in doing so determined the image of the group and its identity. Government funding did not create this process, but it did sustain it, especially over the last two decades. The paradox is that funding only got underway quite late in the story, just at the point when minorities policies, with all the rhetorical room for diversity, was particularly aimed at the 'harder' aspects of integration and when socio-economic integration for most postcolonial migrants and their children was, if not quite complete, at least well on the road to being so. The background to the support for this postcolonial identity politics was the belief that the scope given to the call for recognition of the colonial past would foster redemption and inclusion and, consequently, advance integration. This is an appealing vision, but one that is difficult to validate empirically.

POLITICAL PARTICIPATION

Apart from providing fulfilment or careers for professional representatives, minority organizations served to bring to the fore the interests, concerns and desires of their grassroots. However, their political influence was limited, with the exception of a small number of large Indisch organizations such as NIBEG. The weight of these Indisch organizations was partly explained by the massiveness of their organized grassroots and the popularity of their standpoints in a land where solidarity with the 'victims' of Indonesian nationalism was still strong. No less pivotal were the excellent connections these organizations had with The Hague politicians and, indeed, the royal family. This was a lesson in political mobilization. However, that favourable conjunction would not be repeated.

With the exception of the Moluccans, postcolonial migrants were, on the whole, already Dutch citizens when they arrived in the Netherlands, with either an active or passive right to vote. Access to the Dutch political system, with a view to representing potentially specific interests, could be achieved by seeking out kindred spirits in the political parties, by playing an active part in one of these parties, or by founding specific political parties. Constant efforts were made to achieve the first option, also by using their own organizations to this end. The second strategy seems to have been successful over the last few decades, although the elected politicians rarely operate primarily on the grounds of their postcolonial backgrounds. The third route, founding one's own political party, held little chance of success and was never seriously taken up by postcolonial migrants.[33]

Up until the early 1990s, established political parties had few postcolonial migrants on their election lists.[34] Since then they have caught up at a remarkable rate. Even if the number of parliamentarians went down after the 2010 elections (to 13 out of 150), we may still conclude that over the past decade or so the Lower House of the Dutch parliament reasonably represented the diversity of the population – far more, for example, than the 'colour blind' republic of France.[35] The first member of parliament with a Moluccan background was John Lilipaly (social democratic party PvdA, 1986), the second was Usman Santi (PvdA, 1998). Twelve postcolonial politicians from various parties were of Surinamese descent, starting with Dowlatram Ramlal (Christian democratic party, CDA, 1992). Only three members of parliament, again from different parties, were from Antillean backgrounds; the first was Hubert-Geronimo Fermina (the liberal democratic party D66, 1994).[36] Over the last decade, the overall representation of migrant communities in the Lower House went up, but the earlier postcolonial domination receded – to only three out of a dozen parliamentarians with a 'non-Western' background today.

Politicians with an Indisch background have been left out of this brief overview. Yet, in the years immediately following the Second World War there were many politicians from Indisch backgrounds or experience of the Dutch East Indies. They helped to give a political voice to the interests of the repatriates and, in vain, opposed Indonesian independence and the later transfer of Dutch New Guinea to Indonesia. Most of these politicians were right of centre – as were the repatriates, many of whom blamed the social democratic PvdA for the loss of the East Indies in the first place.[37]

These members of parliament represented an Indisch world that was politically finished. In later decades there were politicians in the Lower House who had some kind of Indisch background, but this rarely impacted noticeably on their election or performance, though they sometimes popped up later on the boards of Indisch organizations. This was also true of prominent politicians whose Indisch past was already a generation behind them, such as Jan Kees Wiebenga (of the conservative-liberal party VVD), chair of the *Indisch Gebaar*, or Winnie Sorgdrager (of the liberal democratic party D66), board member of the Indisch Herinneringscentrum (Indisch Memorial Centre) in Bronbeek. The association of the political right with the Indisch community would remain intact for some time, with a particularly strong position in the conservative-liberal VVD party. The barely visible 'Indisch' representation in the current parliament reflects a broader picture of completed emancipation, in which ethnicity no longer plays a noticeable role in elections or performance.

The First Chamber of the Dutch parliament has remained, to this day, an overwhelmingly white bastion of power. Since the war, there have been fourteen senators who were born in the Dutch East Indies, but only one of them was Moluccan (Samuel Portes, the green party Groen Links, 2001) and one of Surinamese descent (Joyce Sylvester, PvdA, 2003). Something similar applies to the government. There have been no ministers from non-Western backgrounds since the war, though there have been four state secretaries. The first, the Surinamese Philomena Bijlhout (Pim Fortuyn's populist-right party, LPF, 2002), had to step down after a few hours because she had given false information about her role in the Bouterse military regime in Suriname. Bijlhout was succeeded for just a few months by Chinese-Dutch Khee Liang Phoa (LPF, 2002). The two people from non-Western backgrounds appointed state secretaries were Ahmed Aboutaleb (PvdA, 2006), originally from Morocco, and Nebahat Albayrak (PvdA, 2006), originally from Turkey. The right-wing cabinet-Rutte inaugurated in 2010 has no members with a non-Western background whatsoever.

The postcolonial minorities have been prominent for much longer at a local level, logically mainly in the big cities. Initially they were to be found in parties associated with left-wing, anti-racist views, though now they are found across the political spectrum.[38] Tara Oedayraj Singh Varma was the first city councillor of Surinamese descent (Amsterdam, Groen Links, 1983). Many migrants followed from an array of countries, with representativeness being achieved in the larger cities in 2000. The postcolonial domination among these migrant politicians was, once again, short lived.[39]

This applies particularly to the number of city councillors. In 1994 there were more than 70 migrant chairmen and -women on council executive committees, in 2006 there were more than 300. The number of Surinamese chairpersons of these committees rose from 21 to 38, which is relatively speaking a sharp fall. The number of Antillean chairpersons grew from one to six, remaining, therefore, minimal.[40] There were almost no Moluccan chairmen or -women, and those of Indisch descent were not registered. Amsterdam has had two chairwomen of executive committees from Surinamese backgrounds, Hannah Belliot (PvdA, 2002) and Hannah Buyne (PvdA, 2006). Belliot (1998) and then Elvira Sweet (PvdA, 2002) first served as chairwomen ('mayors') of the Amsterdam district Zuid-Oost. However, since then, other Amsterdam districts have been led by chairpersons from Moroccan backgrounds.

To date, there has only been a small number of immigrant mayors. The first, on government instruction, was Surinamese, Roy Ho Ten Soeng (Venhuizen, 2000). The Indisch magazine *Moesson*, however, delicately pointed out that Indisch Dutch Jos Verdier was made mayor long before this (Huizen, 1995).[41] Considering these small numbers, if there had ever been a point to speaking about a postcolonial dominance, this vanished completely with the appointment of Moroccan-Dutch Ahmed Aboutaleb in 2008 as Mayor of Rotterdam, the Netherlands' second city. He promptly clashed with Antillean organizations because, having earlier used strong terms to address Moroccan troublemakers, he was now outspoken about their Antillean peers.[42]

The voting patterns of postcolonial minorities can only to a certain extent be charted. Little is known about migrants with Indisch roots. However, it can be established that they were more likely to find support for their standpoints and desires on the right than on the left.[43] The turn out of Surinamese and Antilleans at the ballot box has been strikingly low for decades, also compared with other migrant groups. Among these voters there was a general preference for the social democratic PvdA. The spectrum has broadened over the last decade, but it is still dominated by the left. The PvdA has remained by far the most popular party among this group, at least until recently and certainly more so than for other migrant groups. It is doubtful whether politicians of Surinamese and Antillean backgrounds are representative of their fragmented, largely non-voting, ethnic grassroots.[44]

The access of migrants to national and local political parties gradually improved, with a strong improvement over the last decade, due in part to migrants without Dutch citizenship being allowed to vote in local elections since 1985. A number of factors explain this: better integration and consequently better qualified candidates, electoral considerations, and more openness on behalf of the established parties. The initial advantage postcolonial migrants had over other minorities, which was linked to citizenship and a socio-cultural lead, has now disappeared. Their advantage has evaporated.[45]

There is nothing to say that politicians with a migrant past set different priorities to other Dutch politicians. When Lilipaly was installed in the Lower House of the Dutch parliament in 1986, he wore a Moluccan smock, which, he said, was a signal to Moluccans in the Netherlands: 'I am a member of parliament, but also one of you.'[46] However, no single party gives much room to identity politics and parliamentarians from migrant groups largely avoid being identified specifically with minority questions or transnational loyalties. Such a position is harder to achieve at a local level. Considering the proximity of the grassroots, it is electorally far riskier for the party and, above all, the politician concerned, who is often elected by preferential votes from their own grassroots supporters.[47]

The rapid rise of politicians from ethnic minorities in districts and municipalities was accompanied by a surge in disaffection regarding these politicians' qualifications and weak ties to the party line. The same applied to postcolonial politicians and was fed in part by 'scandals' surrounding Oedayraj Singh Varma, Bijlhout, and Pormes.[48] Such disaffection provoked predictable reactions. Politicians with postcolonial roots are consistently reminded of this tension, more than leaders of postcolonial organizations.

AMBIVALENT IDENTITIES

How open was the postcolonial Netherlands to the longing for full citizenship, which was articulated in demands for the acknowledgement of and possible concessions for the colonial past and the (alleged) contemporary legacy? The Dutch decolonization debate is often presented in terms of a series of traumas. With regard to Indonesia, so the cliché goes, everything went wrong. This trauma is supposed to have led to financial and migratory concessions during the transfer of sovereignty in Suriname. When this presumed 'model decolonization' again gave rise to a number of disappointments, the next trauma came, in response to which The Hague adopted a pampering attitude towards the Antilles.

Much of this cliché can be dismissed. The decolonization of the Dutch East Indies may well have been traumatic in the beginning, but this does not mean it influenced politics in The Hague decades on – and even less so that this 'trauma' has found its way into the collective memory of Dutch society. As far as political memory is concerned, the decolonization of Suriname rested more on self-interest than the conviction that the country was much better off without the Netherlands. A degree of guilty conscience about the problems caused by the over-hasty transfer of sovereignty to Suriname may have contributed to a more supportive approach to the Antilles. Yet, the acceptance that the islands would remain part of the kingdom stemmed mainly from the insight that The Hague lacked the judicial and political means to complete decolonization with a final transfer of sovereignty.

The argument that the political trauma surrounding decolonization led to a policy founded on a guilty conscience sooner reflects the way postcolonial migration was handled. Despite the degree of doubt and dissent, the final immigration policy was far broader than legally necessary and was publicly defended by appealing to the rights of postcolonial migrants. The Hague's policy was without a doubt more lenient than that of the British. France initially exercised a more open policy, but with a labour shortage in mind that the Netherlands had not yet been exposed to at this time.

Did a sense of contrition affect the treatment of postcolonial migrants, or minority policy as a whole? It is hard to say. It was pretty soon accepted that migrants from the Dutch East Indies were unable return to Indonesia. Their ties with the colonial regime and the fiasco of decolonization, so it was acknowledged, bore obligations for the Dutch. Surinamese and Antillean migrants were able to return, but did not want to. It took longer for this fact to be reluctantly accepted. Insofar as a Dutch sense of guilt has played any part since then, it has done so mainly in relation to earlier chapters in the colonial past.

Postcolonial migrants brought colonial history back to the Netherlands. It is clear that over the course of time there was a growing willingness on the part of the Netherlands to take a critical look at its own colonial history. This did not necessarily mean that postcolonial minorities were treated any better than other newcomers. One may draw a parallel here with the thesis advanced by Herman Vuijsje, who claimed that the shame of the wartime destruction of Dutch Jewry determined post-war minority policies.[49] One may well believe that this sense of shame existed, but did it really lead to a fundamentally different policy, except at a rhetorical level? This is hard to establish.

What can be established is that, whatever was said behind closed doors, openly xenophobic or racist statements were avoided in Dutch politics until about a decade ago. Even though this discourse has, to a distressing degree, become more acceptable these days, it is rarely directed at postcolonial groups, except occasionally the Afro-Caribbean Dutch. All the preceding debates about restricting the entrance of migrants from the colonies into the Netherlands (based on their capacity and willingness to adapt) were couched in guarded terms or with reference to the financial costs for the Netherlands or the interests of the sending countries. These debates rarely led to practical consequences. Moreover, this discourse did feed a feeling among postcolonial migrants that they were not welcome, as was articulated from time to time by Indisch Dutch in the 1950s and ever since by all postcolonial migrants.[50] This, again, is why many felt aggrieved and frequently express their rancour and, at best, their ambivalent identification with the Netherlands.

Meanwhile, the struggle for full citizenship has shifted from entry into the country to support for integration and, subsequently, to the more immaterial realm of acknowledgement: recognition of the colonial history, of the contribution to Dutch culture, and of the specific place of each of the – increasingly diffuse – postcolonial 'communities' within the multicultural society. The demand for the recognition of an own culture and history is linked to the assurance that postcolonial identity fits excellently within Dutch culture. This is correct, but also implies that playing a postcolonial card tends to lose its effect – even in the 'contrite' Netherlands, which, after all, is primarily concerned about other migrants who, it is angrily claimed, cannot or do not want to integrate.

3

THE STRUGGLE FOR RECOGNITION:
WAR AND THE SILENT MIGRATION

Using a variation of the French warning at level crossings, *Un train peut en cacher un autre*, the French-Algerian historian Benjamin Stora once described how one memory (of the Algerian war of independence) may obscure another (of French colonial rule in Algeria): *Quand une mémoire (de guerre) peut en cacher une autre (coloniale)*. The emotions around the final bloody phase of French colonial rule in Algeria are still so fresh and powerful, that to this day France is barely able to view this period with any detachment – and is, therefore, a long way from being able to explore the preceding colonial history seriously.[1]

The memory wars regarding the Netherlands East Indies are not nearly as extreme. Unlike France, the Netherlands is no longer fiercely divided on the subject of the final years of colonialism in the East Indies. The Japanese occupation is regarded primarily in terms of suppression by an alien power and the suffering of the Europeans. It has been established that Indonesian gangs perpetrated terrible violence during the so-called *bersiap* period of the revolution. At the same time, it has become more broadly and gradually less controversially accepted that during euphemistically termed 'police actions' in the first few years after the war – as if the problem were a case of temporarily maintaining order in a colony – Dutch troops were involved in war crimes and the Netherlands had 'stood on the wrong side of history'. But what about before the arrival of the Japanese? There was colonialism. First there was the voc, then the East Indies. The idea that 'something magnificent' was done in that part of the world is rarely bragged about, but there is no reason not to think it sometimes, quietly, and occasionally to celebrate it in style. The colonial period is neither a taboo nor a black hole.

The fact is that the final stages of the colonial period still attract more attention in the Netherlands than the 350 years that preceded them. This chapter is, above all, about the memory of that final phase, which continues to divide opinion in the Netherlands today, but to a far lesser degree than in

France. Why is this? The decolonization process in Algeria was more bloody and is still more strongly marked by cruelty on all sides. It was also more recent. It is important to note that all the parties who contended in the past are strongly represented in France today. Stora has done the calculations. At the end of the final phase of the war, more than a million French soldiers, a million *pieds noirs*, 400,000 'ordinary' Algerians and 100,000 *harkis* who had fought in the colonial army, were repatriated. They brought their memories with them and passed them on to their children. This amounted to six or seven million people by the beginning of the twenty-first century. One in ten French people had either direct or indirect experience of the war.[2]

There are all kinds of other parallels between the *pieds noirs* and the Indisch Dutch, between the *harkis* and the Moluccans, between the French and Dutch soldiers who fought in a final colonial war. The Dutch lost, the French lost. But where the struggle for independence remained at a remove from the Netherlands, the Algerian war spread onto French soil, carried by terrorist attacks and state repression. And where only the losers were repatriated to the Netherlands, hundreds of thousands of Algerians took up residence in France both during and after the war. This meant the repatriated were constantly reminded of the defeat and of the victors, whose Islamic faith became increasingly seen as an obstacle. All in all, not ideal circumstances for achieving a balanced acceptance of the recent past.

Things passed off more peacefully in the Netherlands. Indonesia was further away, both in time and space. The migration had been more selective and Indonesian views were initially not taken seriously. Even so, Indisch and Moluccan memories of the war, the *bersiap*, the journey and their reception in the Netherlands are still marked by bitter discontent. 'Keeping silent with a visible exclamation mark', is how acclaimed author Adriaan van Dis, himself a son of repatriates, characterized this initial attitude – coercion into silent assimilation. It was not until later that the discontent about growing up in what Pamela Pattynama, a specialist in Indisch literature, called an 'atmosphere of concealed memories' came to be articulated more openly.[3] This chapter focuses primarily on the so-called repatriates' struggle for acknowledgement by the Dutch state. Recognition of their suffering in the East Indies, of their right to full Dutch citizenship, recognition that their immigration had been unavoidable and that their reception in the Netherlands had been unduly chilly. This struggle helped them to forge a sense of 'community'.

Two counterpoints conclude this chapter. First of all a comparison with the exodus from the West Indies, which was hardly unavoidable and which, consequently, provoked revealing silences in the nationalist discourse. Another issue is the late 'discovery' of the Second World War in Suriname and the Netherlands Antilles and the way Second World War commemorations in the Netherlands today are employed as an instrument of integration policy. This policy could quite easily, and understandably, provoke new resentment among the Indisch Dutch.

FROM WAR TO EXODUS

At the end of the 1950s, in *De repatriëring uit Indonesië*, Kraak, Ellemers and Wittermans remembered that immediately after the war, Dutch relief workers in the Netherlands had been irritated by the 'haughtiness and pretensions of the evacuees, their emphasis of their own suffering and their limited interest in the Netherlands' experience of the war'. A few pages later they describe precisely the repatriates' indignation that their suffering was not acknowledged and their forced migration not understood, their resentment that the Netherlands felt no 'moral' obligation to help them. Mutual irritation therefore, based on a lack of understanding of each others' wartime suffering.[4] While the earlier irritations felt by the Dutch are now entirely past history, Indisch Dutch resentment is not.

It is now a good sixty-five years since the disembarkation of the first repatriates and four decades since the arrival of the first *spijtoptanten*, or 'regretters'. This lengthy period cannot simply be summed up in the worn-out motto of 'quiet assimilation' and neither should Indisch Dutch life in the Netherlands be reduced to a resentful narrative of being misunderstood and unappreciated. Yet the demand for recognition was indeed the most important theme behind almost all the initiatives to mobilize the East Indian community: recognition that they had their own identity, recognition of the hardships they had endured, recognition of their right to restitution. The question of what an Indisch Dutch (or Moluccan, or *totok*, or Dutch) identity might actually be will be addressed later in the book. Here I am looking at the struggle for an acknowledgement of the hardships they underwent within the trilogy of war, decolonization and migration, and arrival in the Netherlands.

To briefly sketch this history, in March 1942 the East Indian government capitulated and almost all *totoks* were interned in Japanese camps or taken into forced labour elsewhere; around 150,000 people were interned. A minority of the Indo-Europeans were interned; most, known as *buitenkampers*, remained outside the camps, often in extremely grim circumstances. Conditions in the Japanese camps were brutal; almost a tenth of those interned did not survive the war.[5] Yet, there were even more horrendous circumstances. The Japanese used the Javanese for forced labour. On Sumatra, a majority of these *romushas*, around 200,000 of them, died. This story is suppressed in Indonesia, because it points to Sukarno's role in recruiting Javanese labourers, and in the Netherlands because the repatriates, understandably, only drew attention to their own suffering.

The Japanese surrendered on 15 August 1945; Sukarno and Mohammad Hatta proclaimed independence two days later. In the power vacuum that arose, which lasted until the beginning of 1946, thousands of *totoks*, Indo-Europeans and Chinese were murdered locally by radical nationalists and criminals. The anarchic terror of this *bersiap* period was a traumatic consequence of the dream of 'liberation'. The irony was that the *totok* internees were now in a better position than the Eurasians outside the camps. The former Japanese camps provided protection against rampaging Indonesian mobs who loathed the 'Indisch parasites'.[6]

Dutch authority was temporarily and incompletely restored. Between 1945 and 1949, around 120,000 Dutch troops served in Indonesia. Around 5,000 of them died, a fraction of the number of Indonesian casualties. Most returned safely and would carry the memories of maintaining order and 'police actions' with them for many years to come. It is clear that they had Indisch experiences; the question became whether, back in the Netherlands, they could and would join in the Indisch fanfare. In other words, would they become part of what sociologist and military veteran J.A.A. van Doorn characterized as the 'community in adversity' of the 'Indisch generation'.

Sovereignty was transferred on 27 December, 1949. The exodus of *totoks* had already begun, followed by the Indisch Dutch and troops. Then, in 1951, another chapter unexpectedly opened: the arrival, under unclear and what turned out to be misleading conditions, of Moluccan KNIL soldiers and their families. Almost none of the 'repatriates' were sent back, their reception was frugal but, on the whole, formally correct – it would ultimately be canonized 'cold'. This was very different from the 'open arms of Dutch hospitality' Queen Wilhelmina and Crown Princess Juliana had promised on the arrival of the first ship carrying repatriates from the East Indies.[7]

WAR AND *BERSIAP*

The Japanese occupation had been hard and, for numerous Europeans, traumatic. The repatriates brought different versions of wartime memories 'home' with them. Since the 1980s, there has been a *banjir*, a flood, of camp memoirs and, on a far more modest scale, memoirs of Indisch *buitenkampers* – those who lived though the period outside of the camps and survived. In *Achter het kawat was Nederland*, historian Esther Captain analyzes the memories of the internees. Recurring themes are fear, humiliation, anger, grief and the instinct for survival – emotions the victims found hard to leave behind. The scope available for reconciliation with the 'Japs' is to this day limited, as Jet Bussemaker, daughter of an interned *totok* and a former cabinet member responsible for Indisch affairs recently experienced.[8]

Comparisons with the German occupation are drawn all the time, in the most extreme form in polemics – including between such 'first-hand experts' as writers Jeroen Brouwers and Rudy Kousbroek – around whether the Japanese camps fall into the same category as the Nazi death camps.[9] When the question is narrowed down to this degree the answer, based on survival figures, can only be that they do not. However, this is not the whole story. Former internees in the East Indies either told their story, or kept silent, in a country in which most of the population had been spared any personal experience of violence during the German occupation, had never been separated from their spouse and children, and had never even had to leave their own home; in contrast to the Jewish population, which was almost entirely annihilated, only a small number of the population did not survive the war. Viewed in this light, the average *totok* or Indisch-Dutch person had certainly had a much harder time.[10]

The next nightmare was the *bersiap*, a period that mainly affected the *buitenkampers*. In many recollections, the war and this aftermath flow into one another. And yet this period seems to play a far smaller part in the collective memory. This may be because it is more strongly associated with the difficult story of decolonization than it is with the clear-cut and morally unburdened story of the Second World War. But it is probably also because the *totoks* were far less affected by these reprisals. In post-war debates, the *totoks* frequently drowned out the *Indos*.[11]

The material damage resulting from this period was considerable for all involved. What for most of those involved was an unsatisfactory winding up after the war has recently been exhaustively investigated in government-commissioned historical research – a late gesture of acknowledgement to the Indisch community. Peter Keppy wrote about the war damage and rehabilitation in *Sporen van vernieling*, Hans Meijer about 'back pay' for government employees in *Indische rekening*.[12] The cost of damages caused by the Japanese occupation up to the transfer of sovereignty ran into tens of thousands of guilders, far more than the back pay. The precise extent was as hard to establish as the degree to which any party bore liability for the debt.[13] It soon became clear that of the four governments involved, three – the Dutch, the Dutch-East Indian, and the Indonesian – never seriously considered paying damages. In 1956 Japan, which unlike Germany paid almost no damages after the war, got away with paying very modest compensation of less than 40 million guilders for the internees of the East Indies – no more was ever paid, despite the efforts of the *Stichting Japanse Ereschulden* (Foundation for the Japanese Debt of Honour) founded in 1990.[14]

Few in Indonesia had any illusions about gaining compensation, so this demand soon turned into a final colonial project. No one spoke of Indonesian war victims anymore, Keppy observes, wryly.[15] Repatriates in the Netherlands initially cherished some hope, but were soon confronted with the fact that there were no liable debtors, which made the whole issue 'intangible'.[16] Consequently, all attention shifted to the issue of back pay, which was to become a long, drawn out legal battle. During the Japanese occupation, the East Indian government had not paid any salaries or pensions to East Indian civil servants and KNIL soldiers or East Indian navy personnel. Immediately after the end of the war, these victims demanded payment for their loss of earnings. They regarded this as a right, not a favour, a standpoint they would maintain for over sixty years.

The Netherlands' response was non-committal from the beginning, but the state was forced to change this position. Payments were made in successive rounds, although this never amounted to full compensation. Concessions were viewed as gestures stemming from a moral understanding of the situation, not as the repayment of a government debt. And so the victims' dogged battle took on a tragic air. Although they gradually won more sympathy, their wishes were only met in part, even once their claims had been more or less accepted as legitimate.

A number of different elements stand out in the long history of the battle for back pay, in Meijer's words the *'pièce de résistance* of all Indisch grievances against the Dutch State'.[17] First, there was broad support in their own ranks for the organizations that took the lead on the matter. Bosma remarked that Indisch organizations, unlike Surinamese ones, had (many) paying members. Organizations such as NIBEG (Dutch-Indisch Alliance for Former POWs and Wartime Internees), the *Indische Pensioenbond* (Indisch Pension Union) or the association of former military personnel *Madjoe* and their successors could all count on the support of thousands of paying members, because they did not set themselves abstract targets in the realms of identity, solidarity or conviviality, but actively represented the interests of their members. As long as the prospects for recognition, and therefore financial compensation, were good, the level of syndication remained high, to the degree that the emergence of any new, favourable perspectives immediately led to an increase in membership and the foundation of new organizations. This pattern became evident early on.[18]

It is possible to identify a shift in the government's approach from rejection to half-hearted acknowledgement. The initial starting point, prompted by empty national coffers in The Hague and Batavia (today's Jakarta), was firmly to discourage. Only a very modest concession could possibly be offered, which would, moreover, be charged to the Indisch government; The Hague rejected all responsibility. The Dutch business community that had been active in the pre-war Netherlands Indies was far more generous, but it was put under enormous and effective pressure to reduce the more advantageous arrangements it had proposed. This first round was concluded in 1947 with the resolution to pay a paltry 'rehabilitation' payment equivalent to three to five months salary, an offer that was dismissed in the official organ of the Indo-European Alliance (IEV) *Onze Stem* as an 'ice-cold shower'.[19]

The transfer of sovereignty implied that outstanding claims would be transferred from the Indisch government to the Indonesian government, including rehabilitation payments, few of which had been paid and which inflation had also considerably diminished. As the victims immediately pointed out, for them the road had reached a dead-end. The republic had few means and other priorities and, in the end, would never cover the rehabilitation payments, let alone consider paying all back pay in full. The only possible Indisch strategy was to present their demands directly to The Hague; in the meantime a majority of the claimants had been repatriated.

What helped was the relatively widely-held sympathetic attitude of the political parties, particularly those on the right. However, successive cabinets remained reluctant. The first cabinet of Prime Minister Drees (PvdA) decided, after a great deal of hesitation, to make 250 million guilders available for compensation, in contrast with the several billion guilders of compensation for war victims. The NIBEG, which incidentally had far more *totok* members than *Indos*, described this as a 'distressing disparity'.[20] The victims regarded the payments as pittances which marked only the beginning of recognition. However, new rhetorical opportunities arose: in 1951, through the Minister of Union Affairs and Overseas Territories, L.A.H Peters, the Dutch government, more or less by mistake, made mention of a 'moral responsibility'.[21]

The theme of a debt of honour was deployed more and more forcibly by Indisch organizations and became broadly accepted in the 1970s. Existing organizations, with a collective grassroots of tens of thousands of members, were reactivated. New interest groups, such as the *Stichting Nederland-*

se Ereschulden (Foundation for Dutch Debts of Honour, SNE, 1976) attracted thousands of members.[22]

The Netherlands became more receptive to the appeal of moral obligation; a consequence of the changing zeitgeist, but also evidence of the shock caused by the violent actions of radical Moluccans in the 1970s. Ignoring old colonial rage, read the lesson, not only translated into psychic suffering, but also gave rise to violence. By now, the Netherlands had become wealthier and the empty-coffers argument no longer washed. Hence, support for recognition and, ultimately, more generous treatment grew. First, Indisch internees became entitled to consideration under general measures such as the broad legislation that provided financial support for victims of the Second World War (1972). This was followed in 1981, at parliament's instigation, by benefits for those who had been interned in the East Indies in the form of a one-off, tax-free payment of 7,500 guilders, which was paid to breadwinners who were victims, or to their widows. The parliamentary bill, UIG, now spoke explicitly of a 'moral responsibility'.[23]

Once again the government hoped this would be the end of the matter, and once again it proved an illusion. The commercial arguments of the claimants had remained unchanged. It was not, in their view, a question of favours, but of rights, which had also been recognized by other colonial powers – a solid argument that historian Meijer supports in *Indische rekening*.[24] Only full compensation, many claimants argued, would demonstrate the full acknowledgement of the wrongs that had been done to those who, in the East Indies, had been full Dutch citizens. The amount of money offered by the UIG did not meet this demand. It was far less than many felt was reasonable, even though there was no consensus in this regard among the different Indisch organizations. What was even more crippling was the limited scope of the benefits. The UIG set the criterion of internment in Japanese camps. This excluded the *buitenkampers* and, hence, the majority of mixed-race Indisch Dutch. What in the government's view had simply been a pragmatic criterion – but a useful way of limiting the number of expected claims – inevitably came to be interpreted as evidence of discrimination. Almost all the *tokoks* who were still alive were eligible for this benefit, but only a minority of *Indos*. We may reasonably accept that the intention here was not deliberately discriminatory, but the outcome was, leading to predictable responses. Meijer has transcribed a range of indignant descriptions in the archives: 'pittance', 'dishonourable', 'sickening', 'scandalous', 'unscrupulous', 'humiliating'.[25]

The fight continued, even though the first generation had begun to die out and various organizations that had focused on back pay decided to fold.

Yet, in 1992, nineteen organizations joined together – remarkably, at the government's insistence – as the Indisch Platform, determined not to let up the pressure on the government. Supplementary measures were formulated, which now, finally, directly benefited the *buitenkampers*.[26] What was expected to be the final chapter was *Het Gebaar*, 'The Gesture', which was presented in 2000 by Prime Minister Wim Kok's second cabinet and which explicitly apologized for the 'identified shortcomings of the rehabilitation process'. *Het Gebaar*, among other things, provided compensation of 3,000 guilders for all 'Indisch war victims', that is, every Dutch citizen who had been through the war in the East Indies. The government made 350 million guilders available for this, with another 35 million for cultural, social and academic projects.[27]

It is striking that the government that marked this chapter as closed was the very same one that financed research into the question of back pay. The outcome was paradoxical. The conclusions reached in *Indisch rekening* – neither disputed nor confirmed by the Dutch government – that it had responded too late and inadequately to the demands of the victims, did not lead to any new gestures. The government, therefore, financed criticism of its own performance without feeling obliged in any way to rectify its failings. It is unlikely that any effective support will be found to reopen the issue of back pay, even though the Indisch platform is attempting to do so. For the time being it would seem that *Het Gebaar* and the Indisch Memorial Centre comprise the final settlement in this long and highly emotional battle.[28]

THE 'COLD' RECEPTION

World War II gave birth to decolonization, decolonization to the exodus, and the exodus to the postcolonial Netherlands. There was talk of repatriation, but most so-called repatriates had never set foot in the Netherlands before. The majority would have preferred to stay in Indonesia and experienced the move as displacement. Initially many may have dreamt of returning, but this was to remain an illusion – the illusion of the 'orphans' of decolonization.[29]

Would it really have been impossible for them to remain in Indonesia? The Hague had long claimed that this would have been best, at least for those who were 'rooted in the East Indies'. This group may indeed have wanted to return, but the situation was already difficult and would only get worse. 'The past had gone and there was no future, no structure to build on', is how the 'Indo' Rudy Verheem described his feelings, 'it was a no man's land; no way back, no way forward'.[30] The more Dutch-Indonesian relations deteriorated, the harder it became for Eurasians to survive in the young republic. This did not primarily come down to physical threat or deportation, but there was increasing marginalization, which gave rise to fears of worse to come. Indonesia had little patience with what it regarded as the old colonial community. The politics of *Indonesianisasi* meant the dismissal or demotion of *Indos* who worked for the government or for former Dutch companies that had been nationalized. The Netherlands acknowledged this and accepted that they ultimately had little choice other than to leave.

In the end, almost all Indo-Europeans were 'repatriated'. Since then, numerous biographical chronicles, studies and novels have been published about the journey to the Netherlands, sometimes frightening, sometimes full of expectation, the first impressions of the Netherlands, the reception, which has been canonized as 'cold', and the 'mildly terrorizing' paternalistic metropolitan guidance they were subjected to.[31] The fact that integration itself had been a remarkably successful process was played down, suppressed beneath old Indisch anger and somewhat anachronistic apologies from the Kok cabinet.[32]

Historian Martin Bossenbroek, charged with researching the post-war return to and reception of the displaced in the Netherlands, compared grounds for resentment. Were the Indisch Dutch really so badly received? Relatively speaking, not that badly, he concluded, to the surprise and outrage of many. In *De meelstreep* (2001), Bossenbroek compares the reception of all the groups who returned to the Netherlands at the end of the Second World War: the few Jewish survivors, the resistance fighters and prisoners of war, the forced and volunteer labourers, and the repatriates from the East Indies. The latter, in Bossenbroek's view, were the best received. His explanation is based on the moment at which they returned. By that time the Netherlands was already beginning to claw its way up again, logistically things were working better, and there were once again provisions to distribute – the situation had been very different in the first few months after the war, when the repatriates from other parts of Europe were brought back. He explains the disappointment of the repatriates from the East Indies partly in terms of their high expectations.[33] Bossenbroek agrees that the repatriates indeed received little sympathy for their camp experiences. However, he puts this in perspective by pointing out that even the survivors of the Nazi death camps found that their dreadful experiences frequently fell on deaf ears, if they ever felt able to speak of these at all. It was not until the 1960s that the destruction of Dutch Jewry was truly addressed and given a place within the official history of the Netherlands. Seen in this historical context, the 'cold' reception in this literally cold country does not become warmer, but it does become more understandable.

The fact that the exodus from Indonesia ultimately became inevitable was in part a consequence of an uncontrolled decolonization process. The acknowledgement that there had not been a consistent and visionary Dutch policy placed the responsibility for the repatriates' problems with the Netherlands. For the Indisch community, this was self-evident, but The Hague was slow and reluctant to acknowledge – and only partially remunerated – the Indisch victims of the process.[34] The definitive closure of this long chapter was to be provided by *Het Gebaar*. In separate moves, the two 'purple' (social-democrat and liberal) coalition cabinets under Prime Minister Kok invested several millions in research projects such as '*De geschiedenis van Indische Nederlanders*', '*Van Indië tot Indonesië*', a separate history of the Moluccans, and research carried out by the SOTO foundation, which researched the return and care of war victims and which contained a sizeable East Indian section.[35]

A combination of factors explains why, around the turn of the millennium, the Dutch government decided to make one 'final' gesture of reconciliation, when previous governments, immediately after the war and again around 1980, had thought they had already finalized this history. Much had changed in the Netherlands by this time. In the 1960s, the Second World War was 'rediscovered' in a far more critical light and has provided the moral touchstone ever since. Owing to the strong Indisch lobby, the Indisch dimension of the war had by now become an integral element in this narrative. 'Acknowledgement of past suffering' gradually became a right for any group that could convincingly present itself as victims and, conversely, it became a duty of society to honour this claim.[36] The Netherlands was also becoming ever more prosperous and could therefore permit itself to make gestures that had previously been unthinkable.

Within this context of reappraising the war and its aftermath, arrangements were put in place for all groups that had been affected by the war, beginning with Jewish survivors. This provided a model which the Indisch community then emulated. There was also another comparison which, although not often spoken of, must have played a role. From the end of the 1970s, increasing amounts of government money were spent on ethnic minorities policy, running into several tens of millions of guilders annually, reaching more than a billion euros in the new millennium.[37] The Indisch community was recorded as being outstandingly integrated and did not qualify for any of this money. So, viewed in this light, a more generous concession could also be interpreted as a justified rectification.

If the Indisch community had not forced its way into public opinion and The Hague's political circles, it would have achieved far less than it did. As discussed above, a series of strong organizations had kept the issue of reparations alive ever since 1945. From the 1970s a more immaterial offensive was launched, aimed at gaining recognition within the realm of Dutch memorial culture. More ground was gradually won, always involving an appeal to old alliances and the ensuing debts of honour.

And so, bit by bit, 15 August became transformed from an East Indian commemoration to an official Dutch commemoration, culminating in the unveiling of the national Indisch monument in The Hague (1988). Hence, the fury surrounding what was felt to be an unfair treatment of Indisch history by Lou de Jong in the East Indian volumes of his book, *Het Koninkrijk der Nederlanden in de Tweede Wereldoorlog* (The Kingdom of the Netherlands during the Second World War), was effectively translated into a demand for a new history of the East Indies.[38] The anger provoked by amiable relations with Japan – the visit by Emperor Hirohito in 1971, wreath-laying by Prime Minister Kaifu at the Indisch monument in 1991, the celebration of the 400 years of Dutch-Japanese relations in 1999 – led to furious demonstrations in The Hague which again prompted gestures of reconciliation, including the financing of memorial centres.[39] In the background of this process was the intrigue surrounding the Moluccan community and Dutch soldiers. In many respects these were completely different histories, as will be discussed below. However, the public attention these groups attracted each time helped to keep the aftermath of the East Indies in the news.

The run up to *Het Gebaar* was relatively short compared with the preceding history and was marked by the need of Wim Kok's 'purple' coalition's desire to draw a conclusive line under a series of colonial and World War II issues. In the context of a broader enquiry into remuneration and redress for war victims, which was begun in 1997, the Kok cabinet held discussions in 2000 with the Indisch Platform on the subject of financial reparations, led by Rudy Boekholt. The cabinet responded a month later, 'that this particular history book must never be closed,' and expressed 'sincere regrets and apologies' for the 'excessively formal, bureaucratic and above all cold nature of the redress'. A year later the generously endowed *Gebaar* was launched.[40] *Het Gebaar* was intended to be the tailpiece of more than half a century of compromise; a generous financial and moral settling of the accounts for wartime suffering and a cold reception. However, whether this really is the end of the matter is unclear. It is an illusion to think that everyone – the first generation, the children, the grandchildren – will ever be satisfied. There was immediate criticism, sometimes expressed in none too delicate terms with reference to the Dutch post-war normative model: 'A Jew wouldn't allow himself to be palmed off with a "Jewish tip". Only an *Indo* would!'[41] There was certainly not unanimous enthusiasm. The minister responsible, Els Borst-Eilers from the Ministry for Health, Welfare and Sports, later reported that '*Het Gebaar* had been unable to remove the sting'. Meijer also believes that the 'damages' paid by *Het Gebaar* were unable to dispel the 'bitter emotions'. The question of generation undoubtedly played a role in this. Publicist Amanda Kluveld rejected 'nurturing the same resentments as my parents and grandparents', declaring 'you can count this Indisch daughter out'.[42]

By way of closure, *Stichting Het Gebaar* (The Gesture Foundation) published a beautiful book containing a report on the payments and projects under the title *Eindelijk erkenning?* (Recognition, finally?), so, with a large question mark which was emphatically highlighted throughout by the wide variety of fragments of letters. Even at the festive closing event reference was again made to the 'cold' reception, the suffering that did not go away and the ignorance of people in the Netherlands about anything Indisch. All speeches were pervaded by the spirit of rights, not gratitude, and of the need to remain organized to 'keep the past alive'. A recent statement by Hella Haasse, 'We are not finished with the East Indies by a long chalk', was quoted many times, including by the chairman of the board, Jan Kees Wiebenga.[43] The question is how wide the 'we' community is today and how many will feel affiliated to it in the future.

THE UPROOTING OF THE MOLUCCANS

For Moluccan migrants, the prelude that took place in Indonesia was different, but the end result – permanent residence in the Netherlands – would turn out to be the same. The departure of 12,500 Moluccans (KNIL soldiers and their families) in 1951 had become inevitable, because they did not want to be demobbed in the republic while Indonesia was demanding they distance themselves from the ideal of an independent Moluccan republic (RMS). A military command from the Netherlands was decisive in the end. Moluccan KNIL soldiers were given the choice between army discharge on Java or being shipped out with their immediate families to the Netherlands. They chose the second option. When they arrived in the Netherlands they were outraged to find themselves instantly discharged from the army. The helpless rage this aroused was to hold the Moluccan community firmly in its grasp for many decades.

Event commemorating the 35th anniversary of the Moluccan community in the Netherlands; Prime Minister Ruud Lubbers handing Rev. S. Metiarij the 'Rietkerk resolution', named after the Minister for Domestic Affairs, Koos Rietkerk, who was also responsible for minorities policy. The resolution provided for an annual payment of 2,000 guilders to former KNIL soldiers and others who, in 1951 and 1952, had been brought to the Netherlands 'under the care of the Dutch state' and which counted as (the beginning of) reparations. Queen Beatrix also attended this ceremony. The Hague, Ridderzaal, 25 November 1986. (COLLECTION NATIONAL ARCHIVE)

The 'cold reception' is a cherished cliché throughout the Indisch community. But the resentment among Moluccan Dutch lies less with the reception and care they received than with the evacuation itself and the impossibility of going back. This is a precarious story. There is good reason to accept that the military commanders and the Dutch government in The Hague deliberately issued mixed messages about the 'temporary nature' of the Moluccan soldiers' stay in the Netherlands.[44] However, the protracted integration into the Netherlands cannot solely be blamed on The Hague's policy. Long after it had become clear that Indonesia would not contemplate Moluccan independence and that the Dutch government had no influence in Jakarta, the Moluccan leaders in the Netherlands continued to propagate the old ideals and, thereby, the view that integration was undesirable, or at least of secondary importance.

Moluccan integration was consequently ill-starred from the start, as researchers Smeets and Steijlen make clear in their (state-commissioned) book *In Nederland gebleven* (Lingering in the Netherlands, 2006). The Moluccans' social capital was relatively weak. Of course, they were fiercely loyal to the Dutch Royal family and were overwhelmingly Christian, but their average level of education was low and their command of the Dutch language poor. Their accommodation at separate locations – 'islands of embitterment' (Bossenbroek), such as the former Nazi camp Westerbork[45] and later in separate residential neighbourhoods – reflected the hope of an early return to the Moluccas. This illusion, which was sniggeringly contradicted by the Dutch, formed a tremendous obstacle to integration, which indeed stagnated in all areas, starting with work and education. Two decades after their arrival in the Netherlands, the Moluccans' situation was quite simply depressing. The deep frustration felt by the young was partly directed at the older generation, but above all at the Dutch state. The consequences were serious. Violent occupations (the Indonesian ambassador's residence 1970, the Indonesian consulate 1975, a primary school 1977, the Provincial Government Building in the eastern Dutch province of Drenthe 1978) and train hijackings (Wijster 1975, De Punt 1977), to this day unique events in Dutch history, transformed Moluccan anger into a national concern. Whatever the demands, The Hague saw no way to support the republican ideals and only now made this patently clear.[46]

Integration and pacifying agreements were at the heart of the Dutch government's new Moluccan policy, an approach that would provide a model for minorities policy in a broader sense.[47] It brought the Moluccan community recognition – in the sense of 'redress' – its own 'pillar' or compartment in minorities-land and, a bit later, a unique Moluccan historical museum in Utrecht (Museum Maluku, Utrecht, 1990) as well as a government-financed written history. Moluccan integration improved, by fits and starts, in part thanks to a focused government policy and a broader acceptance that return to the Moluccas had become an illusion. No less important is the demographic integration: increasing numbers of Moluccans have found life partners outside the Moluccan community.[48]

In the battle for recognition, the political, transnational element of the RMS has faded into the background somewhat since the end of the 1980s, while the first generation's argument regarding the Dutch 'betrayal' has remained prominent. This appears to contain a certain inconsistency – if one accepts that the RMS had never been a realistic ideal, what could have been an alternative for 'repatriations', other than giving up the ideal? This is a thorny issue which, it would seem, is still difficult to discuss openly. In the meantime, the RMS changed from being a concrete ideal into a more abstract identity symbol, as anthropologist Steijlen has put it, including for the Moluccan youth; a turn towards a less binding engagement with the Moluccas.[49]

The Moluccan community, therefore, remained separate from the Indisch community, just as it had been in the East Indies. The extension of *Het Gebaar* to the Moluccan Dutch was therefore not a self-evident outcome. But it did correspond with the gradual integration of Moluccans into the postcolonial Netherlands. Consequently, in the late 1970s, it was possible for the Dutch parliament to offer its apologies to the Moluccan community, employing such notions as 'dishonourable treatment', 'cold and impersonal attitude' and 'debt of honour'. No reference was made to the familiar Indisch theme of the sloppy processing of KNIL pensions and reparations.[50]

VETERANS AND THE INDISCH COMMUNITY

For the Indisch community, the Japanese occupation, the *bersiap*, decolonization, the forced exodus from the East Indies, and the cold reception in the Netherlands were an ongoing story. During the 1945-49 conflict – the middle part of the story – 120,000 Dutch armed forces entered a colonial history in which they had previously, at most, played an indirect role. They arrived as defenders of the colonial order and, hence, of the *totoks* and Indisch Dutch. Back in the Netherlands, following a futile struggle, they would go on to play their own part in the way the Dutch processed the war and decolonization. Their role was ambivalent, as was the relationship between the Indisch community and these former soldiers.

The army comprised not only professional soldiers and national service conscripts, but also KNIL fighters. Their joint task was to restore a colonial order that was still undisputed back in the Netherlands. The number of conscientious objectors was therefore small. The general feeling was that the East Indies were of crucial importance to the Netherlands, economically and geopolitically, but also that the Dutch had a developmental and ethical mission to complete. Because the republic was associated with Sukarno, Sukarno with Japan, and Japan with Germany, the conflict also had an idealistic and revanchist character. For four years, parley and combat alternated, or sometimes ran simultaneously. From a Dutch perspective, the conflict was an inglorious defeat. The war turned out to be much more violent than expected and, moreover, futile, because the Netherlands found itself increasingly isolated in the diplomatic arena. Hence, the illusion of a restoration of the East Indies and, later, of a special relationship with Indonesia had to be abandoned.

The soldiers came back to a country that found it hard to live with the defeat, right into the highest echelons of society. But soon, since nothing else could be done, the rancorous noises subsided and the Netherlands turned its attention to the order of the day – the post-war rebuilding of the country. This is also how the German occupation had initially been 'processed' – by avoiding any self-examination. The critical re-examination of the war on Dutch soil gained momentum in the 1960s, followed a little later by re-appraisals of the last war in Indonesia.

This moment can be very precisely dated: 17 January, 1969. In a current affairs programme by the TV broadcasting company VARA, *Achter het Nieuws* (Behind the News), the veteran J.E. Hueting spoke frankly of atrocities committed by Dutch troops.[51] His testimony struck like a thunderbolt, leading to vehement discussions and the setting up of an enquiry committee. Its 'Excesses Report' – a pregnant title – concluded that the army was not guilty of 'systematic atrocities'; insofar as any evidence of torture and worse was found, it related to isolated incidents. This conclusion was met with divided opinions. A year later, war veterans J.A.A. van Doorn (the sociologist cited several times above) and W.J. Hendrix described this report in *Ontsporing van geweld* (Tracking violence) as a 'shameful document' that played down the systematic terror. The assessment remained controversial, concluded historian Stef Scagliola in *Last van de oorlog* (Troubled by the war), as did the government's stance and the question of whether the successive governments that had protected the veterans might also have had something to hide themselves.[52]

This episode bore contradictory consequences. First, there was a deep division among the former military themselves. The majority thought more in terms of having carried out their duties to the best of their abilities and in an orderly fashion, rather than of excesses or an immoral war, but their recollections were extremely diverse. The perspective that justified the war corresponded largely with the Indisch view, in which the only conceivable answer to the post-war anarchy and the nationalists had been firm, but righteous intervention. However, in retrospect, the broad publicity attracted by conscientious objector veterans and the few, like Poncke Princen, who defected for their principles, casts the post-war years and, hence, the colonial order that was being defended, in another light. Thereafter it was impossible to commemorate the 5,000 Dutch soldiers who died in Indonesia without mentioning the multitudes of Indonesian victims, or to speak of the loss of the East Indies without putting the legitimacy and justifiability of the colonial order up for discussion.[53]

The Indisch community had complained for a long time about a lack of interest and recognition. Now that more was finally being said about the last years of the colony, the mood was mixed and the tone often strident. Alongside sympathy for the repatriates' departure from Indonesia, their homesickness and the resentment they felt, an image of the Indisch Dutch now emerged as a pre-eminently privileged class of the 'wrong' colonial kind. The Indisch community might at this point have turned, sulkingly, in on itself. But the opposite occurred. It was precisely after this episode that the battle for acknowledgement really got underway. And even though complete redress was their most concrete aim, the focus was increasingly on defending the old order and the Indisch role in it against allegations of self-serving, unjust, violent colonialism.

Consequently, an uncomfortable split arose, which generated striking silences. Where there was talk of discrimination, it was the Indisch Dutch who were the victims of Dutch racism with little being said about their own pre-war attitudes to the 'natives'. Where post-war violence was discussed, the Indisch community spoke of the *bersiap* period, not of Dutch war crimes. Distressingly, in the memories of veterans, it is often precisely the Indisch and Moluccan troops who are deemed to have been violent. This, naturally, never became a popular theme in Indisch and Moluccan circles.[54]

The East Indian veterans were given their own monument in 1988 in Roermond. It was unveiled by Prince Bernhard, prince consort to the former Queen Juliana. This was a remarkable delegation of duties considering Queen Beatrix had unveiled the Indisch monument in The Hague a couple of weeks earlier. A Veterans' Platform was established and the government set about developing a veterans policy. In 1990, the Dutch government, through the Minister of Defence, Relus ter Beek, offered the East Indian veterans the government's apologies for showing them insufficient understanding and guidance on their return to the Netherlands. An apolitical acknowledgement which did not raise the justification for and the point of the war.[55]

Van Doorn included the veterans in what he described as 'the Indisch generation'. There is much to support this stance in the sense that they contributed to keeping the East Indies alive in the Netherlands and, like the Indisch community, continued to influence Dutch government policy on Indonesia for a long time and were deeply offended about what they felt to be a lack of recognition and appreciation. But were they really Indisch in a sociological sense, a community with a shared fate? This is doubtful. Ultimately, the veterans were too transient and had no ties to the pre-war East Indies. Partly because of this, decades later many of them were to become more critical of the old colonial order and the attempt to restore it. The public case of

POSTCOLONIAL NETHERLANDS

the veterans was, above all, whether their devotion to duty as soldiers was fully appreciated, which was quite separate from any personal pride, shame or trauma.[56]

MEMORIAL CULTURE

The call for recognition reflects a desire to be accepted completely and to belong – in the case of the 'Indisch generation', to belong to the imagined community of the Dutch nation. Soldiers and *totoks* could assume they were accepted as Dutch; for them it was quite simply a question of whether their experiences were taken seriously. The Indisch Dutch doubted, correctly, whether their citizenship was taken seriously. They had always viewed their ties with the metropole as family relations, as Ellen Derksen, the driving force behind the enormous annual fair in The Hague, the *Pasar Malam Besar*, put it. It is striking how soon and how bitterly the metaphor of second- or third-class citizens – or 'pseudo-Dutch' (Tjalie Robinson) – took root in Indisch circles and how often complaints were made about 'disloyalty' and a lack of solidarity in the Netherlands.[57]

The Hague's reactions evolved from dismissive through non-committal to accommodating, but the ambition to finally draw a line under the period 1942-1949 remained intact. In 1965, *Pelita* – the foundation charged with payments to war victims, which had been founded in the East Indies – was almost dissolved, 'because people cannot remain war victims forever'.[58] However, Pelita continued, more payments were made, but many continued to be resentful. Fifteen years later, vvd senator Wiebenga called upon the Indisch community to close the issue of back pay, 'also for their own spiritual welfare'. The same Wiebenga later became chairman of *Het Gebaar*, the discontinuation of which he oversaw in 2009, while at the same time describing the government's gesture as 'late and limited'. It remained difficult for all parties to find a middle way between acknowledgement and closure. Historian Cees Fasseur established in 1985 that the war never ended for many of the Indisch generation; a quarter of a century later the generation is greatly diluted, but the emotions remain.[59]

The struggle for acknowledgement also had an immaterial aspect – and again it was a long time before a space was forced open to allow for an Indisch perspective. The national World War II monument in the central Dam Square in Amsterdam was initially only intended as a European memorial. However, at the insistence of prominent Dutch from the East Indies it was decided that an East Indian urn should be added to the design. The urn,

The first major commemoration of the war in the East Indies took place in The Hague on 15 August 1970, twenty-five years after the Japanese surrender. More than 10,000 people attended, including Queen Juliana; the Minister of Culture, Recreation and Welfare, Marga A.M. Klompé; the Minister of Finance, H.J. Witteveen; and the last Governor General of the East Indies, A.W.L. Tjarda van Starkenborgh Stachouwer. This photograph of the entry of Tjarda and his wife evokes an image of colonial nostalgia. (COLLECTION NETHERLANDS INSTITUTE FOR WAR DOCUMENTATION)

which was added in 1950, brought a layer of symbolism to this national monument which, above all, reflected the experience of the *totoks* – Dutch who had just happened to be somewhere else. There was nothing to show that the KNIL had largely consisted of indigenous soldiers or that the Indisch Dutch had also suffered during the war. Thus, the 'monument on the Dam' also symbolized Dutch ignorance of the Indisch world and its wartime experiences.[60]

The memorial culture around the Second World War became more critical from the 1960s onwards, substituting concern about Jewish and other victims, collaboration, traumas and ethical dilemmas for a previous insistence on national heroism.[61] And, gradually, as the Indisch community became more organized and expressed its grievances and desires more openly, more space was demanded for the Indisch wartime experience. Invariably, it was the repatriated Dutch who took the initiative for monuments, but along the way it also became clear that the war in the East Indies was not only an issue for the *totoks*. It took a long time, but in the end 15 August, the day of the Japanese capitulation, became a national day of commemoration. Once again Indisch organizations took the lead, led by G.S. Vrijburg, the man who was later behind the *Stichting Nederlandse Ereschulden* (Foundation for the Dutch Debt of Honour).

In 1970, a memorial ceremony was held at The Hague Congress Building attended by around 10,000 people; guests of honour included Queen Juliana, Princess Beatrix and the last Governor General of the East Indies, A.W.L. Tjarda van Starkenborgh Stachouwer. The day was felt to be a great success. Tjalie Robinson wrote in *Tong Tong* of an 'atmosphere of pride in the Commemoration', but also that it was to be 'the first and last' such ceremony.[62] This turned out not to be the case. The first Indisch monuments were unveiled in Apeldoorn (1971) and Bronbeek (1975). Many books were published and exhibitions held. In 1980, the new 15 August 1945 Foundation organized a national memorial ceremony in Utrecht, attended by 11,000 visitors including Queen Beatrix, members of cabinet and the Indonesian ambassador. The crowning moment of the foundation's work was the unveiling of the Indisch monument in The Hague, once again in the presence of the Queen and members of the cabinet (1988). Ever since, 15 August has been a national day of remembrance, a day that is marked not only in The Hague, but throughout the land at relatively recently constructed monuments.

The tenor of all this remembering does not seem to have undergone any great development: starting with the Japanese, ending with the cold reception, and including the long and never truly won battle for acknowledgement. The scope of the attention paid to victims has broadened along the way to include *totoks* – who, remarks Captain, became more Indisch through the process of remembering – Indisch Dutch *and* Moluccans.[63] The impact of the war on the vast majority of the 'native' population of Indonesia has never been a central issue. The memory remained Indisch.

That the war in the East Indies would not simply go away had become quite clear. But the acknowledgement that was being demanded raised new questions, which were posed more and more forcefully, about the way the

The Hague, 15 August, 1999. Prime Minister Wim Kok and Minister for Health, Welfare and Sport, Els Borst-Eijers, head the procession at the Indisch monument. 15 August became a national day of remembrance in 1988, forty-three years after the Japanese surrender. Both politicians were closely involved in establishing *Het Gebaar* for the Indisch and Moluccan communities in 2000. (COLLECTION ANP)

war was commemorated in the Netherlands: why continue to remember and, now that the generations who lived through the war are fading away, how should it be done? The answers to these questions recall the German occupation and revolve largely around the dual themes of 'Auschwitz never again' and respect for minorities; in this sense they are forward looking.

The memory of the Japanese occupation is less easy to bring up to date. The annual commemoration at the Indisch monument in The Hague on 15 August has attracted on average 2,000 people over the last few years. Dutch television dedicates considerable airtime to the ceremony, which is very different from what tends to happen with, for example, the national commemoration of the slave trade and slavery on 1 July.[64] There is no longer a lack of recognition surrounding Indisch war-related suffering. However, this has not meant that ceremonial commemoration has become truly national, nor that ceremonial commemoration will long outlive the Indisch generation. The opposite is more likely to occur. Historical monuments and ceremonies tend to become anachronisms once the generations who shared the experiences being commemorated have died out. Those who attend the Indisch monument in The Hague still form an impressive gathering, but their number is nothing compared with the numbers that attended in 1970 and 1980.

To prevent forgetting, and after the inglorious demise of the earlier Indisch House in The Hague, the government decided in 2007 to set up the Indisch Memorial Centre (IHC, *Indisch Herinneringscentrum*) on the country estate of Bronbeek in the east of the Netherlands. This is a home for veterans of the East Indies and a museum primarily about military colonial history. The museum, which after many delays finally opened its doors on 16 August, 2010, focuses on the modern history of the Indisch community, with particular emphasis on the war and its aftermath, including the exodus and integration in the Netherlands and elsewhere. The target group, the Indisch community, is very broadly described as 'anyone who has links with or feels connected to the Dutch East Indies or Indonesia' – this broadening of the scope, like the set up of the IHC itself, is evidence of the realization that the existence of such a community and an Indisch identity is less and less a matter of course. The complaints about Dutch forgetfulness and frugality remain, but it is the duty to remember that is increasingly being hammered home. Erry Stoové, chair of the IHC and, among other things, former chair of *Pelita*, speaks of a history that 'must continue to be narrated and represented. For ourselves, by way of solace, and for our children and grandchildren, to provide them with something to hold on to'. The current chair of the Indisch Platform, Herman Bussemaker, has frequently used similar expressions.[65]

How long will this incantation continue to work and what can such a memorial centre mean today, now that a fourth generation is growing up? For how long will the scores of memorials that have been built continue to be visited and understood? Like monuments to the Holocaust, in their appeal to remember, not to forget, they attest to the fearful realization that more and more is forgotten forever and that not only the memory, but also the remembering community, eventually vanishes.[66]

What in any case will remain, besides individual memories passing down and changing from generation to generation, is the collective historiography. Piles of books have been written over the last few years, paid for by public money, aimed at presenting a balanced Indisch history. This written memorial would not have come about without a strong Indisch lobby, which initially crystallized around the anger about what was felt to be a one-sided account in the Indies' sections of Lou de Jong's semi-official history of the war.[67] It is, moreover, striking that almost the entire corpus of the new official history of the Dutch East Indies that has come about in this way was written by (male) historians with no previous personal ties with the colony.[68]

Examining the history of the struggle for recognition, several things stand out. First of all, that Van Doorn's 'Indisch generation' never became united. The parameters, of course, became more inclusive – *totok* domination disappeared and the Indisch voice became stronger – but the Moluccan community remained relatively isolated, also in terms of organizations. This was even more the case with the Dutch soldiers.

A sense of incompatibility also forces its way to the surface. The bitterness of the first Indisch generation remained, regardless of how often the government exhibited regret or how many more 'gestures' it made than it was initially inclined to. These concessions were not won without a battle, nor indeed without a strong lobby of organizations and spokesmen (and they were predominantly men). The Indisch organizations were in part as strong as they were, because they were able to mobilize their grassroots for concrete and, to a degree, legally underpinned aims: it was not a matter of simple acknowledgement or appreciation, but financial demands with real value. Their ambit within Dutch administrative circles was considerable because prominent members of Indisch organizations often occupied prominent positions in Dutch society and came into contact with high-ranking administrators who could boast of East Indian experience. This made it easier for them to identify with each other within a notion of shared citizenship and all the duties this entailed, particularly duties they ascribed to the Netherlands.

Of course, the Dutch government never fully met the demands. There is still disagreement surrounding the legitimacy or fairness of The Hague's position. A cynical view would be that Indisch representations revolved around self-interest, with little concern for the destitute conditions of the indigenous population of Indonesia in 1945 (or later). That, in other words, harping on about their own citizenship was a continuation of a colonial discourse of inequity and racism. The Indisch perspective was very different. It saw the Netherlands as always holding the purse strings, as highly cautious about stripping colonial citizenship of its predicate 'colonial', which would lead to it being confronted with financial consequences. Many *Indos* experienced this as racial discrimination, an accusation that hits home harder in the postcolonial Netherlands than it once did in the East Indies.

At the same time, it will not have escaped the attention of many Indisch Dutch that The Hague not only began to spend serious money on development aid to Indonesia, but, moreover, began to transfer increasingly large sums of money to the Caribbean territories, starting with a few hundred guilders per capita in the early 1960s to several times this amount in later decades – expenditures that would far exceed all the compensation that was ever paid to repatriates.[69]

WEST INDIAN AND DUTCH STORIES AND SILENCES AROUND WAR AND EXODUS

History is told through ordering; through remembering and commemorating, but no less through forgetting and suppressing. Conscious and unconscious choices by diverse groups and individuals lead to very different stories about the past. If we compare the wars in the Dutch East Indies, the Netherlands and the West Indies, the factual differences are enormous. And these differences are reflected in collective memory. If we look further, in this case into West Indian memory, characteristic silences emerge. Suriname and the Antilles were the only 'free' (although, of course, still colonized) parts of the Kingdom of the Netherlands during the war. Allied troops ensured this status and enabled the Surinamese bauxite industry and the oil refineries on Aruba and Curaçao to make an important contribution to the allies' war industry. The colonies supplied volunteers and mariners, many of whom were killed. Several dozen West Indians, who were living in the Netherlands at the time, joined the resistance; a number of them were shot by the Germans or died in concentration camps, like Surinamese Anton de Kom, Aruban Boy Ecury and Curaçaoan George Maduro. This is a footnote in the grand narrative of the Second World War, but a source of Caribbean pride and, therefore, a story that took on a new strategic value, alongside the inherent emotional one.[70]

Shortly after the war, George Maduro's parents put up the starting capital to build the permanent exhibition in The Hague of the Netherlands in miniature, Madurodam (1952). It was not until 2006 that Anton de Kom came to be remembered in stone, in controversial exotic nudity in Amsterdam Zuid-Oost. By now, the Caribbean community in the Netherlands had grown enormously and the willingness to accommodate Suriname and the Antilles in World War II commemorations had correspondingly increased. A war pension was finally paid to West Indian veterans in 2003. The first exhibition and publication on the theme, *Wereldoorlog in de West* (World War in the West) dates from 2004. The civilians and military personnel who were interviewed delivered the message that West-Indian solidarity during the war led to Dutch obligations today.[71]

In Indisch history, repatriation is directly linked to the war and decolonization, something that was inevitable and which therefore generated rights – the right to find refuge in the Netherlands and, above all, the right to expect more than a chilly reception. A similar story cannot be told of the colonies in the West. The war did not bring collective suffering, but rather some prosperity and an opening to democratization and controlled decolonization. As Elfriede Ferrol-Macintosh, from Suriname, powerfully summed it up: 'We celebrated the war.'[72]

The exodus from the former West Indian colonies began much later, had nothing to do with the war and can hardly be described as unavoidable. More than a third of all Surinamese voted against independence with their feet, out of free will, unimpeded by the Netherlands. Antilleans – voters and politicians alike – have rejected independence for decades. Despite, from a regional perspective, enjoying a materially privileged existence, more than a third of Antilleans have decided to settle in the not-much loved, but much more prosperous and freely accessible metropole.

There are no heroic tales to tell about this either and so the dominant West Indian explanation for the migration revolves around rights linked to citizenship: the right to unhindered access; the right to work and enjoy the collective rights awarded every Dutch citizen; and the right, in all respects, to belong. But in stark contrast to the Indisch narrative, the exodus itself is not a popular theme. It is painful, not because things were so bad for the Caribbean community, but because the migration is marked by choice, not the absence of the alternative: to remain at 'home'.

The Netherlands learned to live with the Caribbean exodus. This is less relevant for the second generation of Surinamese and Antilleans, but what was the situation for the first generation? Constructing a narrative remained a delicate affair. The easiest option was the construction of forces beyond one's control, a strategy employed by Asian Surinamese: migration as flight from independence, which was dismissed as 'that Creole thing'. It was only a small step to the dramatic words spoken by Hindustani Surinamese politicians in the Dutch parliament on the eve of independence: 'Hail [Dutch prime minister] Den Uyl, masters, we who are about to die greet thee!'[73] But in the end, Surinamese Dutch of Asian descent retained just one story to tell their family and friends who stayed behind in Suriname. Not a political story of forced exile, but a story of greater opportunity and prosperity.

Early Afro-Surinamese nationalists had the most difficult narrative challenge. How can you celebrate independence when you have chosen to live in the Netherlands, how can you continue to propagate nationalism through organizations like *Ons Suriname* (Our Suriname) which fail to tempt Surinamese Dutch back to Suriname? The rhetorical way out lay in denial. Organizations like the *Landelijke Federatie van Welzijnsstichtingen* (National Federation for Welfare Foundations) initially talked a lot about a temporary stay and imminent remigration, an attitude that the Dutch government soon criticized as naive and counterproductive to integration in the Netherlands.[74] The horizon yielded. In the end, most Surinamese of the first generation – with children and grandchildren who were rooted in the Netherlands – began to think about return as a possibility for their retirement. The most popular rhetorical solution, even among Surinamese nationalists, was simply to snuggle down. The Surinamese exodus became something that, silently, went without saying. But within that silence lay a bias that verged on hypocrisy. While much has been said over the last few years about colonial trauma, especially around slavery, the exodus from the distant republic of Suriname was rarely spoken of in such terms. As if that exodus were not really a deep trauma, on both sides of the ocean. The theme was – and perhaps still is – apparently too close, too painful, too confrontational. It was easier to blame the Netherlands for the abrupt farewell to Suriname and for everything that preceded it than to judge one's own community and oneself.

A similar avoidance of the exodus as a subject for debate can also be found in the Antilles community. Unavoidability and coercion are not the issues, but choice and rights. And here the narrative goes one step further. Antilleans on both sides of the Atlantic were strongly opposed to independence, because one consequence would be the closure of the path to the Netherlands. This is as clear and understandable as it is problematic, from a nationalist viewpoint, and is the reason it is not much spoken of except in vague allusions to the role the 'seventh island' (the Antilleans living in the Netherlands) might play for the islands in the Caribbean.

Surinamese and Antilleans were able to relate more easily to new Dutch attitudes to the Second World War. The war and its memory have been constantly reinvented since 1945, by degrees less nationalistically, more self-critically and with more room for the colonies. Strikingly, a recent programme from the Ministry for Health, Welfare and Sport, *Erfgoed van de Oorlog* (Heritage of the War), was immediately and unprecedentedly directed at all parts of the wartime Kingdom. This kind of initiative, generously supported by the government, further shapes the memory of the war as a signal of recognition and inclusion for the postcolonial migrant. This acknowledgement is appreciated, though the absence of collective West Indian wartime suffering will not have passed unnoticed in the Indisch community. Sceptical Indisch views have, however, seldom been expressed in public.

The institutionalized commemoration of World War Two has acquired an increasingly explicit contemporary significance over the last few decades. The dictum of 'Auschwitz, never again' has become a warning against xenophobia and racism at home. Incidents during remembrance ceremonies and wider concerns about, primarily, Moroccan-Dutch youths have led to another broadening of war commemorations. Increasingly, the global nature of the war is emphasized as a way to draw a range of ethnic minorities into our war, our history, our commemorations. The Netherlands Institute for War Documentation (NIOD) has been actively involved in the publication of such books as *Allochtonen van nu & de oorlog van toen* (Contemporary immigrants & past war, 2004) and *Oorlog op vijf continenten* (War on five continents, 2008).[75]

Such projects developed from the best of intentions, but raise many questions, firstly about their effectiveness, but above all about the contrived use of history for contemporary ends. Over the last few years a lot of attention has been paid to the tens of thousands of Moroccans who fought with the Allies to free Europe and of the several dozen Moroccan soldiers who died in or near the southern Dutch province of Zealand and who lie buried there. This a story that might serve inclusionary purposes, but it is a one-sided story. The number of Allied troops of other nationalities who are buried in the Netherlands is incomparably higher – thinking in terms of contemporary migration, we might mention the 500 or so Poles who lost their lives here. But it is not just about numbers. In the lead up to the Second World War, 30,000 Moroccan troops helped the Fascist General Francisco Franco to overthrow the Spanish Republic, Moroccan cavalrymen fighting for the Allies were guilty of raping and plundering, and anti-Semitism was rampant in Morocco. Only telling half the story is not a serious option.[76]

A broad, explicitly non-nationalistic approach to the commemoration of war can raise very different concerns among postcolonial migrants. Their struggle was to get their own history accepted as part of national remembrance. Their war has a strategic value – right from the start for the Indisch community and more recently for Surinamese and Antillean Dutch. Yet, the wider the bounds are set around an historically linked community in the Netherlands, the less particular the colonial ties become and the more the postcolonial communities may be seen as just another group among so many 'immigrant' minorities. Again, this leads to the loss of the postcolonial bonus.

4

THE INDIVIDUALIZATION OF IDENTITY

Repatriates from the Netherlands East Indies arrived in a country that had almost no experience of ethnic diversity within its own borders and where anyone who was not white was regarded peculiar and labelled as such. There was little patience for difference and the pressure to assimilate was great. No wonder Tjalie Robinson, in his constant struggle against that pressure to adapt, rendered Indisch identity through crass expressions: 'Nations are made, ethnic groups are born: the *Indo* character is inherited and has little to do with logic or the thinking of "an orderly state".'[1]

Fifty years later, while such a characterization is considered scientifically unsustainable, it also resonates little with later generations of Indisch Dutch. For them, Indisch is more a vague feeling than the fixed 'ethnic character' portrayed by Tjalie Robinson. This relaxed approach to putting things in perspective reflects both generational change and the transformations the Netherlands as a whole has meanwhile undergone. In a multicultural society, the scope to define oneself as different on grounds of ethnicity or culture has become more a matter of individual choice than it used to be, a choice that no longer needs to be defended in the essentialist terms 'Tjalie' needed to employ in the 1950s. 'Indisch identity' has become more acceptable, but less clear-cut; the same goes for Moluccan, Surinamese or Antillean identity.

The space that is openly available for the commemoration and experience of postcolonial identities has become tangibly greater over the past few decades. This has also meant that previously 'alien' elements now form part of the nation's self image. Since the opening of the Moluccan Historical Museum in 1990, the government has supported various other institutions for the history, culture, and identity of postcolonial communities.[2] This is remarkable, considering that by the 1980s there was no longer a policy of subsidizing minority languages and cultures. But because of the centuries of historical bonds, postcolonial minorities were allowed some leeway over other immigrants.

The Netherlands East Indies, in particular, became part of the national memorial culture. In 1996 the decision was taken to found an Indisch Memorial Centre (*Indisch Herinneringscentrum*); in 2001 this turned out to have been a failure marked by internal conflict, accusations of nepotism, and mismanagement. Nonetheless, an Indisch House (*Indisch Huis*) was opened, once more in The Hague, but this institution suffered an equally inglorious demise, primarily due to mismanagement.[3] Yet again the decision was taken to start up a new centre. After many delays another *Indisch Herinneringscentrum* opened its doors at the former home for veterans of the colonial army at Bronbeek on 16 August, 2010. A National Institute for the Study of Dutch Slavery and its Legacy (NiNsee) opened in 2003. While focusing on the Afro-Caribbean population, NiNsee also seeks to build bridges to wider society. Only the Asian Surinamese and smaller minorities, such as the Indisch Chinese, have not been given a national, publicly funded, 'identity house'; but neither have they fought hard to get one.[4]

IDENTITY: INDIVIDUAL PERCEPTION, PUBLIC SIGNIFICANCE

Bridging and bonding have become interchangeable in all these memorial institutions. Anyone following the ins and outs of these publicly funded establishments – and certainly the numerous, largely self-generated and self-financed cultural festivals, gatherings, artistic expressions, publications and web sites that celebrate a specific ethnic and/or historical identity – will find that the perception of bonding carries a lot of weight. There is a deeply held sense of a shared, unique identity, often accompanied by the realization that this identity and therefore also the cohesion, sense of security and continued existence of the community is under pressure. The celebration of a specific character begins to take on a defiant air, not because it is actively threatened from outside, but because its significance quietly evaporates.

'Identity' is a vague concept. Like the earlier notion of 'race', it has evident street value in everyday language usage, but it lacks scientific clarity. The concept is such an ambiguous mixture of 'hard' (essentialist) and 'soft' (constructivist) meanings that it now barely functions as an analytical concept.[5] Amidst the stream of publications over the last few decades on the subject of identity and identity politics, a consensus has emerged that collective identity can better be understood as a process, in constant motion, rather than as a fixed result.

Academic consensus on the constructed nature of a specific form of collective identity, namely the sense of nationhood, is not automatically widely endorsed. This was made particularly apparent by fierce response to a comment made by Princess Maxima, the Argentinian-born wife of the heir to the Dutch throne, when she said that 'the Dutch person does not exist'. We, so it appeared from many critical reactions, quite simply like to feel some certainty around the question of who we are.

That 'we' presumes a sense of solidarity, of belonging to a national community. And part of this is an 'identity', frequently defined in cultural terms, that should be expressed in 'cultural heritage'. Wherever ethnic communities stress their own identity, the question immediately arises of how they want to relate to the broader society, to what extent there is also room for communality. Political and academic debates resonate with a need to complement the sharp outlines of the state with a social, cultural, and ideological dimension – to use Benedict Anderson's influential expression, to construct an 'imagined community', through which individual citizens may feel part of an entire nation, even if they regard themselves as belonging to a separate group.[6]

Homogenous nation states do not exist, even if only because there is such a thing as class differentiation. Yet it is easier for countries with limited ethnic and cultural diversity to conceive of 'the nation' as being more or less uniform. Migration made the post-war states of Western Europe more heterogeneous, a process which, far from passing off soundlessly, was the source of heated debates on the subject of the nation – Maxima's contested statement was made at the presentation of a report by the Scientific Council for Government Policy (WRR), which introduced profound subtleties to the idea of Dutch national identity.[7]

No sensible person could possibly claim that national identity does not (or should not) change. Many of the debates revolve particularly around what the fundamental principles of such an identity might be, how many and what changes are acceptable, and who should be allowed to have the final say. The state does not have a monopoly as such, but in a formal sense it does have the last word, whether in terms of establishing and monitoring national symbols and canons, or defining the space for cultural difference within the nation. Debates about multiculturalism revolve around the question of how much freedom should be granted to different views and customs, especially with respect to migrant communities, and whether characteristics specific to those newcomers can be sufficiently accommodated within what up to that point had counted as the national identity – and, indeed, whether they might be able to contribute anything worthwhile to this identity.

Where newcomers are able to muster sufficient demographic and socio-political clout, they begin to play an active part in the game of identity politics. The more minority groups there are that articulate such claims, often in strongly essentialist terms, the more complicated is the situation that arises, with desires that may be partly at odds with earlier views of the national identity and which, moreover, may also be mutually exclusive. No wonder then that in France, a country with a strong, state-centered nationalist tradition, there is much grumbling about the threat of a 'Balkanization' of the national identity and an undermining of the values of the French Republic.[8]

The Netherlands has a less assertive tradition of nationalism and a greater tolerance of diversity, which in part is attributable to the phenomenon of *verzuiling* discussed above. Post-war migrants, therefore, landed in a society that was used to diversity within its own borders, but where cultural difference related mainly to differences between different Christian traditions and between Christian and secular citizens. Two contradictory developments began to emerge from the 1960s. Increased secularization reduced the importance of *verzuiling*. On the other hand, non-Western migrants brought new religions, Islam in particular, which marked a return of religion into the public domain. This question has come to dominate the Dutch debate on migrants and multiculturalism and has also fed a political penchant for 'culturalizing' citizenship, requiring migrants not only to integrate at a functional level, but also to adopt 'our' norms on immaterial issues. 'Islam' has become a hot potato in this area.

The question at the heart of this chapter is how postcolonial migrants experienced and performed their own identity and what role they played in the national game of identity politics. On their arrival in the Netherlands, their colonial backgrounds distinguished them from other Dutch people and, as it would turn out, from other (later) migrants. This gave postcolonial migrants cause to emphasize their own character without it interfering strongly with their identification with wider Dutch society. Their call for their own identity to be acknowledged did not fade away, but gradually began to rub up against the practical process of integration, which eroded the significance of their colonial baggage.

What remained was ambiguous. On the one hand, as an extension of the experience of being different and the need to hold on to what was one's own, protagonists in postcolonial migrant communities pushed more explicitly to the fore the discourse on the enrichment of post-war culture by postcolonial cultures, which had already been employed by Tjalie Robinson. On the other hand, there remained an awareness, which was less enthusiastically voiced, of endemic 'ethnic' problems which were often related to class distinctions.

Migrants from the former colonies had the advantage of the 'postcolonial bonus' over other migrants from non-Western countries. This bonus ranged from full citizenship to a familiarity with Dutch language and culture. The weight of the European component in their colonial culture varied greatly, however, and was divided along partially overlapping lines of ethnicity and class. East Indian culture was a perfect example of a mixed culture; it is no wonder that Tjalie Robinson liked to compare this Eurasian culture with the *mestizo* cultures of Latin America.⁹ The cultures of Suriname and the Antilles too are perfect examples of centuries of creolization; yet when they arrived in the Netherlands, most Caribbean migrants were not regarded as 'Dutch' – probably less so even than the *Indos* – and probably also felt themselves not to be.

The appreciation of 'mixed' cultures and creolization has undergone a remarkable change over time. Such cultures were long considered a corruption of the European norm. It was not until the twentieth century that the ideological re-evaluation that had made such an impression on Robinson, and which in Latin America was strongly nationalist, became dominant. In the postmodern world, where there was no longer a place for 'race', the notion of a 'mixed culture' lost all of its stigma and the 'hybrid cultures' of colonial history even came to be extolled as the predecessors of a globalizing 'creolizing world'.¹⁰

Often missing from this praise of creolization is an understanding of the enduring significance of class. The continuum (African-European, Asian-European), along which new, mixed cultures developed in the colonies, was never neutral. They remained hierarchies in which the European pole corresponded with respectability and progress. In this sense, these mixed cultures indeed served as functional corruptions: the farther away from the European 'norm', the more 'bastardized' they were considered and, hence, less reputable. Respectable social advancement was and continued to be largely dependent on the extent to which the colonial citizens adopted European norms. Colour could be manipulated only to a limited degree and, in a direct sense, only over time through hypergamy, by 'improving your colour' – a widespread and, to this day, recognizable alienating strategy. Conduct and habits were somewhat easier to steer at an individual level. Social advancement was linked to internalizing and practising European norms. For ambitious individuals and families in colonial societies this opened the path to respectability and prosperity, followed by status: 'money whitens'.

Whenever cultural dynamism is praised in migrant societies, it is often in relation to culture in the narrowest sense of the word – art forms such as music and dance, literature, the fine arts, but also religious or cultural enrichment." Reference is also made to physical characteristics and aesthetics; while for centuries the derogatory term 'half-blood' was used, nowadays there is also praise for the postmodern biracial, or 'double-blooded' citizen, to use a term common in the Netherlands today – a rhetorical strategy that does not necessarily penetrate very deeply and which, in any case, continues to clash with the legacy of centuries of racism.

Less is said in this context, and certainly less jubilantly, on the significance of class. Considering the unmistakable continuity between the colonial context and the progress of integration, this is problematic. The closer to the European norm, the greater the chance of satisfactory integration into the receiving country, and vice versa. Concretely, a poor knowledge of the language – Dutch in the Netherlands – low levels of education and employment qualifications, often combined with strongly authoritarian or unstable family relations, was part of the colonial heritage that postcolonial migrants from the lower classes brought with them. Such dysfunctional characteristics also belong to cultural heritage.

INDISCH IDENTITY, FROM TJALIE TO INDO4LIFE

The feeling of being misunderstood and unappreciated by a cold and denigrating Dutch society is a leitmotif that runs through Indisch history – this shared understanding was to become fundamental to the sense of being part of a permanently distinct community. Responses to this sense of being misunderstood and undervalued varied enormously. For Tjalie Robinson, as his biographer Wim Willems makes clear, a refusal to resign himself to the situation led to an impressive struggle to defend individuality – against misjudgement, forced assimilation, loss and, thereby, not only against Dutch society, but also against those in his own circle who adapted in silence. His ambition was great: he wanted his own people, including the *Indos* to 'learn that the *urge* to live more freely is stronger than the *pressure* to live a confined existence'.[12]

It had initially been in the interests of the Indisch Dutch to stress how Dutch they had always been, even in the East Indies, where they were said to form the 'backbone of the colonial society'.[13] This was, after all, the premise of the argument for unrestricted access and the strategy for rapid integration into a society that had little regard for other cultures. The feeling of being different and the resentment at the lack of understanding and appreciation in this respect was mainly expressed in private. Tjalie Robinson was therefore relatively isolated in the 1950s with his emphasis on cultural spec-

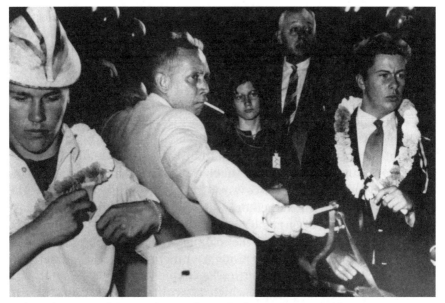

Tjalie Robinson at a fairground catapult stand, The Hague, Pasar Malam Besar, 1959. Play and posturing fitted perfectly with 'Tjalie's' predilection for Indisch *branie*, or bluster. The catapult was removed from the Pasar Malam in 1984, as the police regarded it as an offensive weapon – a striking sample of the domestication of Indisch culture that Robinson so loathed. (COLLECTION TONG TONG FOUNDATION, THE HAGUE)

ificity. Assimilated *Indos* retaliated by saying that clinging onto the Indisch identity was a 'dead end' that would only hinder integration – his popularity could not be compared with that of a crossover artist like the popular Indisch singer Anneke Grönloh.[14]

But this did not deter the indefatigable Jan Boon, alias Tjalie Robinson, alias Vincent Mahieu, from continuing his battle, supported by his wife Lilian Ducelle (pseudonym for Lilian van Zele) and a gradually expanding network of supporters, some recruited from his own family. In the end their struggle would help to make Indisch culture appreciated socially. But what was this culture? To begin with Robinson had hoped that the Indisch population would manage to survive in Indonesia as a distinct people with its 'own language, customs and traditions'. Later he came to regard the Indisch community that had moved to the Netherlands as the bearer, in Willems' words, of a 'transnational identity [...] before this term had been coined'.[15]

But what Robinson defined as 'Indisch' remains a mystery, at least for the – by him almost routinely detested, uncomprehending – outsider. At times he used a description that bound Indisch to blood lines and 'race': 'The *Indo* character is hereditary.'[16] He was more cautious elsewhere, but no more concrete. His Indisch was a mixture of pride and security, full of nostalgic references to a bygone colonial era, a hymn of praise to the fruits of a mixed Eurasian culture, a deep understanding of the internal contradictions ('that so subtly and sentimentally bedevil the Indisch') and of his own weaknesses (lack of ambition and enterprising spirit). The *Indo* mindset, he wrote shortly before his death, is 'typically universalist' – but this, of course, raises questions about what was ultimately so unique about Indisch identity.'[17]

Tjalie Robinson's struggle for the recognition of the Indisch identity was primarily a struggle for the Eurasian *Indo*, but it did not exclude the *totok*. Even if only for strategic reasons, he wanted to erase the divisions between the partially overlapping categories of class and colour. When it came to forging a single Indisch generation he revealed himself to be an optimist. He observed *totoks* in the Netherlands becoming more Indisch, while the so-called assimilated *Indo* 'didn't become a jot more Dutch'. He regarded the rapid increase in exogamy as even less of an impediment to the continued existence of the Indisch identity, which, after all, was a mixed culture. For him it was evident that Indisch culture was and would remain unique, even if outsiders, on the whole, were unable to understand this.[18] As was written in a brochure published by the *Indische Kunst Kring* (Indisch Fine Art Society), in the spirit or, perhaps, even by the pen of 'Tjalie': 'whoever grew up – or worked [in the East Indies], can never forget it. He has been stamped with a mark that is fixed in his blood, anchored in his heart'. This applied to both *totoks* and *Indos*.[19]

It was incontrovertible to Robinson and his supporters that maintaining an individual identity posed no obstacle to integration in the Netherlands.[20] This conviction was not only a prelude to the later ideology of multiculturalism, but also advanced a thesis that was to be born out in the decades that followed. Meanwhile, these early struggles generated a small, but literarily and journalistically fine oeuvre by Boon himself, written under the pseudonyms Tjalie Robinson and Vincent Mahieu, but also in the *Indisch Kunst Kring*, the annual Pasar Malam Besar fair and 'The only Indisch paper in the world', the *Tong Tong* (previously *De Brug*, later *Moesson*) which was confidently extolled as '*Trouw-Branie-Ondernemend*' (Loyal-Plucky-Adventurous).

Tjalie Robinson died in 1974, but his work was continued by his third wife, Lilian Ducelle, his son Rogier Boon, his daughter-in-law Ellen Derksen, and his granddaughter Siem Boon. From the 1970s on, scope for the public expression of Indisch identity increased dramatically, as did the apparent need to disseminate it more widely. This was initially organized using private means and personal energy. When in the 1990s the celebration of In-disch identity became more closely linked to the struggle for compensation for wartime suffering, the government became more of a generous funder. And so the financing of Indisch heritage became a political issue, but, at the same time, this heritage was gradually stripped of its sharper edges.[21]

Where the Indisch sociologist Guus Cleintuar wrote in about 1960 that it was 'at least doubtful as to whether the so-called Indisch Dutch are Dutch, feel Dutch and are felt to be Dutch', a few decades later an ostentatious em-brace of Indisch culture confirmed their complete inclusion.[22] What Lizzy van Leeuwen in *Ons Indisch erfgoed* defines as the 'struggle for culture and identity' becomes something of a symbolic catch-up manoeuvre. The em-phasis on an Indisch identity, which had been so natural in the East Indies that there were no words needed to describe it, helped to bond the commu-nity, provide security and pleasure, but was also fed by rancour.

This rancour was a response to the incomprehension and delayed ac-knowledgement that met them – Ralph Boekholt wrote furiously of the lack of recognition for Indisch 'roots without which we could not exist'. Resent-ment was often also felt later towards more assertive and sometimes prob-lematic migrants. Resentment that they were thought to have been given so much more scope, sometimes jealousy that they seemed able to disseminate their culture so much more easily. And, of course, frustration that the Dutch continued to confuse 'Indisch' and 'Indonesian'. Edy Seriese, director of the *Indisch Wetenschappelijk Instituut* (Indisch Academy) in The Hague sighed: 'Colonial history, no one knows anything about it! If "Indisch" gets mixed up with "Indonesian", it just shows that the Dutch know nothing of their own history!'[23]

Meanwhile, an understanding of the differences of colour and status re-mained alive within the Indisch community. Migrants from the East Indies brought with them a legacy of at times undisguised racism against the 'in-digenous' population, but equally in relation to colour distinctions among themselves. This was carried over into the Netherlands. While the postcolo-nial label 'Indisch Dutch' may have come to be used more freely over time, the colonial distinctions between origin and colour were not forgotten within the community and only began to ebb away somewhat in later gen-erations.[24]

The resentment at the lack of appreciation for the suffering they endured under the Japanese occupation and upon their settlement in the Nether-lands was not expressed in terms of a distinct culture. But where frustration regarding politicians' lack of willingness was expressed, references to the colonial era always slipped in. In the Netherlands, so the complaint went, *totoks* were also privileged above the *Indos*. Class and colour were on the table, but it rarely went further than mutual grousing. The strategic unity among repatriates took priority; the struggle for recognition and compensation for the hardships they had endured fuelled the desire to form a community, despite everything else.

Integration itself only strengthened this. The much discussed process of 'silent assimilation' consisted in part of a pragmatic reinforcement of the Dutch component in Indisch culture. The world of the *totoks* in the East Indies was compared with 'Hilversum [an affluent village in the centre of the Netherlands] in a heat wave'.[25] The life of the *Indo* community was far more varied; Hilversum was one extreme, the *kampong* (village), the other. The *kampong* had to be erased in the Netherlands. Malay, or the Malay- and Dutch-based mixed language Petjo, slipped further into the background, the religion was and remained Christian, and Indisch attire became purely folk costume, from high to low. With no way back, adaptation was by far the best strategy; this is why the repatriates, despite all their irritations regarding Dutch ignorance and paternalism, proved themselves willing to become 'potato guzzlers'.[26]

The more Dutch an *Indo* became, the more the culture of the lower Indisch class began to lose significance. Of course, there remained a class distinction among the Indisch Dutch, but it gradually came to resemble more closely the hierarchy that existed in the society as a whole. What was left of an internal struggle took place largely in private. Meanwhile, from the 1950s on, the Indisch Dutch began to assert themselves in mainstream Dutch popular culture, starting with singers like Anneke Grönloh, followed later by *Indo* rockers like the Tielman Brothers and the Blue Diamonds, who broke through with a largely Western repertoire. The praise expressed at the time – 'rock 'n roll is in the *Indo* blood', Indisch Dutch have the gift of dance 'that can never be forgotten' – sounds awkward today, now the metaphor of hereditary culture is no longer appreciated.[27]

In the decades that followed, the East Indies would continue to penetrate further into Dutch culture, starting with literary awards for Tjalie Robinson/Vincent Mahieu and ending with what Lizzy van Leeuwen describes as the 'Indisch Rococo' around 2000: besides the annual mega-festival of Pasar Malam Besar, numerous incidental and commercially successful initiatives sprung up, like Indisch Zomer in The Hague (2005) and a long series of nostalgic television and feature films about the *Tempo Doeloe* period of around 1870 to 1914 (*De stille kracht, Max Havelaar*), about the war and decolonization (*Oeroeg, Gordel van Smaragd*), homesickness and integration (*De stille intocht, Het land van mijn ouders*). Indisch heritage has become a leading cultural brand. In the end the government also provided funding for an Indisch Memorial Centre, thus fulfilling a long-held desire. However, results so far have been mixed at best; the first two centres were closed down due to an ignominious history of mismanagement.[28]

'Indisch people', even the second generation, remained sceptical about the acceptance of their community, of their own identity. This is revealed by the genre of witness literature, full of depictions – ranging from ironic to bitter – of the defensive way the repatriates were treated and the resulting parental resentment.[29] Such Indisch authors as Alfred Birney, Reggie Baay and, above all, Marion Bloem (*Geen gewoon Indisch meisje*) have been representative of this new, postcolonial genre since the early 1980s. The renowned Dutch author and media personality Adriaan van Dis (*Nathan Sid*, *Indische duinen*), born in the Netherlands of Indisch parents, but white in contrast to his *Indo* half-sisters, was trickier to place and even became the subject of debate: was he Indisch enough? And was the Indisch 'character' acceptable as portrayed in a popular television show by the repatriate Wieteke van Dort using a thick *Indo* accent? There were many of these, often vehement debates: about how harsh the occupation and *bersiap* had really been; about how deep colour consciousness and mutual racism had been and still were (publicist Rudy Kousbroek versus Tjalie's granddaughter Siem Boon); and on the changing meaning of the Indisch identity for later generations.[30]

These debates revealed growing differentiation in Indisch circles and raised the question of whether there was still any point to speaking of a single community with a single identity. Spokespersons of the second generation accused their parents of clinging onto the war and *tempo doeloe*, they also wanted to rebuild ties with contemporary Indonesia; but how deep this all went is unclear.[31] These were also debates that largely passed wider society by – which inevitably brings Tjalie Robinson to mind, venting his spleen on Dutch ignorance and disinterest. And so it was precisely the 'taste and smell of Indisch cuisine' that was recently praised by the Dutch National UNESCO Commission for being a textbook example of immaterial cultural heritage and striking proof of the degree to which migration has enriched Dutch culture. With such well-intentioned constrictions, writes Van Leeuwen, Indisch culture becomes not only 'impoverished' and depoliticized, but also almost entirely stripped of the dimensions of class and colour.[32]

Nonetheless, it is clear that over the past few decades the Indisch community has played a crucial role in the broadening of the notions of what comprises Dutch culture. The Indisch struggle for the recognition of an own identity formed a prelude to the arduous process of multiculturalization. A symbol of its success is the Pasar Malam Besar. Recently renamed the

With a strike on the *tong tong*, Queen Beatrix opens the 50th Pasar Malam Besar,
The Hague, 21 May, 2008. On this occasion, Ellen Derksen announced the name change
from Pasar Malam Besar to the Tong Tong Fair. (COLLECTION ANP)

Tong Tong Fair, this Indisch festival has grown into the largest 'multicultural' festival in the Netherlands and the largest Eurasian event in the world,
attracting around 135,000 paying visitors to the 50th edition in 2008. Florine
Koning subtitled her history of the Pasar Malam *'een Indische onderneming'*,
an Indisch enterprise. This underlines the extent to which the organizers –
originally the Indisch culinary author, Mary Brückel-Beiten, and Tjalie Robinson, quickly joined by volunteers from Robinson's own family, in particular Ellen Derksen and Siem Boon – deliberately ran this event as a commercial
enterprise, without receiving any external funding worth mentioning until
recently. The Pasar Malam was a gift not from, but to The Hague. This established 'the Indisch' – as their advocates had been declaring for decades – as
self-confident, enterprising, enriching, a testimony to the 'uncompromising ambition' of (*dixit* 'Tjalie') 'free, enterprising Indos'.[33]

Nevertheless, considering the changing of the generations and the high levels of exogamy that occurred from the beginning, the existence of a single
community with a shared identity cannot be taken for granted – in fact, less
so by the day. Esther Captain writes that within the Indisch community,
identity is linked to the war, (pre-war) Indisch background, or a combina-

tion of both. She believes 'that "Indisch" culture and identity will probably, in the end, outlive manifestations as war victims.'[34] This is convincing; but the biggest question remains how long 'Indisch' will continue to be a determining factor in the lives of descendants at all.

Recent research into the second and third generation – funded again by the government as part of The Gesture – documents a 'community' that is highly aware of its own 'dilution' and, moreover, speaks of it in very matter-of-fact terms.[35] What is summed up as typical of the Indisch identity is generally positive (good manners, hospitality, warmth, politeness, respect for elders, family values); there is naturally less scope for negative, colonial stereotypes (indolence, culture of gossip, inferiority complex). But what is expressed is staggeringly unspecific: 'Indisch is a feeling', just as The Hague Pasar Malam is celebrated because 'once a year you can be yourself in your own niche'. What remains is nostalgic-sounding criticism of the cold Dutch culture, which varies little from the views of other migrants from other non-Western countries, while at the same time the understanding that the Indisch identity has become increasingly a matter of individual choice.[36]

One may assume that Indisch history will end with the fading away of the generation that experienced the East Indies first hand, or via their parents, or perhaps even their grandparents. As Indisch spokesman Huub Deetman once put it, 'Indisch was there and then, not here and now'. Such a decisive rejection of postcolonial continuity passes over the way in which, precisely in the Netherlands, the need to distinguish oneself as Indisch grew in response to what was experienced as a cold reception – and how it was later felt to be imperative to emphasize ethnic uniqueness in a society that gradually became more accepting of diversity. This is still not past history. Captain has demonstrated that among (grand)children of the first repatriates the need to identify with the Indisch remains strong; Deetman's dismissal was perhaps somewhat premature. On the other hand, the identification Captain describes is so broad – aimed at the past or the present, at *Indos* in the Netherlands, Indonesia or Asia, or a dash of all them mixed together – that the question arises how distinct and communal that Indisch feeling still is. 'The main tendency,' writes sociologist Marlene de Vries in *Indisch is een gevoel*, 'seems primarily to be assimilation.' In which case, the notion 'Indisch community' is gradually, quietly losing relevance, despite Tjalie Robinson and his unremitting polemic against assimilation.[37]

There is something paradoxical about this. The Indisch community entered into ultimately successful confrontations with a society that showed little tolerance for diversity. It wrested more room for the recognition and experience of a unique Indisch identity, which was appreciated as both 'strange and familiar', and thus fended off the pressure to assimilate with increasing success. Later migrants profited from the battle the Indisch pioneers had fought for multiculturalism, long before this word existed. Indisch Dutch still state their pride in their identity.[38] But this identity has become gradually more diffuse, particularly since the Dutch elements of the Indisch identity, which were already prominent, have simply become stronger in the subsequent, 'diluted' generations. Contemporary web sites reveal how the younger generations present themselves as 'Indo4Life' or 'Proud to be Indo', demonstrating a continuity, the transfer of an older, mixed culture. But even the *Indisch Netwerk*, founded by highly educated youngsters of the third or fourth generations, has observed that 'there is now a large group of *Indos* of our generation that is completely uninterested in what we are doing.'[39] To which one may add that the free, noncommittal, individual choice to join Indo4Life is a far cry from the 'hardcore' version of Indisch identity that Tjalie Robinson once brought out into the open.

MOLUCCAN IDENTITY AROUND AND AFTER THE RMS

Among the small group of Moluccans who took up residence in the Netherlands after decolonization, the majority had previously no strong ties with Europeans in the East Indies – neither *totoks* nor *Indos* – beyond the realm of work, particularly the colonial army (KNIL). It is therefore not surprising that this lack of mutual involvement continued to play a significant role in the Netherlands, regardless of how much communality is celebrated (Pasar Malam Besar), commemorated (VJ day on 15 August) or how much recognition is enjoyed today (The Gesture). This recent 'communality' is largely the result of government policy – whether there is rapprochement at an emotional level as well is less clear.[40]

As will have become clear, the meaning of Indisch identity is disputed. The Indisch community that took shape in the Netherlands after the war remained divided along lines of class, status and colour. In subsequent generations the meaning of both 'the community' and its 'identity' became more diffuse. It produced fascinating and often exceptionally sophisticated debates within Indisch circles, but provided no foregone and certainly no uncontested conclusions.

Compared with this, the story of the Moluccans in the Netherlands is easier to survey. The identity of this small and more homogeneous community was better defined. Apart from a small, well-educated Moluccan elite in the colonial service, the majority of the male heads of households had served in the KNIL, usually in the lower ranks. However much was made in the East Indies of their *Oranjeliefde* (love of the 'Orange' monarchy and the Netherlands) and the eternal loyalty of these soldiers to the colonial authority, the culture of these KNIL personnel and their families was not so much a mixed culture as a primarily Moluccan military, 'indigenous' culture which, apart from the Christian faith of the vast majority, only contained superficial Dutch elements.

The refusal to give up what had rapidly become an illusory ideal to return to an independent (South) Moluccan republic (Republik Maluku Selatan, RMS) held integration back by at least a generation. Clinging to their own, politically defined identity made it hard to break with their own culture, even where certain elements proved dysfunctional in the Netherlands, for instance, using their own language, Moluccan Malay. Political radicalization reinforced the feeling that they were fighting for their own, clearly defined aim. Group pressure, which had been a crucial factor since settling in the Netherlands, as well as the need for security, helped to keep the community together, as did the lack of understanding and above all support from the Dutch political establishment. Following the violent actions of the 1970s, hostile reactions from the wider society may have underscored this sense of community.

The abandonment in the 1980s of the ideal of the RMS, or at least the dream of ever being able to settle in an independent RMS, created room for a less imperative and politically more symbolic interpretation of identity.[41] The orientation towards the islands, however, remained strong, far more so than for the Indisch Dutch. The Moluccan identity thereby preserved a strongly transnational dimension. But later and, as yet, incomplete improvements in the social position of the Moluccans are linked to a stepping away from the original colonial baggage – from the Malay language, from the dream of remigration, and from strict familial and communal discipline.

The route to integration and social improvement thus took on something of the character of an escape from the (grand)parents' small community. Demographically, this took shape through many mixed relationships; geographically, through leaving segregated housing and neighbourhoods; and culturally, through participating in Dutch youth culture, among other things. From the mid-1970s, the Moluccan band Massada scored hits with music that tied in with American, Latin-influenced pop music. In the early 1980s Amsterdam's pop temple Paradiso put on monthly concerts under the title *Moluccan Moods*; the musicians and a large section of the audience were Moluccan, but the music was predominantly international pop.[42]

As in the Indisch community, the reorientation of the younger genera tions did not require them to completely distance themselves from the identity of their (grand)parents. Moluccans often claim pride in their identity, which is different from simply being Dutch or Asian, let alone Indisch.[43] On a more symbolic level, the ideals surrounding the RMS, and certainly engagement with the Moluccas, remained alive. In the 1980s there was even mention of a counter reaction among some youths, a tendency to define Moluccan identity more stringently around such issues as a command of the Moluccan-Malay language and knowledge of the traditional *adat* (customs, traditions). In addition, older differences within the community resurfaced, such as ties with particular islands and communities and the separate existence of a Muslim minority.[44]

Over the last two decades the Moluccan community has nonetheless become more Dutch, out of necessity, but also through exogamy and choice. Giovanni Mataheru, grandson of a KNIL soldier and himself in the Dutch army, observed matter-of-factly that the third generation is 'completely integrated. Most of my peers are not even aware of this history. So, you should just let it be.' This last sentence poignantly expresses how identity is nowadays less and less experienced as an exclusive choice, an observation that is highlighted by Smeets and Steijlen, even though they also stress that a sense of difference still remains.[45] This feeling of distinctness, of an own identity and associated obligations may explain why the involvement of the Moluccan community with their islands of origin remains so strikingly strong to this day. And this bond is no longer seen as incompatible with integration – neither by the Moluccan community, nor by society at large.

It is over sixty years since the arrival of the first Moluccan KNIL personnel and their families in the Netherlands and there has been much reflection on the arduous process of integration. Every year around the commemoration of the founding of the RMS it becomes repeatedly apparent how strongly Moluccans feel about 'preserving' their identity. The former director of the Moluks Museum, Wim Manuhutu, recently remarked that a once 'closely structured society, a community that was relatively ordered from the top', had become 'considerably more individualistic'.[46] The debate around this tension has never abated in Moluccan circles. Meanwhile, almost all studies of Moluccan culture and identity have been written by 'outsiders' – certainly in this sense, Moluccan integration has not been successfully completed.

DIVERSITY WITHOUT UNITY: CARIBBEAN IDENTITY

Leading post-war Surinamese politicians presented an ideal of national unity to their strongly ethnically divided country under the motto 'unity in diversity'. This motto, based on the so-called *verbroederingspolitiek* ('fraternization politics') was limited in its success, but it did help to prevent serious ethnic tensions from building up – no minor achievement in a country that was so strongly segregated along ethnic lines. No one has ever remotely claimed that there is such a thing as an homogeneous Surinamese identity, nor is there an homogeneous Antillean identity, as identities are primarily experienced as island-related. Neither can one speak of a strong sense of a shared Afro-Caribbean identity among the descendants of enslaved Africans in the former Netherlands colonies.[47]

It was many years before these contrasts began to dawn on the Dutch – a logical consequence of a long history of neglect. The fact that all inhabitants in the Western colonies were granted Dutch citizenship in 1892, a privilege that was only granted to a fraction of the population of the Netherlands East Indies, did not reflect any special appreciation for West Indian culture or subjects. The Netherlands simply saw no local alternative in the Western colonies – the elite regarded themselves as Dutch – and was unimpeded by worries about population size, which was small, or the existence of radical anti-colonial movements.

The label 'West Indian' concealed the heterogeneity of the inhabitants of these colonies, the extent of which only became really clear with postcolonial migration. Prior to this, people in the Netherlands were not generally aware that Suriname was ethnically and culturally extremely diverse; that the Antilles were made up of different, fairly dissonant islands; that relations between Antilleans and the Surinamese were not necessarily easy; or even that they spoke different languages. Their Dutch citizenship made them a little more similar to each other, but to all other Dutch citizens as well.

It soon became apparent that West Indians continued to organize themselves along regional and ethnic lines, and certainly not because the Dutch authorities stimulated this. However, it also became clear that class was at least as pivotal to social integration and that culture and class were closely related, at least in the case of Afro-Caribbean migrants. This generated all kinds of dilemmas. What precisely were 'our own things', to use the expression of the Surinamese nationalist movement *Wie Eegie Sanie*, and how could they help the Surinamese to secure a place in Dutch society? Inevitably questions arose as to how widely that 'own' could be shared; how useful, for example, had the Creole language Sranantongo been in the colony and how useful was it going to be in the Netherlands – for the first generation, but even more so for later generations?

The history of slavery is a pillar of Afro-Caribbean identity; that understanding, the commemoration and the struggle for the recognition of that history help to strengthen a sense of community. But where slavery generates images of a black and white dichotomy, Caribbean history has been marked by creolization and the emergence, also in the Dutch West Indies, of mixed cultures. Here too, creolization was transected by class distinctions. Internalizing Dutch culture and mastering the Dutch language were conditions for upwards social mobility in the colonies. Meeting such Dutch standards became even more important upon arrival in the Netherlands, where it soon became painfully clear how unequally the postcolonial bonus was distributed.

Afro-Surinamese culture, in a narrow sense, initially reached the Netherlands as a black, Dutch-speaking culture with a funny accent – in the 1950s the musician Max Woiski made it to the charts with his song '*Oh Nederland, geef mij rijst met kouseband*' (Oh Netherlands, give me rice with [typically Surinamese] yard-long beans). The exodus also brought the 'working class', who peppered Dutch with more Sranan and thick accents, who assimilated less silently than the Indisch Dutch or the earlier middle-class Surinamese immigrants, and who were often more challenging. The Surinamese band Trefassi came with a provocative variation of the Woiski song by demanding '*O Nederland, geef mij WW [werkloosheidswet] à contant*' (Oh Netherlands, give me my dole in cash).

In the 1970s, Afro-Surinamese culture came into ill repute through reports about broken families, absenteeism from school, an inadequate work ethic, and drug abuse. The concerns were, it seems in retrospect, one-sided and exaggerated. However, there are indications – though remarkably little solid research – that integration was not successful across the board for the Surinamese Dutch and, specifically, that persistent problems have continued to mark the lower echelons of Afro-Surinamese communities. Anthropological research has revealed striking continuities between a self-perpetuating Creole culture of poverty in Suriname that has carried over to the Netherlands.[48]

In wider Dutch society, Afro-Surinamese culture has at best indirectly claimed a space for itself. In the 1970s, Edgar Cairo wrote hilarious, often tragicomic columns in the national daily *de Volkskrant* in which he helped himself in abundance to Sranantongo and Surinamese-Dutch; writers like Astrid Roemer (*Neem mij terug Suriname*, Take me back Suriname, 1974) and Bea Vianen (*Het paradijs van Oranje*, The Paradise of Orange [orange being the colour of the Dutch monarchy], 1973) turned the exodus into a literary theme.[49] They painted a picture of a world of huge cultural differences, enormous mutual incomprehension, of alienation and a 'life between two worlds'. Since then, the Netherlands and Suriname have come closer together, a growing number in the 'Surinamese' community has been born in the Netherlands and the Netherlands has become multicultural. Publications by contemporary authors of (part) Surinamese origins reflect this. They are more (multicultural) Dutch in theme, tone and vocabulary.

And what else? Today's urban youth culture borrows some phrases from Sranan, the annual Kwakoe Festival attracts tens of thousands of visitors every summer to the Bijlmer district of Amsterdam, popular TV personalities like Jörgen Raymann bring a touch of Surinamese flair to Dutch living rooms. Yet is is striking how limited the visibility of Afro-Surinamese culture is in popular culture. The youth in Britain embraced ska and reggae many decades ago, as French youth did *zouk*, but Suriname's *kaseko* music has never broken through to the Dutch mainstream. The fame of many successful musicians of Surinamese origin rarely rests solely on specifically Surinamese work. What they and other Creole performers and their fans mainly excel in is their participation in an international, North American and British dominated black culture.[50]

It is hard to say which image of Afro-Surinamese identity now dominates in wider society. It is clear that within 'the community', besides pride in their origins, many still feel hugely frustrated about certain negative clichés and racism that prevail, for instance, the raw nerve of what many feel is the racist tradition of *Zwarte Piet* (Black Pete).[51] This was recently graphically expressed by the anger that arose in response to the statue of the radical Surinamese nationalist and writer, Anton de Kom. At long last a monument was being erected to celebrate this Surinamese hero and was to be sited in the Amsterdam-Bijlmer square which had been renamed after him. It then transpired that the Dutch sculptor had rendered him for posterity as a half-naked noble savage, an 'honour' that would never befall a white politician or writer. The reactions in the Dutch press ranged from understanding to irritation and pity for such over-sensitivity, just as they had a few years earlier around the tumultuous unveiling of the Slavery Monument in Amsterdam. However, now there was no longer a Dutch 'us' opposing a Surinamese 'them'. No less striking was how broad the range of reactions from black Dutch people was.[52]

What may be regarded as typically Surinamese has never been very clear; ethnic pluralism and respect for diversity remain as common as they are vague denominators, the old theme of the relationship with the Netherlands has broadened to become the theme of transnationalism. The label of 'Surinamese' has continued to be primarily bound to Afro-Surinamese, a point that is not lamented by the Asian, and certainly not the Indian (Hindustani) Surinamese.[53] Successful Afro-Surinamese usually simply present themselves as Dutch with a different skin colour, a few different habits and somewhat stronger (read: richer) emotions, in which Christianity stills occupies a significant position. None of this refers to large, let alone insurmountable cultural differences.

Where discourse around a unique identity tends to speak of quintessential difference, the Afro-Surinamese, like the Indisch identity, continues to be more diffuse and more strongly linked to the Dutch colonial past, certainly more so than the (British) Indian a.k.a. Hindustani Surinamese identity. This soon marked the disintegration of the notion 'Surinamese'. Wherever the Indian Surinamese community speaks of identity and heritage, it always refers to its own group and links identity directly to ethnicity, religion and tribal land: relatively firm and far stronger criteria for a definition of self. This view of identity provided ideal foundations for self-organization and was not felt to be problematic by the wider society; it was even facilitated in the Netherlands, which had meanwhile begun to lean towards a moderate multiculturalism.

The way the Indian-Surinamese community experiences and disseminates its own identity through the celebration of religious festivals and the annual Milan Festival in The Hague (around 70,000 visitors), in part under the auspices of the umbrella organization Lalla Rookh, outlined a paradox. On the one hand it situated Indian-Surinamese identity outside Dutch colonial history and culture. The religion and bond it shared with India was the determining factor, Suriname was merely an intermezzo; the move to the Netherlands, therefore, an historical accident. On the other hand, its own culture, with its Calvinistic-like respect for family, discipline, learning and work, were presented as perfectly suited to Dutch society. Hence, so the argument goes, the remarkable success of the Indian Surinamese: spiritually different, but also successful because of their particular culture. This perpetuated an implicit discourse of difference and often superiority with regard to Afro-Surinamese culture. And, just as in Suriname, this was expressed out loud in private, but at most sniggered in the public arena – although such authors as Kanta Adhin, Chan Choenni, Ruben Gowricharn and Anil Ramdas have become increasingly less restrained in this respect.[54]

While any discussion about Afro-Surinamese culture cannot ignore the dysfunctional elements of the culture of the lower classes, the discourse around Indian culture harps on about the glorious nature of their roots culture, for all classes. The fact that less positive elements – authoritarian fathers and spouses, sexual and alcohol abuse, homophobia, high suicide rates – are only spoken of reticently, should not come as a surprise; as had earlier been the case with the Indisch Dutch, the motto was 'don't air your dirty laundry in public'.[55] Politically oriented Hinduism is not an issue, even less so than in the United Kingdom.[56]

The latter is, in itself, an interesting fact in a society that, bearing Islam in mind, has begun to judge religious difference largely in a negative light. A minority of Indian-Surinamese is Muslim, as is the majority of Javanese Surinamese. As the Dutch integration debate has become increasingly bound to concerns about Islam, the fact merits attention that there are no indications that Surinamese Muslims had problems integrating. Neither group has a distinct, individual voice, neither in the Surinamese community, nor in the world of Dutch Muslims. Indian Surinamese identify primarily with fellow Muslims who share a similar migration history from 'Hindustan' (in what was then British India), rather than with Muslims from the Arab world or Turkey. However, the current, intensely anti-Islamic tendency in the Netherlands may yet serve to shape Surinamese Muslim identity.[57]

Thus there is no such thing as 'the' Surinamese identity or community beyond this diversity and the relationship with colonial history and the metropole. Rather, the question is whether and how the different ethnic communities, which are easy to distinguish in Suriname, will each be willing and/or able to ensure their continued existence. The picture that begins to emerge here is at first a demographic one. Exogamy is traditionally strong among Afro-Surinamese, which at least at the moment contrasts starkly with the Asian Surinamese – a pattern that can be observed elsewhere in Europe.[58] In the realm of religion and, by implication, choice of life partner, the latter have continued to cherish their non-Western traditions in the Netherlands and there are few indications that this is changing.

This would suggest that the Afro-Surinamese community is becoming less separate, both demographically and culturally – a logical consequence of Western-oriented creolization stemming from the colonial era. From the perspective of integration, problems continue to centre on lower-class culture. The colonial view that this was a dysfunctional variant of Western culture was internalized more completely by the Creolized middle class. Class rather than ethnicity per se was seen as the problem, and not without justification. This problem seems to remain unabated within the urban minorities' culture of the big cities. However, the majority of Dutch people with Afro-Surinamese origins has withdrawn from this situation and feelings about identity and community will presumably come to link them less and less to those who stayed behind. Identity is increasingly experienced as an individual choice and this choice is becoming freer. Consequently, the space and motivation to bind an ever more diffuse community together around themes of a colonial past, cultural (slavery) trauma or a separate *kulturu* is declining.

That the cultural-political history of the Asian Surinamese in the Netherlands took such a different course reflects the more exclusive and rigorous definition of what is considered a distinct identity, which in turn implies serious objections to exogamy. There is no reason to postulate that this will remain the case in future, but for the time being the various Asian-Surinamese groups continue to operate more as separate (but not oppositional) communities. This does not preclude an appreciation of the fact that a 'Hindustani' may have multiple identities, nor does it preclude criticism from within – there are signs that the second generation is distancing itself from the rather authoritarian, patriarchal culture of the first.[59] It is striking, but not surprising, that in contrast to the Afro-Surinamese the Surinamese of Asian descent associate their identity so little with colonial history and resistance: their cultural singularity is simply older and more defined as it is.

Neither is there much point in using such terms as 'identity' and 'community' to define Surinamese and Antilleans of African descent as a single community. What they do share is the history of Dutch colonialism and slavery, the legacies of which some believe continue to disadvantage the descendants today, both in their emotional lives and in their social participation. Institutions such as the NiNsee attempt to unite them along these lines, but the continuing relevance of that past for the present is probably the most contentious issue discussed by leading members of the Afro-Caribbean population.[60]

The features that divide the Surinamese and Antilleans from one another are stronger: divergent local histories, a different relationship to the country of origin, and, above all, language. Where Dutch has become the dominant language for all Surinamese on both sides of the Atlantic, Papiamentu defines the Antillean identity to the extent that it even surpasses concerns of colour difference.[61] And this is the greatest dilemma facing the Antillean community. The language keeps the community together – far more so than, for example, the fact that most Leeward Islanders are Roman Catholic – but at the same time the dominance of this unique Creole language seriously impedes educational performance and the overall integration of lower-class Antilleans.

Dilemmas have been piling up over the last few decades. Independence was rejected on sound, pragmatic grounds. However, the affinity with Dutch culture and politics has not grown any stronger, especially not now there is a feeling that the Netherlands is recolonizing the islands, while at the same time secretly hoping to be rid of the Antilleans who live in the Netherlands. This exacerbates the need of Antilleans on both sides of the Atlantic to defend what they see as their own identity. Papiamentu is the defining trait here; but the absence or rejection of a postcolonial language advantage has turned out to be disastrous for a large group of disadvantaged Antilleans. This dilemma was sketched many times and many years ago, but the issue was tackled badly and only exacerbated the problem. Antillean youths in the Netherlands now have a very poor reputation. Where in the case of other problematic minorities reference is made to a culture shock and an insurmountable generation gulf, here the opposite is true. Poor language skills and school results, low employment levels, teenage pregnancies and matrifocality, and crime: these serious social issues did not arise in the Netherlands, they were simply transplanted from a lower-class culture of poverty, primarily from Curaçao.[62]

An Antillean identity can, therefore, only be celebrated eclectically and sometimes blinkered. The Antillean culture of the higher classes has generated unique music and literature. Discovered by the Netherlands and regarded there as exceptionally rich, it has also become part of Dutch heritage. Curaçaoan waltzes and mazurkas and the work of Antillean authors such as Boeli van Leeuwen, Tip Marugg and Frank Martinus Arion were met with widespread appreciation. On the other hand, the reach of Afro-Curaçaoan folk culture in the Netherlands has remained very limited – Papiamentu-language music plays virtually no part in Dutch music culture and the annual summer carnival in Rotterdam, which attracts more than a million visitors, is beginning to lose its exclusively Antillean character.[63] For outsiders, Antillean culture remains primarily linked to an unintelligible language and the problems surrounding migrants with no prospects – something that is, of course, not taken lightly by Antilleans who actively cherish their origins.[64]

A community is held together through emphasizing its own identity and through endogamy. The latter is no longer the norm for either Antilleans or Afro-Surinamese, but even the former is now under pressure. A division is clearly discernible between well-integrated Antilleans – who by definition speak good Dutch as well as Papiamentu – and the lower and underclasses. This perpetuates the divide characteristic of Curaçao. For successful Antilleans in the Netherlands, identity will increasingly become a matter of choice, perhaps a choice of distancing, with the better integrated

Antillean Summer Carnival to mark the close of the *Kunstmarkt* (Art Market) in Rotterdam, 24 August, 1986. The Rotterdam Carnival began in 1983 and has become ever larger and more commercial. In 1988 'Antillean' was dropped from the title, allowing room for other Caribbean, Latin American and Cape Verdean participants. Recent Carnivals have consistently attracted almost a million visitors. (COLLECTION ANP)

Antilleans simply enjoying greater freedom of choice. Whether they will continue to teach their children – often the products of mixed relationships – Papiamentu remains to be seen.

The parallels between Antillean and early Moluccan history are striking and might offer the Antillean community food for thought. When they arrived in the Netherlands, the Moluccans scored poorly in terms of the postcolonial bonus of the Dutch language. Moreover, they clung onto the illusion of remigration, which led them to postpone adopting Dutch as their official language. This served to bind the community together, while at the same time seriously delaying its integration into the Netherlands, with consequences for social mobility that are still discernible today. It is difficult not to read this as a warning for the Antillean community.[65]

Historian Hans Blom appositely characterized the Netherlands of the early post-war years as a country of 'discipline and asceticism' – today we may add that it was a time of almost inconceivable provincialism.[66] Yet, the country regained its international orientation, its population became more diverse and more space was created for the expression of ethnic identities. This was not a linear process. The last decade has seen a hardening of the integration debate and a tendency towards the culturalization of citizenship. However, because this reaction has primarily been directed against Islam, it has been less significant for the postcolonial communities, who instead were treated to a series of official, inclusive gestures.

In recent Dutch minorities discourse there is endless talk of cultural differences, frequently narrowed down to issues around Islam, rather than class. A multicultural culture of extreme tolerance is denounced as having undermined the fundamental values of Dutch society. Postcolonial migrants play a peripheral role in these debates. They are seen to be generally well integrated and, above all, are not viewed as presenting a threat to the social order. The first conclusion too easily steps over the existing problems associated with class and discrimination that have by no means been resolved. The second conclusion is correct; over the last 65 years, apart from the now concluded, moderate Indisch lobby against the Republic of Indonesia and the short period of violent Moluccan actions, there has been no radical political mobilization by postcolonial migrants.

From this perspective it might seem remarkable that it is precisely in the last few decades that Dutch politics has acknowledged and provided support for all kinds of demands in the realms of postcolonial identity, memorial culture, museums and cultural institutions and the canonization of (colonial) history. Furthermore, repatriates from the East Indies, unlike migrants from the Caribbean, were able to appeal for financial compensation for the war, *bersiap* and the 'cold reception'.[67] The background to these gestures was an understanding of the reasonableness of such demands, but also the view that acknowledging the postcolonial communities would make it easier for them to positively identify with Dutch society. A slogan such as 'Bound in Freedom' – the motto promoted by the government for the commemoration of slavery – evocatively expresses this aim.

In this sense, the widespread attention for (post)colonial culture and history, spurred on by well-integrated postcolonial lobbies, can also be understood as the conclusion to a process of facing up to the colonial past. Once again the critical issue is the extent to which the postcolonial communities are still able or want to define themselves as separate; where the struggle for the recognition of an own identity has more or less been won, the question of how 'separate' one really is becomes all the more pressing. Emphasizing postcolonial identity thus increasingly becomes a matter of choice – assuming society at large respects that freedom of choice. Yet there is little here that can be taken for granted. Societies are not colour blind and are almost always sceptical about newcomers and their descendants. The freedom they are granted, both individually and collectively, to preserve aspects of their own identity and to express it publicly varies greatly. The same applies to the domestic willingness to loosen the definitions of national identity and to allow room for multiculturalism.

The Netherlands has changed a great deal in this respect. In the early post-war decades, the Indisch pioneer Tjalie Robinson experienced the 'pillarized', but ethnically fairly homogeneous society as suffocating. The attitude to 'coloureds' was at best uncomfortable. Much post-war literature revolves around the confrontation with a culture that was regarded as homogeneous, petty, parochial, and often harbouring an aversion to being tainted by outside influences. The sense of alienation and frustration that resulted from feeling misunderstood and rejected would continue to form part of the collective postcolonial memory.

In the decades that followed, the Netherlands became less provincial, even though the codes for the national identity only changed slowly. Much about national identity remained unexpressed, a vagueness which for a long time was actually considered to be a wise approach. In the mid 1990s, prominent historian E.H. Kossman qualified the notion of national identity as 'an enormous jelly fish on the beach', best avoided: 'too complicated, too multifaceted and too fickle'.[68] With this Kossman positioned himself in opposition to essentialism, but perhaps he also disregarded the codes that confronted migrants in Dutch society. In the meantime, a shift towards being more explicit had begun to emerge. In the edited volume *Het nut van Nederland* (The use of the Netherlands, 1996), the influential intellectual Paul Scheffer rejected the 'boundless taking for granted' of the national identity and the negligent treatment of national history and symbols. 'What perhaps best typifies the Netherlands', he wrote, 'is a self-importance that is believed to have no need of words'. He added, programmatically in view of his later interventions in the multiculturalism debate, 'Perhaps those words are needed now'.[69] With his own work, starting with an essay in the leading Dutch national broadsheet *NRC Handelsblad*, 'Het multiculturele drama' (The multicultural drama, 2000) and culminating in *Het land van aankomst* (The country of arrival, 2007), Scheffer has exercised an enormous influence over the Dutch debate on national identity that has flourished over the last decade.

The identity issue has meanwhile become crucial. The evolution of colonial history stands out. Typical for the time, *Het nut van Nederland* did not reflect on the impact of this history or postcolonial migrations on Dutch identity at all.[70] Since then there has been continual rediscovery and recognition, in a gradually more relaxed, inclusive atmosphere, often accompanied by paradoxical self-congratulations regarding an apparent absence of pride in a national history. Critiques of colonialism *there* and parochialism *here* were contritely endorsed. If the national identity was being undermined at all, it was certainly not by postcolonial migration, as Scheffer also suggests in *Het land van aankomst.*[71]

Recognition will advance identification and hence integration, the new adage had it. Working from this philosophy, more concessions were made to the identity politics of postcolonial migrants. A number of memorial institutions were granted, from the Moluccan Historical Museum to the NiNsee and the Indisch House: from apologetic gestures ('we were in the wrong') to conciliatory ones ('now you really belong'). Consequently, it has become less acceptable over the last few decades to exclude (post)colonial literature from the official canon; museums, theatres and the media have hesitatingly paid more attention to colonial history and culture and to postcolonial artists; and accordingly more space is dedicated to the colonial past and its legacies in the new official canon of Dutch history.

Viewed from the perspective of 1950 or 1975, these changes were radical. They answered the demands of postcolonial migrants which were articulated by their own leaders and organizations or representatives. The 'struggle' for recognition was almost always moderate and – with the exception of the Moluccan actions – largely took the orderly route of demonstrations, media appearances and political lobbying. The mobilization of the grassroots for the struggle also served to bind communities together, to reunite them. There was broad political support; only right-wing populist political leaders Pim Fortuyn, Rita Verdonk and Geert Wilders explicitly opposed radical Afro-Caribbean claims – what is striking is that Verdonk and Wilders, champions of an extreme assimilation policy, both have links to the Dutch East Indies through their parents. Perhaps for this reason they feel an affinity with the normative tradition of 'silent assimilation'.[72]

However, we cannot attribute the apparent end of the cycle of recognition to this political headwind. With the passing of the generations, high degrees of exogamy, in short, with the decline in the uniqueness of postcolonial communities, the experience and above all expression of a postcolonial identity becomes increasingly a matter of choice. This also applies to the struggle for separate memorial cultures. The immediate post-war denigration and rejection of the cultural identity of Indisch migrants unintentionally served precisely to strengthen the sense of community. Where postcolonial identities later became more vague, less exclusive and more accepted, identity politics could no longer be taken for granted. Hammering away at the anvil of a distinct identity increasingly served to camouflage its loss or embodied the effort to compensate for this loss.[73]

The challenge for wider society has become far greater. Is it possible to formulate a view of Dutch identity which accommodates all migrants, without jettisoning traditions and visions that are still considered important, and which resolves more recent contradictions that no longer revolve around the colonial past? This debate has become highly polemical around the issue of Islam over the last decade. Where Moroccans and, to a lesser degree, Turks are being stimulated by a harshening of the social climate to see themselves more as faith communities and perhaps also national communities, this particular challenge passes the postcolonial migrant by.[74] Oversimplified criticism of Hinduism does not occur, while harsh words about the problems within the Afro-Caribbean population sooner lead to divisions within this group. This is partly because these issues are strongly class related; better integrated Antilleans and Surinamese have sufficient room to be able to distance themselves from the problems. Unlike the United States, or even the United Kingdom, 'black politics' – mobilization based on race – does not exist in the Netherlands.[75]

A broadening of Dutch self-identification has been underway for quite some years now. Where this relates to history, the postcolonial migrants are a step ahead; the rediscovery of a shared past is still fresh and based, moreover, on obvious grounds. That cultural advantage has disappeared in most other areas. Indisch, Moluccan Surinamese or Antillean authors no longer have a monopoly on the theme of nostalgia and the 'life between two worlds'; the enrichment of the language is no longer restricted to words lifted from Malay, Sranan or Papiamentu; government policy for the 'preservation' of cultural heritage is now aimed at all minorities. Just as in politics, migrants from Islamic countries form an increasingly distinct presence in the world of literature, theatre, the visual arts and the media, because that is where there is talent, but also because the same inclusive governmental reflex is now aimed at newcomers from the Islamic world – because cultural policy in the broadest sense is simply also political and because the better-integrated postcolonial minorities are no longer a priority.

Being a priority in a minorities policy is, by definition, bad news. But even so, this offers scant comfort. Many Dutch from a postcolonial background are unhappy about what has been achieved to date and continue to demand more appreciation of their own histories and cultures. The mobilization of partners in the face of adversity is the most obvious way to bind a community together. That solidarity still exists and is preserved in memories – less now of the country of origin and more of arrival and integration in the Netherlands – and identifications with an own heritage. These emotions will remain, but will become increasingly less noticeable in a multicultural society. Bonding can create space for bridging.[76] Where identification becomes increasingly a matter of choice, where all citizens are increasingly able to reinvent themselves within multiple identities, the scope for postcolonial migrants to organize collective struggle diminishes. The need for a political translation of postcolonial desires ebbs away and, following the same logic, the notion of the 'postcolonial community' evaporates.

This sobering conclusion might be contradicted with reference to the numerous expressions of postcolonial identity among the young, to the series of recent studies of which grateful use has been made in the above, to the memorial institutions which will combat precisely that forgetting. But appearances can be deceptive. The players in the game of identity politics (claim to) speak for a grassroots that is losing its cohesion; academics analyze their expositions, but grope around in the dark trying to find out how representative they are. Where the struggle against erosion is chronicled, the process of erosion itself can be overlooked. However legitimate or refreshing it may be, a biased focus on community and identity politics conceals more fundamental processes of integration and loss of exclusive significance for (postcolonial) identities.

5

IMAGINING COLONIALISM

A few years ago, in an unguarded moment of visible irritation, the then Dutch Prime Minister, Jan Peter Balkenende, allowed himself to be drawn into appealing to the country to follow the positive example of the *Verenigde Oost-Indische Compagnie* – the Dutch East India Company (voc). The footage of these words being spoken in the Lower House of the Dutch parliament suggest that he too was somewhat shocked by his own bold comparison. 'Don't you think?', he added in slight hesitation. Mild embarrassment seems to have descended on the parliament, accompanied here and there by disbelief and derision. The political and media reactions were predictable: there are so many painful questions surrounding the voc that the Prime Minister should never have referred to it so lightly. And that is where it ended. Parliament does not debate history, unless it really cannot be avoided.[1]

What was more remarkable, however, was the almost complete absence of comment from Indisch Dutch and Moluccans. Praise of the voc, while not endorsed, was not experienced as insulting, it would seem. Perhaps the more critical minds were still too fatigued by the 2002 voc anniversary celebrations to regurgitate the familiar counterstory for the umpteenth time. Perhaps the fire had quite simply gone out.[2] On the other hand, Surinamese organizations protested in a demonstration and sent an indignant letter to Balkenende demanding 'apologies, atonement and restitution for the voc era he so praised', especially as this was also the era of the West Indian Company (wic) and its slave trade.[3] Thus, a couple of rhetorical turns transformed an unfortunate remark about the voc into an unforgivable insult of the Afro-Surinamese. Antilleans were not mentioned at all.

This turn was typical, or at least characteristic of sensibilities in the Netherlands at the beginning of the twenty-first century. Things had been different in the past. Then we were expected to be proud of the voc and what succeeded it. Little was said or written about the wic or more broadly about colonialism in the Atlantic region, not so much out of a sense of shame, but because that particular history was considered unimportant and not very interesting. As an overture to his book *De laatste eeuw van Indië* (The last century of the Dutch East Indies, 1994), the acclaimed Dutch sociologist J.A.A. van Doorn, referring to the loss of Indonesia, dryly wrote, 'The Netherlands reverted to being small country on the North Sea with a few, insignificant territories in the Americas.'[4] Regardless of how controversial van Doorn often was, here he articulated a broadly held and, in empirical terms, defensible view. Only his use of the word 'insignificant' can really be regarded as contentious, a vague echo, perhaps, of the designation *islas inútiles*, useless islands, with which the Spanish had disqualified the Antilles centuries before. But, above all, it was an implicit refusal to employ the jargon of 'equality' and 'reciprocity' that had dominated post-war relations between the Netherlands and the former Caribbean colonies. Employing that jargon and, moreover, avoiding such terms as 'insignificant' became more advisable as Surinamese and Antillean communities in the Netherlands grew. Van Doorn was, apparently, unconcerned about such sensitivities.

THE COMPANIES

The contemporary Dutch memory of colonialism reflects something of that distant past, but also, and perhaps more so, serves as a gesture towards the postcolonial communities that feel particularly involved with this history. Such gestures may easily come at the expense of historical consistency. The contrast between the 2002 celebration of the VOC and the public atonement for slavery and, thereby, the WIC is a striking illustration.

We can be brief about the WIC (1621-1792). The company was economically far less successful than the VOC (1602-1798), did not have a monopoly and focused on a part of the world where the Republic of the United Netherlands was only a modest player. Its early colonies appealed more to the imagination – North-eastern Brazil and what is today New York and the surrounding area – but these were lost early on. The remaining prizes of Atlantic expansion, Suriname and the Antilles, by the late nineteenth century had become awkward properties it might have been better to jettison. This is illustrated by the fact that a large part of the first WIC's archives was sold to a rag-and-bone man in 1821 – worthless papers from an insignificant past. The company's feat of arms that most appeals to the imagination is the conquest by Piet Hein of the silver fleet in Cuba's Bay of Matanzas in 1628.[5]

Insofar as there was any memorial culture around the WIC in the Netherlands, it continued to be completely overshadowed by the VOC. Although doughty Dutch heroes like Michiel de Ruyter, Maarten Tromp, Piet Hein or Witte de With conquered Atlantic waters, they also conquered other seas. Only Hein has been remembered down the centuries for his Caribbean exploits, though there are few today who know what the nineteenth-century song *Hij heeft gewonnen de zilvervloot* (He won the silver fleet) – so popular until recently in football stadiums – is about. The only recent statue of Hein, unveiled more then ten years ago in the Bay of Matanzas, simply reflects the hobby of a few Dutch business people and the Cuban state's intention to develop tourism on the island. Such an initiative would be unthinkable in the Netherlands, considering the association of Hein with the WIC and, therefore, the Atlantic slave trade, which is the only thing the company is remembered for today.

In the same spirit, a Dutch entrepreneur on Curaçao was promptly forced to retract his proposal to call his restaurant 'The West Indian Company' – in the end he called it 'The Governor'. Around the same time, a Chinese businesswoman in the old port of Jakarta opened a restaurant using the name and the coat-of-arms of the VOC without meeting any opposition. This is because few Indonesians have any idea what VOC means. The situation is different in the Netherlands. Balkenende associated the company with 'commercial spirit, entrepreneurial drive and the courage to sail the seas'.[6] This is the usual image of the company. The preceding government, a 'purple' coalition under Labour Prime Minister Wim Kok, had assessed it no differently. The spirit of 'Four hundred years of the VOC' was a festive and proud celebration, which was, of course, not entirely unfounded; the VOC was in many respects spectacularly successful.[7]

It is easy to be critical of the VOC celebrations. Yet it would be as remarkable to ignore such a milestone, as it is natural to investigate what the anniversary taught us about memorial culture in the Netherlands.[8] What strikes one immediately is the paradox that the celebrations to mark the 'first multinational', a company that transformed a small country into a major player on the burgeoning world stage, were extraordinarily provincial. However much the Netherlands attempted to disguise the element of celebration and to emphasize equal exchange, countries like South Africa, India and Indonesia experienced the project as colonial, chauvinist and consequently insulting. They did not take part in the celebrations. The Ministry for Foreign Affairs eventually instructed the embassies in those countries to steer clear of VOC festivities. The embassy in Jakarta organized an event that allowed plenty of room for criticism of the VOC and, thereby, the Netherlands. The question, in retrospect, is whether the business community was particularly happy with this attempt to use the anniversary to help Dutch enterprise nestle deeper into Asian markets.[9]

The celebrations attracted negative attention in Indonesia, which allowed little room for the subtle differences between the VOC administration and the later colonial Dutch East Indies – following the example set by Sukarno in 1931. Indonesian web sites published radical texts about the violent nature of Dutch colonialism and demanded apologies. At the eleventh hour, the Indonesian ambassador refused to attend 'the celebration of our own colonization' in the Ridderzaal (Knight's Hall) in The Hague. His embassy published a book full of severe criticism of the Netherlands' role in Indonesia since the arrival there of the VOC. The Hague administration looked on in embarrassment.[10]

However astonishing it may seem, that The Hague failed adequately to anticipate this predictable criticism, such lacks of stately empathy are not unusual. The Spanish made a spectacular blunder with their 1992 celebration of the 500th anniversary of Columbus' arrival in the New World. The original plans for celebrating the *descubrimiento* (discovery) were so chauvinistic that the former colonies protested en masse. In the end, another more neutral notion, *encuentro* (meeting), was decided upon. But in reality the events held in Spain remained explicitly nostalgic and triumphant. Something similar happened a few years later with the Portuguese celebration of Vasco da Gama's discovery of the sea route to India. The chauvinistic tone of the celebrations inflicted considerable diplomatic damage on Portugal, in the view of Indian historian Sanjay Subrahmanyan.[11]

The problem that confronted the Netherlands, Spain and Portugal is not unique. Every remembrance associated with colonialism provokes these kinds of issues and tensions. Every former colonial country is constantly being reminded of that past and accused of triumphalism and concealing the 'dark pages' of its history. Its former Caribbean colonies continued to remind France for years that the subject of slavery was completely ignored during the celebrations marking the bicentenary of the 1789 revolution. It is also difficult for Great Britain today to celebrate the fact that it once ruled the waves without admitting that this had sometimes dramatic consequences for distant continents. Commemoration has become a perilous undertaking and will doubtless remain so in the future, also as an element in international diplomacy.

Back in the Netherlands, the festivities were coordinated by the *Stichting Viering 400 jaar VOC* (Foundation Celebration 400 Years of the VOC), chaired by the conservative-liberal member of parliament, Enrique Hessing. The foundation had a budget of 4.5 million euros, furnished mainly by the government, but also by donations from the business community. Many events were privately financed. 'The Company' was commemorated with academic conferences, exhibitions, web sites, debates and a pile of new and reprinted books. Wherever a link of any kind could be found with what one of the publications described as the VOC's 'illustrious past', the jubilee was blithely celebrated with concerts, fairs, culinary arrangements and whatever else could be thought up. This merchandising would be inevitable, anywhere: culture and commemoration are, after all, dynamic branches of industry.

What was striking about the content of these celebrations, certainly compared with the concurrent discussions around the WIC, was the lightness of tone. This was made easier by the decision to place most emphasis on the early period of the VOC (1602-1620) and its maritime and commercial aspects, rather than its function as a violent protocolonial state. In doing so the Netherlands remembered a different VOC from the one remembered by a country like Indonesia, where the *kompeni* is seen as the predecessor to the nineteenth- and twentieth-century colonial state of the Dutch East Indies. Admittedly, at a late stage the Foundation Celebration 400 Years of the VOC decided to pay explicit attention to the 'shadowy sides' of the Company's history such as violent suppression, the slave trade and slavery, in ways that included a public debate. However, it is clear that this critical reflection continued to play no more than a subordinate role within the celebrations as a whole, a ceremonial concession to 'politically correct twaddle'.[12]

What domestic sensitivities did the foundation have to consider? Remarkably few. The dominant view of the VOC in the Netherlands is a positive one, somewhat in the tone of the evergreen book for young readers by Johan Fabricius, *De scheepsjongens van Bontekoe* (The Ship's Boys of Captain Bontekoe) – and this appreciation had not diminished by 2002. Critical voices sounded from the academic world, but the Indisch Dutch and Moluccan communities remained remarkably silent. A few web sites vented anger and there were some critical meetings and small demonstrations opposing the celebrations.[13] However, all in all, the anniversary provoked little in the way of emotions and objections. A more striking illustration of the gulf separating the Indisch community in the Netherlands from Indonesia is hard to imagine.

On closer inspection, the gulf is all too understandable. The Indisch Dutch community was not angry about colonialism so much as about the way it came to such an abrupt end, leading to the exodus and the – at best – lukewarm reception in the Netherlands. This contrasts strongly with both the way Indonesia now regards colonial history, including the VOC, and the feelings of the Caribbean community in the Netherlands. Among Caribbean Dutch, the understanding of the colonial past that dominates is so explicitly critical that few can be left untouched by it. A '400 Hundred Years of

WIC' celebration is virtually inconceivable today and this is likely still to be the case in the jubilee year 2021.

These contrasts in memory communities made it possible for the queen and the prime minister to express their regrets about the WIC in 2002, while at the same time celebrating the VOC. Socially understandable and perhaps also sensible, but from an historical perspective far from consistent. It is not about establishing that the VOC was 'good' and the WIC 'bad', or the other way around for that matter, nor is it a question of affected political correctness. The point is that commemoration should also be about drawing informed comparisons and should not be an exercise in the art of bending over backwards to give everyone what they want to hear.

'SOMETHING MAGNIFICENT WAS DONE THERE!'

With the collapse of the Dutch Republic at the end of the eighteenth century, the companies also disappeared from the stage. Around 1815 the United Kingdom of the Netherlands took over the management of the colonies. It was not long before the East Indies became economically, politically, scientifically and culturally crucial to the metropole. At the same time, hope evaporated of making profitable colonies of Suriname and the Antilles. They disappeared from view and did not return into focus until after the East Indies had been lost and particularly with the Caribbean exodus to the Netherlands.

If the colonial system had been unashamedly directed towards the interests of the metropole, at the end of the nineteenth century its course, in theory, shifted. The Netherlands, in the words of C.T. van Deventer, had a 'debt of honour' to pay.[4] Put more positively, the new 'ethical politics' saw as its task the elevation of the natives and bringing economic development to the colony. The planned modernization process coincided with the – where necessary – violent pacification of the archipelago, which was more or less completed by about 1910. More than a hundred years after first contact and settlements, the Dutch finally controlled the entire archipelago, although this colonial hegemony was only to last three decades. The Dutch East Indies were in all respects heterogeneous, with arbitrary borders and a fragile configuration that were direct consequences of a colonial history that might have turned out very differently.

Dutch interest in the East Indies is often reduced to the frequently invoked contemporary metaphors of the 'cork' that kept the Dutch economy afloat and the worry that without its Asian colony, the Netherlands would plunge to the 'rank' of smaller European countries such as Denmark. Cork and rank were constantly referred to in selfish arguments against relinquishing the colony. The first, in retrospect, was an unnecessary spectre; the second more relevant. However, there was a third, less self-interested argument, namely, that the Netherlands still had an enormous modernization project to complete before it could leave the East Indies. Looking back in December 1949, cabinet member J.H. van Maarseveen said in parliament, 'The East Indies were our pride. We governed the Dutch East Indies in a way that provoked admiration everywhere.' Hence, 'We had a job to do in Indonesia and we are ethically bound not to abandon this task.' This mission was a mixture of concrete infrastructural and social programmes and a paternalistic civilizing offensive – not that different, when scrutinized, from the pretensions of other late-colonial powers or post-war development aid. The Dutch East Indies had become a state project.[5]

This image of a grand mission was canonized in 1941 in Van Helsdingen's *Daar wèrd wat groots verricht...* (Something magnificent was indeed done there...).[6] The title of this huge book, a variation on a statement by the pioneering (and brutal) governor Jan Pietersz Coen more than three centuries earlier, was intended to boost spirits in the Netherlands already occupied by the Germans and to offer something of a prelude to the changes in Asia. After the war the slogan '*Daar wèrd wat groots verricht!*' would become a superb cliché of Dutch arrogance. But the underlying question of the real significance of the Dutch colonial project has remained the subject of serious academic and political debate in the Netherlands.

Initially the debate took place primarily among people who held quite similar views, people who had close ties with the Dutch East Indies before the war and repatriates. The dominant view was that a good mission had been abruptly interrupted in an unfortunate way. It was not until 1970 that a much more critical interpretation came into vogue, articulated for a broad public by the official historian of World War II, Loe de Jong. In the draft version of his volume on the war in the Indies, de Jong passed harsh judgement on Dutch post-war military actions ('war crimes'), but he also painted an extraordinarily critical picture of pre-war colonialism, which he linked to exploitation and racism.[7] This was a harsh blow for the Indisch community and provoked a well-organized response led by the *Comité Geschiedkundig Eerherstel Nederlands-Indië* (GENI, Committee for the Historical Rehabilitation of the Netherlands East Indies). The deep resentment that splutters off every page of the book *De staat, dr. L. de Jong en Indië* (The State, Dr. L. de Jong and The Dutch East Indies), published by Ralph Boekholt soon after de Jong's book came out, is articulated in biting sarcasm about de Jong's work that was qualified as 'deliberately incomplete, one-sided, negative, grievous and un-scientific'. Since the transfer of sovereignty, wrote Boekholt, the Indisch community 'had either been hushed up or distorted in books, articles, and television programmes into a world of white colonial suppressors who bled the population dry while Eurasians and others of mixed-race wandered around in between, looking up to the Dutch and down on the Indonesians and who otherwise had nothing better to do than talk about food in broken Dutch'. De Jong had now canonized this image and confirmed Dutch paro-chialism. 'Stupidity, which initially had been received with a smile, in the meantime had grown into a tumour of the soul. East Indians too have self-respect.'[18]

The 'courageous and honourable struggle' (Boekholt's own words) for a drastic revision of the representations of colonialism and the Indisch world, as canonized by de Jong, was fought and lost in a five-year long courtroom battle. It was, nevertheless, reasonably successful. In the definitive version of his book, de Jong was milder in his judgement of the military interven-tion and there was no more mention of 'war crimes'. More importantly, the plaintiffs broadened the platform on which their views could be publicized. All later government support for research into the Dutch in the East Indies was issued in answer to the unrelenting demand of the Indisch community to have their story told 'properly'. This proper rendering was diametrically opposed to the view that the repatriates had been 'on the wrong side', as if, to quote Lillian Ducelle, 'the war in Asia had been a kind of punishment for our sinful (colonial) life! Which the Netherlands, of course, had no stake in!' Thus, not only the struggle for recognition and financial compensation, but equally the battle against imputations of morally wrong colonialism, unit-ed *totoks* and *Indos*.[19]

The battle for historical legitimacy turned on two main issues – pre-war colonial society on the one hand and, on the other, the Japanese occupation up until the move to the Netherlands and the alleged chilly reception found there – and was fought by a community built around the task of remember-ing. We can be brief on the subject of the latter issue, which was discussed at length in the previous chapter. The government repeatedly conceded on symbolic acknowledgement and financial concessions. Although this may never have been enough for the plaintiffs, The Hague's gestures went much further than could have been conceivable in 1950 or 1970. The beneficiaries, in the end, were the Indisch generation as a whole: *totoks*, Indisch Dutch, Moluccans and veterans. They found one another in a shared defence of their memories and truths and ended up being closer to another than had ever been the case in the Dutch East Indies. Yet the memories remained divided, even within the various categories of the Indisch generation: former internees on just how terrible the Japanese camps really had been, veterans on the justification and nature of the post-war military intervention, and so on.

From the 1970s, public and academic interest in pre-war colonial history resurfaced. Opinions continued to be divided over the question of the legitimacy of colonial society. The enormous historical value of the Dutch East Indies to the Netherlands was taken for granted, and with good reason. Insofar as this was at all a matter for dispute, disagreement was less about the facts than about their assessment: should all that profit give cause for shame?

The opposite question gave rise to far more debate: what good did the Netherlands do the colony (and by implication could have continued to do if the work had not been abruptly cut short)? This is a far more difficult question. It is not only about good intentions, but also about what became of them; not only what the colonial authorities finally brought about, but whether this was impressive when looked at from a comparative perspective; not only about establishing what had been good work, but also drawing up the balance between what was give and what was take.

In academic research, the last word has not been spoken on any of these questions. For a brief moment among Dutch historians there was a kind of battle of directions, in which scholars from the University of Amsterdam supposedly adopted a more critical stance, while their Leiden colleagues were said to be more conservative, moderate or whatever. In retrospect, this is a rather ludicrous division, which says a lot about academic egos and the importance attached to scientific support for personal memories or political standpoints. An uncritical, pro-colonial school of historians does not exist. While debates about colonialism outside academia are saturated by moral issues, the historiography of colonialism in the Dutch East Indies and Indonesia has taken a clear distance from moralizing.[20]

In wider society, colonialism is still an issue replete with questions of ethics and judgement. The pattern here has long been predictable. Older experts with experience of the Dutch East Indies defended the colonial order and, thereby, their own role. Complainants were politicians and historians like de Jong, who before the war had shown little interest in the Indies. And finally there was the baby-boom generation, discovering all kinds of parallels between the decolonization of Indonesia and the Vietnam war. The 'pro-colonial' Indisch generation would partially lose this battle with the government's statement in 2005, expressed by Minister for Foreign Affairs, Ben Bot, that the Netherlands 'had stood on the wrong side of history' in its dealings with Indonesian nationalism. Meanwhile, the controversy on the more complex question of the character of pre-war colonial society has still not been settled and seems to attract ever less attention as the Indisch generation passes into oblivion.

This trend of depoliticization was appositely illustrated by the events surrounding the renovation of the Amsterdam Van Heutsz monument, one of the many monuments that have been carved in stone over the years in praise of colonialism." J.C. van Heutsz's brilliant military and administrative career was crowned with the post of governor-general. He acquired considerable fame as the ruthless 'pacifier' of Aceh; the young Queen Wilhelmina admired him. Yet, his reputation was controversial, not least because the subjection of Aceh cost tens of thousands of Acehnese their lives. The posthumous monument in his honour, unveiled by the queen in 1935 in Amsterdam's Olympia Square, not only glorified Van Heutsz, but was also a monument to the beneficial work carried out by the Dutch in the East Indies. By the 1960s, his reputation as an old war horse had become problematic for the monument, which from then on regularly became a site of actions and vandalism.

In 1998, the *Comité Herdenking Gevallenen in Nederlands-Indië* (Committee for the Remembrance of the Fallen in the Dutch East Indies) attempted to have the decayed monument restored with the intention of giving it a new purpose. The Amsterdam borough of Oud-Zuid voted in favour of this plan and work began on a thorough research and discussion process, which drew on opinions from a range of historians. Where other participants in the debates frequently played on the emotions of 'pride and shame', most professional historians avoided them. The outcome of much nattering and palavering would have been practically unthinkable thirty years earlier: the monument remained intact, but was renamed *Monument Indië Nederland* (Monument East Indies Netherlands), 'representing the many memories of our colonial past, while pointing to the future, with respect for Indisch heritage'. A number of monumental elements were added that refer to the history of the Dutch East Indies between 1598 and 1949. What these additions share, above all, is that five of them are twentieth century, that they do not refer to Indonesia and that not one of them forms any provocation for the Dutch who had been involved. Hence, the Dutch Indies landed softly, almost meaninglessly, inoffensively in a renovated monument that was soundlessly unveiled at the end of 2007 – and with its back to Indonesia."

Something similar continues to characterize the history syllabuses in Dutch schools. The history of the Dutch East Indies/Indonesia has been on the syllabus four times since 1976 – which incidentally means that this part of Dutch history has only reached a limited proportion of all pupils over the past few decades. Consequently, pupils who opted out of history, but also the vast majority of those who did choose to study history, left school with only a cursory knowledge of any aspect of Dutch colonial history whatsoever.

The emphases of these four rounds of Dutch East Indies history varied and there was always room for critical reflection on the performance of the Dutch. However, what disturbed professional historians was the bias towards the Indisch dimension of the history of colonialism in Indonesia – a gesture to the Indisch community in the Netherlands.[23] This rendering of Dutch East Indies history demonstrated, on good grounds, that Dutch national history is incomplete without its colonial chapters. Unintentionally, an uninformed pupil might easily get the impression that the majority of the 'natives' were mere onlookers in the story. This was once again the complaint heard from specialist journals when colonial history was last on the school syllabus in 2007. Yet, one cannot say that there was a heated discussion – perhaps because the Republic of Indonesia itself only rarely speaks out about the ways the Dutch deal with this 'shared' past.[24]

What is remarkable about these and similar representations and debates is not only what is said and the constant moralistic bickering, but also what remains unsaid. Thus, post-1942 history seems to be imprinted far more firmly on the retinas of repatriates and Moluccans than anything that went before. The first story is one in which injustices were done to them that need to be put right. The pre-war history seems to evoke nostalgia for a lost paradise and the old days, *tempo doeloe*, rather than critical reflection.

This nostalgic image belongs to a controversial repertoire in which the colonial system was 'good', but it would also appear to evoke an all too rosy image of the life of the Eurasian Indisch population. Recent studies have convincingly dismissed the image that all those in the colony who were legally European were well off. They reveal the great heterogeneity of this population and the increasing threat the lower Indisch classes felt exposed to from the *totoks* above and the 'natives' below. Colour and 'purity' of lineage were not the only factors at play here; as in almost all colonial societies the rule 'money whitens' applied here. It is nonetheless crystal clear that colour indeed mattered and gave rise to enormous personal dramas and social contrasts.[25]

In post-war Indisch memories, such social distinctions based on colour seem to have receded or been smoothed over. In the Japanese camps the *totoks* still looked down on *Indos*. But once in the Netherlands, in the battle for recognition of their Dutch citizenship and the accompanying rights, the colour distinction was downplayed 'as the joint label of "war victim" began to serve as a great equalizer', Wim Willems commented. But when it looked as if recognition and concessions were far more likely to benefit the *totoks* than the *Indos*, the latter once again complained loudly about discrimination. In so doing, they implicitly drew a parallel between the attitude of the *totoks* in the Dutch East Indies and the government in the Netherlands. But this did not bring about an organizational rupture, which from a strategic viewpoint would have been extremely injudicious for both groups. If they had not been easily identifiable as two strictly divided groups in the East Indies, once in the Netherlands history, integration and the struggle for recognition brought them even closer together, despite the lingering legacies of colonial colour casting.[26]

If racial discrimination was discussed openly at all, it usually related to the Dutch population and the Dutch government in particular. Complaints like these were constant and often justified.[27] However, it is at the very least ironic that a group that in the Dutch East Indies had held a privileged and colour-conscious position in a society divided along colour lines, should be so disturbed by discrimination in the Netherlands.

There are many such remarkable silences. The traditional narrative of the Moluccan community revolved around 'centuries' of loyalty to the colonial regime and the post-war betrayal by the Netherlands. Although the story has some truth to it, one could ask whether after the war the Netherlands was in a position to set a different policy from the one it did and whether 'betrayal' is therefore the appropriate term. Either way, critical reflection about the Moluccans' own role in the Royal Dutch East Indian Army (KNIL), as accomplices to an oppressive colonial regime, did not become a popular theme in the community. This became even more remarkable in retrospect, when the radical second generation began to identify itself with the wars in Vietnam and Angola and movements like the Black Panthers in the United States. Rhetorically this was resolved by characterizing the Suharto regime as a continuation of the violent colonial order. Yet this was precisely the order their parents and grandparents had served and defended.[28]

The pattern of all this remembering is relatively straightforward. The various groups of the Indisch generation all made claims on Dutch memorial culture and, therefore, had to lobby the Dutch government, both directly and through the media. It was a long time before Dutch society and politics were able to face up to this dimension of the nation's history. The repatriates took it for granted that their history should be included in the narrative of the Dutch past, but this was experienced differently in the Netherlands. The veterans could be included, of course, but the futile post-war struggle was best forgotten. The *totoks*, fine, but without to much whingeing. And it took decades of struggle before the Indisch Dutch and the Moluccans started to become part of the imagined community of the Dutch nation.

The main grievance of large sections of the Indisch generation was the lack of understanding they faced in Dutch society. The struggle for recognition was primarily directed at the government. This was logical. Even though the government is limited in the amount of scope it has for looking at its citizens through an alternative lens, the government does have the means to shape a memorial culture and to make material gestures. Consequently, the entire post-war game of Indisch identity politics was directed at The Hague. Although the government did become more forthcoming over time, it saw itself up against limits the Indisch generation regarded as less important: governmental relations with Japan and Indonesia. The Hague's policy strove to strike a balance between respect for the repatriated new Dutch, and maintaining good diplomatic relations with both of these former enemies – the occupiers and the nationalists.

In post-war relations with Japan the second consideration was decisive from the start, to the great frustration of the Indisch generation. The visit of Emperor Hirohito (1971), the laying of wreaths by President Kaifu at the Indisch monument (1991), state visits back and forth, questions concerning a Japanese debt of honour and apologies, laborious attempts at collective reflection on the past – time and again emotions ran high. The main problem was that Japan was far less self-critical and conciliatory than Germany had been. The dismissive Japanese attitude continued to provoke incomprehension and irritation, not only in the Netherlands, but also in other Asian and European countries. Nevertheless, The Hague consistently put diplomatic interests above concessions for repatriates.

In relation to Indonesia, The Hague allowed itself to be led by Indisch sensibilities for far longer – and it helped that in the first decades after the war these meshed with its own frustrations. This gave rise to a constant bilateral diplomatic friction. But for our present purposes, another question is of more interest, namely, whether and how Indonesian perspectives were accommodated at all within Dutch memorial culture. The answer to this question is short and final: hardly at all. Where Indonesian history was discussed in the Netherlands, it was almost always in relation to the colonial history, about an assessment of Dutch colonialism, and increasingly about the history of the repatriates and their exodus to the Netherlands. The growing acknowledgement of the importance of this last subject is evidence of the growing inclusion of the Indisch community as an inherent part of Dutch history. But this inclusion had the side effect that the Indisch world has continued to dominate the Dutch perspective of the archipelago, not Indonesia as it is today.

The contrast with state-sponsored history in Indonesia could not be greater. Of course, in historiography and education much time is given to the struggle for independence, but apart from that, the Dutch 'intermezzo' is only paid scant attention, even though it was crucial to the modernization and formation of the state. A lot of consideration is given to such topics as regional history, the relation of the regions to the central authority, social history ('bottom up') and the position of the archipelago within its Asian surroundings. Hero worship – though not of Dutch allies – dominates the treatment of these subjects and certainly the turbulent history of the republic. Many lacunae and distortions can be identified, so much so that some now declare it is time for a decolonization of Indonesian historiography.[29]

However, what is most striking compared with Dutch memorial culture is that in Indonesian representations of the past, the history of the (Indo-) Europeans and Moluccans, including their exodus to the Netherlands, plays no role whatsoever, neither in research, nor in education.[30] From an Indonesian perspective, the minority who left was just a marginal group. This contrast highlights the ambivalent position of those Dutch who are 'rooted' in Indonesia: simultaneously claiming full Dutch citizenship and a separate identity, while being alienated from a country of birth that quickly erased them from its collective memory.

Dutch debates about the rights and wrongs of colonial times, about the years 1942-1949, or about the repatriates and their place in the Netherlands were, and are, above all significant for the local society. They mean little to Indonesia, so little in fact that Indonesia kept out of the Dutch debates entirely. It is alert to what it regards as colonial demonstrations, such as the voc celebrations, but has never demanded apologies or reparations for the colonial period. This particular piece of decolonization was concluded at an earlier stage, no doubt made easier by the fact that the republic won the final and decisive battles.

This separation of memorial communities is also reflected in their reading cultures. The Dutch language is almost forgotten in Indonesia, the number of historians that draw on Dutch-language sources and literature is small. English-language literature is only read to a limited degree. Indonesian historians publish primarily in Indonesian, are not translated into Dutch and rarely into English, and are only read outside their own country by a handful of specialists. Professional Dutch historians publish a lot in English, but translations into Indonesian are the exceptions – where this does happen it never works with an Indisch orientation. The number of

Dutch professional historians who have a good knowledge of Indonesian is greater than the other way round. Mochtar Lubis' *Het land onder de regenboog* (The land under the rainbow, 1979) is still the only Indonesian history written for a broader Dutch reading audience.

This is no less succinctly expressed in belles-lettres and diaries, autobiographies, memoirs, travel logs and so on. The production and success of the Indisch generation and its offspring within Dutch literature is considerable. The pre-war Indisch canon is beginning to wane, just like older Dutch literature on the Indies, but the nineteenth-century authors Louis Couperus and especially Multatuli – hardly ever read nowadays in Indonesia – still hold their own. In contrast, the work of the leading Indonesian author Pramoedya Ananta Toer, with his anything but nostalgic view of the Dutch East Indies, enjoys only a small circle of readers. Modern Indonesian literature is rarely translated. For many years now, the number of students signing up to study Indonesian languages can be counted on two hands. The Dutch East Indies are far from forgotten and Indonesia is barely in the picture. The same is true from the other side: Indonesian interest in Dutch literature is non-existent.

THE WEST INDIES: WITHOUT PRIDE

Van Doorn once described the Dutch East Indies as 'the way in which Europeans, and in particular the Dutch, have given shape to the natural landscapes and native societies they encountered in the archipelago'.[31] It is immediately clear that a history of the East Indies thus understood only comprises a small part of the history of Indonesia. Hence the exaggerated, but nonetheless now proverbial comparison coined by nineteenth-century author Willem Walraven, that Dutch cultural influence amounted to little more than 'scratches on a rock'.[32]

A formulation of the Dutch West Indies has to cast the net more widely. With the arrival of the Europeans, Caribbean history in all respects began anew with the development of an immigration society. The Dutch colonies were not unique in this. The western colonies only had small 'native societies'; the Amerindians in Suriname could be counted by the thousands and on the islands by the hundreds. In colonial times, everything revolved around the plantations and hence the import of labour: initially mainly slaves from Africa and, after abolition, Asian indentured labour. The islands were unsuitable for plantations, but in the eighteenth century Curaçao and St Eustatius became trading centres and slave depots, populated by

Africans. Only limited numbers of Europeans were drawn to the Dutch colonies in the West.[33]

So, the history of the Caribbean that is relevant to most of the population there today – and to the Caribbean community in the Netherlands – only began in the second half of the seventeenth century with the activities of the WIC, slave traders and so on. Dutch colonialism in the West soon lost its ambition. After 1800, Suriname and the Antilles never came out of the shadows of the East Indies. By this time an unpleasant paradox had arisen. As far as the Netherlands was concerned, the East Indies grew steadily in significance, while the mark made by the colonizer there remained limited. In the West, the Netherlands was responsible for the creation of completely new societies, which would bear a far stronger European identity. But the motherland saw little economic or political use for these colonies, and showed equally little appreciation or consideration for the culture of these Dutch-made colonies.

To a far greater degree than in the East Indies, the colonizer and colonized shared a single history in the West. Everything that had happened since the seventeenth century was in some way or another linked to colonialism. Where repatriates from the East Indies were carriers of a history that ended in Indonesia with their departure, Surinamese and Antilleans on both sides of the ocean represent the same history. The verbal battle that was fought over that past for years was about interpretation and often about moral assessment, but never about who the players were in that history. In the West Indies there was only one history, a colonial one.

Of course, from a colonial perspective, there were constantly reasons for concern, in part because the subjects did not conform as easily as the metropole would have liked. However, from a Dutch perspective, the western colonies were only of marginal importance, especially after 1800. Throughout the late colonial period, there was little interest in, and still less admiration for Caribbean culture or history. Consequently, little scholarly attention was paid to the West Indies and Dutch colonial institutions – from the Ministry for the Colonies to academic institutions – regarded Suriname and the Antilles as peripheral at best. Real interest and pride and a genuine sense of mission were reserved for the Indies, which in Dutch no longer required the prefix 'East' – 'Indies' now sufficed.

It therefore seemed that real colonial history came to an end with the loss of the East Indies. In the long, drawn-out run up to the 1954 Charter of the Kingdom consisting of the Netherlands, Suriname and the Netherlands Antilles, prominent administrators who had earned their spurs in the East Indies administration often found it hard to conceal their frustration about the premises and great pretensions of this final accord with the western colonies. While old colonial institutions and education extended their range to 'underdeveloped countries', only a few institutions like the Royal Institute for Southeast Asian and Caribbean Studies in Leiden (KITLV) kept to the former colonies and would gradually upgrade their interest in the West. A certain disdain continued to exist, even in academia, for what the acclaimed Dutch novelist W.F. Hermans had mockingly characterized as the 'final remains of the tropical Netherlands'.

Indeed, from the second half of the nineteenth century on, there had been regular proposals to give up or sell the Caribbean colonies, although only Elmina was ultimately handed over to the British. Money was always having to be pumped into the Dutch West Indies and plans for development failed. Minister for the Colonies, Hendrik Colijn lamented in 1935 in the Senate that, 'Everything that has been tried in Suriname has [...] quite simply failed'.[34] Things began to improve for Aruba and Curaçao in the late 1920s with the construction of the oil refineries; however nothing truly 'magnificent' was done there. It is, therefore, no wonder that the mood changed in the Netherlands around 1970. It was time, so the metropolitan argument ran, for Suriname and the Antilles to become independent. Suriname did, but the hope that the Antilles would follow Suriname's good example was ultimately, reluctantly abandoned. Dutch politicians abided with the Antillean refusal to accept independence; Dutch popular opinion continued to regard a farewell as the best solution.

Few interests, few ex-pats and little traditional interest; consequently there was far less emotion invested in the West. This is why there was almost no desire for a post hoc defence of colonialism. There were no angry repatriates to defend the honour of colonialism and, hence, their own pre-war lives. The growing number of Dutch West Indians settling in the Netherlands had little flattering to report about a colonial era dominated by slavery, indentured labour and the like. Almost all the Dutch could honestly say was that they knew nothing of that history and had no personal involvement in it. This made humility a lot easier.

More books about the history of the Antilles and especially Suriname have been published over the last two or three decades than in the three centuries before. It is Dutch, not Surinamese or Antilleans authors, who have dominated this catching up, and most of those authors who are from Caribbean descent live in the Netherlands. The rediscovery of the western colonies is a particularly postcolonial phenomenon, directly related to the exodus and the emergence of postcolonial identity politics. Only now did the Netherlands 'discover' the former colonies, only now was there a hesitant acceptance that this past too belonged to Dutch national history. And one topic would become the leading narrative of Dutch West Indian history: the African slave trade and slavery.

Yet, one single complaint continues to unite Surinamese and Antilleans on both sides of the Atlantic: 'We always had to know everything about the Netherlands, while the Dutch knew, and know, almost nothing about our history.' Those who live in the Netherlands can also add that, 'we are here only because you were there'. This argument of historical ties helped Suriname and the Antilles to keep The Hague politically engaged. So while the Dutch had hoped, to no avail, that Indonesia would find the argument of a 'shared past' enticing, the same 'shared past' argument helped West Indians to prevent the Dutch from disentangling themselves from the Caribbean.

It is not surprising that the slave trade and slavery are the subjects most discussed in Caribbean colonial history. Not only because it is, in the negative sense, the most conspicuous episode, but also because it spans more than two centuries and, thereby, the greater part of Dutch colonial history. Half of all Surinamese and the majority of Antilleans descend from Africans who were once imported as slaves. But there is more. No other theme in the shared history lends itself better to an appeal for Dutch gestures of reparation and no other theme is linked to such powerful ideas of contemporary legacies for which one or another should pay.

And so slavery came to dominate the story of Caribbean history. This produced a remarkable distortion for the Antilleans, and more so for the Surinamese. A story in which not only half of the population, but also the ethnic plurality of the society remains underexposed. This is not strange. Indian and Javanese Surinamese organizations do not need to look back on a painful past in slavery. They also did not articulate competing, accusatory claims of identity. This is not to suggest that they attach no importance to their own culture and history; quite the contrary, judging by the large number of organizations in these circles. However, the accent is on religion and culture, not on historical injustices and even less so on a battle for acknowledgement or reparation. In Caribbean Indian discourse there is little room for victimhood or bitterness. Characteristically, initiatives from this community to create space for their history and culture were often self-financed. The smaller Javanese community barely speaks up at all.

A view of the history of Suriname therefore developed that was more clearly divided along ethnic lines than was the case in the country of origin.[35] The unsteady ideology of a single, undivided nation – articulated from Anton de Kom via the nationalist movement to the 'revolutionary' regime of Desi Bouterse – continued to lose credibility in the diaspora. The annual celebration of independence fell into oblivion and the celebration of ethnically defined holidays became more important. As a consequence, the Surinamese community in the Netherlands became increasingly more divided in terms of its memorial culture. In Suriname, 1 July, Emancipation Day, is a national holiday; in the Netherlands, only Afro-Surinamese and a few white Dutch mark this day. The same thing applies to commemoration as to religious and family festivals: Surinamese in the diaspora have less to do with compatriots of other ethnicities than is the case in Suriname.

Looking back on recent (post)colonial history, there are two remarkable silences. In 1975, Suriname voted for independence by a narrow majority. The development of the republic was not a bed of roses and this, in part, is why the Antilles refused to take the same step. At the same time, the exodus was already underway, with serious political and economic consequences and no less drastic personal consequences: insofar as one can speak about Surinamese and Curaçaoan 'communities', they are divided by the Atlantic ocean and those on the European side are materially better off. This was a delicate episode and certainly a painful one for ardent nationalists – Surinamese voting with their feet against independence, Antilleans simply rejecting the option of independence. One cannot help but remark that this outcome is hardly ever discussed within the same moralizing repertoire that is applied to the preceding colonial era.

COLONIAL SLAVERY, POSTCOLONIAL SETTLEMENT

The Netherlands has had a National Slavery Monument since 2002 and the abolition of slavery in Suriname and the Antilles in 1863 is commemorated on 1 July every year.[36] Surinamese Dutch have dominated the commemoration of slavery, as was illustrated once again recently in the choice of Sranantongo as the language for the motto: *Keti koti*, or broken chains. An unsuspecting newspaper reader could be forgiven for thinking that the whole of Surinamese history is about slavery and that all Surinamese descend from Africans who were once shipped to Suriname as slaves. This is not the case. Half of Suriname is Asian in origin, their forefathers arriving in Suriname after the abolition of slavery. A large number of the 300,000 descendants of slaves living in the Netherlands are from Antillean descent.[37] Moreover, slavery also played an important part in the history of the VOC and the Indisch Dutch. The fact that this is rarely depicted says less about colonial history than about the way in which postcolonial migrants have settled in the Netherlands.[38]

The Atlantic slave trade and slavery have never been forgotten. Memories, which gradually become stylized, distorted and canonized, are passed on from generation to generation by the descendants. However, it was not until the late twentieth century that this history became more widely recognized in the western world through world leaders and heads of state who were rightly conscious of an historical guilt. Slavery and the slave trade have been addressed by Dutch historiography for a long time. One cannot speak of active silencing, but neither of a broad understanding. In the end it was not professional Dutch historians, but descendants who placed the subject on a broader and political agenda.

There was a build up to this history in which the Surinamese immigrant Anton de Kom played a crucial role. His seminal book, *Wij slaven van Suriname* (1934, We Slaves of Suriname) was simultaneously an anti-colonial history and a radical left-wing nationalist manifesto. Almost all the elements in the contemporary discourse around slavery – exploitation and reparation, racism, dehumanization and trauma, self-liberation – were addressed in this remarkable book.[39] *Wij slaven van Suriname* put into words the deep emotions surrounding the legacies of Surinamese slavery, such as the 'inferiority complex' of his 'race', nurtured by a 'history education in which only the sons of another people are named and praised'. It took a long time, de Kom wrote, 'before I had freed myself of the obsession that a Negro was always and unconditionally the lesser beside any white person'. With his book he aimed 'to awaken Surinamese self-respect', because only then, 'once the old slave mentality has been banished from our hearts will the Surinamese gain true human dignity'.[40]

De Kom was arrested as a member of the Dutch resistance during the war and died in a Nazi concentration camp. *Wij Slaven van Suriname* became a canonical text for young Surinamese nationalists after the war and the book took on political significance for the independence struggle. Later, long after 1975 and primarily in the Netherlands, it would once again be inspirational in the battle for Dutch recognition of and atonement for the history of slavery. However, de Kom's memory could not become the posthumous figurehead of the struggle. He was born after slavery and, moreover, being Surinamese, held little appeal for Antilleans.

Suriname and the Antilles developed very different commemoration traditions. On 1 July, 1863, the abolition of slavery in both colonies had been orchestrated as an exercise in thankfulness to God and King. The correct use of freedom was deemed to be piety, obedience, dutifulness, monogamy and a respectable family life. This was the civilizing meaning attached to the first of July. In Suriname, the celebration of emancipation developed into an

Amsterdam, 1 July 1963. Surinamese Dutch celebrate the abolition of slavery exactly 100 hundred years earlier. The banner slogans speak of freedom, but also of respect for one's own people. 1 July has remained the day of commemoration under the motto *keti koti* ('broken chains') for Surinamese on both sides of the Atlantic. However, many Antilleans prefer to commemorate 17 August, the day of the great slave uprising on Curaçao in 1795. (COLLECTION INTERNATIONAL INSTITUTE FOR SOCIAL HISTORY)

ambiguous folk festival, a shifting mix of dedication to the faraway monarch and racial awareness, an Afro-Surinamese festival which after the war was renamed a multicultural Day of Freedom for all groups in the population, though it was later reduced to the celebration of the one freedom, a marker in interethnic relations.[41]

Slavery lived on in private memory on the Antilles, but less so in the public sphere. One explanation should probably be sought in the realm of ethnicity and politics. In Suriname commemoration of slavery was an element in Afro-Surinamese identity politics vis-à-vis compatriots of Asian descent. On the islands, where Dutch and Antilleans of European origin held the reins of power until well into the twentieth century, there was little enthusiasm on the part of the authorities to recall this past. So, the celebration of Emancipation was dropped from the calendar and it was not until more than a century later, on Curaçao, that an alternative celebration came in its place: 17 August, the day in 1795 when Tula gave the sign to start the largest slave revolt in the history of the island.[42]

It is unsurprising, therefore, that emancipation celebrations in the Netherlands were introduced by the Surinamese community. Following the call by the journal *Sranan Krioro Suriname*, around 1,000 people took part in the celebrations in 1962. A year later, in 1963, the centenary of the Emancipation was marked by a parade through Amsterdam.[43] Such celebrations would have had a strong element of bonding within the as yet small Surinamese community. This element of bonding through joint celebration has remained ever since; the Moravian Church in the Netherlands still organizes an annual Emancipation celebration and the annual Kwakoe Festival in Amsterdam made room for 1 July celebrations.

In the 1990s a group of Surinamese activists took the lead in the politicization of the celebrations. Not only has 1 July been celebrated in the Amsterdam square Surinameplein since 1997, 30 June has also become an occasion for a solemn commemoration of the victims of slavery. The name '30 June and 1 July' deliberately alludes to the Second World War dates 4 and 5 May, respectively Remembrance Day and Liberation Day – two central dates in Dutch commemorative culture. The *Stichting Eer en Herstel Betalingen Slachtoffers van Slavernij in Suriname* (Foundation Honour and Reparations for the Victims of Slavery in Suriname, 1997) operated in the same spirit – the name referring to the persecution of the Jews in a strategic comparison which had begun to gain currency among Indisch Dutch too.

Within a short space of time the number of organizations with a similar aim grew appreciably. In 1998 the Afro-Surinamese women's organization *Sophiedela* submitted a petition to the Lower House of the Dutch parliament requesting a national monument. Around that time, in the weekly paper *De Groene Amsterdammer*, the renowned Curaçaoan author, Frank Martinus Arion, argued the case for a gesture from the Dutch state. This provided the Prince Claus Funds with the impetus to publish the book *Facing up to the past*, an appeal for remembrance, reflection and the physical erection of a monument. Clearly, the time was ripe. Parliament and the Dutch government, under Prime Minister Kok, responded positively and asked the parties to join as a single representative organization. Out of this came the *Landelijk Platform Slavernijverleden* (LPS, National Platform Slavery Past), with Suriname-born activist Barryl Biekman, chair of *Sophiedela*, at the helm. In 2002, the National Slavery Monument was unveiled in Amsterdam's Oosterpark.[44]

All the organizations involved aimed at bridging gaps.[45] They wanted to commemorate slavery not only in their own circles, but also as a theme of

On 1 July 2002, the National Slavery Monument was unveiled in Amsterdam's Oosterpark in the presence of Queen Beatrix, Prime Minister Wim Kok and other politicians. An annual commemoration of slavery is now held at the monument, which was made by Surinamese sculptor Erwin de Vries. The date refers to the day, 1 July 1863, on which slavery was abolished on the Antilles and in Suriname. In 2008, Prime Minister Jan-Peter Balkenende attended the commemoration and celebration on behalf of the Dutch government. (COLLECTION ANP)

national importance. The fact that the national government, and subsequently local governments and various social and cultural institutions, were found willing to make a symbolic gesture underlined how much this lobby had already achieved. This success is therefore also indirectly evidence of successful integration: there were enough people who themselves had authority or who were able to gain access to government and politicians. The result was a cautious mainstreaming of a theme which, until then, had always been regarded from the traditional centre as 'your thing'.[46]

It is some ten years since the decision was taken to erect a national monument. Through the Queen, Crown Prince and ministers, the Dutch government on several occasions has expressed 'deep regret' for the suffering inflicted by the slave trade and slavery. Local gestures followed. In Middelburg, the logistical centre of the slave trade, a monument was unveiled in 2005. In 2006, the then Mayor of Amsterdam, Job Cohen, had a plaque attached to the facade of his official residence declaring that one of the first residents of the house had been the director of the slave trade for the WIC. Subsidized TV documentaries followed, teaching aids, exhibitions in major museums, a pile of books, theatre projects and much more. A 'dynamic' monument followed in 2003: the National Institute for the Study of Dutch Slavery and its Legacy (NiNsee).

The speed at which the theme of slavery became acknowledged as a dark page in the nation's history is remarkable. A questionnaire carried out under the auspices of the monthly *Historisch Nieuwsblad* (History Newsletter) revealed that between 2000 and 2008 increasing numbers of respondents pointed to slavery as the most shameful period in Dutch history. The inclusion of the Atlantic slave trade and slavery as one out of fifty items in the historical canon commissioned by the Dutch government was, in this sense, the pinnacle of the battle for acknowledgement. Ten years earlier the theme had played no part at all in the debates around national identity and history.[47]

This does not mean that the lobby to have this part of colonial history acknowledged as national history has been fully successful. That a space has been conquered for what until then had been a marginal theme is a remarkable success for the activists and is evidence of the conciliatory attitude of the authorities. However, a tension remained between expectations held by the West Indian Dutch and the openings offered by the government. The authorities reasoned in an atmosphere of acknowledgement and gestures, which were intended to close this chapter once and for all, hence the official mottos of inclusion and looking forward, such as 'Bound in Freedom'. The parallel with the way in which the government dealt with the desires of the East Indian and Moluccan community is clear.[48]

There were great expectations among the descendants. The politicization of the past was expressed in a radical discourse ('Black Holocaust', slavery trauma) and in demands (reparations) which provoked incomprehension and resistance among the wider population. Within The Hague's policy there was little room for radical movements and more moderate partners were selected with which to erect a national monument and to found NiNsee.[49] Ultimately the NiNsee found itself caught in an uncomfortable dilemma between demands from a radical grassroots and the task of connecting with society at large and building up respectability. A constant and hugely difficult balancing act between bonding and bridging.

What conflicting interpretations and expectations were at stake here? Did solemn words mean the same to all parties? Are spoken expressions of regret sufficient? Are they implicit apologies, or are explicit apologies needed? What is atonement in this context? How much public attention has to be organized to shine sufficient light on the subject? What is 'sufficient', both in terms of money and time, when judged according to the historical 'accuracy' of the information? Who determines what it accurate, can it be left to academics to decide or do descendants deserve a greater voice in this? Is it right to follow the American example and speak of a 'Black Holocaust'? Should reparations be made? Are the wounds inflicted by slavery so deep that one can or should speak of a trauma that can be used to explain the problems of today? Is it at all possible to close this chapter?

It is not surprising that these questions provoke strongly conflicting answers, in which the lines of division not only run between 'descendants' and 'the rest'. How widely the call for acknowledgement is supported within the Caribbean community in the Netherlands is almost impossible to establish. It is equally difficult to know the extent of the support in this community for those organizations – and their discourse and policies – that the government regards as its partners. The NiNsee has not researched this, neither have outsiders. One gauge is the active participation in particular moments of commemoration. A few, large manifestations that preceded the national commemoration, the consultation rounds to choose a monument, exhibitions and the 1 July celebrations have consistently attracted a few thousand visitors in recent years. Lectures and debates at the NiNsee have generally attracted far fewer visitors. The same goes for the alternative commemoration in Amsterdam's Suriname Square or at the Zeeland monument.

If we compare attendance of the 1 July celebrations with the early 1960s, the proportion of active participants from the Caribbean community has declined dramatically. This is, of course, a thorny issue. When challenged to respond to this fact, the NiNsee chairman Eddy Campbell argued that there was no decline in the level of interest. 'The remembrance event at the slavery monument will continue to exist as long as the one at the war memorial in Dam Square!' Other Caribbean participants commented that 1 July should also become a national holiday. Some acknowledged that attendance might be lower than expected, but that the same applies to the 'all-Dutch' national commemoration of the Second World War on the 4 May.[50] This is, of course, true and also applies to the East Indies commemoration on 15 August. The generation that has experienced the war firsthand is dying out and it is proving a difficult task to attract later generations to take part in the commemorations. Precisely for this reason, all those involved in commemorations know that support from the government and the media is vital to ensure some kind of continuity.

There is a pattern to the way postcolonial migrants attempted to elevate their displeasure about historical episodes to a national level. If Dutch society were finally to understand what we have been through, so the argument ran, acknowledgement and gestures – symbolic and material – will follow. The frame of reference was explicitly 'domestic', in the sense that it was tied to the post-war moral discourse in the Netherlands around being 'right' or 'wrong' (read: resisting or collaborating) during the Second World War.

The Indisch struggle was about full citizenship; acknowledgement of the fact that they had always been Dutch; drawing the war in Indonesia out from under the shadow cast by the war in the Netherlands; compensation for lost income and possessions; an appreciation of their uprootedness; confirmation that their resentment and bitterness were not unfounded. The demands were concrete and to a certain extent could be met. But for many it was too little too late and they remained aggrieved. Yet, this was a clear story about a recent injustice and targeted compensation for material losses was discussed.

Around the subject of slavery other, less familiar discourses were articulated which provoked more resistance than Indisch desires had done. Slavery was regarded as concerning distant ancestors, not first generation immigrants; the sympathy white Dutch people are able to muster for claims relating to the injustices of a distant past has remained limited. If the Indisch Dutch were told in the 1960s that the subject of the war had to be closed once and for all, black Dutch were told even more frequently not to 'keep focusing on the past'.

Many descendants of enslaved Africans experience slavery precisely as an unfinished history. The reasoning is that a traumatic history dating back centuries left lasting scars that still cry out for acknowledgement, atonement, catharsis, liberation. Consequently, this debate has become no less sensitively charged than commemorations of the war. There was talk of the trauma of slavery that thwarted individual happiness and the ability to function within society; of the need to 'de-traumatize'. Links were sought with international African-American movements and Dutch society was confronted with a call for recognition that was often felt to be excessive.

The discourse of trauma never really caught on beyond the realm of slave descendants and even there it remained highly controversial.[51] There are no scientific grounds – or refutations thereof – for the notion of a trans-generational transfer of slavery trauma. The problem with this discourse is not only conceptual and empirical, it also raises the simple question of how long the debts of a bygone era can remain open and whether today's society is in a position to do anything about possible psychological legacies. It is clear in this respect that a line was drawn by government policy: there was room for symbolic acknowledgement, but scepticism concerning the trauma discourse and no question of financial compensation.

The forthcoming attitude of the government in The Hague seems sooner to have provoked a counter position rather than a widely shared sense that a lot more still needed to be done. Populist right-wing politicians made forceful statements about what they called victimhood (Pim Fortuyn) and ridiculous concessions to people who drag down Dutch honour (Rita Verdonk). Their own grassroots, they will have rightly thought, would gladly support this view. The discourse around the view that misdeeds perpetrated centuries ago should be translated into far-reaching demands in the present – beyond symbolic acknowledgement – remained marginal in the Netherlands.[52]

Views on this varied greatly among the descendants, but once again it is difficult to establish which voices are representative. Only a small number of Afro-Caribbean Dutch were actively involved in the debates around slavery. And even within this group opinions were greatly divided. There is a moderate group, which focuses on acknowledgement and closure and which is therefore barely distinguishable from the government line. At the other pole is a radical group for whom the past is far from over, which sees the slavery monument as just the beginning, which regards the NiNsee as too cautious and continues to demand substantial 'reparations' for the 'Black holocaust'.

These contradictions often reflect views about how 'bad' the past really was, how 'wrong' the Netherlands was, how important the slave trade and slavery were to the countries involved and how far the shadow stretches. (White) historian and activist Alex van Stipriaan has spoken of a radical 'black' versus a moderate 'white' discourse. Those who have been involved in the often heated debates of the last few years will recognize this division. However, it is almost impossible to explain outside this circle and there is little sympathy for the radical school of thought.[53]

This is unlikely to change. Slavery came home to the Netherlands with the arrival of Caribbean migrants and was then, finally, acknowledged. But as far as the well-meaning government is concerned, and probably most Dutch people, symbolic recognition is the end of the matter. Slavery has largely remained a topic for a minority of around 300,000 Dutch people, less than 2 per cent of the population. The black population on the Antilles, another quarter of a million souls, barely feature in Dutch consciousness, even though they live in the same Kingdom of the Netherlands. It is therefore unlikely that 1 July will ever become a national holiday in the Netherlands. This is not just a question of small numbers, but also the historicity of the national perception. The Jewish population in the Netherlands was almost 200,000 before the Second World War; today it numbers around 45,000. Yet Dutch remembrance culture pays far more attention to the lot of the Jews. This reflects the enormity and historical proximity of the Holocaust, but also the fact that, as part of the story of the German occupation, Jewish history seems to be experienced far more as a national concern than the colonial past is.

So, although the acknowledgement of slavery has become a national affair, the experience of it has remained an emotional and politically charged issue mainly among the descendants. The way the press has reported on the commemorations and celebrations over the last few decades has been indicative of this. It was not until the late 1990s that the media began to pay more attention to the history of slavery. The tone was sympathetic. The widespread reporting of the disastrous unveiling of the national monument on 1 July 2002 was typical. A series of mistaken logistical decisions, miscommunication and plain bad luck led to the unveiling act itself presenting an image of major divisions. The immediate vicinity of the monument was cordoned off for a select group of invitees, black and white; this gathering departed to a party tent after the unveiling. The monument and the ceremony were largely obscured for the thousands of people who had come to take part and who began to protest ever more loudly. To make matters worse, it rained solidly throughout the whole ceremony. As a result, this first 1 July was far from being a feast of reconciliation, whatever the speakers said. The press presented a devastating picture of a partying establishment and frustrated descendants – with a great deal of sympathy for the latter.

The media has covered this annual commemoration ever since, but 1 July has never again been such big news. The reports today fit within a broader press policy which more or less obliges it to cover ethnic festivals. 1 July is not a national holiday. Conversely, the Indisch commemoration on 15 August in The Hague is now covered extensively in the national media, in imitation of Remembrance Day on 4 May and Liberation Day on 5 May; 1 July news reports are at best flashes. An arresting coincidence: at the exact moment of the slavery commemorations on 1 July, 2009, the national public broadcasting company broadcast a programme for schools that sang the praises of the voc.

Within the circles of those who are most actively engaged in commemoration it has become common to speak of slavery in terms of an actively 'silenced' history. A recently published inventory of the legacies of slavery, in part initiated by NiNsee, was given the programmatic title *Op zoek naar de stilte* (In search of silence).[54] This view fits within a broader understanding that Dutch society has deliberately kept colonial and especially Dutch Caribbean history out of the picture, because it conflicts with the flattering self-image of a progressive, humane, tolerant society.

Slavery has indeed long been a neglected theme in Dutch memorial culture. However, this does not mean that the 'forgetting' was part of a deliberate policy. There is nothing in the history of slavery to be proud of; even abolition in the Netherlands and its territories came late and was imposed from outside. This could have led to active suppression. However, it is more probable that slavery simply remained too far away in space and time, too marginal to need a policy. It was not until the descendants began to arrive in the Netherlands that Dutch society at large became confronted with its own slavery history. This was a shocking contrast with the rosy self-image, but the link with contemporary 'whitewashing' racism that is often suggested is, at best, speculative in this context.

In the meantime, the contemporary discourse on slavery has also produced its own silences. The slave trade and slavery in the VOC's trade zone have been forgotten, because no descendants have asked for recognition. Most attention paid to the 'West' goes to Suriname, simply because the Surinamese community in the Netherlands has been the most outspoken. The images of slavery that now appeal most to the imagination are, on the one hand, of extreme repression ('Black Holocaust') and, on the other, heroic resistance – the more typical shades of grey remain underexposed.

Where descendants and their organizations ask for a 'shattering of the silence', they not only long for more attention, but also for room for other perspectives and conclusions. Such desires belong to all emancipatory movements. However, they carry the risk that new truths will be claimed, the assumptions and content of which are at odds with empirical fact. A heated debate has erupted in the Netherlands over the past few years around such questions as the defining power of scholarship and the question of whether there is such a thing as a distinct black perspective and if so, whether that should be privileged. Where is the middle ground between a radical black perspective that 'you wouldn't let a Nazi write the history of the Nazi concentration camps either' and the positivist view that the background of a postcolonial researcher is completely irrelevant? In the almost entirely white world of Dutch historians the overwhelming conviction is that, with all the room there is for multivocality, there are still standards for scientific quality against which historical research can and should be tested and in which the background and emotions of the researcher may only play a subordinate role. In many respects this discussion recalls the laborious and almost impossible closure of the moralizing in debates about resistance and collaboration in the Netherlands during the Second World War.[55]

As already mentioned, all of this presented NiNsee, which has educational, research and collecting tasks, with a huge dilemma. Radical groups from its own grassroots demanded room for their visions and truths, referring to their origins and the unpaid debt. Opposite them stood a circle of people who were involved, but who had little truck with a separate 'black perspective'; administrators, because they linked acknowledgement to social cohesion; and researchers, because they seek out the nuances of the past and its legacies. NiNsee found itself more or less sentenced to following a middle course, which then prompted the question of what exactly made the institute individual and innovative.

From a government point of view this was not a pressing question. Commemoration, monument and institute existed within the framework of a moderate multiculturalism with mottos of solidarity and social cohesion. No different from the succession of gestures towards the East Indian and Moluccan communities, the administrative attitude to black Caribbean frustrations and desires can also be described as a policy of pacification. In this sense, descendants' lobby was taken seriously. Some had expected much more in gestures (apologies, a national holiday, reparations) and in results (addressing social problems, 'de-traumatizing', and more aid for the former colonies). These expectations, we can safely state, ten years down the line, were set too high. What remained were modest gestures of inclusion and pacification.

PLEASING EVERYONE, ALL OF THE TIME?

Where do we stand now in terms of a wider Dutch familiarity with, and understanding of the colonial past?[56] Over the last few years a lot has been said on the canon of Dutch history, which is an authoritative collection of the most important elements in our national history. Formulating such a canon is a perilous undertaking. What is presented as the core of history reflects – ideally – the state of academic research, but also, and probably more so, the social demand for a recognizable story about the past.

That is where the shoe pinches. Where historians have strongly contradictory views of the past, even among themselves, the questions and desires of society are even less univocal. This assessment is all the more tricky where significant meaning is attached to the canon, which here and elsewhere in Europe is used as an instrument for the culturalization of citizenship. In the multicultural Netherlands, the call for an authoritative historical canon is linked to the need for intellectual and normative anchors for a nation that is apparently adrift, confused by the blurring of its own borders and identity by 'Europe' and immigration.[57]

In its elucidation of the canon of Dutch history, the state-commissioned Van Oostrom Commission rightly gave short shrift to the high expectations surrounding the usefulness of a canon. There is, it wrote, no direct link between this canon and the advancement of a national identity and only a modest relation between the canon and assimilation. Moreover, the commission also stressed that there are legitimate alternatives for its proposals. With this the canon was modestly laid down, not as a 'state pedagogy' but as a beginning or, more precisely, a record of a particular moment which in time will be replaced by a new formulation of 'what every Dutch person should know about national history'.[58] The canon will continue to be controversial – the directors of the forthcoming National History Museum, Erik Schilp and Valentijn Byvanck, have already expressed their serious doubts.[59] But, for the time being, the Van Oostrom canon will continue to serve as a guideline for public opinion, as there is no officially recognized alternative – hence, perhaps, the somewhat more assertive tone of the committee's final report.[60]

This makes it all the more interesting to see what space this canon offers to colonial history and it legacies. Colonialism appears to be relatively generously distributed across five of the fifty 'windows' (topics). There are windows on the voc, on slavery, on *Max Havelaar*, a nineteenth-century novel criticizing colonial rule in Java, and on Suriname and the Netherlands Antilles. Various other windows – for instance on King Willem I of the Netherlands – have a colonial dimension that is mentioned more in passing. All in all far more attention is paid to colonialism, particularly in the West, than would have been the case only a few decades ago. How can this be explained? Do we now know more about that past? Undoubtedly. But considering we know more about almost everything to do with the past, this is not a useful explanation. The incorporation of colonial history into the contemporary canon reflects a general distancing from a narrow Eurocentrism, but above all the fact that this past has come into view with the arrival of postcolonial migrants in the Netherlands, thus becoming the history 'of us all'.

The post-war rediscovery of the colonial past fits within a broader pattern of making room, often with a guilty conscience, for the descendants of the victims of our history. The social and, thereby, political willingness to acknowledge old injuries and the resultant 'trauma' and to deliver justice has dramatically increased, partly with a view to inclusion and pacification.

Representatives of groups involved also know how to demand this space and to utilize it. This is a good game of identity politics. In this way, new perspectives of colonial history and colonial legacies have found their way into the canon, including in the Netherlands.

Precisely which aspects of colonial history should be canonized is strongly disputed and depends on the perspective adopted and the meaning that people today attach to that perspective. In the Netherlands, as indicated above, one more remarkable division comes into play. To make a bold generalization: the pain among migrants from the East Indies has less to do with colonialism than the way it ended so abruptly. Migrants from the Caribbean, at least those with African roots, have far more difficulty with colonialism itself and slavery in particular. In this respect the most recent history raises surprising new paradoxes. Among Caribbean Dutch there are now frustrations about the sudden farewell to Suriname and the perceived 're-colonization' of the Antilles. The expectations surrounding acknowledgement are contradictory and consequently, not everyone can be satisfied. This will continue to be the way with an unfinished colonial past.

Ever more groups are demanding room for their story in the imagination of a national past. At worst this leads to memory wars, to a debate in which the players are only interested in their own perspective: a Balkanization of the past in which everyone adds their own story, obscuring the greater narrative behind lots of smaller discourses. This is an unattractive postmodern panorama. At best, cautious attempts are made to reconstruct a broad national narrative, placed in a European perspective with a pinch of world history thrown in and a bit of extra space for colonialism and migration stories. This is the path chosen by the canon commission. The outcome is somewhat surprising. The rediscovery of colonial history has had a considerable effect on the canon. The *verzuiling*, 'pillarization', which the first post-war generations grew up with, has been shifted into a section about the multicultural Netherlands. And colonialism, about which they heard almost nothing when they were at school, is now strongly represented. Thus, the canon reflects the shifts in our historical understanding, which in part was brought about by the postcolonial migrations. It is said that the canon reflects a worried climate in which the Netherlands has 'mentally withdrawn behind the dikes'. But is this the case? Even if the rediscovery of an 'own' colonial past has something 'national' about it, it at least testifies to an increased willingness to interpret 'national' more broadly than the Netherlands-on-the-North Sea.[61]

The postcolonial broadening of the canon reflects a willingness to include 'newcomers' who have in fact been fellow citizens for ages. It is a wonderful aim yet absolves no historian, or anyone else who is involved in any way, from the responsibility of striving for a certain balance in the reconstruction of the past, including the colonial past. Trying to please everyone all of the time is never a serious option.

6

TRANSNATIONALISM: A TURNING TIDE?

Long gone is the time when migrants, embarking on a new life overseas, bade farewell to their homeland forever.[1] Technological developments, greater prosperity, and the enormity and complexity of post-war migration flows have resulted in transnationalism, in permanent and often intense relations between citizens of the countries of origin and immigration. This phenomenon has led to a boom in debates and publications over the last few decades. A degree of consensus has taken shape around the proposition that migrants in foreign countries (are able to) develop multiple orientations that connect them simultaneously to their countries of origin and immigration, as well as to ethnic or religious groups, or political movements elsewhere. Yet a key question has remained as to whether, in the context of widespread integration, the transnationalism of the first migrants would hold strong or lose its intensity over subsequent generations.[2]

Studies in transnationalism stress that migrants are able to maintain a range of relations between countries of origin and host countries. This leads to 'social spaces' that transcend geographic, cultural, and political borders, involving and changing not only the migrants, but also those who stay behind. The migrant community does not only send money 'home'; there are also political, social, and cultural remittances. Transnationalism thus contains a significant component of community (belonging) and identity. It is therefore not surprising that governments in the countries of origin often attempt to get a grip on their overseas citizens and whatever they send home in terms of money, goods, ideas, and emotions.[3]

Countries of immigration respond in different ways to this transnationalism. Interference by foreign governments regarding migrants in a country of immigration are seldom appreciated. The space granted to transnational engagement by migrants varies enormously; the worry that transnationalism may stand in the way of integration is an important factor in this. National policy in a general sense corresponds with the degree to which multiculturalism is accepted, but more particularly with indications of political or religious radicalism. The idea that transnationalism is more or less supplanting the traditional nation state is not convincing in this light. Koopmans and Statham defend the opposite view on good grounds, namely, that the amount of space a host country provides is a crucial determinant of the strength of transnationalism found there.[4]

Dutch postcolonial migrants maintained transnational relations with their countries of origin to varying degrees. The question is what these relations meant and what they continue to mean today for individual citizens and organizations, and for the countries themselves. Comparative studies of different postcolonial communities indicate that there are clear distinctions between them and that these are in part rooted in both colonial history and the changing of the generations. The strength of transnational bonds, so the argument of this chapter runs, is currently diminishing, which in turn is linked to the disappearance of a sense of community among postcolonial migrants in the Netherlands itself.

The various national governments involved have determined the amount of room that is available for transnational engagement. The space that the Dutch state made available for transnationalism was relatively large, aided by the fact that the thorny issue of dual nationality was of minor importance to postcolonial migrants. Cultural transnationalism and private development aid was not obstructed and has even been praised over the last few decades. Yet the space that was granted to political engagement was also quite generous – remarkably more so than other migrants receive today, especially those from Islamic countries. The initial tolerance of Indisch revanchism and the struggle for the RMS was not so much evidence of realpolitik than of the metropole's frustrations about losing the East Indies; the desire to keep the country's own minorities happy only began to play a role from the 1970s on. Yet the postcolonial bonus began to lose its strength here too. The importance of good international relations and domestic order came to prevail.

Conversely, Indonesia offered almost no room for the Indisch community, nor for Moluccan transnationalism; this frustrated Moluccan RMS nationalism in particular.[5] What follows below illustrates that Surinamese transnationalism was far more significant. This did not lead Paramaribo to a specific policy; the Surinamese political line can be described as floating between sympathy and ambivalence, but is, above all, passive. The Antillean and Aruban governments so far seem to have felt little, if any need to develop a vision for relations with the 'seventh island' – the Antillean community in the Netherlands.

DECOLONIZATION, MIGRATION CIRCUITS AND GENERATIONS

We may presume that migrants' orientation to their country of origin declines with the generations. Memories and loyalties carried by migrants do not necessarily vanish in later generations, but they do fade. The recent stream of studies on transnationalism provokes the need for a more nuanced interpretation of the break, but does not undermine the belief that distance and time simply do their work, even in an age when technology and prosperity have reduced the meaning of distance.

Measured against passenger traffic, migration, material support, and political or cultural influence, relations maintained by the postcolonial community with Indonesia are far weaker than relations with Suriname or the Antilles. This assessment confirms the assumption that transnational relations decline in intensity over time, but this is not the whole story. Migrants from the Netherlands East Indies were anything but a reflection of the Indonesian population as a whole; hence their departure cannot be described as anything other than a break. The situation for Caribbean migrants was and is utterly different.

Between 1945 and the beginning of the 1960s, almost the entire European population of Indonesia left the country – both *totoks* and those who were described as being 'rooted in the East Indies'. By far the greatest majority of these 'repatriates' settled in the Netherlands, while substantial minorities settled elsewhere, particularly in the United States and Australia. Remigration not being an option, they were forced to shut the door behind them: there was no place for them in the Republic of Indonesia. This applied not only in the public realm. Because the Indisch community emigrated en masse, albeit in phases, there were only a limited number of significant, enduring family ties with Indonesia.[6] With the exodus of the Indisch community, Indonesia lost a small portion of its population, in terms of numbers, whereas most of the migrants lost all their concrete ties with their homeland. The usual anchors in transnational relations – family and friends, possessions and investments, a realistic chance of return – did not exist, and political relations remained extremely difficult for many years. By the time international relations had become normalized, a majority of the Indisch community in the Netherlands belonged to the second or third generation; there was, by definition, no chain migration; and a significant number of Indisch Dutch were the products of mixed relationships.

The development of the Moluccan community was very different because of the nature of its migration history. At the core of the community were demobilized soldiers who would never reconcile themselves to the voyage to the Netherlands, which had more or less been forced upon them, to their subsequent dismissal from the army, and to relinquishing the idea of an independent Moluccan republic, the RMS. The transnational orientation of the Moluccan Dutch remained strikingly pronounced. This not only says something about the strengths and risks attached to political ideas, but also the pressure of continuing family ties and local loyalties, even when there were almost no new migrants to swell their numbers. From the Dutch camps and, later, housing estates where they lived, many Moluccans kept in contact with the islands, villages, and communities of villages (*pela*) they came from. The hope of return remained a receding horizon, but the sense of being connected to much larger communities in the Moluccas was kept alive, even in the third generation, a large number of whom made short visits to the land of their grandparents.

The Caribbean communities in the Netherlands date from a little later, but distinguish themselves primarily in that they are both pre-eminently transnational. Around 40 per cent of all 'Surinamese' and 'Antilleans' live in the Netherlands. By definition, almost all Surinamese and Antillean Dutch have large numbers of family and friends in the country of origin, and vice versa. Unlike the Indisch Dutch and Moluccans, the Caribbean community in the Netherlands is crucial to those who 'stayed behind' in many ways. There are also considerable differences within the Caribbean communities. Firstly, between the Surinamese and the Antilleans. Almost thirty-five years after independence, relations between the Surinamese and the Dutch Surinamese populations are still close, but the question of whether this will continue is beginning to make itself felt. However often people fly back and forth today, to-ing and fro-ing migration has declined drastically, in particular due to the legal restrictions imposed at the Dutch end and the economic and political problems at the Surinamese end. There is increasingly less evidence that the second and subsequent generations will hold on to the orientation of their (grand)parents. By contrast, the decision to continue Kingdom relations still enables Antilleans to settle freely in the Netherlands, and vice versa. And there is indeed a lot of to-ing and fro-ing in terms of travel and living; most Antilleans in the Netherlands are still first generation. There are other contrasts within the Surinamese and Antillean communities, which are mainly linked to ethnicity and perhaps class for the Surinamese Dutch, while for the Antilleans it is primarily class and island of origin that are important.

Apart from whether or not the possibility of return was cut off or not, the language factor was crucial to relations between the postcolonial communities and the country of origin. When they left the Dutch East Indies, most Indisch Dutch spoke reasonable Dutch, albeit perhaps peppered with Petjo;

the Moluccans spoke mainly Moluccan Malay, or 'barracks Malay' among themselves.[7] Language politics in Indonesia soon made Bahasa Indonesia the national tongue of the archipelago, over and above the numerous regional languages. Dutch was marginalized and is now a dead language. Conversely, among the Indisch and Moluccan communities in the Netherlands, only one or two speak modern Indonesian. Among the later generations of Indisch Dutch, the Malay-Dutch language Petjo is rarely ever spoken. The command of *Malayu sini* (literally 'Malay from here') among younger Moluccans is very limited, while High Malay is now only used in church services. The ability to communicate back and forth – a condition vital for a transnational community to exist – therefore declined within the space of only two generations. The question is whether English – used by many young Moluccans today as their lingua franca for new communications channels such as Facebook and the Dutch social networking site Hyves – will come to compensate for this.

The situation is utterly different in the case of Suriname.[8] Here, too, each ethnic group had its own language, with the Afro-Surinamese language Sranantongo serving as the lingua franca. Over the course of the twentieth century, Dutch won ground as a consequence of higher levels of education and increased local pragmatism. A good command of Dutch was considered essential to social advancement, but was also the only language that was acceptable to all ethnic groups as a national language. The quality of one's Dutch continued to be linked to class, but most of the Surinamese who emigrated around 1975 had a fairly good command of the language. It goes without saying that the standard of Dutch improved in the Netherlands in the generations that followed and boosted their integration. More importantly, in the Republic of Suriname a uniquely local, but otherwise recognizable form of Dutch maintained its position after 1975 and even gained ground. Language therefore presented no barriers to transnational ties.

The language situation in the Antilles was more complex.[9] During the colonial period, Papiamentu developed as the lingua franca of the Leeward Islands. This is one of the few Creole languages that has no stigma associated with lower social class or peripheral ethnicity attached to it. Dutch only became more broadly used over the course of the twentieth century through the colonial education system. However, unlike in Suriname, it never became widely spoken by the people and to this day Dutch is primarily used in education and government. Its domination is in fact limited even in these areas. A command of Dutch continued to be strongly associated with the middle and upper classes. A majority of pupils in primary and lower level secondary education leave school – prematurely or otherwise – with a scant knowledge of the language of the metropole. It is unsurprising, then, that the switch from elite to mass migration from the Antilles also transplanted the islands' linguistic and educational issues. This has not benefitted integration and has meant that the ability of the communities on either side of the Atlantic to communicate has continued to depend on Papiamentu, rather than Dutch.

Hence, a command of Dutch unites postcolonial migrants in the Netherlands – with each other and with the rest of society – but, paradoxically least of all with other Antilleans, even though it is precisely the Antilles that have remained part of the Kingdom. Most importantly for transnationalism, it was only the Indisch and Moluccan communities who found themselves confronted by a deep language gulf. This severely hampered their ability to maintain personal relationships, to follow the media, or to collectively reflect on the meaning of colonial and postcolonial history. Where their use of the media is concerned, postcolonial communities are also extremely well integrated. The image of satellite dishes in the Netherlands' larger cities aimed at distant countries of origin (Morocco, Turkey) – an expressive argument against multiculturalism – is irrelevant in these cases.

CITIZENS AND THEIR TRANSNATIONAL ORIENTATIONS

The intensity with which migrants from the former colonies and their (grand)children maintain relations with the country of origin varies from group to group and, we may assume, from generation to generation. Relevant indicators for establishing the importance of transnational relations at an individual level are physical and virtual contact, financial and other material relations, and the extent to which current affairs are followed.

Transnational relations are least important to the Indisch community. This is logical considering the rupture that decolonization and migration inflicted on this community. Almost no studies have been carried out on this subject. In the early days, all kinds of relations must have been maintained: some of the earliest repatriates clung onto the illusion of being able to return for a long time; later they put their effort into bringing over those who were 'rooted in the Indies' and *spijtoptanten*. They followed the news through correspondences and the media. Little is known about material support sent to those who stayed behind. It is unlikely that this involved large sums, if only because the majority of repatriates were far from well off themselves.

In the 1970s, bilateral relations between the Netherlands and Indonesia were normalized and the Indisch community was regarded as having successfully integrated into what was an increasingly prosperous Netherlands. People could now permit themselves to travel as tourists to Indonesia. This was largely one-way traffic of a strongly nostalgic nature. This tourism grew in fits and starts, more or less echoing the rhythm of political relations between the two countries. Here and there this led to support from rediscovered families or communities; however, this was never more than moderately significant. Information about developments in Indonesia was initially provided by the community that had stayed behind; once again it was Tjalie Robinson who set the tone with his *Piekerans van een straatslijper* (Musings of a gadabout) among other writings. But with the last of the repatriations in the early sixties, this source dried up and news had to be followed primarily through the Dutch media. Tjalie's *Tong Tong* magazine had a huge readership and carried 'Indisch' news, which inevitably became increasingly Dutch; only later did magazines such as *Moesson* and *Archipel* dedicate space to the modern Indonesia. Because of the language, this Indisch press, by definition, had no significance in Indonesia itself beyond the 1950s. In the generations that followed, the split between the Indisch community and Indonesia grew larger rather than smaller with the arrival of new media, from television to Internet, where the choice of language is the determining factor.

Illustrative of the gulf separating the Indisch community from contemporary Indonesia is the destination of 35 million guilders' worth of project funding from *Het Gebaar*. Almost none of this money went to projects in Indonesia; the rare exceptions involved memorials and care for *warga negara*, Indisch who had stayed behind.[10] When asked about how individual payments were spent – primarily paid out in the Netherlands – only a few said they spent the money on family in Indonesia or even on a visit to that country.[11] The Indisch response to a recent survey among prominent postcolonial migrants and organizations was typical. Questions regarding a current and future sense of transnational community were answered in a markedly less positive way than by respondents from other groups.[12]

The focus of the Moluccan community on the islands of origin was stronger for longer. From the late 1970s on, the ideal of the RMS was silently abandoned, at least as a prospect for Moluccans in the Netherlands; the hope of remigration was relinquished. The normalization of relations with Indonesia opened up travel opportunities, which paradoxically confronted the visitors with the gulf that now separated them from the islands' inhabitants. In the decades that followed, a small number of Moluccan Dutch visited the islands. A relatively large number of Moluccan organizations and individuals continued to direct their aid to the islands they originated from. The scale of this material help is unknown, but can only have been of limited significance for the population of the Moluccas as a whole, which numbers more than two million.[13]

The Moluccan Dutch were as unrepresentative of the population in the country of origin as the Indisch Dutch were. The Moluccans in the Netherlands were overwhelmingly Protestant, while the Christian population on the Moluccas, which was initially slightly in the majority, is no larger than the Muslim population today. Furthermore, the KNIL personnel, who formed the core of the Moluccan migrants, had often served long periods on Java or Sumatra and not infrequently had found wives there. Transnational solidarity was not, therefore, simply a matter of course and language became a divisive element here too. Moluccans in the Netherlands acquire their information about the Moluccan Islands increasingly from media – from the periodical *Marinjo* to contemporary web sites – that exclusively use Dutch, even if it is nostalgically peppered with Malay. On the other hand the small Moluccan community in the Netherlands is not at all a point of focus for the inhabitants of the Moluccan islands. Previously, the censored press on the islands ignored their overseas cousins, while today, apart from tourist visits, they are both distant and, literally, hard to understand.

The contrast with Surinamese transnationalism is enormous. Since the exodus around 1975, almost everyone in Suriname has friends and relatives in the Netherlands. Falling airfares and growing prosperity in the Netherlands has led to spectacular growth in the number of flights people take between the two countries, especially Surinamese living in the Netherlands. The value of annual remittances in the form of money and goods in the 1990s was estimated to be in the region of 70 million US dollars, almost a third of Suriname's GNP at the time. In 2006, half of all Surinamese households received money from the Netherlands, mainly from family members; in that year this amounted to between 100 and 125 million euros. The total magnitude of these legal donations is feasibly greater that the 'dowry' given to Suriname by the Netherlands on independence – in 1975 valued at 3.5 billion Dutch guilders, which today would be way over 3.5 million euros – and almost certainly more important to the alleviation of poverty. However, people on both sides of the ocean realize that the continuation of this solidarity by later generations of Surinamese Dutch cannot be taken for granted.[14]

Surinamese on either side of the Atlantic also had growing access to information about the political goings on in both countries. The dominance of the Dutch language was crucial in this. During the prelude to the exodus, Surinamese organizations in the Netherlands brought out magazines, such as *de Koerier* or *de West-Indiër*. These were published in small editions and did not last long, but they did serve a social and political purpose. During and after the mass migration, the Dutch press began to publish more about Suriname, in part based on reports in the Surinamese press. Even now, a quarter of a century after independence, reports about Suriname are still usually reported on the domestic news pages of the Dutch nationals. As the Surinamese population grew, so too did the number of 'ethnic' periodicals. These were often short-lived, sometimes longer-lasting and, like *Weekkrant Suriname* (1980-2004), had a broad outlook. Since 1983 there has even been a scientific journal for Surinamese studies, *Oso*, in which Surinamese and Dutch from both countries publish.

Radio and television were not left behind and broadcast a lot of news from Suriname, sometimes taken from local media, but often gathered independently. Alongside this, the number of local Surinamese-Dutch radio stations increased dramatically from the 1970s and Surinamese presenters, musicians, actors and sportsmen and -women penetrated the mainstream media. Conversely, Surinamese media gradually began to report not less, but more news about the Netherlands and, ultimately, adopt entire programmes from Dutch television. Moreover, the Dutch world service RNWO (*Radio Nederland Wereld Omroep*) has for decades been a popular intermediary with its considerable offering of Dutch and Caribbean news. Since 2000, the number of web sites where information is exchanged about Suriname and Surinamese in the Netherlands has grown enormously. In brief, a ramified and busy information network developed that virtually bridged the gulf in the Surinamese community.

The Antillean community in the Netherlands only began to grow strongly in number in the 1980s. Prior to this, the expectation of most migrants – and certainly students – was that they would return to their home island. Then there followed the exodus. Statistics about the rapid growth of the community somewhat conceal the circular character Antillean migration has retained: levels of remigration are still substantial. This is not only explained by the relative prosperity of the islands, but also the related fact that the islands are still part of the kingdom. People are able to change their minds, more than once if necessary. This mobility also conforms with the migration traditions of the region, where temporary labour migration has been common since the abolition of slavery.

Hence, in the 1990s the 'Antillean' community – in fact mainly Curaçaoan – became transnational. Here too there was a dramatic increase in the number of flight movements and, one may assume, intensive virtual contact. But unlike Suriname, there are no indications of large-scale material support being sent to the Antilles. In view of the absence of any systematic research, we can only assume that the level of remittances – perhaps leaving aside the drugs-related black market – has never been high; recent research confirms this.[15] This may be explained by the fact that the differences in income within this transnational community are minor. Measured against Dutch standards, Antillean migrants are relatively poor; Antilleans on the islands are relatively well off compared with the migrants, but also compared with living standards in Indonesia or Suriname.

Antilleans, at least those from the Leeward Islands, communicate with each other in Papiamentu. It is therefore not surprising that one of the first Antillean publications in the Netherlands, the student magazine *Kambio; Portabos independiente antijano*, bore a Papiamentu title, even if most of the articles were in Dutch.[16] Papiamentu would continue to bond the Antillean community while sometimes isolating it from its broader surroundings. Antillean organizations in the Netherlands nowadays usually choose Dutch for their publications, even though Papiamentu continues to be the language they use to communicate with each other.

A paradoxical development has taken shape since 1990. An increase in Antillean migration to the Netherlands was counterpointed by an increase in the Dutch presence on the Antilles – (indirectly) governmental, economic, but also demographic, and through a steep rise in tourism. This led to increased mutual interest, which was reported largely in the Dutch media. Once again the *Wereldomroep* (World Service) served as an intermediary. Moreover, on the islands new Dutch language papers were launched and Dutch television gained access to Antillean homes through BVN, the Dutch language world service TV: the schizophrenic linguistic situation thus became accentuated even further. For decades news from the islands could be followed in the Netherlands through the news gathering of the Dutch national press. Later, local digital newspapers and a large number of web sites were added, in both Dutch and Papiamentu. The question for the distant future is how long Papiamentu will be sustained in the Netherlands. In time it might become a second language for Antillean Dutch – vital mainly to maintaining relations with the islands of origin.

POSTCOLONIAL ORGANIZATIONS AND TRANSNATIONAL POLITICS

As early as 1934, Anton de Kom wrote in *Wij slaven van Suriname* of 'the hope and courage contained in that one mighty word that I learned abroad: organization'.[17] He was not alone in referring to his stay in the land of the colonial ruler as a political education. Regardless of which colonial power we look at, in the pre-war years migrants from the colonies wrote crucial pages in the history of anti-colonialism. Sometimes these were workers, more often intellectuals who began to articulate criticism of colonialism while studying in the mother country. This relation remained intact in the early decades after the war: migrants worked for decolonization and regarded their stay in the metropole as temporary. A remarkable turn then occurred, in the Dutch context as well. Independence lost its lustre and return became less and less an obvious option.

It is not surprising that migrants from the Netherlands East Indies were the least anti-colonial of all; their privileged existence was, after all, closely intertwined with the colonial system. Insofar as nationalism existed, it was articulated by Indonesian (prior to Indonesian independence) organizations and individuals, seldom by Indisch ones.[18] The split came about after the war. The number of Indonesian students and other migrants soon declined; they wisely kept away from political agitation. The rapidly growing Indisch community, on the other hand, objected strongly to decolonization and were often extremely resentful about having to accept the loss of the East Indies. The Indisch lobby developed in three phases, which became gradually more focused on the Netherlands. The first phase, resistance to the nationalist assumption of power, was more or less completed by the transfer of New Guinea in 1962. The bitterness felt towards Indonesia remained, but politically was of little more than symbolic significance. Meanwhile, a new aim was being striven for: the right to 'repatriation' and an adequate reception for the entire Indisch group. These efforts were rewarded during the course of the 1960s. After this the Indisch lobby focused mainly on symbolic recognition and financial compensation for the suffering and damages incurred in the period after 1942, but for a long time it also argued against the establishment of warmer interstate relations with the republic.

Insofar as the Indisch community demonstrated any kind of transnational political engagement, it was primarily reactionary. In the period leading up to the transfer of New Guinea's sovereignty, affiliations were largely found with political parties on the right which, in Lijphart's famous characterization, had also failed to leave 'the trauma of decolonization' behind them.[19] Never did a postcolonial lobby find such a receptive ear in Dutch politics; but the aims were soon superseded. What remained was a symbolic battle, in which Indisch veterans also asserted themselves. Sukarno remained an anathema, reciprocal state visits were vehemently opposed. It would be 2005 before the Dutch government reluctantly admitted '1945' (the year of the nationalist proclamation of independence) rather than '1949' (the year for the formal transfer of sovereignty) as the date marking the end of its rule. State visits to and from Japan likewise faced fierce objections. Attempts to appease the Indisch community put a spanner in the works of a 'normal' foreign policy for decades. It did not help that the Indonesian government was exceptionally sensitive to 'reactionary tendencies' within the Indisch community, and for this reason even boycotted the Pasar Malam Besar in The Hague for several years.[20]

Dutch politicians gradually began to distance themselves from this revanchist politicking, regardless of how much symbolic recognition and how many gestures the Indisch lobby harvested at the same time. Relations with Indonesia and Japan were normalized, all parties preferring to ignore the stickiest issues in bilateral relations rather than stir them up. And wherever witnesses to Dutch 'excesses' during the war of decolonization did turn up, and they frequently did, they were met with fierce opposition from the Indisch generation, albeit primarily from the veterans. The recent issue of Dutch war crimes perpetrated in the Javanese village of Rawagede in 1947, discussed at length in the Dutch media, are typical of this. The Dutch government finally expressed its deep regret and offered surviving relatives a number of development projects by way of modest and indirect compensation. However, apart from a few exceptions, the Indisch organizations remained silent.[21]

The transnationalism of the Moluccan political elite remained longer and more violently scarred by the traumatic course of decolonization; this gave rise to radical political actions that are unique in the history of the postcolonial Netherlands. The hope that their stay in the Netherlands would be temporary, merely a transitional phase en route to remigration to an independent (South) Moluccan republic (RMS), was clung onto for many years. Initially Dutch politicians, particularly on the right, were sympathetic towards the Moluccans' frustration regarding their forced demobilization in the Netherlands and the struggle for the RMS. However, this was not accompanied by concrete assistance and by the 1960s The Hague had already begun to pursue an integration policy. This gave rise to considerable frustration in the Moluccan community and ultimately, in the 1970s, to violent hostage taking and hijackings carried out by youths of the second generation. These actions were met with complete incomprehension and rejection across the political spectrum and resulted in a domestic policy aimed precisely at boosting integration into Dutch society. The government was wary about putting its fragile relations with Indonesia at risk for the RMS, which it viewed as a completely unrealistic dream.

Moluccan activists surrender after briefly occupying the official residence of the Indonesian Ambassador in Wassenaar, near The Hague, 31 August, 1970. This action was carried out on the eve of what was, also for Moluccans, the highly controversial visit of President Suharto of Indonesia to the Netherlands. The young activists unsuccessfully demanded a meeting between Suharto and the RMS president-in-exile, J.A. Manusama. A meeting between Prime Minister Piet de Jong and Manusama did take place later, but to little effect. This possibly contributed to the violent actions that followed later. One policeman was killed during the occupation. The 'Wassenaar 33' were later convicted and imprisoned with sentences ranging from four months to three years. Their popularity in Moluccan circles was considerable. (COLLECTION INTERNATIONAL INSTITUTE FOR SOCIAL HISTORY)

Reluctantly, and often silently, most Moluccans by the 1980s had begun to see that neither the RMS nor remigration were realistic objectives. The 'struggle' shifted into a demand for the right to self-determination for the Moluccas, a position that Steijlen has termed 'caretaker nationalism'.” After this, radical political transnationalism seemed to be heading for extinction: regardless of how much pent-up sectarian rage fuelled the internal struggle, or how frantically the old leaders clung on to the ideal of the RMS, their influence within the wider Moluccan population was declining. Very recently, the new 'president of the Moluccan government-in-exile' John Wattilete openly distanced himself from the necessity of a Moluccan Republic when he took office – a revisionist view that is not unrelated to the fact that he is also the first 'president' of the second generation.²³ But none of these shifts signalled the end of the engagement with the islands. The bloody riots between Christians and Muslims on the Moluccas from 1999 to 2001 provoked great agitation in the Netherlands.

This *kerusuhan*, which left five to seven thousand dead and hundreds of thousands of refugees, led to a renewal of Moluccan Dutch identification with the islands of their (grand)parents, which many young people had by now also visited. Money and equipment was collected, national events were organized in which thousands of Moluccans took part, and attempts were made to get Dutch politicians involved. This once more underlined how strong Moluccan Dutch transnationalism had remained compared with other postcolonial migrants.

For a moment it seemed as if the 1970s had been let out of the bottle, as radicals once again began to make threats against Dutch politicians and scholars who they accused of being too lenient towards Jakarta and too little concerned about the Moluccas. The Dutch government found itself forced to meet regularly with a new generation of Moluccan Dutch to discuss an issue over which it had no jurisdiction. By appealing to the safeguarding of international human rights – always a thorny issue in the relationship with Indonesia – they pressed the Indonesian government to intervene. Order in the Netherlands was preserved, a few minor incidents notwithstanding, and the political consequences of these actions remained limited. The Hague, after all, allows itself few liberties when it comes to Jakarta, especially with regard to sensitive questions such as the Moluccas or Papua (New Guinea).²⁴ Whether, in this discouraging context, a new generation of Moluccan Dutch will grasp ahold of the renewed orientation is unclear. Yet, it is remarkable how often the annual commemoration of the proclamation of the RMS continues to be accompanied by rioting by disaffected youth, who claim that the Netherlands has always let them down.²⁵

Compared with the Indisch and Moluccan communities, Surinamese in the Netherlands have had a longer and, on the surface, more successful history of political activism. Writer and politician Albert Helman published the melancholic *Zuid-Zuid-West* (South-Southwest) in 1926 in the Netherlands, with its biting Multatulian epilogue, in which he declared that the Netherlands was responsible for the 'whithering' of his homeland. While Helman requested greater national engagement, Anton de Kom – not much later – formulated the demand for independence. This desire was picked up by students of *Wie Eegie Sanie* in the 1950s and was brought to fulfilment, in part by them, in 1975.²⁶

Demonstration for the independence of Suriname, Amsterdam, 1971. In these years, demonstrations in favour of independence took place on a fairly regular basis, often with strongly-worded slogans. Most photos from the time show Afro-Surinamese and indigenous Dutch, rarely Indian or Javanese Surinamese. This is not surprising. The majority of the 30,000 Surinamese who lived in the Netherlands around 1970 were Creole; moreover, the pursuit of independence fell on sympathetic ears mainly in Afro-Surinamese circles. (COLLECTION INTERNATIONAL INSTITUTE FOR SOCIAL HISTORY)

However, a paradoxical development occurred at this point. The success of the nationalists led indirectly and unintentionally to the exodus to the Netherlands. The Surinamese who went to the Netherlands after 1970, not only distanced themselves from their country in so doing, but also, silently, from the dreams of the nationalist generation. This was complained about in Suriname. A few years later Surinamese prime minister Henck Arron himself – who had addressed several thousands of compatriots in Amsterdam in 1974, 'You do not belong here! You belong in Suriname!' – in an unguarded moment let slip that his country could survive without the 'schorriemorrie', or riffraff who had taken shelter in the mother country. Opposition leader Lachmon, too, spoke frankly of the gulf created by choosing one citizenship or the other.[27]

Among Surinamese in the Netherlands – and somewhat more in Afro-Surinamese periodicals like *Famiri* than in Indian Surinamese ones, such as *Aisa Samachar* – lip service was initially paid to the doctrine of remigration, much to the irritation of the Dutch government who wanted to follow a policy of integration. Surinamese questioning the illusion of return were often treated to furious and, in retrospect, naive reactions.[28] After a short revival immediately following the military coup, optimism about the republic and remigration dwindled completely. Migration became primarily a one-way affair, but the nostalgia remained.

Although there were demonstrations in the Netherlands in favour of independence, the influence of Surinamese in the Netherlands on the actual negotiations was negligible.[29] It was not until 1980 that the Surinamese community began to become more politically active. The military coup in 1980, the 'December Murders', or brutal execution of fifteen political opponents in 1982, the guerrilla war, with the absolute trough of the massacre at the Maroon village Moiwana in 1986, and the fragility of the subsequent democratization process in Suriname brought an end to the many illusions about *switie Sranan* (Sweet Suriname) and remigration. Key Surinamese-Dutch figures and organizations attempted to influence Dutch government policy. This took place in part behind the scenes, which, for instance, benefitted opponents of the military regime by securing a relatively generous admittance policy. At the same time a small number of radical left-wing (former) students remigrated to lend their support to the 'revo'.

Most Surinamese organizations were dedicated to democratization and were therefore opposed to the military regime. This is all the more logical in view of the fact that the Netherlands admitted many prominent opponents of the military regime after 1980.[30] That the prosecution for the December Murders has continued to be higher up the agenda than the horrors of Moiwana reflects the 'urban' character of the Surinamese resistance in the Netherlands, in which Maroons were barely represented. Surinamese lobbyists had little difficulty in persuading Dutch politicians, who at this time were still strongly and often paternalistically engaged with Suriname, to support them. Their dilemma about devoting themselves to prompting Dutch action was that it inevitably brought a degree of loss-of-face. In the period when democracy was restored between 1985 and the early 1990s, Dutch assistance was explicitly welcomed by the old parties; thereafter sensitivities about sovereignty and interference began to play a significant role once again.[31]

Insofar as the Surinamese community in the Netherlands has lobbied for political goals in Suriname since then, their aims have been more specific, for instance the prosecution of military leader Desi Bouterse and company, the restoration or continuation of the development aid relationship, or cultural cooperation. The aim was to maintain a 'special' relationship, with the underlying view that Suriname could not manage without the Netherlands. However, the turnout for political gatherings declined after the restoration of democracy (1987-1990).[32] Efficacy was also limited: with the changing of the political generations in The Hague, the Netherlands shifted towards more businesslike relations, while Paramaribo aimed to avoid any suggestion that it was paying too much attention to what was going on in the Netherlands. The recent election of Bouterse as president, in spite of his violent putschist past and his conviction in absentia in the Netherlands for drugs trafficking, has only widened the gap.

While The Hague took the route of pragmatism and thereby detachment, around 2000 the big cities entered into direct cooperative relations with Paramaribo, often to the displeasure of the Ministry for Foreign Affairs. Thus municipal authorities in Amsterdam, Rotterdam and The Hague were able to demonstrate their engagement – with Suriname, but also with the Surinamese-Dutch electorate. Politicians and civil servants of Surinamese origin often played a leading role in this; their political hue in the Netherlands seems to have been less relevant.[33]

The outcome is that Surinamese organizations and politicians in the Netherlands have come to focus more on the Netherlands, from issues of representation and antiracism to the struggle for the acknowledgement of a shared past. Fewer and fewer Surinamese organizations focus primarily on projects in Suriname; this number fell drastically in Amsterdam between 1970 and 2000.[34] Even solidarity shaped by shared ideals came under pressure. Where independence was celebrated between 1975 and 1990 by 10,000 or more Surinamese Dutch, this declined thereafter, in part due to decreased funding, until the celebrations quietly became marginal.[35]

At the same time, and doubtlessly also in response to diminishing engagement, a greater detachment began to take shape on the part of Suriname. Surinamese Dutch were no longer referred to as 'riffraff' or 'traitors'. These emotional descriptions were part of the initial phase of painful separation. Since the 1990s, Suriname has been far more pragmatic and held few illusions about the political significance of the former compatriots. It has therefore also been more critical: clamourous or prying armchair politicians from the Netherlands were not appreciated in Paramaribo. Former Surinamese Prime Minister, Jules Sedney, appositely summed up this feeling some years ago as, 'He who wants to sit at table should at least be prepared to stand in the kitchen. Affinity has to be proven.'[36] Surinamese political parties have traditionally had branches in the Netherlands. How much influence they had in the past can no longer be confirmed, but their current significance is not rated highly in Suriname. They generate a bit of money for the parent party's coffers, it is said, and major donors in the Netherlands deliver a degree of symbolic status and perhaps some material benefits, during visits, but no more. Conversely, the era in which the major Dutch parties

Antilleans demonstrating in The Hague, 1 June, 1969. Two days earlier, on 30 May, a labour dispute had erupted into a small, politically motivated revolt against the local administrative and economic leaders. Large areas of Willemstad's city centre went up in flames. The Dutch army restored order by force of arms – pictures of this seemingly colonial intervention were dispatched around the world. This episode led to a rapid change of direction in The Hague towards independence for Suriname and the Antilles. Many demonstrations would have supported this aim, but ultimately Curaçao and the other islands continued, successfully, to resist independence. (COLLECTION KITLV/ ROYAL NETHERLANDS INSTITUTE OF SOUTHEAST ASIAN AND CARIBBEAN STUDIES AT LEIDEN)

had separate committees for Surinamese issues (sometimes combined with the Antilles) and maintained contacts with the sister parties across the ocean, is long gone.

There has to be some doubt about whether the few who have remigrated really form a long-term bridge between the two countries. Surinamese Dutch who remigrated, or temporarily returned for work, often met ignorance and opposition. The resulting frustration has been consistently expressed since the 1970s. Authorities in Paramaribo are clear. Remigration is not an issue in contemporary Surinamese politics; almost no one in Suriname expects productive and enterprising Surinamese Dutch to remigrate on any significant scale. Some may regret this, but it is accepted. Anyone who does return, in most cases for a short time and under good conditions, must be sure to avoid any hint of paternalism. Black Dutch too have to prove themselves.

There is little evidence of an Antillean political transnationalism. There is no pre-war tradition; the few Antilleans who did spend any amount of time in the Netherlands as a rule belonged to the local elite and kept their distance from political issues, with the exception of those who were members of the resistance and were killed during the German occupation of the Netherlands, such as George Maduro and Boy Ecury. After the war, at the time that *Ons Suriname* and *Wie Eegie Sanie* began to propagate nationalist sentiments, the Antilles remained quiet. It was not until the 1960s that this began to change. Various prominent figures and sympathizers of the Curaçao uprising on 30 May, 1969, developed critical opinions of neocolonialism, racism and the local elite as students in the Netherlands. On the other hand, support for the short-lived Curaçaoan revolt was immediately signalled by demonstrations in The Hague. The magazine *Kontakto Antiyano*, for which the acclaimed Curaçaoan novelist Frank Martinus Arion wrote, declared itself in favour of independence.[37]

The uprising had paradoxical political consequences. The Netherlands was shocked to be reminded of the apparently still acute responsibilities it had for the other parts of the kingdom and turned, almost from one day to the next, to a radical policy of decolonization. Suriname went along with this and became independent in 1975, but the Antilles resolutely rejected the 'gift' of independence. Insofar as there had been any anti-colonialism at all in the Antilles, it soon fell silent, both on the islands and in the Netherlands. The political struggle of the Antilles has ever since revolved around the right to remain within the Kingdom of the Netherlands, the right to break up the six islands, the right to maximum autonomy, and the right to unhindered access to the Netherlands. On the first two fronts, The Hague would ultimately give up its own policy – the independence of the Antilles as a unit of six islands. In 2010, the former six-island non-sovereign country of the Netherlands Antilles was subdivided into three countries (Aruba, since 1986; Curaçao; and St Maarten), while the three remaining islands have attained a semi-municipal status within the Netherlands; all six refused to consider independence. Meanwhile the constant bickering over the limits of autonomy has continued. Much has been said on the subject of restricting Antilleans' access to the Netherlands – for decades behind closed government doors in The Hague and over the past decade openly in parliament, often using harsh words – but this has not so far lead to restrictive legislation.

What is striking about these political trajectories is not only the absence of serious political mobilization among Antilleans in the Netherlands, but also the apparent lack of a need to do so. Considering the structure of political relations, this should not come as a surprise. By virtue of the Charter of the Kingdom, the Dutch government has to do business with the overseas national government(s). The formal negotiating position of these bodies used to be strong, so there was generally little need to make Antillean political wishes heard separately in the Netherlands as well. Conversely, there was little desire on the part of the Antillean community in the Netherlands to distance themselves from the standpoints being articulated on the islands. Radical anti-colonialism, or open criticism of Antillean politics, were rarely articulated in the Netherlands; political engagement among Antilleans is limited anyway.[38]

However, the Netherlands did provide a new platform for Antillean politics in one respect, namely, to emphasize the individual characters of the different islands. An Aruba Day has been celebrated in the Netherlands every year since 1976. This is not just a social event, it was also explicitly part of the struggle for a *status aparte*, separate status, for the island. Once this ideal was achieved in 1986, this annual day of celebration became a way of keeping the Aruban community on the Netherlands involved with the island. Bonaire, Curacao, and the Windward Islands soon followed. Such festivals presented an opportunity to experience the 'island feeling', but also offered a platform for setting them apart from the fiction of a united nation of 'the Antilles' always dominated by Curaçao.

In other respects, political transnationalism remained limited to a few moderate initiatives, in which Antillean and prominent Dutch figures politely supported Antillean interests. Examples are the informal advisory committee supported in the 1990s by Minister Plenipotentiary 'Papi' Jesurun, the *Stichting Vriendschap voor de Nederlandse Antillen en Aruba*, the *Stichting ABC Advies* and the *Comité 2004* chaired by member of the Royal House Pieter van Vollenhoven; bodies with a certain amount of prestige, intellectual capacity, and access to The Hague elite, but without the need or scope to adopt radical positions. The same applies to the now defunct Antilles commissions of the political parties: consultation and thinking together, not confrontation, was the motto.

Organizations like the *Antilliaans Netwerk* (2000), the OCaN mentioned earlier, and MAAPP created a more distinctly 'Antillean' profile for themselves,

Whereas The Hague had set course for the speedy independence of the six islands of the Netherlands Antilles after 1970, the aim of the islands was precisely the opposite: to remain part of the Netherlands. Support for separatism from the other islands grew and tied down the Dutch government. Aruba served as crowbar and gained *status aparte*, separate status, as a new country within the kingdom. Years of demonstrations and negotiations had preceded this. The small Aruban community in the Netherlands did not allow itself to be ignored, as can be seen from this demonstration at Schiphol in 1977. The demonstrators are welcoming the champion of separate status, Betico Croes, on his way to The Hague to put his case to the government. (COLLECTION NATIONAL ARCHIVE)

but their influence on kingdom relations was very limited – administrators on the islands at times let it be known that they did not appreciate receiving unsolicited advice about their political activities from these 'Dutch' groups. However, there is one area in which the Antillean parties on both side of the ocean have found themselves joining forces: to resist any change to Antilleans' right to unhindered access to Dutch residency and to fight the separate registration of Antillean migrants. Here too The Hague was forced to withdraw its intended change of course – in response to Antillean pressure on both sides of the Atlantic, but also to serious criticism by Dutch institutions on the legal and ethical flaws of restrictive legislation.

It all remained at the level of polite string-pulling and only a radical change in direction of Dutch politics will change this. The balance is clear.

The consistent and successful Antillean rejection of independence was not a consequence of political agitation in the Netherlands; it did contribute to the transnationalization of the Antillean population; and this last development more or less obstructs the route to any future transfer of sovereignty. The Antilles are not unique in this: the relation between France and its Caribbean *départements* is comparable in terms of migration, as is the relationship between the USA and Puerto Rico. The same tensions arise in these cases: a resentment towards the metropole that cannot be translated into a meaningful struggle for independence; local aversion to migrants interfering in island politics; united resistance to any hint of limiting migration; and numerous latent doubts about how long the migrants and their (grand) children may continue to be regarded as members of the imagined community whose roots are on the islands.

CULTURAL TRANSNATIONALISM, 'DIASPORA' AND COMMUNITY

Transnationalism stems from a solidarity between migrants and those who stayed behind. Emotions around a divided identity loom large. There is little that can be taken for granted when it comes to the notion of identity, and postcolonial migrants are not an exception to this rule. What is certain is that an awareness of a divided identity does not necessarily or primarily need to be linked to a relationship between two countries. Turkish and Moroccan migrants settle in many countries; they are able to identify with their country of origin, but also with compatriots in the host country and/or other European countries, with other citizens of their host country, with others of the same religious persuasion all around the world, or they combine several of these identities at the same time. When the term diaspora is used, it refers not only to a long-term, perhaps permanent state of 'being away from home', but also to dispersion across many lands – the Jewish Diaspora being the original model.[39]

The latter does not apply to the postcolonial communities in the Netherlands. The vast majority of migrants from the Dutch East Indies, Suriname, and the Antilles settled exclusively in the former metropole. Their cultural and/or political identity was already strongly linked to the Netherlands. Questions of identity and identification now acquired an even stronger bilateral character: how did they then relate themselves to Dutch culture? The only groups that showed themselves to be in any way linked to a broader diaspora were the Chinese migrants from the colonies and the Surinamese of British Indian origin.

The Indisch Dutch left a country that rapidly and successfully erased almost all cultural traces of Dutch colonialism, with the exception of what is still a considerable Christian community. 'Europeans' in the East Indies, once they had made the journey to the Netherlands, discovered that they were not nearly as Dutch as they may once have thought. While they conquered a cultural space for themselves in the host country, they lost the connection to modern Indonesian culture. Interest in the republic remained, but the distance grew. There is no longer a cultural 'homeland' and neither does the Indisch community exercise any significant influence on Indonesian culture. It is doubtful whether the work of Tjalie Robinson will really serve as a 'blueprint for transnational [Indisch] identity' for later generations, as Wim Willems suggests.[40]

When they arrived in the Netherlands, the Moluccans were culturally far less European, which enabled them to hold on to the cultural links with their islands of origin. In retrospect, cultural transnationalism does not apply here: there never was any *reciprocal* cultural influence – in general terms Moluccan transnationalism is more unilateral than is the case for Suriname or the Antilles.[41] But from the perspective of the Moluccans in the Netherlands, the cultural gulf between the successive generations also became wider – because the Moluccans became more firmly integrated into Indonesia, but, above all, because the Moluccan Dutch became more Dutch.[42]

The Surinamese community in the Netherlands seems not only to have become more Dutch over the last few decades, but also more explicitly ethnic, more Afro-Surinamese, Hindustani or Javanese – and thereby less 'national' than in the country of origin. In Suriname, under the motto 'unity in diversity', all were supposed to live up to the ideal of building a nation; in the Netherlands the various groups increasingly went their own way. The name 'Surinamese' became narrowed down to apply to the Afro-Surinamese – a step back in time. The surprising gesture by the black players in the junior Dutch football team in 2007, who on winning the European football championships did a lap of honour carrying the Surinamese flag, was promptly welcomed or condemned as 'proof' of continuing solidarity with the land of their parents. But regardless of what the true meaning of such a symbolic claim to an identity might be, this display of the flag propagated 'Surinamese' as primarily belonging to Creole Dutch.

This return to colonial modes of ethnic pillars (*verzuiling*) became apparent in ethnic organizations and in the handling of cultural heritage, first and foremost advocated in the Hindustani Surinamese press.[43] Inherent to this was a strong contrast between external orientations. The history of the African diaspora is suffused with spiritual 'back-to-Africa' movements. In

the Netherlands too, such pioneers as Anton de Kom and *Wie Eegie Sanie* exhibited an orientation towards the Black Atlantic, long before the phrase
had been coined. However, this African orientation has remained diffuse
among Creole Surinamese. There is no demonstrable country of origin and,
moreover, events on that continent for many years gave little cause for pride.

This contrasts strongly with the spectacular surge in enthusiasm for India and Indian culture among the Hindustani Surinamese, from classical
culture to contemporary Bollywood. Looking back, hints of this could already be found in the way in which Hindustani Surinamese organizations
focused on religion and culture from their inception, just as they had in Suriname. In the Netherlands, Hindustani Surinamese began more distinctly
to form part of a wider diaspora, which linked them to 'overseas Indians' in
numerous countries around the world and, for the majority, with Hinduism. Where the first generation was initially focused predominantly on Suriname and only in a spiritual sense on India, for subsequent generations
the sense of a diaspora seems to have become more important. It cannot be
presumed that Suriname will remain the main focus of their attention in
future.[44]

A similar development is conceivable for the Muslim Hindustani Surinamese minority and for the Javanese Surinamese. They were initially predominantly identified as Surinamese, later predominantly as Muslims.
They too organized themselves along religious lines as soon as they arrived
in the Netherlands, but within their own (linguistic) community and did
not join up with other Muslims from Turkey or Morocco. Yet in both groups
there seems to be evidence of a slight increase in curiosity for the country of
origin, in part fed by a degree of interest from India and Indonesia. Even so,
integration in the Netherlands and an orientation towards a world religion
will have a greater impact on them in the long-term than the Surinamese
intermezzo or their ancestors' country of origin. Consequently, Surinamese
Muslims have become active in umbrella organizations where, thanks to
the postcolonial language bonus, they are often able to serve as mediators.
Once again the conclusion that thrusts itself forward is that an overarching
'Surinamese' identity in the Netherlands – which sixty-five years ago was
obviously and almost exclusively Creole, thirty years ago still evidently so,
but with broader ethnic overtones – will lose its significance within a few
generations.

The colonial construction of the six islands of the Netherlands Antilles
never gave rise to a strong sense of nationhood. It is therefore unsurprising
that Antilleans in the Netherlands also mainly identify with their own islands. Nonetheless, language drew the inhabitants of the three Leeward Is-

lands closer together as only they speak Papiamentu (or, in the case of Aruba, the slightly different variant of Papiamento). But within one, or at most two generations, Antillean Dutch will have to answer the classic question: what is the price they are willing to pay to hold on to a dysfunctional language in a new society – the question also arises in a less extreme form on the islands themselves. What is striking, though not surprising considering the central position language occupies in the Antillean identity, is that the dilemma is so little discussed by Antilleans in the Netherlands. For the time being, Antillean transnationalism, in its more recent manifestation – continuing two-way traffic, and the language factor – is strong at an individual level, but already becoming comparatively weak in the fields of organizations and political engagement.[45]

For all other groups of postcolonial migrants, transnationalism appears to wane or, in the case of the Indisch Dutch, to disappear almost entirely. This is unsurprising in light of the lessons of migration history – rather it is extraordinary that Moluccan transnational engagement, despite the lack of realistic political prospects or remigration, has remained so strong for so long.[46]

Transnationalism not only binds migrants to the country of origin and vice versa, it also connects – harmoniously or otherwise – migrants, their families, networks, and organizations: after all, they share an interest in, concern about, and identifications with the country of origin. The weakening of transnationalism, therefore, also implies a vanishing sense of community among postcolonial migrants in the Netherlands. In this sense, the persistence of Moluccan (trans)nationalism, which not infrequently was enforced by the Moluccan community, is also understood as a means that was deployed – deliberately or otherwise – to keep Moluccans in the Netherlands together as a community. This worked for a long time, but even this exceptionally tight-knit group has become increasingly undermined by simultaneous integration.[47]

7

AN INTERNATIONAL PERSPECTIVE

The Dutch experience of postcolonial migrations was not unique. A number of other countries found themselves confronting migration flows from their former colonies at the end of the Second World War. In Europe this particularly applied to the United Kingdom, France and, somewhat later, Portugal. Mass migration unexpectedly brought these countries – and the Netherlands – face to face with their colonial histories, with the issue of integration, and the position of colonialism and postcolonial migration in the nation's imagination. There was more room for the latter in the British and Dutch model of moderate multiculturalism than there was in France and Portugal.

Postcolonial migrations were part of a far broader migration process which dramatically changed the face of post-war Europe. It also brought Islam to Western Europe on an hitherto unprecedented scale. In France, a large proportion of the postcolonial migrants were Muslim, which was not the case in Portugal or the Netherlands; the United Kingdom occupied the middle ground in this respect. This was to give rise to remarkable differences in the debates about integration and postcolonial nationhood.

A comparison between the Dutch experience and the experiences of the United Kingdom, France, and Portugal lies at the heart of this chapter. A number of other countries are also discussed, particularly former European colonial powers which were not confronted with postcolonial migrations. The question is whether these countries, unhampered by a postcolonial lobby, developed different views on colonialism.

The phenomenon of postcolonial migration to the former metropole is not limited to the old Europe. The United States, as well as Japan and Russia, received millions of post-war repatriates who were mainly migrants from their former colonies. In the case of the United States there are many parallels with Europe, both in issues surrounding integration and in debates about colonialism and postcolonial relations. It seems typical of a completely different approach to history that such debates were virtually absent in Japan and Russia.[1]

MIGRATIONS IN POST-WAR EUROPE

Viewed from the perspective of 1945, the post-war changes Europe was to undergo were almost inconceivable. The war had cost the lives of millions, among whom six million murdered Jews. The devastation was immense in other respects as well. Europe was destitute and disillusioned.

Migration was one response to this situation. Millions of people migrated from Western and Southern Europe to distant continents. Millions from Eastern Europe, while they still had a choice, chose the West in preference to the newly developing Eastern Bloc. Millions of *Volksdeutsche* (Germans living abroad), fleeing or having been expelled from Central and Eastern European countries, moved to West Germany. Migrants sought refuge across the borders; borders were repositioned over the heads of local populations. Shortly after the war, European states were ethnically more uniform than they had been for centuries. Furthermore, until 1989, the new map of the continent was marked by a deep and apparently stable political divide.

In less than two decades, most West-European colonial empires collapsed. The outcome was not the economic catastrophe gloomily predicted by many. Instead, Western Europe experienced three decades of spectacular economic growth. This miracle was in some measure possible due to the mass migration of low-skilled workers from Southern Europe, the former colonies, and Turkey and Morocco. But, by the mid 1970s economic growth had stagnated and the transition to a postindustrial society had begun to take shape. Opportunities for low-skilled labour dwindled. Western European countries now had a mind to curb immigration and encouraged labour migrants to return to their countries of origin. The opposite occurred. The reuniting of families and chain migration to all Western European welfare states led to a sharp increase in 'non-Western' populations, which further expanded with the immigration of political and economic refugees from sub-Saharan Africa and Asia.

The unintended and undesired creation of multicultural societies in the western part of Europe from the 1970s on, from Sweden to Spain, became the subject of increasingly anxious debates. The fall of the Berlin Wall and the opening up of the Eastern Bloc not only meant political upheaval, it also set in motion a new, now westward, wave of migration. Consequently, the population of the 'old' Europe became more multicultural, while most of 'new'

Europe attracted almost no migrants and remained ethnically relatively homogeneous, or at least quiet – former Yugoslavia being the shocking exception here.

Much has been said about 'traumatic' events in recent European history. Notwithstanding the sometimes absurd inflation of this concept, it is clear that the traumas suffered and kept alive were not the same for the whole continent. Almost all of Europe had been involved in the war. Bitterness and sorrow abounded everywhere. Humiliation was a common feature of the memory, except in the United Kingdom and the Soviet Union. Shame – about crimes committed, collaboration, 'looking the other way' – were only addressed later, that is, in the West.

In part as a consequence of the war, Western European states lost their colonial empires. This was indeed experienced as a 'loss' and often described in terms of trauma. With the exception of Russia, Eastern Europe had no colonial history. Contrastingly, Eastern European countries did have a history of being 'colonized' – by the Ottoman and Hapsburg Empires, and then by the Nazis and the Soviet Union. In the Soviet era, the memory of the war and the Holocaust was narrowed down to a comprehensive narrative in which communism had conquered the fascist excesses of capitalism. Only after 1989 did it become apparent that the 'new' Europe above all had to deal with what was broadly experienced as forty-five years of oppression by the Soviet Union. Eastern Europeans saw themselves as victims; there was little room for critical reflection on anti-Semitism, let alone the treatment of such minorities as the Roma. Later accusations of collaboration referred sooner to collaboration with the Soviet Union than the Nazis.

European memory accordingly remained completely asymmetrical, as has been convincingly argued by historian Tony Judt in *Postwar*, in the sense of there being sharply contrasting views of European history. But the ways in which migration from outside Europe and ethnic differences are viewed also turned out to vary enormously. If postcolonial immigration was met with great scepticism in Western Europe, in Eastern European countries there is little knowledge and even less affinity with the history that preceded it – and therefore, it seems, little sympathy for the logic of postcolonial migrant communities in Western Europe. How this tension will be resolved is unclear. The outcome will be decisive in relation to the question of whether modern Europe, in the spirit of Judt, can really be, or become, an example for the world at large.[2]

The former colonial metropoles lay to the west of the Berlin Wall. After the Second World War, four countries received considerable numbers of migrants from their former colonies – if we limit ourselves to the migration flow directly linked to the decolonization process, this amounted to between five and six million people.[3] Two of these countries – France and the United Kingdom – had a serious labour shortage immediately after the war and welcomed these migrants. The Netherlands began recruiting labour in the 1960s, but almost none from its colonies. Portugal was traditionally an exporter of labour; its late decolonization process did not lead to immigration until the 1970s. Hence, the context of postcolonial migrations varied enormously. This is also true of the histories that preceded them: the presence in France and the United Kingdom of migrants from the colonies had always been more significant. Moreover, the French and British had both made extensive use of colonial troops in both World Wars.

Postcolonial migration is not the same as labour migration and the degree to which both kinds overlap varies considerably from country to country. This is also true of other potential overlaps. The Western-European minorities debate has increasingly become a debate about Islam. This may be one-sided and nonsensical, but it is a fact. From this perspective, it is relevant to note that the vast majority of postcolonial migrants in France were Muslim, while this overlap is small in the Netherlands and negligible in Portugal; the number of Muslims among British postcolonial migrants lies between these two extremes.

A close look at the sending countries also reveals a highly varied picture. Most Southern European migrants have settled in France. The former French, part colonial, part informal empire in the Maghrib generated not only a large number of migrants to France, but also to other European countries. From Turkey, which had no European colonial history, migrants spread to almost all Western European countries. Migrants from the French and Dutch Caribbean migrated almost exclusively to their own metropoles. The largest proportion of migrants from the British West Indies, however, has settled in the United States, rather than the United Kingdom. The decolonization of Asia and the Middle East generated a relatively modest stream of migrants, with the exception of the Dutch East Indies and British India. The migration most directly linked to the decolonization of sub-Saharan Africa headed for Portugal, Belgium, and the United Kingdom; in the case of the latter, the migrants were mostly 'twice migrants', ethnic Indians who had settled in Africa. Alongside Africa and Asia, Eastern Europe has also become a major supplier of labour over the last two decades. Many of these migrants will no doubt eventually become Western Europe citizens too.

Europe's history of post-war migration therefore generates a mosaic that cannot be encapsulated in a single formula. This also applies to the four countries – France, the United Kingdom, the Netherlands and Portugal – which faced large-scale postcolonial migration, within which a distinction can be made between European 'repatriates' and former colonial subjects.[4] By way of throwing the Dutch context into relief, the following paragraphs sketch the migration histories of these three countries and their relationships with decolonization, their societies' reactions to it, and the place of colonial history in the debates about national identity.

FRANCE: REPUBLICAN DILEMMAS

Unlike most countries on the European mainland, France became a land of immigration as early as the late nineteenth century.[5] Successive governments and political majorities explicitly encouraged this immigration. Natural population growth was low, especially compared with its great rival Germany, which put France at an economic and military disadvantage. Immigration could compensate for this. Migrants had to become French citizens as quickly as possible, for this to work, which initially meant they had to make the French language and culture, including republican values, their own. Immigrants consequently became part of a far larger project to turn all the inhabitants of the highly divided 'hexagon' into French citizens. But this was still a long way off. On the eve of the First World War, half of the citizens of France spoke poor French, if any at all.

The migrants initially came from Belgium and Italy, later Poland and Spain and, after the Second World War, mainly Portugal. There were violent incidents of local resistance to the newcomers. Generally speaking, however, the settling and assimilation of these immigrants passed off relatively smoothly. The process was retrospectively labelled a success story; *le creuset français* – the European version of the (supposed) American melting pot. The explanations are obvious. On the whole there were enough jobs and if there were not, the migrants moved on; the immigrants had no social or political rights that put them in a position to negotiate as a separate group; there was no strong ethnic or cultural difference between the immigrants and the French 'norm', which was itself in rapid development.

The French political, intellectual, and academic elites of the republic long regarded *le creuset français* as the most relevant national narrative of migration and assimilation. France supposedly welcomed immigrants, as long as they were willing to convert to republican values and norms. The immigrants were thus guided in the same direction as the inhabitants of France's extremely diverse regions. What determined this socialization process were the strictly centralized education system and a solemn, at times quasi-religious glorification of the magnificence of the republic. After all, it had given the world the ideals of *liberté, equalité, fraternité* and could, therefore, claim the moral high ground. Thus, President Charles de Gaulle was able to speak gladly of a pact between the magnificence of France and the freedom of the entire world.[6]

There are other, very different stories to be told of this enlightened state, especially if we take the colonial dimension into account. Long before the French Revolution, France had already established a number of colonies. The opportunity to allow the new ideals to take root overseas during the revolutionary period was deliberately repulsed. For a moment, France was the first country to abolish African slavery in the New World, but this revolutionary decision was not implemented and Napoleon revoked it. French colonialism made a second start after 1830, first in the Maghrib and South-East Asia, later in sub-Saharan Africa. Colonization was in many cases accompanied by bloody wars and oppression. Later in the nineteenth century a new, noble ideal was brought to bear, broadly supported by the republican elite: French colonialism had a *mission civilisatrice*, a civilizing mission. How fortunate the colonized peoples who were touched by the civilizing offensive of the superior French culture!

Even if the link with exemplary republican ideals was unique, the idea of a civilizing offensive was not exceptional. The British spoke of 'the white man's burden', the Dutch, somewhat later, referred to a 'debt of honour' and the resulting task of 'ethical politics'; other countries employed similar arguments. Meanwhile, this colonial discourse above all served to justify a policy in which the international power positions, prestige, and wealth of the colonial powers took priority. Britain and France would also make extensive use of colonial troops during both World Wars. France was unique in the sense that it also regarded its colonies as a source of labour for the metropole itself. Hence, shortly after the slaughter of the First World War, several hundreds of thousands of workers from North Africa and Indo-China were brought to France – always explicitly on a temporary basis and as second choice after Europeans.

After the Second World War the French authorities opted for a strict immigration policy. Immediately after the war there were extensive discussions about whether migration from outside Europe, primarily from the French colonial world, was acceptable. There was widespread agreement that European immigration was infinitely preferable. However, the argument that non-Europeans would be insufficiently able to adapt was eventually swept from the table: it was felt that the nation's institutions were robust enough to sustain the French integration model. The argument was also a pragmatic one: they had little choice, because the flow of Europeans would never be large enough.[7]

Thus, concern about migrants from the (former) colonies would dominate immigration and next the French migration debate. In the first three decades after the war (*les trentes glorieuses*) the French economy expanded enormously and there was an almost constant demand for more labour. There was still labour migration from within Europe, now primarily from Portugal, but its relative significance declined. Demand was largely met by spontaneous migration from French Algeria and the former Maghrib protectorates of Morocco and Tunisia, as well as state-organized migration from the French Caribbean provinces of Guadeloupe and Martinique. The bloody war of decolonization in Algeria, which ended in 1962, also led to the 'repatriation' of a million French citizens (pieds noirs) who had settled there and more than 100,000 *harkis*, colonial troops and their families, who were predominantly Muslims. The history of the pieds noirs is reminiscent of that of the Indisch Dutch, while the history of the *harkis* resembles that of the Moluccans.[8]

As long as the economy grew, migrant labourers had enough work and did not leave much of an imprint on society, either demographically or culturally, this (post)colonial migration passed off relatively peacefully. All this changed in the mid 1970s. Economic crisis and restructuring led to a drastic rise in unemployment, which in turn led to laws aimed at curbing immigration. In the circle around President Valérie Giscard d'Estaing, migrants from the Maghrib were now referred to in candidly xenophobic terms.[9] Restrictive legislation was ineffective and even had the opposite effect: migrants who had already settled stayed and now also brought over their families. In the decades that followed, France, now a welfare state, experienced a strong influx of asylum seekers and economic refugees from Africa, Asia, and Eastern Europe, a number of whom never acquired legal status. Meanwhile, a second and then third generation of 'migrants' was growing up who were legally and, in part, culturally French, but who fell socio-economically way below the French average. A disproportionate number was living in the worst parts of the *banlieues*, suburbs, of the big cities, especially Paris, Marseille and Lyon.

Where the 1980s and '90s saw tentative experiments in a previously inconceivable broadening of the meaning of citizenship (*le droit à la différence*), by 2000 this debate had already become less relaxed. On the one hand there was severe criticism of the alleged unwillingness of the Maghrib communities to adapt. On the other there were fierce debates about the significance of

Islam and colonial history for the nation; the primacy of the secular state remained intact, but the debate inevitably marred the lofty image of grandeur and the colonial *mission civilisatrice*.

Then there were the massive riots in the autumn of 2005, which gave rise to fierce debates. Had the French model failed? Were non-Western migrants really willing and capable of fully integrating? What role does Islam play in this and how does it relate to *laïcité*, laicization, a principle that was only made law in 1907, but which derives from a 1789 revolutionary principle that religion belongs in the private domain? Should national identity be strengthened, redefined?[10] Under President Nicolas Sarkozy, himself the son of a migrant, assimilation continued to be the motto. In 2007, he established a new ministry for Immigration and National Identity, with identity explicitly defined in the term of the classical republican tradition.[11]

What is striking is that participants in the debates about 'the nation' are primarily French (and white), while broader studies of background and the current significance of migration and ethnicity in post-war France are often written by Anglophone foreigners. Striking, but it would seem also typical of a rather introspective national elite, which for so long relied on the self-evident superiority of the French integration machine and which was unable or unwilling to see the numerous other signals. This was exacerbated even further by the rejection of much-loathed Anglo-Saxon multiculturalism and objections to the identification of separate ethnic groups, let alone the registration of their socio-economic, cultural and other characteristics. After all, this does not fit the image of a nation that thinks along the lines of equal citizens rather than a segmented society.[12]

This attitude also explains why, right up to the present day, only very rough and contradictory estimates exist of the numbers of first, second and third generation non-Western 'migrants' in France – more than five million French citizens among a total of sixty-four million, most originating from the Maghrib, others from the French Antilles (around 500,000) and French Indo-China (100,000 – 150,000). Most migrants from sub-Saharan Africa come from the former French colonies in that region, many of whom were unable to acquire citizenship in the first generation. In sharp contrast to the Dutch situation, in France the category 'non-Western' overlaps almost entirely with 'postcolonial' (the most important exception being 400,000 Turks) and 'Muslim' (with the exception of the Antilleans). Both facts play a major part in the French debates.[13]

Long before the riots of 2005, the English-language literature warned of a dangerous geographical concentration of socio-economic deprivation, in particular youth unemployment, poor living conditions, and frustration regarding discrimination and police conduct.[14] Following the 2005 riots, it was widely believed that it was not the background or the course of the riots that was new, but rather the vast scale and long duration. Most of the academic analyses did not place 'Islam' high on the list of causes. The profile of the rioters was of young, French citizens who had no issue with French culture as such; who identified themselves firstly as French, and only secondly as something else (and then more in terms of country of origin than religion); and who above all felt angry and aggrieved because in their experience the republic did not live up to its promises of inclusion. Furthermore, it has been noted that there was a complete absence of leadership or political articulation: the riots were in this sense literally unguided.[15]

Reactions from the French government were contradictory. Sarkozy, then still a minister, spoke in militant terms about scum who had to be firmly clamped down upon; while President Jacques Chirac, in a moving television speech, expressed sympathy for the underlying frustrations, thereby opening doors for a more pragmatic approach to minority issues. This was also because factors such as ethnicity and discrimination could now be named. France therefore gradually turned away from a 'colour blindness' which had been self-inflicted in the name of lofty republican ideals. Even a pragmatic interpretation of the Anglo-Saxon model of multiculturalism could now be discussed: *diversité* cautiously became the motto.

This does not mean that the principles of national unity and *laïcité* have been jettisoned. On the contrary, the debates in the French media about Islam and, above all, the need to exclude it as much as possible from public life, continue unimpeded. The outcome of the protracted 'headscarf crisis' (1999-2004) proved that France is considerably more principled than other European countries and consequently continues to reject more firmly the wearing of religious symbols in state institutions. The republic will not allow itself to be overruled that easily. A significant symbol of the wide range of interpretations of integration, even among immigrants is that the black headmaster who refused to allow Muslim girls wearing headscarves into his school is himself originally from Martinique.[16]

The position of Afro-Caribbean migrants is ambivalent. Coming from the overseas provinces, like Antilleans in the Netherlands, they have free access to France. In the 1960s, Antilleans were actively recruited to ease the labour shortage, but also to reduce the populations on the islands. Traditionally they had a strong postcolonial bonus in the areas of language and religion, which translated into a relatively smooth integration process, but also into a tendency to feel superior to other migrants. However, the real benefits declined in the second and subsequent generations and it is now often observed that Antilleans in France suffer from racism and exclusion almost as much as other 'migrants' – which in turn has led to a stronger tendency towards identity politics and a distancing from a republican ideology that has not lived up to its own pretensions.[17]

Amidst this tense atmosphere, an even fiercer debate erupted not long ago on the subject of the colonial past. What is striking, from a Dutch perspective, is how broad these debates were and that they were held at such an elevated intellectual level, but also the polemical tone they set. With good reason people speak of a *guerre de mémoires*. By far the most sensitive theme is the Algerian bloody war of independence, which had such a traumatic impact that it took three decades before a public debate was possible at all.[18] That ferocity, it would seem, not only affects France's resentment regarding the darker side of its own history, it also reflects the slowly dawning, painful realization that the republic, internationally and morally, is no longer the enlightening example its elites believed it for so long to be. The aversion to 'identity politics' by ethnic minorities within its own borders fits in a republican tradition which allowed little scope for difference. But it also reflects legitimate concerns regarding the disappearance of French identity ('Balkanization') and the 'tribalization' of history.

THE UNITED KINGDOM: BRITISHNESS AND MULTICULTURALISM

The debate about national identity in the United Kingdom also has a long history, which was not initially related to either migration or Europe, but to the relationship between the centre and periphery of the United Kingdom itself: dominant England on the one hand and on the other hand Scotland, Wales and Northern Ireland – and, of course, Ireland prior to its independence.[19] This tension has never abated and has even grown over the last few decades, as revealed by the report *Citizenship and belonging: What is Britishness?* (2005). Inhabitants of Scotland and Wales defined themselves in the first instance not as British, but as Scottish or Welsh. White English identified themselves as English, followed by British. Only one category of British citizens described themselves as being in the first instance British: ethnic minorities in England, who use 'British' as an appropriately broad term and associate 'English' with what in the Netherlands is called the autochthon population, and some associate Englishness with racism.[20]

The United Kingdom has a long colonial history and ruled over an empire that was larger and mightier than any other European empire ever. The history of British immigration history stretches way back and from the beginning was partly linked to the colonial empire. However, up until the Second World War, the largest numbers of new Britons came from Ireland and continental Europe. After the war, immigration soared. This was in part a consequence of the dynamic of decolonization – an estimated 300,000 to 400,000 Britons returned to the metropole.[21] Next, the number of labour migrants grew rapidly. Throughout virtually the whole of the post-war period, the majority of these continued to come from Ireland and continental Europe; a new development was the substantial influx of migrants from the (former) colonies, initially mainly from the British Caribbean, and later British India and Africa. Citizens of the British Commonwealth had unrestricted access to settle in the UK between 1948 to 1962. This permission was revoked in response to a surge in migration from the (former) colonies. In the decade that followed the law was tightened ever further, so that postcolonial migration henceforth became extremely difficult.[22]

As on the continent, the restrictive legislation of the early 1970s coincided with the end of a long period of economic growth, rising unemployment, and concerns about ethnic tensions. And in the United Kingdom, immigration continued: where in the 1960s and '70s there was an emigration surplus, the immigration volume has been growing ever since.

In British statistics, as in the United States, colour and/or ethnicity have been documented for several decades without restraint. This was considered indispensable to the formation of an effective minorities policy.[23] In 1959 the number of non-whites was estimated to be a few tens of thousands, in 2001 this was 4.5 million, around 8 per cent of the 55 million British citizens.[24] Besides postcolonial migrants and the later flow of refugees and labour migrants from Africa and Asia, Eastern European migration became more significant after the fall of the Berlin Wall in 1989 and the subsequent expansion of the European Union; the number of migrant Poles alone is estimated at around a quarter of a million.

By far the majority of non-white immigrants comes from the former colonies. Until the 1960s these were mostly Caribbean migrants, since then there have been more Asians: more than two million British citizens have roots in the former South Asian colonies, more than half a million in the Caribbean. The overlap between 'postcolonial' and 'Muslim' is smaller than in France. More than half of the more than two million Britons of South Asian heritage are Muslims (mainly from Pakistan and Bangladesh), the rest are Hindu or Sikh (and mainly from India). The British of (Afro-)Caribbean descent are on the whole Christian.[25]

Early on immigration gave rise to unadulterated racist reactions and race riots, which resulted in the Commission for Racial Equality (CRE) being set up as early as 1976. The CRE was charged with identifying sources of racial tension and advising both government and society on anti-racist policy. Its foundation demonstrated that the issue had been recognized and was a first step in the direction of a multicultural policy. The CRE remain intact even under the long-lasting reign of the Conservative Party, first under Margaret Thatcher, followed by John Major. Although not endorsed by central government, the traditionally left-wing big cities adopted a policy of multiculturalism, which became the norm in the 1980s. And when Tony Blair came to power with New Labour in 1997, a moderate multiculturalism became standard across the country.[26]

This multiculturalism, inspired by the Canadian and to a lesser extent American models, strived for integration but either did not make cultural assimilation a top priority, or rejected it entirely as a concern of government policy. In the meantime, a growing degree of differentiation between the different postcolonial communities was beginning to take shape in the new generations. Hindus and Sikhs were socio-economically most successful, while Muslims from former British India were the least successful; the Caribbean British come in between.[27] Where once the terms 'white' and 'black' were used, today the minimal and again hopelessly inadequate differentiation between 'white, black and Asian' is used.[28]

The debate about British multiculturalism revolved not only around the question of the diverging socio-economic development of the different groups, which brought with it such issues as school dropout rates, (youth) unemployment, potential ghetto forming, and deviant behaviour. Questions of social cohesion, marginalization, and identification with British culture were also debated. The discussion intensified after 9/11 and especially after the bloody London Tube and bus bombings on 7 July, 2005. Besides a call for repressive, stricter immigration restrictions, the question was inevitably raised again about whether multiculturalism had underestimated the need for social cohesion – and whether integration was indeed possible without a certain degree of assimilation.

Among the things that emerges from these debates is that many prominent participants in the debate themselves come from postcolonial backgrounds and that they hold highly conflicting viewpoints.[29] Both these characteristics underscore the fact that the public debate in Britain is far more sophisticated than in continental Europe. Moreover, the prominent role played by British institutions – which still include the CRE, now part of the Equality and Human Rights Commission – stands out, as does the fact that successive prime ministers have explicitly been involved in these debates. The breadth of the debate is in line with Britain's early embrace of a pragmatic multiculturalism, which for many years was a complete anathema in France and surrounded by many more question marks elsewhere in continental Europe.

In the self-image of the United Kingdom, the colonial empire has traditionally occupied an important and positive position. After the Second World War this was augmented by the proud realization that it was the only country among the European Allies that had not been occupied and that it had made major sacrifices to achieve victory. This image of the war has remained intact and continues to buoy up a particular British sense of pride.[30] Conversely, the colonial past has also been subjected to highly critical assessment over past decades, far more than in most former colonial metropoles – perhaps with the exception of the Netherlands.

That precisely British colonialism should be so thoroughly examined in part arises from the sheer range of the Empire and the apparently banal fact that it left behind English as the language of intellectual debate wherever it went – in the academically prominent USA, but also in India, the Caribbean, and so on. Also pivotal was the influence of postcolonial migrants, including scholars from West Indian backgrounds, such as Stuart Hall and Paul Gilroy, who founded the British version of Postcolonial Studies. Recently, the extensive critiques of colonialism and its legacies led, rather predictably, to an academic revisionism, which re-emphasized the positive role of Empire.[31]

Much earlier than in France, and probably the Netherlands too, colonial history and postcolonial migrants were key themes in all debates about multiculturalism and the nation. Recent British debates about social cohesion and nationality have given rise to a paradox in this respect.[32] Where the rediscovery of the colonial past in France led to fierce polemics, the same history no longer seems to play such a divisive role in the United Kingdom today. It appears the country has come to terms with the past: there is a relatively broad acceptance that the acknowledgement of (the darker aspects of) colonialism is important as an inclusive gesture to contemporary citizens of colonial heritage. This was most strikingly illustrated by the massive and self-critical commemoration of the bicentenary of the abolition of the Atlantic slave trade (1807-2007).[33]

This confessional self-criticism on the part of the state clearly does not stand in the way of a positive approach to British heritage. Not long after his government had distanced itself from more radical interpretations of multiculturalism, Blair declared that the core of the national identity comprised certain essential values, which included 'British heritage' – he then added that this would always include room for multicultural diversity.[34] Nonetheless, the message was clear: in the service of social cohesion, a national identity that is rooted in the past should be talked about more often and with greater pride, without this leading to the exclusion of minorities.

It is ironic that Blair's successor, Gordon Brown, was just as unable to define national identity more precisely than 'that Britain has something to say to the rest of the world about the values of freedom, democracy and the dignity of the people that you stand for'.[35] This is a view that is close to the French self-image of being a moral compass to the world. Somewhat later, in the memorandum *The governance of Britain* (2007), the Labour government declared that the British self-image was far less clearly defined than the French one and that this was precisely why a description of national identity was called for. This was to be sought in history, institutions, values, and mentality – the parallel with the debate held in the Netherlands over the last few years is manifest.[36]

The question in the British debates is not so much whether the high values of the colonial empire were met – there are few who would make that claim – but whether this colonialism is discussed openly enough today and whether postcolonial migrants and their children have been given equal opportunities. Postcolonial intellectuals like Gilroy, a severe critic of New Labour, believe this is absolutely not the case. However, even according to his own analysis, he appears to occupy a lonely position in the political and intellectual debate.[37]

Meanwhile, the increasing diversity between and within groups of postcolonial and other migrants makes it ever harder to plausibly forge direct and generalized continuities between colonial and postcolonial experiences. Spokespersons for various groups have emphasized exactly these differences – the joint 'black' antiracism of Asian and Caribbean Britons already made way for distinctions between them in the 1980s. Opposite 'Black Britons' – from the Caribbean or Africa – are the 'British South Asian, or 'BrAsians' for short, but within this last category Sikhs and Hindus resist association with the Muslim community.[38] For the purposes of everyday policy, the notion 'postcolonial' as a description seems to be becoming ever less relevant – colonial background is not even discussed in the report *Our shared future* (2007) by the Commission on Integration & Cohesion.[39]

PORTUGAL: RELUCTANT RE-MIGRANTS

After five centuries of colonialism in Asia, Africa and Brazil, by the end of the Second World War Portugal retained possession of two large African colonies (Angola and Mozambique) and a series of smaller colonies in Asia and Africa. Most Asian enclaves were taken over by India or China in the decades that followed. These take-overs spurred the small-scale migration of the Eurasian elites to Portugal, where they integrated silently. East Timor was occupied by Indonesia for many years (1975-1999) after its independence; the scale of migration to Portugal was small. The independence of Portuguese Africa, on the other hand (1975), led to a massive migration of more than half a million Portuguese *retornados*. The immigration of Africans from the former colonies – primarily Angola and the Cape Verde Islands, far fewer from Mozambique – occurred later and was not directly related to the decolonization process; this applies a fortiori for the recent growth of the Brazilian community. Together these groups are estimated to number less than 150,000. Like earlier *retornados*, these migrants speak Portuguese, but they do not immediately acquire Portuguese citizenship when they arrive. Over the last few years they have had to compete with a similar-sized influx of Eastern European migrants.[40]

These successive rounds of postcolonial migrations broke with a long tradition in which poor Portugal had predominantly been a country of emigration: initially to its own colonies in the interwar years and mainly to France after the war. The decolonization of 1975 was directly related to the Carnation Revolution (1974), which brought an end to a prolonged dictatorship and opened the way for modernization and accession to the European Union (1986). The unforeseen arrival of large numbers of *retornados* to the still poor Portugal bore many parallels with the Indisch migration to the Netherlands: dissatisfaction regarding their cold reception, but also rapid integration. Unlike the Indisch Dutch, however, the *retornados* were overwhelmingly white and were not recognizable as a separate 'ethnic' group. The initial fear that they would undermine the still fragile, young democracy turned out to be unfounded.[41]

Portugal has now integrated into Europe and has developed strongly in many ways. Today there are considerable ethnic minorities in the country, from elsewhere in Europe and from the Maghrib. Once again the rapid emergence of a multicultural society has led to debates about the position of migrants and the nature of national identity. Insofar as colonial history has been accommodated within this, it is certainly not with the same tone of self-criticism – rather, it appears there is a certain nostalgia for the time when Portugal still belonged to the vanguard of European colonialism.[42] Any retort from the (re-)migrant groups is limited; not least because the *retornados* were so closely linked to colonialism, albeit in the final, already anachronistic phase. Again their history recalls the pieds noirs and Indisch Dutch.

POSTCOLONIAL NETHERLANDS

The combination of contrite acknowledgement and symbolic gestures not only typifies the Dutch attitude to slavery, but equally that of the British and French. The United Kingdom commemorated the bicentenary of the abolition of slavery with a deluge of memorials, exhibitions, television programmes, research projects, publications, educational projects and more.[43] The mood was humble, very different to earlier commemorations which, with their emphasis on abolition, presented a heroic image of British humanity and somewhat obscured the preceding centuries of unabated slave trade and slavery.[44]

Expressions of regret (no explicit apologies) marked the commemorations in 2007. There was plenty of room for critical reflection on British traditions and for the West Indian community – around half a million souls in the UK – to participate and express their views. No other government in Europe has provided so much support or made so much money available – more than two million euros – to such ends. The efforts of Tony Blair's Labour Party reflected a symbolic multiculturalism; the expression of regret was a sign to descendants of their inclusion in the British nation. Institutions like the Church of England and the BBC made explicit contributions. Here too successful integration preceded the lobby: 'Black Britons' already occupied prominent positions in both the cabinet and the national church and broadcasting corporation. There was of course criticism, on the one hand complaints about exaggerated self-criticism and a glossing over of African complicity in the slave trade, and on the other that there was too little attention for African or Caribbean perspectives. The dilemma is in part a question of presentation – how much misery and anger can be dispensed upon an unprepared white audience without it simply switching off? – but also of conflicting interpretations of the past and how that should be commemorated today. The debate around black-versus-white perspectives, so frequently conducted in the Netherlands, cropped up here too.

Divisions also remained on the question of whether and how the past affects the present and whether this gives rise to obligations. These are in fact political questions. Are contemporary racism and the unmistakable deprivation suffered by many Black Britons rooted in the slavery era? Does British society have a debt to pay, should a form of reparation be part of this, and if so who should receive it? The answers to such questions varied enormously, as the British government had predicted.[45] The familiar dilemma was that radical standpoints were incompatible with the intention to make '2007' a truly national commemoration. All in all, the year of commemoration in the United Kingdom does seem to have offered a lot of scope for conflicting views without looking to force a consensus. That openness squares with Britain's relatively long experience of multiculturalism.

In France, the nation's involvement in the slave trade and slavery was publicly rediscovered late on; during the 1989 celebrations marking the bicentenary of the French Revolution with its lofty ideals, this delicate subject was basically ignored. The situation was very different in 1998, 150 years after the abolition of slavery. Demonstrations began in the former colonies, but the largest was a march in Paris in which 40,000 Antilleans took part demanding official acknowledgement of France's involvement in slavery. That such a massive march was needed to break through the government's aversion to identity politics is very telling. The British and Dutch governments, which both operate more within a tradition of moderate multiculturalism, did not require such robust encouragement – a calm lobby and a couple of petitions sufficed.

Evidently, the Chirac government was now prepared to make resolute gestures. It supported a private member's bill by Christiane Taubira, member of parliament for the overseas *département* of French Guyana, which condemned the slave trade and slavery as crimes against humanity. With its unanimous parliamentary acceptance of the bill, which also stipulated that the subject should be given a 'suitable' place in education and research, the French government went much further on paper that its British and Dutch counterparts.[46]

The Taubira law became a symbol of redress for the Antillean population, not only for the citizens of the overseas Caribbean provinces, but also for the half a million Antilleans living in France.[47] It is also in line with a broader debate about integration issues and the dissatisfaction of postcolonial migrants, in which a consistent argument is that the republic does not live up to its lofty principles. And yet this bill did not mention apologies or concrete reparations. The call to give the past a 'suitable' place remained vague. In this sense the law seemed to be an uncontroversial, but also fairly intangible gesture. To illustrate: at the commemoration of Haiti's bicentenary (2004), the colony which had liberated itself from France and slavery, the French government refrained from any significant engagement.

In 2005, the Taubira law hit the headlines once again. In that year the French parliament adopted a second colonial commemoration law – this one called for school curriculums to emphasize the positive role of colonialism, especially in Algeria. This provoked heated discussions not only on the merits of that particular law, but also on the wider question of whether the French state should be allowed to define past events and prescribe what French citizens should think of them. Is this not in the first instance the task of historians and secondly a question of personal judgment? And so the debate turned from slavery to 'history laws'. Two more such laws had meanwhile been adopted – the first regarding Holocaust denial, antisemitism and racism, the second the Armenian genocide – and the way seemed open for an inundation of many more bills.

The debate began not so much with the Taubira law, but with the law about the 'positive role' of colonialism. A triumph for a lobby of Algerian pieds noirs, a triumph for the chauvinists, and an open invitation to polarization. A storm of protests followed, initially only directed at the law itself. But it was not long before President Jacques Chirac himself vetoed the law in 2005, declaring that it was not the responsibility of the state to tell historians how to interpret the past. This has not prevented his successor, Nicolas Sarkozy, on several occasions from explicitly demanding attention for the positive aspects of colonialism.[48]

Logically, the debate continued: if a law that praised colonialism was unacceptable, was a law condemning slavery appropriate? In the French press various letters were published from prominent historians who rejected any form of governmental interference in the business of history. After all, so the argument went, we do not live in a totalitarian state. The debate was carried out with a great deal of passion and erudition. Its ferocity reflected broader concerns about the sustainability of the republican ideal of an undivided nation, a certain distaste for including the memories and views of migrants in the discourse about the nation, but also, quite rightly, concerns about intellectual freedom.[49]

This last concern was only reinforced by a bizarre court case brought by a radical Antillean organization against a respected historian, Olivier Pétré-Grenouillé. He had publicly rejected the term 'genocide', had pointed to the existence of slavery in numerous cultures, in particular Arab culture, and had underlined the role played by African merchants. He was promptly charged with defending the European slave trade and slavery and thereby denying a crime against humanity. This led to furious polemics in which the Taubira law came under fire as 'state-led pedagogy'.[50]

The court case, which was eventually thrown out, did no service to the 'business' of the commemoration of slavery and colonialism in general. Touches of intolerant fanaticism and totalitarian practices began increasingly to stick to the otherwise legitimate rediscovery of colonialism and slavery. And so Pierre Nora, the great man behind the project of lieux de mémoire that has been imitated around the globe, co-authored a furious Pamphlet, Liberté pour l'histoire. As chair of the foundation of the same name, he and his vice-chair, Françoise Chandernagor, wiped the floor with any attempt at state-led pedagogy. Historical research can only thrive in a climate of complete and utter intellectual freedom, accordingly, abolish the ridiculous laws that restrict this freedom and, above all, do not devise any new ones, their argument resounded. Keep the realms of memory (*mémoire*) and history (*histoire*) separate and press historians not to fall into the trap of becoming lackeys for minorities who want to render their collective memory the status of truth.[51]

No well-meaning person would dare say that Nora or Chandernagor were wrong, at least when it comes to freedom of thought and interpretation. Yet, respected opponents, such as Benjamin Stora and Patrick Weil, argued that it was not so much intellectual freedom that was at stake and that the issue of expressions of regret was, in fact, marginal. According to their view, the state, by definition, determines which key moments from the past should be commemorated and how. Just look at all the historical monuments, the school books, the annual celebrations on 14 July or the remembrance of the two World Wars. It is no good suddenly screaming blue murder just because all sorts of new and more critical desires are being articulated around national memorial culture.[52]

What the long-term effect of the Taubira law will be is hard to say. As in the cases of Britain and the Netherlands, 'rediscovery' initially received broad support, but friction soon arose around more radical views and expectations. The pacification and symbolic inclusion of postcolonial migrants were also the driving force behind government policy in France. Hence, the emphasis shifted from Africa and the Caribbean to Europe. This was appositely illustrated by the date chosen for the annual commemoration of slavery and its abolition by a national commission in Paris: 10 May. This date bears absolutely no relation to colonial history and slavery and simply refers to the day on which the French senate unanimously accepted the Taubira law.[53]

The comparison between the commemoration of slavery in these three countries generates a picture largely of parallels. The presence of descendants who acquire sufficient influence to put the subject on the agenda; the official emphasis on shame and regret, while simultaneously avoiding apologies that might lead to compensation claims; the provision of modest means which are deployed for general, mainly education goals; the tension between radical demands and expectations, on the one hand, and a moderate governmental policy of pacification on the other; and issues surrounding white-versus-black perspectives. The most obvious differences between the United Kingdom and the Netherlands on one side and France on the other is the issue of how flexible society, government, and intellectuals are in their responses to a discourse that undermines a nation's positive self-image. The French debate reveals more pride in the nation's history, but also more defensiveness.

Other comparisons can also be drawn. No less striking than the sudden trend for recognition in these three countries is the continuing silence elsewhere in Europe. Portugal was the frontrunner among trans-Atlantic slave traders and slavery was not abolished in the Spanish colony of Cuba until 1886, later than in all of the other European colonies. And yet in these two countries there is no question of a national debate or signs of recognition. The same applies to Denmark, which also once trafficked slaves between Africa and its own slave colonies in the Caribbean. This silence is largely explained by the absence of communities of slave descendants who could put this issue on the agenda. Moreover, the view of the relatively distant past for these two Iberian lands might be obscured by their more recent histories of civil war, dictatorship and poor development – the memory of an illustrious colonial past is cherished like balsam on an open wound.[54]

The question of whether 'the descendants' – regardless of the African and the Caribbean countries involved – have much to gain from gestures or acknowledgement can barely be answered. Concrete measures have remained limited and it seems improbable that anything fundamentally different will follow. The likelihood of reparations really being paid is minimal. What remains is recognition, which is expected to have an inclusive effect, easing the way for Afro-Caribbean citizens to identify with the nation. The effectiveness of this approach seems obvious, but is almost impossible to verify. Even less certain is whether social gestures of contrition and self-criticism will lead to the 'self-liberation' of the descendants, to a break with an alleged cultural trauma.

Thus considered, the recent rediscovery of slavery remains somewhat noncommittal and the West-European memorial cycle seems to be nearing completion. Slavery has been actively recalled, but has remained in the past tense; a history, moreover, that is not important to everyone to the same degree. This ending could hardly be any different in a multicultural society with diverse memorial traditions. Between a single undivided national discourse and the dividing up of the past into innumerable ethnic narratives, there are many possible compromises. But the stronger the heterogeneity of the citizens, the more impossible the task to construct a national narrative that is satisfactory to all.

COLONIAL PAST AND POSTCOLONIAL MIGRATIONS:
A BROAD COMPARISON

The presence or absence of substantial postcolonial communities have had a major influence on the public debate about the colonial past. This assumption lends itself to a broader examination than just the memory of slavery. Beyond the four 'key countries' named above – the United Kingdom, France, the Netherlands, and Portugal – there is a handful of other European countries with a colonial history. Their treatment of the past, or rather their scant interest in it, would seem to support the hypothesis of a link with postcolonial migration.

Of the remaining European countries with a colonial history, only Belgium was still a colonial power at the end of World War II. On the eve of independence in 1960 around 95,000 Belgians lived in Belgian Congo and Rwanda; the majority repatriated and fitted without too much difficulty back into a life in what for most was the land of their birth. The number of African migrants from the former colonies has never been large in Belgium and is today estimated to be no more than 15,000 to 20,000. Their numbers are nothing compared with the number of Belgians with roots in the Maghrib or Turkey. The African migrants do not play a leading role in reflections on Belgian colonialism. The dominance of white repatriates among the postcolonial migrants provides the most obvious explanation for the absence, at least until very recently, of a debate on Belgian colonialism.[55]

Spain is a special case. With Portugal, Spain was the pioneer of European colonialism in the Americas, but also in Asia and Africa. Around 1900, what remained of the colonial empire was broken up, except for the enclaves Ceuta and Melilla in Morocco and the African colonies which had been acquired late in the day. Equatorial Guinea became independent in 1968, Spanish West Africa was handed over to Morocco in 1976; this did not lead to any migration worth mentioning. Up until the 1970s, Spain was a country of emigration. This rapidly changed thereafter, in line with the country's modernization. The majority of the migrants were European, followed by Spanish Americans and Africans, mainly from Morocco.[56] The sizeable Spanish-American migration flow was a reversal. Until 1970, many millions of Spaniards had settled in Spanish America, while the number moving in the opposite direction had remained minimal. The recent reversal was led by economic factors, which for Spanish-American migrants includes the postcolonial bonus in terms of language, religion, and conditions for legalization.

The Spanish view of its own colonial past is traditionally marked by pride and perhaps nostalgia. The *quincentenario* of Columbus' landing in the

Americas (1492) had been organized as a major celebration of national pride and an optimistic confirmation of the role Spain might play as a leader of the international *hispanidad*. It soon became clear that this nationalist discourse would have to be toned down and the emphasis was moved from 'discovery' to 'meeting'. At the same time space was created for a more critical approach to colonization, in particular with a nod to the indigenous population. However, these compromises were primarily aimed at appeasing the Spanish American republics, rather than 'postcolonial' minorities in Spain itself – they let little of themselves be heard in this context, their primary concern being to acquire Spanish nationality and thereby European citizenship.

The colonial pasts of Denmark, Italy, and Germany seem almost forgotten, because they are almost a century behind us and because there is no postcolonial community to keep this history alive. Danish expansion stretched for centuries across Scandinavia, Iceland, and Greenland. Denmark also played a small part in the African slave trade, possessed a few plantation colonies in the Caribbean from the early seventeenth century, and had a trading post in India. When Denmark sold its Caribbean Virgin Islands to the United States in 1917, the curtain fell on the tropics for the Danes bringing an early end to this colonialism, no postcolonial migration and, indeed, almost no debate about its colonial past. The history of Danish involvement in the slave trade and slavery seems to have been entirely forgotten beyond a small circle of historians. Insofar as there is a vague Danish memory of the Caribbean, it is nostalgic rather than critical. This is all the more interesting because the Danish self-image lies fairly close to the Dutch: a small, progressive country which places a great deal of importance on human rights.[57]

Italy's modern imperialist era did not last long. At the end of the nineteenth century it colonized Somalia and Eritrea, followed by Libya (1912) and, under Benito Mussolini, Ethiopia (1935). During the Second World War Italy was forced to relinquish its colonial possessions, after which several hundred thousand Italians were repatriated; they did not amount to an influential community. There were almost no African postcolonial migrants to Italy.[58] This colonial history has attracted little interest outside a small academic circle, even though colonialism was closely related to the formation of the Italian nation, both in the early republic and under Fascism. The few researchers working in this field almost unanimously speak of deliberate silencing. This 'forgetting' corresponds with the link to Fascism, with the abrupt break during the war which meant that Italy was not itself actively involved in the decolonization process, and with the absence of mass immigration from the former African colonies.

Some overtures by Prime Minister Silvio Berlusconi towards Libya therefore seem surprising. As a consequence of earlier political expressions of regret (1991) for the excesses of Italian colonialism in Libya, in 2008 Berlusconi agreed to pay a kind of compensation, which is unique. The Italian gesture of five billion US dollars' worth of investments cannot be explained as a response to domestic pressure and certainly not to pressure from a postcolonial lobby, but should probably be put down entirely to geopolitical considerations. Berlosconi's counterpart, Colonel Muammar Khaddafi, promised Italy would be given priority when it came to investment in Libya's gas and oil industry and Libyan support in tackling illegal immigration. Doubts about ethical motivations are strengthened by the fact that there is no question of Italian overtures to other former colonies where Italian colonialism was far more invasive – including the use of nerve gas by Mussolini's troops in Ethiopia.[59]

It was not until the 'scramble for Africa' in the late nineteenth century that Germany became a colonial power.[60] However, it was forced to give up its African colonies after the First World War. There was almost no migration from the colonies to Germany during the few decades of its colonial rule. German historians have recently rediscovered the colonial past, which has since been given a modest position on school curriculums. The question often posed in this context is whether or not there was a continuity between colonial racism and the violence of Nazism that followed later.[61] A hundred years on, in 2004, the German government acknowledged the brutal suppression of the Herero and Nama peoples in Namibia as genocide, but did not link this to compensation.

That it was so long before the colonial past was reflected upon and that it is still rarely the subject of broader debate, can in part be attributed to the short duration of German colonialism and the absence of a postcolonial community. No less important here is that fact that the German culture of *Vergangenheitsbewältigung* (roughly translated as the struggle to come to terms with the past) was almost entirely focused on the legacies of the two World Wars, particularly the second, and the Shoah. Then, after 1989, there came a string of new historical and moral questions around the subject of East Germany – it seems the national memory has been more or less saturated by self-examination.

The picture therefore seems to be clear. Wherever there is an absence of substantial postcolonial migrant communities, the chances are that the colonial past will be forgotten or silenced. Where such communities do exist, memory and their desires for commemoration will vary depending on their previous relationship with the colonial system. Where primarily voices critical of the colonial past are put on the agenda, the response of governments and intellectual elites reflects how great the influence of the ideology of multiculturalism is.

All this has limited relevance to a notion of memorial culture outside Europe. The formation of the Soviet Union can be understood as a Russian colonial project; the implosion of the USSR was followed by the repatriation of millions of ethnic Russians, coinciding with smaller-scale emigration of ethnic minorities from Russia. However, in the smaller, now ethnically more homogeneous Russian core of the former Soviet empire, this did not lead to a national debate about the merits of the Soviet Union as a colonial project and even less so to a discussion of special treatment for these postcolonial migrants.[62]

Something similar applies to Japan, which colonized Korea in the early twentieth century and, in the 1930s, violently occupied part of China during the prelude to the Second World War. After the Japanese surrender in 1945, millions of Japanese colonists were repatriated, mainly from Korea. The integration of these postcolonial migrants passed off relatively smoothly. But there was no room for their stories and even less for a broader critical reflection on the colonialism that preceded it, or on the role of Japan as an aggressor during the war.[63]

Postcolonial memorial culture in the United States has more in common with what in Europe is gradually becoming a familiar mix of self-criticism and regret, without being accompanied by many concrete gestures, than with the Japanese and Russian aversion to such critical self-examination. However, unlike Europe, the US was chiefly concerned with 'colonized' domestic minorities, namely, the indigenous population and the descendants of enslaved Africans. The influence of postcolonial migrants on the debate about nationhood was not great. Strictly speaking, this context only relates to post-war, ongoing immigration from the self-governing Commonwealth of Puerto Rico associated with the United States, which has many parallels with Antillean migration to France and the Netherlands. Puerto Rican intellectuals have had some influence on the American multiculturalism debate. Inevitably, considering the enormous diversity of this debate, their voice has remained modest.[64]

TYPICALLY DUTCH?

So, every country has its own characteristics. What might we describe as being typically Dutch in this context? We might first look at the nature and scale of postcolonial migrations. In terms of the demographic significance for the country as a whole, the parallels with the British, French and Portuguese experiences are clear. In terms of the diversity of postcolonial migrations, relating to the location and nature of the former colonies, France and the United Kingdom are comparable with the Netherlands. In almost all cases, postcolonial migration was an unintended spin-off of decolonization; the Netherlands experience is no different. Like France, the Netherlands is still politically tied to a number of its former colonies, which means postcolonial migration is ongoing; herein lies a parallel with the United States too.

The characteristics of postcolonial migrants varied greatly and so too their integration. The most relevant comparisons involve the three principal European countries. In all cases the migrants benefitted from a postcolonial bonus, at least in terms of a right to settle, but also more often in terms of cultural capital; the significance of this bonus by definition declined with the generations. Measured in terms of socio-economic class and education levels, repatriates from the Dutch East Indies were by and large better off than migrants from Suriname and the Antilles. This translated into the somewhat distorted image of an entirely 'smooth assimilation'. The similarities between the Indisch Dutch, the pied noirs, the *retornados*, and, perhaps, repatriates from the British Empire, also extended into a less critical, sometimes plainly nostalgic relationship with the colonial system.

Postcolonial communities were – in part internally – divided along partially overlapping lines of class and ethnicity. As in all other countries, migrants met a great deal of incomprehension and silent, everyday racism in the Netherlands. However, unlike France and the United Kingdom, there were almost no race riots. Besides, what continues to be peculiar to the Netherlands is that only a minority of postcolonial migrants are Muslim, whereas a large majority of other non-Western migrants are Islamic. This is similar to the situation in Portugal and in stark contrast to the British and French experience. The more the minorities debate in the Netherlands comes to revolve around 'Islam', the more accepted non-Muslim postcolonial migrants probably become.

In all cases the meaning of the notion of 'community' and thereby 'postcolonial identity' became more problematic with the changing generations. Again, levels of exogamy had a major impact here. In all cases exogamy was high among Afro-Caribbean migrants. Religion turned out to be a crucial factor. Exogamy is low among British and Dutch Muslims and Hindus, higher in France, but also there it is lower than among Antilleans. Moreover, the example of Hindus, and in Britain Sikhs, illustrates that low exogamy is not necessarily a hindrance to successful socio-economic integration.

Integration did not always proceed smoothly. The Moluccan group arrived in the Netherlands with a disadvantage similar to the *harkis* in France; their drawn-out engagement with the struggle for an independent Moluccan republic is, however, unique. The integration of a large proportion of the Afro-Caribbean population of the Netherlands was more successful than many pessimists had predicted; however, a considerable underclass has perpetuated a culture of poverty. Here the parallels with the French and, above all, the British Caribbean communities is painfully clear. Of the Asian-Surinamese communities, it would seem that the Hindu majority are most successful in socio-economic terms; here lies an obvious parallel with Hindus in the United Kingdom.

With the exception of the short-lived Moluccan actions, the Netherlands had no experience of militant postcolonial resistance to the status quo. Insofar as postcolonial migrants integrated only moderately well – measured according to concrete criteria such as education and employment – this was not a reflection of any resistance, but rather a reflection of some mix of incapability and discrimination. Ethnic subcultures highly critical of colonialism and the postcolonial Netherlands did develop, but this did not amount to a radical rejection. In the Netherlands, as in other parts of Europe, this type of radicalism was exclusively expressed in Muslim fundamentalist circles, which in the Netherlands did not stem from colonial history.

Conversely, government policy for postcolonial migrants in the Netherlands was inclusive and aimed to promote identification. This initially just involved immigration and integration policies, but later, through the decision to adopt a mild form of multiculturalism, also symbolic gestures in response to the identity politics of the different communities. Hence the Netherlands, like the United Kingdom and somewhat more flexibly than France with its strongly unitary republican tradition, became enriched by postcolonial monuments and institutions, festivals and memorial days. Accordingly, this history and its aftermath became canonized. As it turned out, this was all the more defensible, because none of the postcolonial groups voiced positions that were incompatible with broadly held interpretations of the values and norms of society at large.

In this light, there is little reason to think that the recent widespread criticism in the Netherlands of multiculturalism will lead to a different treatment of postcolonial migrants – after all, the debates are largely about

Islam and the alleged rejection of acculturation by large groups of Muslims. This suspicion does not pertain to postcolonial 'communities', which are gradually becoming more integrated and, through exogamy, more diluted, and who for decades have fought for recognition precisely from within an explicitly Dutch frame of reference.

8

'POSTCOLONIAL' (IN THE) NETHERLANDS

Post-war, the Netherlands became richer, less segmented (*verzuild*), ethnically more diverse, and more embedded in Europe. Immigration and migrants have been controversial subjects of debate for sixty-five years now, but nevertheless, in that time the Netherlands admitted vast numbers of newcomers and became multicultural. This change raised the issue of how migrants and their children related and ought to relate to Dutch culture. Inevitably, the question that then had to be answered is what that culture, or identity, actually was. The answer has remained controversial; that the answer in 1945 would have been different from the answer in 1975 or 2005 is obvious.

The post-war rebuilding of the Netherlands was initially tackled with backs turned to history. In the early post-war years of 'discipline and asceticism' there was no time to dwell on past suffering – this attitude was also made easier because the section of the population that had been most hit by the war had been exterminated elsewhere and by others. It was not until well into the 1960s that the few surviving Jews began to be heard and the persecution of the Jews became part of the nation's memorial culture. In the decades that followed it was precisely the Holocaust and the powerlessness or unwillingness to prevent this genocide that set the benchmark for moralizing debates about the nation's history, the nation, and the treatment of post-war migrants. The lot of the Jews became a horrible frame of reference, but also a model in the struggle for symbolic and financial reparations.[1]

The discovery that yet another traumatic wartime history was alive on Dutch soil took a long time to emerge. Only in the 1980s did the repatriates from the Netherlands East Indies begin to make strides in their battle to win a place in national World War II commemorations. For strategic reasons, at times rationalized in shockingly opportunistic ways, reference was made to the earlier acknowledgement of recent Jewish history, including the material compensation that had been paid. This comparison reflected the deeply-held frustration about suffering that was not understood and rights that were denied. The expression of such emotions was increasingly felt to be justified and publicly and politically legitimized. And, indeed, remorseful gestures of recognition have been an essential feature of Dutch politics since the 1970s. Recognition of past suffering, recognition of society's shortcomings, recognition of the right to symbolic and perhaps financial gestures; this was to become a model for postcolonial identity politics.[2]

Meanwhile, emotion began to penetrate further into the heart of a society that had previously been reputed for its level-mindedness and which was still a privileged nation where it was rare for anything to happen that affected the citizenry as a whole. The arrival of television played a major part in this. By far the largest post-war disaster, the North Sea flood (watersnood) of 1953, which cost the lives of 1800 people in Zealand, was only processed and remembered in private silence for decades. And yet more recent and, in terms of the number of fatalities, considerably less disastrous calamities – plane crashes on Tenerife, in Faro and Eindhoven, or the firework-factory disaster in Enschede – were immediately surrounded by far more public attention. Wherever immigrants were involved in an air crash, the commemoration took on the character of a political gesture of inclusion, as highlighted by the royal displays of sorrow and speeches by politicians following the crash of a Surinam Airways flight from the Netherlands just prior to landing in Suriname, and after the Bijlmer Disaster in which an El Al cargo plane crashed into a block of flats in the predominantly black south-east area of Amsterdam. Even a recent, small plane crash in Suriname, more than thirty years after the transfer of sovereignty, elicited condolences from the Queen and the Prime Minister.[3]

Suffering and grieving became ritualized, as witnessed in the many silent marches against 'mindless violence', or even trivialized, as in the funeral of the popular Dutch singer André Hazes (2004). All this is evidence of a far-reaching popularization of taste and fashion, but also the democratization of public memory. The criteria have become ever less clear. Where more space is granted to accommodate the recognition of individual suffering, the need for arbitration grows if the risk of losing meaning and communality in commemoration is to be avoided. Which stories of the past ought to be considered important today? The time has passed when politicians and intellectuals from the dominant political or spiritual trends served as self-evident authorities on national identity. As their authority waned, the discourse of inclusion came under pressure, marking the end of a politics of 'reasoned tolerance', in which a matter-of-fact adoption of diversity was broadly, if not always enthusiastically accepted. Typical of this was the way the Van Oostrom Commission itself spelled out that even its official canon of Dutch history was a result of choices and historicity; even more typical is the curtailing of its breadth ever since, from being prescriptive to at best directional for Dutch schools.[4]

Where the intellectual approach to identity is characterized by qualifications and room for diversity, in the 'street', and recently in politics, the tone is much harder – among migrants who demanded space for their own cultures and views of the past, and who used to find a willing ear among politicians, but equally among large sections of the non-immigrant white Dutch who have long ceased to blindly follow politically-led instructions for a broadening of the idea of 'national identity'. The leading radical-right political leader, Geert Wilders, tellingly translated this sentiment in his criticism of Princess Maxima's perfectly defensible qualification of the idea of a homogeneous Dutch identity as 'well-meaning, politically-correct poppycock'.[5]

POSTCOLONIAL MIGRANTS:
INTEGRATION, IDENTIFICATION, COMMUNITY

The population of the Netherlands doubled in the space of sixty-five years, partly through immigration, creating a society that was more ethnically diverse than ever before. This process was ushered in by the repatriations from the Netherlands East Indies. The cliché of the smooth assimilation of these repatriates is not unjustified; their social integration ran smoothly, in part due to their strong postcolonial bonus. Yet this highly diverse group of 'repatriates' nurtured many misgivings about the culture of the country of arrival, with its poor understanding and lack of interest in its East Indian history. This must have hindered their identification with the Netherlands – ironically, but also painfully for a group which, in the East Indies, had always identified with the 'mother country'.

And yet there was no question of willfully keeping a distance from Dutch society. On the contrary, from the start exogamy was so strong that while there is already a fourth generation of Indisch Dutch, it has become ever more inappropriate to regard the Indisch 'community' as a distinct group. 'Indisch' came increasingly to be seen as a non-exclusive choice of identity, which was further enhanced by the fact that transnational ties are weak – there is far more nostalgia for the lost East Indies, or something vaguely Asian, than there is meaningful engagement with the Indonesia of today.

The indignation surrounding the lack of understanding and compensation for their wartime suffering, along with the presumably 'cold' reception in the Netherlands, led to an ever better organized and more successful struggle for symbolic recognition and financial compensation from the 1960s on. Its success – though still scandalously modest, according to many in the Indisch group – reflected a heightened sensitivity in Dutch society, certainly in political circles, for the identity claims of minorities. In the case of the Indisch Dutch, such gestures also reflected an appreciation of their smooth integration. Throughout this history it was crucial that the Indisch community was represented by authoritative members of high social status, considerable cultural capital, and excellent contacts among the elites of the post-war Netherlands.

What anthropologist Lizzy van Leeuwen refers to as the Indisch 'struggle for culture and identity' was a struggle on two fronts. Besides the political disputes surrounding the way things were settled after the war, there was the recurring issue of the recognition of a unique identity, embodied by Tjalie Robinson. The silent continuation of Indisch traditions and the organization of events such as Pasar Malam Besar were very important for opening up a national culture that, although *verzuild*, in all other respects was fairly homogeneous. Indisch emancipation slowly evened out, but now the path had been laid for the moderate multiculturalism that followed. Indisch cultural broker Ellen Derksen expressed this appositely in her speech to open the thirtieth Pasar Malam (1988): 'The Indisch Dutch have not silently assimilated away, they have silently imprinted their mark on Dutch society.'[6] In the meantime, the paradox has only become more pronounced: the more recognition Indisch culture and identity acquired, the less clear its significance for the next generations became.

The integration of the Moluccan community passed less smoothly. It was a long time before there was room to identify with the Netherlands, alongside and instead of identifying with the Moluccas. This laborious integration process was in part due to the low levels of education among the first generation. The problems were exacerbated by the engagement, sometimes enforced, with the struggle for an independent Moluccan republic (RMS). The decision to choose this political identity obstructed engagement with the Netherlands for many years.

No other postcolonial migrant group battled so militantly for recognition – although the struggle for an independent RMS was never a realistic aim and only later, hesitatingly, was reformulated as a call for respect and space for a Moluccan identity in the Netherlands. The Hague's attitude towards the Moluccan community developed from neglect and distance to inclusionary engagement in response to militant Moluccan actions. Concerns about Moluccan integration gave an important impulse to the formulation of an integration policy. All the Dutch parliament's gestures revolved around recognition, inclusion, and support for integration, but stayed well away from the political struggle.

In the Moluccan community too, the question began to arise about what constituted Moluccan identity, beyond the RMS, and, above all, to what degree one could speak of a shared identity distinguishing Moluccans from other Dutch citizens. This debate in part developed as a consequence of generational change. The time when the vast majority of Moluccans lived in camps, then housing estates, is over. Exogamy is also high now among Moluccans. Once again, there is little that can be taken for granted in the terms 'community' and 'identity'.

More than two decades passed before the next postcolonial influx arrived. The Surinamese exodus took place at the same time as Mediterranean migration got under way and the Netherlands became irrevocably multicultural – and was reeling from the shock. The integration of the Surinamese migrants in the end proceeded better than initially expected and certainly better than was the case for most other non-Western migrants. The postcolonial bonus did its job, even though the Surinamese community remained more strongly divided along class lines than the Indisch. Soon only lip service was being paid to the ideal of remigration. This strengthened identification with the Netherlands, all the more considering the rapid growth of the second generation, which is now already producing a third.

The Moluccan community was relatively homogenous when it arrived in the Netherlands, the Indisch community more strongly divided along class-colour axes. But these differences were nothing compared with the contrasts in the Surinamese community. Colonial Suriname was described as an ethnically *verzuild*, segmented society. This *verzuiling* was not simply perpetuated in the Netherlands, but even enhanced: the nationalist discourse of ethnic fraternization served no purpose here. This was not so much a process of active avoidance, even less of conflict among the various segments, but simply of each group going its own way. Only in terms of political engagement with the country of origin was there something resembling a 'Surinamese' voice, especially in the protests against the military dictatorship in the 1980s, but this later subsided.

Consequently, there was no such thing as an undivided Surinamese community, but at most ethnic subgroups none of whom resisted integration in the Netherlands and who all showed every sign of identifying with the country they had arrived in. There were also clear contrasts. The integration of the Afro-Surinamese group occurred partially along demographic lines: exogamy was and continues to be high. The Afro-Surinamese were more outspoken than the Indisch Dutch about their right to retain their own identity; this could be more easily accommodated in a society that was now moving towards moderate multiculturalism. The official acknowledgement of the Dutch slavery of the past fitted within this framework. But again, one must question how relevant it is to speak of a separate, Afro-Surinamese community and identity, now and certainly in the future.

If a strong and fairly demarcated, unique postcolonial identity applies anywhere, then it applies to Surinamese Dutch with Asian ancestors. Of course, this affirms very traditional views of frozen ethnicity. The Hindu majority of Hindustani Surinamese has continued to link its own identity to the religion, and towards India and the Indian diaspora. Muslim Hindustanis and Javanese Surinamese continue to link their identity to their religion, which does not seem to interfere in any way with their identification with the Netherlands. However, exogamy among Dutch of Asian-Surinamese origin is far lower than in any other postcolonial group, the effect of which is at least a delay to the weakening of community ties. Besides, it is remarkable that these groups have only rarely articulated a desire for recognition or political gestures. Apparently the room available to practice identity was sufficient and there was no urgent need to demand apologies for the colonial past.

Due to the continuing status of non-sovereignty, the final stage of postcolonial migration, from the Antilles, has not reached its conclusion. The Antillean community shares its slavery history with Afro-Surinamese Dutch, but in itself is also a fragmented community. This is largely a consequence of the language gap. Apart from the memory of slavery and colonialism, the perception of identity within the Antillean community to a large extent revolves around Papiamentu and, moreover, the island of origin – the vast majority of Antilleans stem from Curaçao.

The fact that Papiamentu is the first language for the great majority of Antilleans in the Netherlands severely devalued their postcolonial bonus. The Antillean community is also divided along class lines. This, combined with high levels of exogamy, raises questions about how long it will make sense to speak of an undivided Antillean, or even Curaçaoan community and identity in the Netherlands. Complicating this further is the fact that Antillean migration continues to be circular, so that both communities continue to influence each other.

This short summary of the developments of the last six decades underlines the stark contrasts that exist, but also suggests clear convergences. An erosion of the meaning of 'community' and 'identity' is apparent in most groups, facilitated by a turn towards Dutch culture that may or may not stem from the colonial era, and by the changing of the generations and high degrees of exogamy; only the Asian-Surinamese communities require subtle distinctions to be made within this conclusion. The degree of transnational orientation here varies from group to group, but is on the decline everywhere; in the past, transnationalism only obstructed an identification with the Netherlands in the case of the Moluccan Dutch.

The postcolonial bonus worked for all migrants from the former colonials, but to differing degrees. All benefitted from unhindered access to the Netherlands, but the cultural capital that was tied to the Netherlands was unequally distributed. In the first instance, this was a question of class, but also of other colonial legacies, which were unfavourable for Moluccans and later Antilleans. The significance of the postcolonial bonus diminishes with the changing of the generations, at least in its supporting role during the process of integration. All second generation migrants, whether they stem from Morocco, Turkey, Suriname, or wherever, enjoy Dutch citizenship. Formally, opportunities are evenly distributed, the education system corrects, at least in part, the inequalities that used to exist and in so doing eradicates the potential linguistic and cultural bonus that migrants from the former colonies used to enjoy.

What remains of the bonus will ultimately be no more than a rhetorical element: 'We are here because you were there.' Spokespeople from the postcolonial communities have made good use of that comparative advantage. Their access to the media and politicians highlights the fact that these claims did not so much precede integration, as follow it; that is how the bonus worked. With identity issues finally on the agenda, colonial history, little by little, gained a more prominent position in the reformulation of the nation's history. Yet, when it comes to expanding the view of what is Dutch culture, the postcolonial element appears to have lost its advantage over other migrant cultures.

'Race' has played almost no part in this book, neither has racism. This is not to say that there was or is no racism in the Netherlands, nor that this was irrelevant to integration and identification with the Netherlands. All postcolonial migrants were confronted with racism and xenophobia, in all cases this led to frustration and anger, which ultimately stimulated the articulation of identity claims. However, the question is how far racism played and, above all, will continue to play a role in binding the various postcolonial communities together.

We might begin by arguing that racism in the past did not determine how postcolonial migrants were treated. The bonus of the unhindered right to settle in the Netherlands – even after the transfer of sovereignty in some cases – remained intact for a long time, despite xenophobia and despite the fact that the admittance of postcolonial migrants served no economic purpose. Postcolonial concerns about state respectability were decisive, even if the admittance of postcolonial migrants was and is judged more negatively by many Dutch. At the same time, this broader society learnt how to deal with migrants of a different colour from the former colonies. It has often been remarked that beneath the gloss of proverbial Dutch tolerance there often lay and lies avoidance, indifference and, sometimes, unadulterated racism. Yet at the same time, the growing acceptance of ethnically mixed relations, precisely with partners with colonial roots, illustrates that this zeitgeist is neither universal nor immutable.[7] That exogamy has remained relatively low among Hindustanis and Javanese Surinamese primarily stems from their own religiously motivated rejection of such mixed relations, not of imposed isolation.

The space accorded postcolonial migrants to publicly express their own identities has noticeably increased over the last few decades and is reflected in the debates about Dutch culture and history. With this the government attempted to stimulate identification with the Netherlands – there is a reason why commemorations of the colonial past so often emphasize contemporary 'bonding'. While this is difficult to substantiate, it would appear that all this postcolonial acknowledgement and commemorating has indeed fulfilled the purpose of building bridges between old contradictions. The source of frustration surrounding metropolitan denial has certainly receded considerably.[8]

Dutch debates around minorities and nation have hardened over the past decade or so. Wherever borders are drawn more sharply, a renewed ethnicization soon takes shape. Opposition can have the effect of slowing down the erosion of communities. Something similar threatens to take shape – unevenly – in the Netherlands through the over-simplification of the minorities debate to a problem around or with Islam. It is possible that the small minority of Muslims among postcolonial immigrants may feel that they too are being addressed and may consequently develop a stronger need to highlight their religious identity.

What is striking about the debates over the last few years is that postcolonial migrants have figured only rarely, and when they have, it has usually been in a positive sense, as in the exemplary assimilated Indisch Dutch and the Surinamese, who are believed to be heading in the same direction. The most discussed postcolonial problem revolves around Antillean youths, but this is a debate in which not culture, but class should be seen as the prime factor. A widespread backlash against postcolonial communities is not on the cards, which is good news for these groups. The flip side of this seems to be that, in the absence of a political offensive to isolate them, the erosion of these communities will continue.

NEW IDEAS ABOUT THE 'NETHERLANDS'

The contemporary view of Dutch history and culture grants far more space to the (post)colonial dimension than was the case in 1950 or 1970, at least insofar as this image is directly or indirectly set by the government. The identity politics of the different postcolonial communities has played a decisive factor here. This is not to say, of course, that the average Dutch citizen attaches the same importance to the colonial past and its legacies as citizens with roots in the colonies. Interest, knowledge, and above all the emotional value associated with this vary enormously.

It is therefore not simply a question of postcolonial migrant versus 'the rest'. As little as postcolonial migrants have distinguished themselves in demonstrating any particular engagement with other migrants – and why should they? – equally, nothing attests to mutual interest, let alone solidarity, among the different postcolonial communities. Just as no ethnically defined group has such a homogenous identity that it necessarily leads to identity politics, it is equally absurd to expect there to be a single postcolonial voice.[9]

The complaint that 'the Dutch' know, understand, and appreciate so little about their colonial history and about the resultant cultures is part of the standard repertoire for all of these postcolonial groups. However, anyone attending any postcolonial commemorative events will immediately notice that the people who are present, alongside the members of the community involved, are primarily white Dutch. Caribbean Dutch have no interest in Indisch commemorations, while Indisch Dutch, Moluccans, or Hindustanis will rarely show their faces at commemorations of slavery, and postcolonial Dutch rarely attend remembrance events marking the Nazi occupation and the Holocaust, and so on – people remember and celebrate, first and foremost, in their own circles supplemented by a few white Dutch who have become involved through personal relations, or who attend in an official capacity. This is a sobering conclusion, which highlights the impossibility of translating all identity-based claims to a memorial culture into a truly shared, national narrative. The government may facilitate and legitimize a broad and inclusive remembering, but it cannot enforce it. Society is simply too heterogeneous and democratic, and the ethnic and historical identifications too diverse.

The post-war struggle for recognition by postcolonial organizations has generated increasing understanding, recognition, and concrete gestures since the 1970s. That the grassroots allowed themselves to be more easily mobilized for concrete causes than for abstract desires is logical and illustrated by the broad Indisch support for the battle for backpay. Perhaps with the exception of the Moluccan ideal of the RMS, the struggle for more idealistic goals remained largely an issue for minorities in each group. Only a fraction of the Indisch 'community' was actively involved in the Indisch House, and the same goes for participation by the Afro-Caribbean population in the annual commemoration of slavery. The irony is that the acceptance of postcolonial identity claims tempered justified indignation about the silencing of the past, while at the same time contributing to the loss of meaning for the postcolonial parties involved – the cry for recognition had, after all, been one of the anchors in the formation of communities and action.

A decisive factor in the treatment of postcolonial identity claims was that they appealed to generally accepted precepts of what in the Netherlands was considered appropriate and morally correct, but also that they were ultimately politically innocent, or at least were made so. It became acceptable and even the done thing, to adopt a critical approach to the colonial past with reference to the self-image of a freedom-loving, humanitarian nation. Indirectly, the wholehearted recognition of the fact that these norms had not been adhered to in the colonies accentuated the self-congratulatory image of an exemplary nation. However, where radical claims were problematic for national interests, pragmatism prevailed over testimony. 'Regret' was frequently mentioned, but 'apologies' never, for fear of compensation claims in the case of the Atlantic slave trade, or war crimes in Indonesia. The importance of good international relations also prevailed over sympathy for the frustrations of the migrant communities – see the rejection of the RMS, the rapid reconciliation with Japan, and the eventual acknowledgement of '1945' as marking the end of colonial rule in the Netherlands East Indies. This last symbolic gesture, towards Indonesia, which had been so long awaited, reflected how long the 'Indisch generation' had exerted its considerable influence.

It is almost impossible to judge what the outcome of sixty-five years of facing up to the colonial past has been, broadly speaking. What this book mainly documents is the struggle for a space for postcolonial perspectives in the nation's image and governmental responses to it, but also in the world of culture, education and science. A picture can be sketched of this official canonization, but it does not answer the question as to whether this has had

Demonstration at the National Monument to Slavery, Amsterdam, 27 October, 2006, in response to the statement about the VOC by then-Prime Minister, Jan Peter Balkenende. Balkenende had praised the 'VOC mentality' in parliament. There was little reaction from the Indisch or Moluccan camps, but this statement provoked great agitation in Surinamese circles. Under the motto that the VOC era was also the era of the WIC, the slave trade, and slavery in the Caribbean colonies, demonstrations were held for 'rehabilitation, apologies, and reparations'. Balkenende later said that it had never been his intention to offend anyone and certainly not to gloss over slavery. (COLLECTION ANP)

an impact on society at large, or not. There has been no systematic research into what the Dutch, of any background, know about history and the diverse cultures in their own country. The couple of surveys that have been carried out over the last few years suggest a certain interest and sensitivity for 'colonial issues', but it is unclear as to how representative this is. It is not evident that the shame about slavery felt by readers of the glossy *Historisch Nieuwsblad* is any more representative of the mood in the Netherlands today than right-wing populist tirades to the contrary.

What is clear is that the current canonical image of colonial history is full of inconsistencies and new silences, in part due to the active input of the postcolonial communities in the game of forgetting, commemorating and silencing. Many examples have been given in the previous chapters: the VOC is remembered with pride, while the WIC evokes only shame; linked to this, the narrowing of colonial slavery to the West and the nonsensical reduction of West Indian history to slavery; and the tendency to reduce the history of the Indisch Dutch to the twentieth century, in particular to the Second World War, repatriation, and a suffering that was silenced or denied for too long.

The postcolonial struggle corrected old silences, but allowed others to persist and generated new ones. The exposure of these old silences was a response to a gradually more self-critical attitude in Dutch intellectual and political circles. Everything revolved around the acknowledgement of neglect and discrimination, past and present. For strategic reasons, recognition could not easily be demanded in anything other than an assertive tone and with indignant reference to past and present victimhood. Yet this attitude was often at odds with critical self-examination. Consequently, the identification of colonialism, racism, and colonial war with the 'Netherlands' obscured the fact that colour distinctions and open racism were inextricably linked to Indisch history, that the Indisch community was a privileged product of that colonialism, that Moluccan soldiers derived their existence and status from their unconditional loyalty to the Netherlands and the House of Orange; or, likewise, that colour consciousness and ethnic distinction continues to characterize Caribbean cultures.

The canonization of decolonization was also half-hearted. First, there were decades of refusing to accept the end of the Dutch East Indies and especially the manner of its demise. This was a refusal to surrender to the course of modern history, an attitude The Hague only dared break with once the first 'Indisch generation', including the veterans, had all but withered away. Next there was the usually self-silenced trauma of the exodus from Suriname. Unlike the repatriates and military from the East Indies, this migration was not forced, but rather reflected a lack of faith in the country and its leadership, and the fiasco of nationalism. The final step was a gradual distancing from the less fortunate compatriots who stayed behind. This is a painful conclusion, which seldom led to open self-reflection and was smothered in silence, buried under discourses of shattering other, older silences, in particular around slavery. The history of the Republic of Suriname served only to strengthen Antillean refusal to move towards independence. There is no room for heroic orations here either and so the Antillean claim on Dutch memorial culture primarily limits itself to the paradoxical combination of stressing centuries-old bonds and the injustice of slavery and cultural suppression alike.

But most striking is perhaps the moralizing that surrounds the writing of colonial historiography and the public image of this past as presented in museums and the media – all the more striking since accusations of silencing and suppressing the colonial past have not subsided.[10] The last few years have revealed a strong desire not only to turn over stones and lift veils, but also to (pre)judge, accuse, pardon, or express sympathy for the past. In this there is only one precedent: the memory of the Nazi occupation of the Netherlands and above all the persecution of the Jews. This penchant for moralizing – which has all but disappeared in studies about class war and the labour movement, about *verzuiling* and a fortiori about earlier episodes of Dutch history – corresponds seamlessly with the context in which the colonial past was rediscovered, a combination of postcolonial identity claims and a willingness to make inclusive gestures.

This imbalance is not surprising; it merely highlights the social construction of canonization. However, in the end, it is not just the historian, but anyone who is interested in national and colonial history and every participant in the debate about nationhood who would be better served by a more balanced representation of the colonial dimension of the nation's history. Hence, one would prefer a picture that is less defined by group perspectives and moralizing ruminations on who and what 'we' were and are.

This point has by no means been reached and the existence of a multitude of voices will undoubtedly remain the rule – and yet the canonizing of national history at the very least demands an open debate on the tension between 'ethnic' perspectives and a shared canon. A recent survey of advocates and organizations in postcolonial communities produced interesting outcomes in this respect and disproved any hopeful belief that the chapter on the symbolic inclusion of postcolonial migrants had meanwhile reached its happy conclusion.[11]

Almost all respondents from all groups answered negatively the question of whether the history and culture of 'their' group was now sufficiently known about and understood by Dutch society, in particular in education and museums. The Netherlands, most believed, is still insufficiently open to colonial history and the background to postcolonial migration. Opinions about the current history canon varied. All groups sensed a certain degree of shame in the Netherlands about this past. Where Moluccans, Surinamese, and Antilleans regard this embarrassment as justified, the views of the Indisch Dutch – not surprisingly perhaps, considering their own entanglement in this history – were divided.

Being addressed as a representative of a specific community, the respondents, of course, answered from that personal perspective. Nonetheless, it is remarkable that even these active and engaged citizens barely identified with other postcolonial groups and displayed only limited interest in them. When asked whether they felt they belonged to a postcolonial community, only a few answered wholeheartedly 'yes'.

A distinct majority of the respondents from all the groups articulated another thorny issue, namely the ongoing sense that the historiography and image of their own group was still not being defined enough by people from their own group. The dominance of 'white' researchers in the established 'white' bastions has been remarked upon for decades, but has indeed changed little. Yet, according to most of those questioned, this does not lead to the outcomes of the research being less acceptable, neither did they believe that researchers from the respondents' own circles would, by definition, produce better work. However, the sense of disadvantage and the idea that the government has not corrected or stimulated enough is strong among active postcolonial citizens.[12]

The most extreme view, in the tone of 'you lot don't understand a thing', was articulated early on and sometimes in plain vitriol, by Tjalie Robinson and others in his Indisch circle.[13] The same argument was more recently expressed by the demand for the history of slavery to be finally studied from a 'black' perspective, a point of departure that is propagated by the National Institute for the Study of Dutch Slavery and its Legacy (NiNsee), among others. In this approach, which has become dominant throughout the 'Black Atlantic', the more intuitive Indisch approach ('they don't understand a thing') is rendered with a heavier theoretical foundation, leaning strongly on developments in the areas of cultural studies and postcolonial studies in the United States. Preferring this dichotomy of black versus white perspectives is, from an academic point of view, at the very least contestable; yet it tellingly illustrates how the rediscovery of the colonial past does not simply revolve around making neutral facts visible.[14]

INTERMEZZO: INTERNATIONAL HERITAGE POLICY

Before the Second World War, in the words of sociologist Jacques van Doorn, the Netherlands East Indies were 'our greatest investment, not only in economic terms, but also culturally and morally'.[15] After 1900, one in forty

Dutch citizens spent time in the colony, far greater numbers of Dutch were indirectly involved with the Dutch East Indies through these 'colonialists' – who included top industrialists and later such statesmen as prime minister Hendrik Colijn.[16] The colony also contributed to the cultural life of the metropole. In the realm of the belle-lettres, these were mainly Indisch and *totok* authors, writing under such pseudonyms as Multatuli or Melatti van Java, or their own names, such as Louis Couperus, Augusta de Wit, or Madelon Szekely-Lulofs. Beyond literature, Dutch interest mainly focused on the indigenous cultures, from the visual arts and music to religion and culture in an anthropological sense. This interest was often orientalist in the way it regarded the indigenous populations as bearers of distinctly strange cultures, but was nonetheless of interest and quality.

Large numbers of Dutch researchers, from the nineteenth century on, built scientific careers on studying the nature and culture of the archipelago. Many members of the Royal Netherlands Academy of Arts and Sciences (KNAW) had worked in the East Indies. A sizeable number of the alumni of Delft and Wageningen found employment in the East Indies and the number of 'Indisch' dissertations in law, literature, economics, and agricultural science was substantial. The government supported the foundation of institutions that were specifically focused on the Netherlands East Indies, such as the *Koninklijk Instituut voor Taal-,Land- en Volkenkunde* (KITLV, today Royal Netherlands Institute of Southeast Asian and Caribbean Studies, 1851), the *Indisch Genootschap* (Indisch Society, 1861), and the *Koloniaal Instituut* (Colonial Institute, 1924). Societies like the *Koninklijk Nederlands Aardrijkskundig Genootschap* (KNAG, Royal Dutch Geographical Society, 1873), focused not exclusively, but predominantly on the Netherlands East Indies. Whether or not the Netherlands did anything 'magnificent' overseas, it certainly benefitted its own scientific and intellectual infrastructure.[17]

The small European/Indisch minority in the archipelago was rarely the subject of political discussion or anthropological interest. Post-war, this contributed to the remarkable situation of the huge lack of understanding the Eurasians encountered on their arrival in the Netherlands. To its indignation, this group was labelled as utterly different from other Dutch citizens – because 'rooted in the East Indies'. They not only looked physically different, it was also thought that their culture would also not easily assimilate. The Netherlands East Indies belonged to the canon of the day, but the *Indo* barely at all.

The little interest there was for the West corresponded with the limited interests the Dutch had there and the small size of the population, but it also reflected the view that Suriname had little cultural value and the Antilles none at all. Illustrative of this is the pre-war acquisitions policy of the Dutch colonial museums, in which there was at most scant attention for the native American Indian and Maroon cultures of Suriname. For Asian Surinamese culture researchers generally preferred to look to the root cultures in Asia itself, whereas the Afro-Caribbean cultures were regarded as corruptions, 'bastard cultures', rather than interesting creolizations of European and African cultures.

It has become commonplace to speak of a post-war suppression of colonial history. Henk Wesseling, referring to the 1960s, spoke of a 'cut-out, banished, vanished' colonial past which had been given no time to be processed into history. Even if this view sometimes seems too routinely tied to the trauma of the abrupt decolonization, it is defended with solid arguments. University curricula for the Indies were discontinued; the Indisch career circuit disappeared; the Dutch East Indies shrunk, even in history schoolbooks; the Indisch dimension of World War II was ignored, and so on. The first post-war retrospectives of the Netherlands East Indies, published by prominent colonial figures, exuded a sense of frustration about a rudely interrupted mission.[18]

Yet it remains paradoxical that forgetting was so widespread at the same time as 300,000 repatriates settled in the Netherlands and almost 120,000 veterans returned home to a country where the pre-war generations had been brought up with the understanding that the distant East Indies were extremely important. The immediate answer is that it was not so much forgetting, at least not for those who had lived in the Dutch East Indies, but that the act of remembrance was banished from the public realm. That silencing, moreover, did not last long. The public rediscovery of this history took place in an atmosphere in which the repatriates who were calling out for recognition suddenly found themselves confronted with moralistic questions about the legitimacy of colonialism. Yet at the same time, the Netherlands was developing a sense of guilt in its engagement with the Indisch Dutch. All this helped the Indisch generation to create an active community of people who had shared the same fate.[19] The Caribbean migrants followed a different trajectory and somewhat later. They had no more forgotten their own history than the Indisch Dutch had theirs. Along with their integration they acquired the space to have this history more widely remembered. The difference, however, was that they were never accused of being colonial, 'on the wrong side of history'. They had the moral advantage of not having been perpetrators or collaborators, but victims of a system that was discredited post hoc.

In the decades that followed, the Netherlands developed a certain sensitivity for migrants from the colonies – hence room for identity claims and a public acknowledgement of their history and culture. Over the last decade the Dutch government began to invest substantial amounts in 'minorities' cultural heritage'. Considering the previous history, it was only logical that postcolonial migrants would be given priority. Indisch Dutch and Moluccans consequently began to receive more attention in museum environments than ever before and institutions such as the Rijksmuseum and Tropenmuseum began, somewhat shamefully, to collect and exhibit Caribbean artefacts, encouraged by The Hague and in the hope of attracting new audiences.

This new interest generated renewed attention for cultural cooperation with the countries of origin. The previous history had been disheartening. The foundation Sticusa, set up immediately after the war to facilitate cultural cooperation between the Netherlands and the (former) colonies, was almost immediately dismissed as colonial by Indonesia. For the former colonies remaining in the Kingdom (Suriname and the Antilles) Sticusa did work for a long time – until 1975 in the case of Suriname and 1988 for the Antilles – but here too its neocolonial image proved fatal.[20]

Cultural and historical cooperation developed in different ways. With Indonesia it ran parallel to a political dynamic that has only recently become more relaxed, partly because The Hague has slowly moved away from unsolicited and misplaced missionary zeal. Apart from projects in the areas of monument conservation, archive preservation, and bilateral historical conferences, there was little room for exchange on the themes of a colonial past, which in Indonesia was now simply regarded as an anathema and completely closed chapter. The republic continued, undiminished, the policy introduced by the Japanese, who had banned the use of the Dutch language and colonial symbols; in the historiography the colonizer was allocated either marginal or antagonistic roles.[21] Bilateral cultural cooperation, as well as Dutch heritage policy, had to be neutral, above all. In practice this came down to a lot of attention for 'refined' art from Java and Bali, 'primitive' art from the former outlying provinces, little of the culture of the vast Muslim majority of the archipelago, almost nothing about the colonial period, and even less about the pre-war Indisch subculture. The gulf between international and domestic Indisch-oriented heritage policy remained huge; it could hardly be any other way.[22]

Cultural exchange with the Caribbean had a different dynamic. Postcolonial sensitivities were no less, while the dominance of the Dutch in the relationship was overwhelming, due to the enormous differences in scale and wealth. However, Dutch interest in cooperation waned after Sticusa was discontinued.[23] Unlike Indonesia, the recent revival of interest in cultural exchange with Suriname and the Antilles – primarily using Dutch funds – fits perfectly with the inclusive gestures made to postcolonial migrants in the Netherlands. This is also easier, because there is no sense of a deep cultural divide between the communities on either side of the ocean.

Only recently, apparently beyond the shame of the last few decades, has The Hague begun to develop an international cultural policy in which the colonial dimension is given a central role. Six of the seven focus countries are former colonies or had colonial settlements: Brazil, Ghana, Indonesia, Sri Lanka, Suriname, South Africa.[24] Countries like the United States, Japan, and China, which in the past were also 'touched' by the voc and wic, are not targeted because strong cultural cooperation already exists here and no extra impulse is needed. Conversely, the exclusion of a country like Guyana – neighbouring Suriname and a Dutch colony until the beginning of the nineteenth century – merely reflects how cultural policy is also explicitly a component in a broader foreign policy. Guyana is inconsequential for the contemporary Netherlands, and there is therefore no strong reason for developing a joint heritage policy.

What is striking about recent Dutch international cultural policy is that, compared with the domestic treatment of the colonial past, moral issues and a moralizing tone are far less prominent.[25] This firstly reflects the composition of the partners. Countries like Ghana, Sri Lanka, and South Africa have no inclination to 'celebrate' their Dutch colonial histories, but do welcome a joint policy for material heritage and research. For a long time Brazil was even the driving force behind the 'rediscovery' of the Dutch period (1630-1654): relieved, the Netherlands could join in with a view in which the wic, and in particular Johan Maurits van Nassau-Siegen, are associated with promising developments, religious tolerance, flourishing arts and sciences, not the slave trade or oppression. The regret expressed on more than one occasion to Ghana for the Dutch involvement in the Atlantic slave trade was more a response to domestic sensitivities than something desired by the Ghanaian government.

Hardly surprisingly, an almost proportional relation seems to exist between the proximity of the colonial past and the burden it bears. No wonder, then, that cultural cooperation with Indonesia has rarely gone beyond running the gauntlet – the turbulence of decolonization has long obscured the view of the colonial history that preceded it. Yet there are signs of normalization and depoliticization, even if they were interrupted by the voc celebrations, which were not appreciated by Jakarta. Since then, The Hague has aimed for cultural cooperation on the subject of the colonial past, but any trace of chauvinism is anxiously avoided. The commemoration of four centuries of Dutch presence in the archipelago is regarded very differently in Indonesia and the Netherlands. Where in Indonesia the significance of colonialism is highly moderated and Indisch or Moluccan history barely addressed, in the Netherlands the 'Dutch East Indies' continue to dominate the memory. Two different versions of the past to serve two different audiences.

The relation between the proximity of the colonial past and the burden of that colonial past is far more influential in the cultural cooperation with Suriname and – in Kingdom relations – the Antilles. The fact that both are Dutch colonial creations and are still seriously dependent on the former metropole only serves to strengthen this. The consequence is paradoxical. The recent revival in The Hague of interest in cultural cooperation on joint heritage also answers the desires of the Antillean and Surinamese communities in the Netherlands. Hence, as more has been researched, written, and exhibited about the West, the centre of gravity has shifted further to towards the Netherlands. Suriname and the Antilles have become increasingly the receivers of research, writings, and exhibitions carried out in the Netherlands, by Dutch who might not have a Caribbean heritage. The conservation of monuments or archives is no different: the means, initiative, and actors come largely from the Netherlands.

Another dilemma is emerging. The communality of the past was set by colonialism, slavery, contract labour and, more recently, the exodus to the Netherlands. Whatever one thinks about that history, it has remained unmistakably decisive and shared. This is why it is possible to focus so much attention on cultural cooperation and why it is done. However, among Antilleans and Surinamese on both sides of the ocean there is a strong penchant for focusing on precisely the culture that is regarded as their 'own' and far less on what is associated with the Netherlands: Sranantongo, Sarnami or Papiamentu, rather than (Caribbean variants of) Dutch; oral traditions, religion outside, or on the margins of, Christendom, and much, much more.

This dilemma does not arise in collaborations with Indonesia. Dutch heritage institutions house innumerable artefacts and a wealth of knowledge about the archipelago and its inhabitants, but there is no question of an Indonesian desire for the Netherlands to continue its early scientific and museological role. Where this is expected, in Suriname and the Antilles, it raises interesting questions about postcolonial cultural policy. Papiamentu has been spoken in the Kingdom for centuries, including on an island (Bonaire) which has recently become a Dutch municipality; should this language have the same status as Frisian? And what about the West-Indian English spoken on the Windward Islands? Does a shared cultural heritage policy

extend to cultural developments after political independence? In Suriname, does the oral history of the Hindustanis in the rice district of Nickerie or
the Maroons in the interior, prior to 1975, belong to a shared cultural heritage, and what followed thereafter not? The answers to these kinds of questions are largely political, as is the issue of what status should be ascribed to
migrant cultures in the Netherlands.

This interlude about foreign policy underlines the fact that cultural heritage is far from neutral; that in the postcolonial Netherlands 'foreign' is
constantly transected by 'domestic'; that in the realm of heritage policy, this
also forces choices to be made that have barely become the subject of public
or political debate. And that, once again, it is clear that the way we treat colonial heritage and colonial history, both now and in the past, reflects most of
all the ever-changing present.[26]

POSTCOLONIAL STUDIES IN THE NETHERLANDS,
A MISSED OPPORTUNITY?

The previous chapter placed the post-war experiences of the Netherlands in
a broader context. That history was unique in the sense that successive,
highly diverse postcolonial migrations were separate from the migration
from Islamic countries that took place on a similar scale. Postcolonial migrants were, on the whole, better equipped for socio-economic integration
and were culturally closer to Dutch society. This translated into a high degree of exogamy and a strong identification with the Netherlands.

Dutch society received migrants neither with open arms, nor without
prejudice. In the 1980s, it was reluctantly acknowledged that the Netherlands had become a multicultural society and a moderate form of multiculturalism was accepted. This has remained more or less intact ever since,
even if attitudes towards Islam over the last decade have become more dismissive. However, this has barely affected postcolonial migrants, a minority of whom are Muslim.

In embracing a cautious multiculturalism, the Netherlands was closer
to the British model than France or Portugal, where there was less acceptance of postcolonial identity claims. In a broader sense, it is remarkable
how much more commonplace a critical reflection on one's own colonial
past and gestures of recognition towards postcolonial migrants became in
North-Western European countries than in the Iberian countries. If we draw
even broader comparisons, what emerges is that Europe and the United
States are far more open to these issues than the former colonial powers of
Japan and Russia. Evidently, something like a 'Western' norm for historical

accountability emerged after the Second World War.

The struggle of migrants, in particular migrants from the former colonies, for their view of colonial history to be recognized is closely linked to pre-war movements such as *négritude* in France and, in the academic realm, primarily the post-war rise of postcolonial studies in the Anglo-Saxon world. Recent studies have remarked upon the fact that even once a debate on colonialism and its legacies had developed, this school found few supporters in the Netherlands.[27] The question is not only whether this observation is correct and what the explanation might be, but if so, whether much has been missed.

Before these questions may be answered, a few exceedingly brief remarks about postcolonial studies are apposite.[28] This is an approach to colonial history and the contemporary legacies of this history with a strong emphasis on taking a 'contesting' view, based on the assumption that most scientific knowledge was produced from an implicitly colonial paradigm and continues to be so. Supporters of postcolonial studies aimed to correct and cross-out that prejudiced Western, colonial gaze, an aim which for most of its practitioners was not only interpreted as an academic task, but also a political one. By extension, postcolonial studies were often explicitly deployed to serve social and political aims, such as anti-colonialism and antiracism. In this a link was drawn to the postmodern approach of cultural studies, which had gained prominence mainly in American universities in the 1980s, but also with the neo-Marxist-inspired subaltern studies in India and elsewhere. The result was a strong focus on the 'holy trinity' of class, ethnicity and gender.

The first question – is it true that postcolonial studies in the Netherlands hardly developed? – can be answered in the affirmative without much equivocation. There is no widespread tradition of reflecting on the colonial past, even less so of an explicitly postcolonial paradigm. Before the Second World War, a number of somewhat dispersed anti-colonial publications did appear in the Netherlands and the colonies, but apart from their political and ideological significance, they had no academic pretensions or reverberations.[29]

The end of the Second World War also brought an intellectual fracture between Indonesia and the Netherlands. Indonesian historiography was marked by a mixture of antagonism towards colonialism and a downplaying of the significance of the Netherlands in the history of the archipelago, but also by scant interest in theoretical reflection and debate. In the Netherlands it was mainly the sociologist J.A.A. van Doorn who devoted studies to continuities between colonial policy in the Dutch East Indies and Dutch minorities policy. However, in this work he remained far removed from the terminology and political positions commonly used in postcolonial studies.[30]

The modest growth in Caribbean studies since the 1970s took place within the context of the exodus to the Netherlands. The centre of gravity was and remained in the Netherlands and the former colonies have continued to be receivers, rather than producers of this academic work. Surinamese or Antillean authors did begin to stir up the debate about the colonial past, but only a few from academic positions. Sociologist Philomena Essed, originally from Suriname, published a number of studies on racism in the 1980s based on a postcolonial paradigm; however, her work met with few positive responses in academia. The Hindustani-Surinamese columnist and author, Anil Ramdas, initially linked himself to postcolonial studies, but then seems to have made a complete U-turn, even if he did remain committed to the idea of identity as choice, a proposition in part derived from the work of Stuart Hall.[31]

Hence, it was a remarkably long time before the paradigm of postcolonial studies won broader support in the Dutch debate about colonialism, though still modest and predominantly by 'white' scholars. Beyond literary and cultural studies, there was no formation of a school. Many historians and anthropologists were later to some degree inspired by postcolonial studies, but only a few, and all female – Frances Gouda, Lizzy van Leeuwen, Susan Legêne, Gloria Wekker – explicitly set themselves up as supporters, even their work is usually fairly removed from the radical Anglo-Saxon version of postcolonialism.

Why is there no strong tradition of postcolonial studies in the Netherlands? The most obvious explanation is the absence of a widely shared colonial and postcolonial experience and language in the former Dutch empire. The colonies had relatively little to do with each other – the course of postwar decolonization underlines this – and there has never been much solidarity or even mutual interest among postcolonial migrants in the Netherlands. The Dutch language disappeared from Indonesia, while in the Antilles it is still unpopular and rarely standard. Only in Suriname did it gradually become the language of the people. Unlike English, the Dutch language does not bond the former empire and serves only to recall colonial domination. There is, therefore, no broad language community that can cast a collective critical look on Dutch colonialism.

Moreover, strategic choices have evidently been made within postcolonial migrant groups. By far the majority of talented postcolonial (and other) migrants chose to study medicine, economics, or law as a passport to social success. The number that chose an uncertain career in the humanities and social sciences was many times smaller. Whether they were then given equal opportunities is open to discussion; preferential treatment was, in any event, rare. Whatever the case, few to date have achieved positions in established academic and heritage institutions, where 'white' Dutch continue to dominate. This has also contributed to the recruitment field for postcolonial studies remaining small. Additionally, where postcolonial studies was explicitly left-wing and anti-colonial, this political orientation was far from typical of the Indisch and Moluccan 'community'.

There might well be another explanation, but it is speculative and all the more debatable. The rise of American and British postcolonial studies took place in polarized societies with a strong racist element, which in the United States was even anchored in law until the 1960s. Postcolonial studies not only aimed to broaden horizons, but also to adopt political positions in a polarized social climate. It is not my assertion in this book that there was no racism, or thinly disguised ethnocentrism, in the Netherlands; the opposite is more plausible.[32] However, there were almost no instances of race riots and open expressions of xenophobia were, until recently, an anathema. This was beneficial to the social climate, but not conducive to the rise of postcolonial studies.

The question 'Why is there no postcolonial studies?' may give the impression that the absence of such a tradition is exceptional and a great lack. As far as the first point is concerned, the popularity of postcolonial studies has remained largely an Anglo-Saxon phenomenon. Even in France, which in view of its long academic tradition of political engagement would seem an obvious candidate, this approach has remained marginal. In Latin America and the Caribbean, the postcolonial paradigm caught on here and there, but primarily through academics who had diverted to American universities.[33]

The question remains as to whether any of this is a great deficiency. Without doubt, the testators of postcolonial studies such as Edward Said had a major influence on the development of a curative 'source criticism' of Western traditions and interpretations of the non-Western world. The unconventional work of West Indian Britons such as Stuart Hall and Paul Gilroy on black culture in a postmodern world provided inspiring reflections on the (dis)continuities between the colonial and postcolonial world. Protagonists of postcolonial studies, moreover, offered academic inspiration and support to the identity claims of postcolonial migrants. All this was important to the postcolonial debate in the Netherlands, which was so slow to get going.[34]

However, on the way, the problems associated with postcolonial studies began to weigh more heavily.[35] First, there was a strong tendency towards uncompromising political correctness, which in practice led to a theoretically contestable strategic essentialism and, at times, to useless black-versus-white thinking.[36] Moreover, the continuities between the present and the past were more often stipulated than proven through references to empirical arguments and with due consideration of the immense range of local variety; the intractability of ethnic contradictions was too easily ascribed to colonialism; and the distinction between 'memory' and 'history' was frequently understated or simply missed. In more extreme versions, the emphasis on the 'multivocality' of experiences and interpretations of (post)colonial reality led to an excessive problematization of the methodological conventions of mainstream scholarship and, thereby, disastrous isolation. The irony is that much of what was explicitly intended to be emancipatory in postcolonial studies ultimately got bogged down in horrible jargon and terminological hairsplitting among insiders. In short then, from a 'conventional' academic perspective this school suffered from a shortage of conceptual clarity and empirical foundations.[37]

Viewed thus, one wonders whether it is really regrettable that the Netherlands developed little in the way of an Anglo-Saxon postcolonial studies tradition. Future research into Dutch colonialism and its effects on the present will continue to consider postcolonial issues, but ultimately it will have to employ solid, empirical, and comparative research – an argument that most supporters of a moderate version of the postcolonial paradigm who are working in the Netherlands will also endorse. Meanwhile, it remains remarkable how 'white' almost all the research and cultural heritage institutions still are and how little representative of postcolonial Netherlands. This is problematic, even if one need not presume that postcolonial migrants would carry out fundamentally different or better research.

THE FUTURE OF THE COLONIAL PAST

Postcolonial communities brought colonial history with them to the Netherlands. This rediscovered past thus acquired a bright future. The space available for this past today may still be too modest in the eyes of many Dutch who cherish their (post)colonial roots, but it is unmistakably greater than it ever has been since the loss of the Dutch East Indies and also more explicitly self-critical than ever before. Established institutions such as the Rijksmuseum and new competitors like the National Historical Museum (now being developed) promise to pay significant attention to the colonies and their migrants. Old colonial institutions such as KITLV/Royal Institute of Southeast Asian and Caribbean studies and the Tropenmuseum extended their mission to include postcolonial history and Dutch citizens with colonial roots. The press, popular and specialized magazines, publications, university courses, exhibitions on the colonies, 'race' and ethnicity, and, of course, the official history canon – all these testify to a new postcolonial sensitivity that has developed over the last ten to twenty years.[38]

This postcolonial debate is an appropriate, albeit not always balanced correction of earlier neglect and distortions. However, this does not in any way mean that a clear course has been set. If we assume that the rediscovery of colonial history and its legacies was rooted in the postcolonial migrations, then we have to ask how long and how profound and effective this impulse will remain. The answer to this question is perhaps sobering. The rediscovery of the past was forced by migrants who derived their identities primarily from that past and old colonial obligations. The irony is that it is precisely their colonial antecedents that gave them the cultural capital to express their desires and to engage in successful lobbying. But what of later generations? To begin with, the high frequency of relationships outside their own communities meant they developed a more layered identity, in which the (post)colonial was merely one dimension. The recognition that the first generation(s) managed to extract through adopting a strategic essentialism is for them a given, the thought that this past might also define them to the bone has become increasingly less self-evident.

Postcolonial identity, in other words, is ever more a matter of choice. Distancing oneself from a one-dimensional choice gradually became easier because the Netherlands, which was becoming ever less uniform, had to begin to accommodate other cultures and other views of national identity. Migrants from the colonies also found a more willing ear because their claims now pertained to a history that had, indeed, been shared for centuries. Certainly, this struggle for recognition was not easy and certainly not linear. However, the strongest counterforce to a broadening of the notion of the Dutch nation has not been aimed at postcolonial migrants, but at Muslims – two categories which share only a small margin of overlap.

But this is not the end of the story. Postcolonial migrants may frequently feel they have an advantage over other migrants and indeed a right to one, but in practice this advantage is declining noticeably – not only in terms of the postcolonial bonus, but also in the realm of recognition. Despite the recent successes of the radical right, a willingness to make inclusive gestures to towards cultural minorities still dominates political thought in the Netherlands. In this context the rhetorical advantage of a notion like 'colonial legacy' over 'moderate Islam' is declining.

The struggle for recognition primarily, and logically, occurred within the nation's borders. The Indisch generation identified almost exclusively with the Netherlands. Radical Moluccans referred to freedom movements elsewhere in the world only for a short while. The Afro-Caribbean call for the acknowledgement of slavery had a more explicit international orientation, with the 'Black Atlantic' as the frame of reference. But here too, political actions had a national focus. The recurring claim was that the Dutch nation, that every Dutch person, was indirectly involved in that colonial past and its legacies – an involvement that began to acquire the emotional charge of complicity.

But the character of the nation that was being addressed was also undergoing rapid change. A confusing diversity arose; alongside a large number of postcolonial citizens, there was a no less significant number of migrant communities from elsewhere. Mutual understanding between the postcolonial communities was limited and there was no natural sense of solidarity with other migrant groups. In a nation where the number of new citizens with no previous ties to the Netherlands was growing, demands for the colonial past to be recognized were increasingly drowned out by other voices in a cacophony of identity claims. But where each group wants to add its own 'thing' to the idea of nationhood, without paying much attention to what is important to other groups, there is little hope for a community of all citizens.

At the same time, the Netherlands became more and more a European country and this also undermined the postcolonial argument. 'Old Europe' was dominated by countries with colonial pasts. This did not mean that these countries were, as a matter of course, more receptive to desires surrounding the recognition of the colonial past – as pointed out earlier, there was resistance everywhere and the amounts of openness varied greatly from country to country. The successes of the postcolonial lobby remained limited and above all national. A broader, European identity politics of postcolonial migrants failed to arise. Conversely, it is striking that although Brussels formulated all kinds of development policies for the former colonies, it took almost no initiative in the area of a shared, *European* colonial cultural heritage – even though there were ample opportunities to do so, both in Europe and overseas, and in terms of material and immaterial heritage. The Netherlands, traditionally firmly oriented towards Europe, made no moves in this direction either.

And this is where the tide for postcolonial arguments also begins to ebb. The new Eastern European countries have no colonial history of their own, rarely show any interest in this aspect of European history, and show even less understanding of the emotions that still circulate in 'Old Europe' regarding special relations with the former colonies, or for compensation claims by postcolonial minorities. The Western European sensitivity around questions of 'race' or ethnicity are absent in Eastern Europe; oppression for these new member states recalls their own experiences with Nazism and Communism, not their own part in the subjection of others, let alone in distant tropical lands. In other words, in the new, enlarged Europe, colonial history and its legacies do not carry the same weight as for the old guard.

New Europe is still in the midst of coming to terms with its painful recent history. As with every imagining of history, it is not just about what is remembered, but equally about what has been deliberately diminished, suppressed, or shut out. This book emphasizes the battle against forgetting (the colonial past), and understanding and sympathy resonate throughout for the postcolonial migrants' desire for their history to become part of Dutch memory. However, within a broader European context we cannot avoid two sobering conclusions. Firstly, that the current exercises in European commemoration underline that forward-looking historiography must also contain an element of deliberate closure – otherwise, in view of the divisions and often extreme violence of the continental past, a mental European unification is inconceivable.[39] Next, where the notion of 'Europe' is so strongly construed around achievements, on the one hand, and the desire to close a dark chapter, on the other, the room available to a discourse that links the rediscovery of Europe's colonial past to moral condemnation and compensation claims shrivels.

The rediscovery of the (post)colonial past is not a new beginning, but the closure of a long history. In the Netherlands as well – and not only because the government likes to see its own gestures as providing closure. The postwar corrections to (post)colonial forgetting and silencing were extracted, in part, as a consequence of successful integration. Now we are witnessing the evaporation of the postcolonial bonus, community and identity. Descendants of colonial subjects of the past have become, in the first instance, Dutch and then European citizens. They will gradually identify less and less with their colonial roots; this ever more distant past will simply be one element in what they consider to be their identity. Where generations succeed each other, where forgetting and silencing make way for recognition and commemoration, the motivation for the organization and collective experience of old wounds has weakened – in this sense the dynamics around 1 July or 15 August are no different than 4/5 May.[40]

The past does not fall silent, it is simply inclined to subside now and then, gradually rearing its head less and less frequently. There is no reason to think that this will be any different for the colonial past in the long term. The Netherlands has, of course, become postcolonial. It is impossible to imagine Dutch society without migrants from the former colonies and their children and their cultural contribution, and there is far greater awareness of colonialism and its after effects today than, say, in 1960 or 1980. It is unclear whether all this has changed the image the Dutch have of themselves or their country. What is certain is that other issues are higher on the agenda now; insofar as these relate to migrants, they relate to different ones, namely Muslims. This too has perhaps made it easier to be a Dutch citizen with (post)colonial roots.

The Netherlands has become postcolonial over the last sixty-five years – almost a lifetime – but at the same time the postcolonial minorities have become Dutch and the significance of their colonial background has begun to evaporate. The postcolonial move to catch up on the debate about national identity is almost completed. Not to everyone's satisfaction, but there is nothing unusual about this either. Consensus about 'the nation' continues to be a receding horizon.

NOTES

INTRODUCTION

1 Schama, *Embarrassment of Riches*.
2 Lijphart, *Politics of Accommodation*.
3 Lechner, *The Netherlands*, 133.
4 Bagley, *Dutch Plural Society*, blurb.
5 This personal observation corresponds with conclusions drawn by Hondius in *Gemengde huwelijken*, 315-8.
6 The term 'multicultural society' can be confusing; I use it descriptively, not as a normative ideal, and assume that a society cannot function effectively if there is no consensus between citizens – regardless of their ethnic backgrounds or cultural characteristics – on the fundamental values of government and society. Cf. Schnabel et al., *De multiculturele illusie*, Entzinger, 'Voorbij de multiculturele samenleving'. For comparative purposes, I have benefitted from the studies on integration and assimilation by Portes & Rumbaut, *Immigrant America*, and Alba & Nee, *Remaking the American mainstream*.
7 Cf. Bernstein, 'Identity politics', Poletta & Jasper, 'Collective identity'.
8 Breman, 'De sociologie', rightly questions the idea of pre-War provincialism. See also the section 'Intermezzo' in the last chapter of this book.
9 Scheffer, *Het land van aankomst*, 185.
10 For a photographic companion to this book, especially chapters 3 and 5, see Oostindie, Schulte Nordholt & Steijlen, *Postkoloniale monumenten in Nederland/ Post-colonial monuments in the Netherlands*.
11 Oostindie & Steijlen, 'Zestig jaar'.
12 Herbert Gans coined the notion of a

nostalgic, political and fairly irrelevant, but keenly felt 'symbolic ethnicity'.
13 Cf. Lammers, *Vreemde overheersing*, 215.

1 DECOLONIZATION, MIGRATION AND THE POSTCOLONIAL BONUS

1 The existence of such a 'bonus' for migrants from the Netherlands East Indies has already been established, using different terminology, by Kraak, Ellemers & Wittermans, *De repatriëring*, 373, and for Caribbean migrants by Van Amersfoort & Van Niekerk, 'Immigration as a colonial inheritance'. For more statistics, see Oostindie, 'Postcolonial migrants in the Netherlands'.
2 Cf. Oostindie & Steijlen, 'Zestig jaar'.
3 Earlier studies include Kraak, Ellemers & Wittermans, *De repatriëring*, and Surie, 'De gerepatrieerden'. A small minority of Moluccans did not belong to the KNIL and consequently had a somewhat different history in the Netherlands, see Van der Mee & Tomasouw, *Andere verhalen*.
4 The name *Indische Nederlander*, 'Indisch Dutch', was already in use in the 1910s in the Netherlands East Indies (Van Leeuwen, *Ons Indisch erfgoed*, 194), but did not become common parlance in the Netherlands until after the war.
5 Van den Doel, *Afscheid van Indië*.
6 Ninety per cent of all those who were legally Dutch left Indonesia. Just under 40,000 Indisch Dutch remigrated, usually via the Netherlands, to the USA and Australia; for more on this transmigration

see Willems, *De uittocht*, 252-329.

7 Until the mid 1970s, they were usually referred to as 'Ambonese'; 'Moluccans' became the norm thereafter (Van Amersfoort, 'De Ambonezen', 109).

8 This characterization is borrowed from Thio, *Genoegens*, 19; cf. Vogels, Geense & Martens, 'Maatschappelijke positie', Yap, 'Het peranakan-gezin'.

9 Vlasblom, *Papoea*, 374, 474, 496-497, 515, 605-606.

10 Obdeijn and Schrover, *Komen en gaan*, 199.

11 Oostindie & Klinkers, *Knellende koninkrijksbanden*, II, 226-227. Cf. Willems, *De uittocht uit Indië*, 126, 148 and Schuster, *Poortwachters*, 112-113.

12 Surie, 'De gerepatrieerden', 79, also 91.

13 Bagley, *The Dutch plural society*, Verwey-Jonker, *Etnische minderheden*; cf. Van Doorn, *Indische lessen*, 91-92.

14 Van Leeuwen, *Ons Indisch erfgoed*, Willems, *Tjalie Robinson*.

15 Willems, *De uittocht uit Indië*, 201; Smeets & Steijlen, *In Nederland gebleven*, 327.

16 Contemporary Suriname has around 475,000 inhabitants, 10,000 of whom are new immigrants from Brazil and China.

17 Wesseling, *Indië verloren*, 303; Oostindie & Klinkers, *Knellende koninkrijksbanden*, II, especially Chs. 6 and 8.

18 Elsevier, 24-8-1974; cf. Van Doorn's warning in NRC *Handelsblad*, 4-11-1972 (also in Van Doorn, *Nederlandse democratie*, 66-76).

19 1972 Census, estimate Statistics Netherlands (CBS) 2007. See Choenni & Harmsen, 'Geboorteplaats', Obdeijn & Schrover, *Komen en gaan*, 250, 255.

20 Liem, *Stapwaarts voorwaarts*, is based on limited research from 1994. Niekerk, *De mier en de krekel* and 'Afro-Caribbeans', established that Afro-Surinamese and Indian Surinamese (Hindustanis) in the Netherlands in the mid 1970s had equal or lower levels of employment and education, but proposed that precisely lower-class Indian Surinamese have strongly improved their position ever since. Sansone, *Schitteren in de schaduw*, painted a bleak picture of the Afro-Surinamese underclass in the Netherlands.

21 Lucassen & Laarman, 'Integratie', set the intermarriage rates of Afro-Caribbean migrants in the first generation at approximately twenty-five per cent, in the second generation as high as around sixty per cent, and less than ten per cent for first generation Indian Surinamese (Hindustanis); cf. also Ramsoedh, 'Surinaamse hindoes en moslims', 143. Cf. Van Heelsum, *De etnisch-culturele positie*, 164 and Hondius, *Gemengde huwelijken*, 74-75, 77-78.

22 Oostindie & Klinkers, *Knellende koninkrijksbanden*, III, especially Chs. 10, 11 and 13, Oostindie, 'Migration paradoxes'.

23 Cf. Grosfoguel, 'Colonial Caribbean migrations', Ramos & Rivera, *Islands at the crossroads*, Oostindie & Klinkers, *Decolonising the Caribbean*.

24 Lucassen, *The immigrant threat*, 1-24, Lucassen, Feldman & Oltmer, *Paths of integration*, 7-23. Scheffer, *Het land van aankomst*, defends a sceptical standpoint about the relevance of previous integration successes to current issues. (Leo) Lucassen and Obdeijn & Schrover, *Komen en gaan* are more positive; (Jan) Lucassen & Penninx, *Nieuwkomers*, and Vermeulen & Penninx, *Het democratisch ongeduld*, preceded them.

25 Lucassen, 'Appendix', 421-426. For pre-war, often only temporary presence of migrants from the Dutch East Indies, see Poeze, *In het land van de overheerser*, Bosma & Raben, *De oude Indische wereld* and Bosma, 'Sailing through Suez'. For Surinamese and Antilleans in the Netherlands prior to the exodus, see Oostindie & Maduro, *In het land van de overheerser* and Oostindie, *Paradise overseas*, Ch. 6.

26 Scientific Council for Government Policy (WRR), *Etnische minderheden* and *Allochtonenbeleid*; *Integratiebeleid*; Schumacher, *De minderheden*, 67, Fermin, *Nederlandse politieke partijen*, 242-247, Fortuyn, *De puinhopen*. Vuijsje more or less predicted this about-turn *Correct* (1997). De Jong, *Een wereld van verschil*, recently defended moderate cultural relativism against the caricatural renunciation that became the vogue in the Netherlands at the time.

27 Blok Committee, *Bruggen bouwen* (Bridge building), 583-584; cf. Entzinger & Fermin, 'Gidsland', 59.

28 Cf. the reflection of Henk Molleman, the first director of Minorities Policy (Molleman, 'Het minderhedenbeleid'). Entzinger & Fermin, 'Gidsland', 53, and Koopmans, 'De politieke mobilisatie', believe that the strong emphasis on assimilation came later.

29 Fermin, *Nederlandse politieke partijen*, 238, Penninx, Schoorl & Van Praag, *The impact*, 214.

30 Lucassen & Köbben, *Het partiële gelijk*, 152, 158. Jones, *Tussen onderdanen*, 228, 261, 296.

31 Ter Wal, *Active civic participation*, 15.

32 Fennema & Van der Brug, 'Nederlandse anti-immigratiepartijen', 70, Coenders, Lubbers & Scheepers, 'Het tolerante land', Sniderman & Hagendoorn, *When ways of life collide*. Duyvendak, Engelen & De Haan, *Het bange Nederland*, defend the opposite standpoint.

33 Entzinger, *Voorbij de multiculturele samenleving* and 'The rise and fall', Snel, Engbersen & Leerkes, 'Transnational involvement', 305. Koopmans believes that, in practice, Dutch policy up to 2002 allowed more room for multicultural measures than British policy; this does not imply that the Netherlands supported a radical multiculturalism (Koopmans, 'De politieke mobilisatie', 130, 132); cf. also Sniderman & Hagendoorn, *When ways of life collide*, 1-2, 8-9, 123-128.

34 Cf. such diverse publications as Duyvendak, Engelen & De Haan, *Het bange Nederland*, De Jong, *Een wereld van verschil*, Sniderman & Hagendoorn, *When ways of life collide*; however, see also Scheffer, *Het land van aankomst*, 178-183. Vuijsje commented more than ten years ago that colonialism did not provide an explanation for the avoidance that he had identified of naming ethnic problems: 'For us, colonialism is remote; it does not provide a significant gauge for personal actions.' (*Correct*, 104-105). Moreover, an early collection of essays, such as Bleich & Schumacher, *Nederlands racisme*, focuses at length on the colonial roots of topical issues and postcolonial migrants.

35 In the 1960s, the recruitment of labour in Suriname and Curaçao was experimented with, however, only in small numbers and the experiment did not lead to significant labour migration.

36 See Jones, *Tussen onderdanen*; Schuster, *Poortwachters*.

37 Lucassen & Köbben, *Het partiële gelijk*, 157.

38 See figures published by Statistics Netherlands (www.cbs.nl) for indicators such as income and education levels; cf. Oostindie, 'Postcolonial migrants'.

2 CITIZENSHIP: RIGHTS, PARTICIPATION, IDENTIFICATION

1 Koning, *De Pasar Malam*, 65.

2 Bloemraad, Korteweg & Yurdakul, 'Citizenship and immigration'.

3 Parliamentary commission report Blok (Blok, *Bruggen bouwen*, 537).

4 Schuster, *Poortwachters*, Jones, *Tussen onderdanen*.

5 Schuster, *Poortwachters*, 101.

6 Quoted in Meijer, *In Indië geworteld*, 334, respectively Jones, *Tussen onderdanen*, 161; furthermore 146-147, 153.

7 Kraak, Ellemers & Wittermans, *De repatriëring*, 152, Surie, 'De gerepatrieerden', 73-74.

8 Jones, *Tussen onderdanen*, 112, 119.

9 Smeets & Steijlen, *In Nederland gebleven*, 327-328, Jones, *Tussen onderdanen*, 339.

10 Oostindie & Klinkers, *Knellende koninkrijks-banden*, II,.8, Schuster, *Poortwachters*, Ch. 3.

11 Oostindie & Klinkers, *Knellende koninkrijks-banden*, II, 237.

12 Jones, *Tussen onderdanen*, 246.

13 Oostindie & Klinkers, *Knellende koninkrijks-banden*, III, Ch. 13, Jones, *Tussen onderdanen*, 293, 307-319.

14 This terminology became broadly accepted, including in administrative circles, through Putnam's work, *Bowling alone*.

15 Bink & Massaro, 'Media en etnische culturele diversiteit'.

16 Poeze, *In het land van de overheerser*, Oostindie & Maduro, *In het land van de overheerser*, Bosma, *Terug uit de koloniën*, 56-100.

17 Bosma, *Terug uit de koloniën*, 203, Bosma & Alferink, 'Multiculturalism and settlement'. 80 per cent of the organizations

traced were registered at the Chamber of Commerce, the rest were mainly religious organizations and informal networks and web sites. See also Van Heelsum, *Migrantenorganisaties*, Van Heelsum & Voorthuysen, *Surinaamse organisaties in Nederland*.

18 In the order of 1:2500 for Indisch Dutch and repatriates, 1:575 for Antilleans, 1:400 for Surinamese and 1:140 for Moluccans (Bosma, *Terug uit de koloniën*, 232).

19 Van Leeuwen, *Ons Indisch erfgoed*, 302-314, Schulte Nordholt, *Indonesië*, 256.

20 The immediate cause was the Linggadjati Agreement (Van den Doel, *Afscheid van Indië*, 171).

21 Meijer, *In Indië geworteld*, 374-377, Willems, *De uittocht uit Indië*, 111-115, 162-167, 171.

22 The founder was the Dutchman Herman Coenradi. At its peak it reached an edition of 40,000, which dropped later to 20,000 (Bosma, *Terug uit de koloniën*, 23).

23 Steijlen & Smeets, *In Nederland gebleven*, 245-246, Bosma, *Terug uit de koloniën*, 176-190, Vogel, *Nabije vreemden*, 177-183.

24 Bosma & Alferink, 'Multiculturalism and settlement'.

25 Vermeulen & Van Heelsum, 'Group- or host state-related?'

26 Almost 30 per cent of the 880 Surinamese organizations in Van Heelsum's research (*Migrantenorganisaties*, 1, 64) were counted as religious, a slightly higher percentage than for Moroccans (24 per cent) and much higher than other groups. This percentage applied to all Surinamese organizations, though the number was certainly higher for the Indian and Javanese communities.

27 Bloemberg, *Tussen traditie en verandering*, Choenni & Adhin, *Hindostanen*.

28 Mahawat Khan, 'Hindostaanse moslims', 134, Ramsoedh, 'Surinaamse hindoes en moslims', 140.

29 After the withdrawal of The Hague plans, ocan chairman Glenn Helberg spoke of 'justice' and in the same breath pressed for 'assistance, and education, work and welfare opportunities' (Dutch world service radio, *Radio Nederland Wereldomroep*, Caribbean desk, 20-12-2008).

30 Blok Commission, *Bruggen bouwen*, 510, 516.

31 Bosma, *Terug uit de koloniën*, 332-338, Bosma

& Alferink, 'Multiculturalism and settlement'.

32 Oostindie & Steijlen, 'Zestig jaar'.

33 A (failed) exception was the *Vrije Indische Partij* (1994. Free Indisch Party) (Meijer, *Indische rekening*, 319).

34 Rath, 'Immigrant candidates', De Haan, 'Over de grenzen', 162-163.

35 Michon, Tillie & Van Heelsum, 'Political participation', 15, Chambon, *Sel de la démocratie*, 89-109.

36 Surinamese-Dutch politicians: four for the PvdA, three for the CDA, two for the VVD, one for GroenLinks and the LPF. Antillean-Dutch politicians: D66, PvdA, Christen Unie (Christian Union).

37 Meijer, *Indische rekening*, 138 and passim.

38 Tillie, *De etnische stem*, 109.

39 Fennema et al., *Sociaal kapitaal*, 1, 12-13.

40 Fennema & Tillie, 'Civic communities', Michon, Tillie & Van Heelsum, 'Political participation', 12.

41 *Moesson*, 1-1-2000.

42 Letter from MAAPP to Aboutaleb, 24-3-2009, consultation OCAN and MAAPP with Aboutaleb, 10-6-2009 (*Antilliaanse Nieuwsbrief*, July-August 2009).

43 Van Doorn, *Indische lessen*, 71.

44 Fennema et al., *Sociaal kapitaal*, 10-11, 37-38, 40, Fennema et al., 'De politieke integratie', 153-154, Fennema & Tillie, 'Civic communities', Michon, Tillie & Van Heelsum, 'Political participation', 4, 6, 11.

45 Van Heelsum, 'Political participation', 29.

46 Quoted in Ensel, 'Multiculturalisme', 171. Cf. also Ramlal, 'Politieke participatie', 209-210, on his experiences as the first Indian councillor in Goudt and, later, member of parliament, *In de gemeenteraad* and Petronilia, *Raadsleden*.

47 Fennema et al., *Sociaal kapitaal*, 28.

48 Oedayraj Singh Varma was suspected of clientelism and fraud, Bijlhout turned out to have concealed her links with the Bouterse military regime and Pormes was believed to have prepared and/or carried out violent acts in the Moluccan cause.

49 Vuijsje, *Vermoorde onschuld* and *Correct*. In the introduction of the reprinted edition of the latter, Vuisje, moreover, identifies a conformist 'passivism', 'perhaps the most

striking "intellectual characteristic" of the Netherlands in the second half of the last century' (*Correct*, XII).

50 Kraak, Ellemers & Wittermans, *De repatriëring*, 372, Surie, 'De gerepatrieerden', 95.

3 THE STRUGGLE FOR RECOGNITION: WAR AND THE SILENT MIGRATION

1 Stora, 'Quand une mémoire'.
2 Stora, 'Quand une mémoire', 60.
3 Van Dis, *Leeftocht*, 333 (from 'Een deken van herinnering', 1998); Pattynama quoted in Koning, *De Pasar Malam*, 167. Cf. Captain, *Achter het kawat*, 340, Willems, *De uittocht*, 15.
4 Kraak, Ellemers & Wittermans, *De repatriëring*, 151, 154-156, 200. Bossenbroek, *De meelstreep*, 72, speaks of a 'deep rift'. Cf. Willems, *De uittocht*, 137-140, 198-201.
5 Meijer, *In Indië geworteld*, 226, 237. He puts the number of Indo-Euroepean internees at 50,000; the number outside the camps at 125,000.
6 Meijer, *In Indië geworteld*, 245, speaks of 3,500 dead and 2,000 missing Dutch citizens, as well as several thousand Chinese and pro-Dutch Indonesians.
7 Bossenbroek, *De meelstreep*, 163.
8 Fasseur, 'Het verleden tot last', 134 ('bandjir'), Captain, *Achter het kawat*, 15, 339-342. At the Indisch commemoration in 2008 she appealed for the war to be commemorated with the Japanese as a way to 'process the trauma'. She referred to the experiences of her father, who had been interned by the Japanese. This cautious appeal was immediately rebutted on live TV by a former internee (and later television personality) Kick Stokhuyzen, who articulated the familiar position that Japan should first show remorse and stop falsifying history (NOS News, 15-8-2008). Compare also the problems with reconciliation quoted in Somers & Rijpma, *Nederlanders Japanners Indonesiërs*, 21, 36-44, 66.
9 Bossenbroek, *De meelstreep*, 535-536, Van Doorn, *Indische lessen*, 71.
10 Shortly after the war, the number of Europeans who died during WWII in the

East Indies was set at about 50,000; in the Netherlands this was 190,000, more than 100,000 of whom were Jewish. (Bossenbroek, *De meelstreep*, 41-42).

11 Bossenbroek, *De meelstreep*, 519-521, 530-531, Captain, *Achter het kawat*, passim, Meijer, *In Indië geworteld*, 269, Meijer, *Indische rekening*, 298, 301.
12 Compare also Bossenbroek, *De meelstreep*, 387-392, 413-417, 424-426, 432-434 and Willems, *De uittocht*, 204-228.
13 Keppy, *Sporen van vernieling*, 232.
14 The foundations had been laid in the US-brokered peace accord of 1951 (Bossenbroek, *De meelstreep*, 413-417, Keppy, *Sporen van vernieling*, 36). The battle for Japanese reparations has never ceased, cf. Somers & Rijpma, *Nederlanders Japanners Indonesiërs*, 41-42. Raben, *Beelden*, presents a broad view of the representation of the issue in Indonesia, Japan and the Netherlands, which, unsurprisingly, is different in each country.
15 Keppy, *Sporen van vernieling*, 233; ook 234-235, 241.
16 Keppy, *Sporen van vernieling*, 241.
17 Meijer, *Indische rekening*, 12-13.
18 Bosma, *Terug uit de koloniën*, 198, Meijer, *Indische rekening*, 134, 192, 245, 248, 261, 319.
19 Meijer, *Indische rekening*, 33, 38-42, 70-72 (business community), 73 (IEV).
20 Bossenbroek, *De meelstreep*, 230, Meijer, *Indische rekening*, 102.
21 Meijer, *Indische rekening*, 142; see also 150, 189.
22 Meijer, *Indische rekening*, 245-248, 254, 257.
23 *Uitkering Indische Geïnterneerden*, UIG. Meijer, *Indische rekening*, 295, cf. 251, 303.
24 Meijer, *Indische rekening*, 82-86, 92.
25 Meijer, *Indische rekening*, 307, see also 315.
26 *Wet Uitkeringen Burgerslachtoffers*, financial support for civilian victims, (1984), *Wet Indisch Verzet*, financial support for Indisch resistance(1986), payment of 7500 guilders net to former KNIL soldiers (1993); Meijer, *Indische rekening*, 318-319.
27 De Ridder, *Eindelijk erkenning?*, 17-22, Meijer, *Indische rekening*, 321, Steijlen, 'Het Gebaar'. The notion 'Dutch citizen' was interpreted in such a way that it included everyone who had been considered Dutch

in the East Indies and those who acquired Dutch citizenship later in the Netherlands, in particular, the Moluccans. In the end, 4000 guilders, tax-free, were paid out to all who fell into these categories.

28 The Indisch Platform does not accept the end of the road has been reached; cf. Steijlen, 'Het Gebaar'.

29 This characterization was provided me by Henk Schulte Nordholt.

30 Quoted in Meijer, *Indische rekening*, 25; cf. also Brand, Schulte Nordholt and Steijlen, *Indië verteld*.

31 Van Doorn, *Indische lessen*, 89.

32 Letter from the Kok cabinet, quoted in De Ridder, *Eindelijk erkenning?*, 18; cf. Bossenbroek, *De meelstreep*, 369.

33 Bossenbroek, *De meelstreep*, 280-284, 378.

34 Surie, 'De gerepatrieerden', 73.

35 'De geschiedenis van Indische Nederlanders' (The history of the Indisch Dutch) was executed under the auspices of the NWO (Netherlands Organisation for Scientific Research); SOTO and 'Van Indië tot Indonesië' (From the East Indies to Indonesia) were financed by the government and executed at the NIOD (Netherlands Institute for War Documentation), and the writing of the Moluccan-Dutch history was financed by the government and carried out at the Museum Maluku.

36 Withuis, *Erkenning*.

37 Blok Commission, *Bruggen bouwen*, 583-584.

38 Published in 14 volumes and over 15,000 pages, this massive series had two volumes on the East Indies, published in 1984 and 1985; see De Jong, *The collapse*.

39 Boekholt, *De staat*, Van Doorn, *Indische lessen*, 67-72, Meijer, *Indische rekening*, 315-323, Scagliola, *Last van de oorlog*, 221-240, Somers & Rijpma, *Nederlanders Japanners Indonesiërs*.

40 Bossenbroek, *De meelstreep*, 564-568, Ridder, *Eindelijk erkenning?*, 17-21.

41 Quoted in Meijer, *Indische rekening*, 322.

42 Ridder, *Eindelijk erkenning?*, 31 (Borst), 55 (Kluveld); cf. Van Leeuwen, *Indisch erfgoed*, 104, 138, 145, 166, Meijer, *Indische rekening*, 338.

43 Ridder, *Eindelijk erkenning?* The final meeting of *Het Indische Gebaar*, The Hague,

Madurodam, 19-1-2009.

44 Smeets & Steijlen, *In Nederland gebleven*, 64-68.

45 Bossenbroek, *De meelstreep*, 246, 587.

46 Steijlen, RMS, 235, Smeets & Steijlen, *In Nederland gebleven*.

47 Whereby the Moluccans lost what had initially been a unique position. This was experienced as 'degrading' (Smeets & Steijlen, *In Nederland gebleven*, 369).

48 Smeets & Steijlen, *In Nederland gebleven*, 371.

49 Steijlen, RMS, 227, 234, 245, Smeets & Steijlen, *In Nederland gebleven*, 375.

50 Meijer, *Indische rekening*, 271.

51 Precisely at this time American war crimes in Vietnam (My Lai,1968) were receiving broad coverage in the news; the parallel was unmistakable.

52 Van Doorn & Hendrix, *Ontsporing van geweld*. See Scagliola, *Last van de oorlog*, 105-115 for a short overview of the debates in the Netherlands about military interventions since 1945.

53 In contrast to the 5,000 Dutch military casualties, 50,000 Indonesians died in 1949 alone. (Van Doorn, *Indische lessen*, 73).

54 Meijer, *In Indië geworteld*, 249-250, Scagliola, *Last van de oorlog*, 38-44.

55 Scagliola, *Last van de oorlog*, 355; also Locher-Scholten, 'Die "Indische Generation"', 75.

56 Scagliola, *Last van de oorlog*, 362.

57 Willems, *De uittocht*, 330 (Derksen), 244 (Robinson), Meijer, *Indische rekening*, 111, 269, 286, 321-322 (ranks), 330 (disloyalty), 315 (solidarity). The notion 'imagined community' is borrowed from Anderson, *Imagined Communities*; in Oostindie, *De parels en de kroon*, it applies to the imagining of the Dutch colonial world.

58 Quoted in Bosma, *Terug uit de koloniën*, 151.

59 Final meeting of *Het Indische Gebaar* (The Indisch Gesture), The Hague, Madurodam, 19-1-2009. Fasseur, 'Het verleden tot last', 134. There is the same need for acknowledgement among the Indisch community in Australia, which in terms of commemoration contexts is also increasingly isolated, Willems has established (*De uittocht*, 318).

60 Bossenbroek, *De meelstreep*, 324-331,

Locher-Scholten, 'From urn to monument', 112-115, Willems, *De uittocht*, 99-101. The monument in Dam Square was not completed until 1956.

61 Bossenbroek, *De meelstreep*, Haan, *Na de ondergang*.

62 Bossenbroek, *De meelstreep*, 531.

63 Captain, *Achter het kawat*, 334.

64 According to statements by the Memorial Foundation 15 August 1945 (*Stichting Herdenking 15 augustus 1945*) (e-mail 5-2-2009) in the years 1999 to 2008 the number of paying attendees at the morning programme fluctuated around 1,250 and around 2,000 at the open memorial ceremony.

65 Indisch Herinneringscentrum Bronbeek, *Nieuwsbrief* August 2008, De Ridder, *Eindelijk erkenning?*, 25 (Stoové). The immediate cause was heart-rending. According to a press release from the Ministry for Health, Welfare and Sport (26-7-2007), the IHC is the 'successor to Indisch House in The Hague, which was forced to close its doors in 2006 due to financial mismanagement'. See Chapter 4 for more about Indisch House; it was intended to be an East Indian pendant to the memorial centres at Westerbork, Amersfoort and Vught. (Captain et al., *De Indische zomer*, 234).

66 Young, *Holocaust memorials*, Van Vree, *In de schaduw van Auschwitz*.

67 The first sentence in the 'Word of Thanks' in Willem's *De uittocht uit Indië* (388) is striking: 'Without Ralph Boekholt, we might have waited many more years before being able to taste this "alternative East Indian history".' Boekholt had previously published a fierce indictment entitled *De staat, dr. L. de Jong en Indië* (1992) on behalf of the *Comité Geschiedkundig Eerherstel Nederlands-Indië* (GENI, Committee for the Historical Rehabilitation of the Netherlands East Indies).

68 The only exception is Peter Keppy. His colleagues are Ulbe Bosma, Remco Raben, Martin Bossenbroek, Hans Meijer, Henk Smeets, Fridus Steijlen, Wim Willems.

69 Oostindie & Klinkers, *Knellende Koninkrijksbanden*, II, 184-185, III, 294. This

comparison continues to be valid, even if we discount the hundreds of millions that were spent on relief for Indisch Dutch in the Netherlands (Meijer, *Indische rekening*, 328).

70 Kerkhof, 'Postkoloniale identiteitspolitiek'; cf. also Van der Zijl's hit novel *Sonny Boy*.

71 Van der Horst, *Wereldoorlog in de West*. The exhibition in the Dutch Resistance Museum in Amsterdam toured to Suriname and the Antilles.

72 Quoted in Van den Oord, *Allochtonen*, 100.

73 L. Mungra, quoted in Oostindie & Klinkers, *Knellende koninkrijksbanden*, II, 141.

74 Bosma, *Terug uit de koloniën*, 165.

75 Van den Oord, *Allochtonen*, Ribbens, Schenk & Eickhoff, *Oorlog* .

76 Both Van den Oord's *Allochtonen* and Ribbens, Schenk & Eickhoff's *Oorlog* sketch a far more balanced picture than was suggested in the press.

4 THE INDIVIDUALIZATION OF IDENTITY

1 Quoted in Willems, *De uittocht*, 243.

2 Renamed the Museum Maluku, or Moluks Museum, in 2008.

3 Van Leeuwen, *Ons Indisch erfgoed*, 225-75.

4 The Indian-Surinamese Sarnami Institute in The Hague is run mainly on donations and by volunteers – the municipality decided to withdraw its funding altogether in 2010.

5 Cooper & Brubaker, 'Identity', argue that views of identity and the use of identity politics are part of social reality, but that researchers can better use such concepts as identification, self-conception or self-understanding, and communality or solidarity. Cf. also Bernstein, 'Identity politics', Sen, *Identity and violence*.

6 Anderson, *Imagined communities*.

7 WRR, *Identificatie met Nederland*; cf. Duyvendak, Engelen & De Haan, *Het bange Nederland*, 17-23.

8 For France see Bruckner, *La tyrannie de la penitence*, Gallo, *Fier d'être français*, Lefeuvre, *Pour en finir*.

9 Willems, *Tjalie Robinson*, 219 passim.

10 Hannerz, *Cultural complexity*, Price, 'The miracle'.

11 As in the five volumes extolling the virtues of multi-ethnic Dutch culture, *Cultuur en migratie in Nederland* (Meijer et al.).

12 Willems, *Tjalie Robinson*, passim; cf. Van Leeuwen, *Ons Indisch erfgoed*, 59 (quote), 51-66 and Surie, 'De gerepatrieerden', 95.

13 Cleintuar, *Indische Nederlanders*, 7.

14 Charles Metselaar, quoted in Captain et al., *De Indische zomer*, 242; cf. Van Leeuwen, *Ons Indisch erfgoed*, 48, 75, 80, Willems, *Tjalie Robinson*, 327.

15 Willems, *Tjalie Robinson*, 198, 213, 315, 541.

16 Foreword in Cleintuar, *Indische Nederlanders*, 3, quoted in Van Leeuwen, *Ons Indisch erfgoed*, 16.

17 Willems, *Tjalie Robinson*, 219, 266, 311, 343 (quote), 372-374, 395, 459, 483-490, 508 (quote).

18 Willems, *Tjalie Robinson*, 480, 484, 488.

19 Quoted in Van Put, 'Den Haag', 172.

20 Cf. also Cleintuar, *Indische Nederlanders*, 54-57.

21 Van Leeuwen, *Ons Indisch erfgoed*, passim.

22 Cleintuar, *Indische Nederlanders*, 5-6.

23 Boekholt, *De staat*, 45, Seriese in *Moesson*, 1-4-1998. Cf. Surie, 'De gerepatrieerden', 45, 77, 91, 95, Seriese, 'Wie dit lees', Van Leeuwen, *Ons Indisch erfgoed*, Willems, *Tjalie Robinson*. In Indisch circles there was much scorn for the pampering of later migrants, cf. Bosma, *Terug uit de koloniën*, 249, 308.

24 De Vries, 'Indisch is een gevoel', 318-319, Willems, *Tjalie Robinson*, 479.

25 Baudet & Brugmans, *Balans van beleid*, 358. Hilversum, a town in the centre of the Netherlands, presently the media centre of the Netherlands, and situated in the rural area 't Gooi, has a long-standing reputation for being home to the rich and famous.

26 Surie, 'De gerepatrieerden', 79; also 77, 85, 91, 99.

27 Poldi Saueressig, respectively Lilian Ducelle, quoted in Captain et al., *Indische zomer*, 118, 120. Cf. Van Leeuwen, *Ons Indisch erfgoed*, 91.

28 Van Leeuwen, *Ons Indisch erfgoed*, 225-275, 282.

29 'Hollands' was understood as far more negative and ethnocentric than the neutral word 'Dutch', De Vries notes in 'Indisch is een gevoel', 184-203; cf. Van Put, 'Den Haag', 174, Willems, *Tjalie Robinson*, 74. A parallel is the qualms migrants to the United Kingdom had with the designation 'English' instead of 'British' (Commission for Racial Equality, *Citizenship and belonging*, 7-8).

30 Van Leeuwen, *Ons Indisch erfgoed*, 195-199.

31 Van Leeuwen, *Ons Indisch erfgoed*, 101, 142-145, 151-152.

32 Van Leeuwen, *Ons Indisch erfgoed*, 20, 346. Tjalie Robinson also liked to use the metaphor of Indisch cuisine, cf. Willems, *Tjalie Robinson*, 284.

33 Koning, *De Pasar Malam*, 12, 41 and passim.

34 Captain, *Achter het kawat*, 359.

35 This image is confirmed by our own research; Oostindie & Steijlen, 'Zestig jaar'.

36 Visitor quoted in Koning, *De Pasar Malam*, 11; De Vries, 'Indisch is een gevoel', 185-209, 317-363. Willems, *De uittocht*, 189-192 presents a range of examples of negative stereotypes. The 'Indische portretten' in Captain, *De Indische zomer*, 239-279, suggest more continuity.

37 De Vries, 'Indisch is een gevoel', 363, Willems, *Tjalie Robinson*; cf. Seriese, 'Wie dit lees', 200-204. A striking observation in a recent survey of contemporary 'Indisch' artists: 'contemporary artists often do not know which other artists are Indisch' (Van Put, 'Den Haag', 159).

38 Oostindie & Steijlen, 'Zestig jaar'.

39 Lucky Oudkerk Pool, quoted in Van Leeuwen, *Ons Indisch erfgoed*, 191.

40 *Moesson*, 15-6-1990 (interview M.F. Mual), 1-2-2000 (interview Wim Manuhutu); e-mail Manuhutu, 17-6-2009.

41 Steijlen, *RMS*.

42 Smeets & Steijlen, *In Nederland gebleven*, 283-286.

43 Oostindie & Steijlen, 'Zestig jaar'. Recently, there has also been an orientation towards Melanesian, rather than Indonesian, as the 'roots culture', (*Wereldjournalisten.nl* 17-6-2009).

44 Steijlen, *RMS*, 186-187, Smeets & Steijlen, *In Nederland gebleven*, 374-376.

45 Quoted in Smeets & Steijlen, *In Nederland gebleven*, 358; cf. 359.

46 *Marinjo*, February/March 2009, 7.

47 Oostindie, *Paradise overseas*, Chs 3 and 5.
48 Sansone, *Schitteren in de schaduw*, Bijnaar, *Kasmoni*.
49 Van Kempen, 'De Nederlandse taal', Hoving, 'Nat hout'.
50 Sansone, 'The internalization of black culture' and 'The making of Suriland'.
51 Helder & Gravenberch, *Sinterklaasje*, Helsloot, 'Het feest'. The character of *Zwarte Piet* is traditionally blacked-up and dressed as a medieval page. He accompanies St Nicholas, *Sinterklaas*, to distribute presents and sweets to children on the feast of St Nicholas.
52 *de Volkskrant*, 24-4-2006. Sculptor Jikke van Loon, supported by members of De Kom's family, retorted that she had wanted to emphasize the strength of the freedom fighter. An interesting detail: the independence of Suriname was celebrated in that very same square, then still called Bijlmerplein, on 25 November, 1975.
53 Choenni & Adhin, *Hindostanen*, 9, Choenni, *Madad Sahára Saháyta*, 131.
54 *Lalla Rookh* 17/1 (1992), 18/1 (1993), 18/3 (1993); Choenni & Adhin, *Hindostanen*,
55 Choenni, *Madad Sahára Saháyta*, 15-19.
56 Koopmans & Statham ('How national citizenship shapes transnationalism', 221) argue that Hinduism leads to almost no political claims; cf. Levitt & Jaworsky, 'Transnational migration', 140. The examples that Thandi gives of recent acts carried out by militant British Hindus ('Postcolonial migrants in Britain') prompt more subtle distinctions.
57 Bal & Sinha-Kerkhof, 'Een Hindostaanse diaspora', 249, Boedhoe, 'Hindostaanse moslims', 112, Mahawat Khan, 'Hindostaanse moslims', 135. Cf. Grasveld & Breunissen, 'Ik ben een Javaan', 99.
58 Lucassen & Laarman, 'Immigration'. Choenni points to a growth in the number of mixed relationships among Indian Surinamese (Adhin & Choenni, *Hindostanen*, 61, however, see 88).
59 Ramsoedh, 'Surinaamse hindoes en moslims', 141, 144, 146.
60 Oostindie, 'Slavernij, canon en trauma', 14-18. Their low level of political participation is also explained on the same grounds

(Fennema & Tillie, 'Civic communities', 36-37; however, see Sharpe, 'Globalization and migration', which looks for an explanation in exclusion in the Netherlands). Cf. also Amsterdam City Archives, transcript of interview with Roy Groenberg (2004), 6-7, 9 on the gulf between the two groups.
61 More radical definitions also exist, in which blackness is compulsory (Oostindie, *Paradise overseas*, 127). Here I am leaving aside the small group of Antilleans from the Windward Islands; also Aruba and the strong rhetoric of difference that shapes Aruban identity in contrast to Curaçao. (Alofs & Merkies, *Ken ta arubiano*, Oostindie, *Paradise overseas*, 123-129).
62 Amesz, Steijlen & Vermeulen, *Andere Antillianen*, Broek, *De terreur van schaamte*, Van Hulst, *Morgen bloeit het diabaas*, Van San, *Stelen en slikken*.
63 Alferink, 'Festivals'.
64 Oostindie & Steijlen, 'Zestig jaar'.
65 Cf. Van Amersfoort, 'De Ambonezen', 132, 139. Another disturbing parallel is with the Puerto Rican-American population group, cf. Duany, 'La nación en la diaspora'.
66 Blom, 'Jaren van tucht en ascese'.
67 There is no political support for paying compensation for the early phases of colonialism, in the East or West, but neither has there been a widely articulated demand for this.
68 Kossmann, 'Verdwijnt de Nederlandse identiteit?', 68.
69 Koch & Scheffer, *Het nut van Nederland*, Scheffer, 'Land zonder spiegel', 13, 29.
70 Oostindie, *Paradise overseas*, 158-179.
71 Scheffer, *Het land van aankomst*. Scheffer was himself 'ambassador' for the monument to commemorate slavery.
72 Ad Verdonk, Rita's father, was a soldier in the Netherlands East Indies and did not return to the Netherlands until 1952. Wilders' mother was born in Soekaboemi, Netherlands East Indies (now Sukabumi, Indonesia).
73 Cf. Cooper & Brubaker, 'Identity', 87, Polletta & Jasper, 'Collective identity'. The Dutch approach, which initially ignored the existence of an Indisch identity, as well

as negligence (Von Winckelman & Willems, 'Zwijgend inburgeren', 180) can also be seen as an unintentional stimulus for the formation of communities.

74 Surinamese-Dutch Muslims are hardly ever distinguished in this way.

75 Koopmans & Statham, 'How national citizenship shapes transnationalism', 219-220.

76 Cf. Sanders, 'Ethnic boundaries', 348-349.

5 IMAGINING COLONIALISM

1 Balkenende in Lower House of the Dutch parliament, 28-9-2006. 'I don't understand why you're all being so negative and unpleasant. Let's just be happy with each other. Let's just say "the Netherlands can do it" again: that VOC mentality. Look across our borders. Dynamism! Don't you think?'

2 Research in the magazines *Marinjo* and *Moesson* (until end 2006) generated no response. The main Indisch web sites were equally blank, or mentioned it once in passing in an article on a different subject.

3 Stichting Eer en Herstel (Honour and Restoration Foundation), letter 30-9-2008 (www.stichtingeerenherstel.nl). According to the press around 200 people walked in the demonstration by 15 organizations three days earlier. The 'noisy procession' began at the slavery monument in Ooster-park and ended at the NiNsee, which was accused of giving a flimsy response. MP Balkenende said he deeply regretted the misunderstanding: 'I never intended to say anything in favour of slavery'. (Radio Netherlands Worldwide, Caribbean desk, 27-10-2008).

4 Van Doorn, *De laatste eeuw*, 11, 9.

5 On the WIC, see Den Heijer, *Geschiedenis van de WIC*. Also compare Oostindie, Paradise Overseas, 1-20.

6 Radio Netherlands Worldwide, Caribbean desk, 27-10-2008.

7 On the VOC see Gaastra, *Geschiedenis van de VOC*.

8 See Raben, 'De VOC', Rietbergen, 'De VOC herdenken?', Bruijn et al., *Roemrucht verleden*, Van Stipriaan & Bal, 'De VOC is een geloof'.

9 Oostindie, 'Squaring the circle', 136, 144-151.

10 Sukarno, *Indonesië klaagt aan!*, 15, Andi Lolo, *De VOC in de Indonesische archipel*, Oostindie, 'Squaring the circle', 146-149.

11 Trouillot, *Silencing the Past*, 138. Sanjay Subrahmanyan, debate University of Amsterdam, 24-6-2002.

12 The KITLV produced a web site about the VOC with a grant from the foundation. As a participant in this project and in my role as director of the institute, I organized a debate about the 'darker sides' in De Balie, Amsterdam, 18-4-2002. Cf. Oostindie, 'Squaring the circle', 153-155. The Rijks-museum had a similar experience, cf. Kees Zandvliet's article in the daily NRC Handels-blad, 12-12-2007.

13 *Marinjo*, November 2001, 8-9, Moesson, 1-5-2002, 1-2-2003, www.blimbing.nl, www.dlm.org/voc.

14 Van Deventer, 'Een ereschuld'.

15 Lecture 8-12-1949, quoted in Fasseur, 'Het verleden tot last', 138-139. Van Doorn, *De laatste eeuw*.

16 Van Helsdingen, *Daar wèrd wat groots verricht...*

17 For a more detailed discussion of the rediscovery of Indisch history, see Van Doorn, *De laatste eeuw*, 11-17 and *Indische lessen*, 63-77, Fasseur, *De weg naar het paradijs*, 252-273, Houben, 'Koloniale geschiedenis', Locher-Scholten, 'Die "Indische Generation"'.

18 Boekholt, *De staat*, 106-107 (initiators), 30, 28, 29 (quotes).

19 Boekholt, *De staat*, 10, Bossenbroek, *De meelstreep*, 533 (Ducelle). Cf. Van Doorn, *Indische lessen*, 75, Willems, *Uittocht uit Indië*, 339.

20 Meijer, *Oostindisch doof*.

21 Vanvugt, *De maagd en de soldaat* (The virgin and the soldier).

22 Geemert, *Monument Indië Nederland*, 62 (quote), De Lange, 'Een spiegelende opper-vlakte', 64-79, Oostindie, *De parels*, 41-43, 105, Vanvugt, *De maagd*, 90-94. The district council commissioned the Clingendael Institute of International Relations to carry out research (Aspeslagh, *Gewenst en niet geliefd*). The opening lines are telling: 'In the Netherlands a discussion has begun

about the way we treat our past. The outcome is uncertain. However, the positive point is the willingness to open the darker pages of our history.'

23 Historian Tom van der Geugten, himself of Indisch descent, published a large number of articles in *Moesson* in 1991-1993 and in 1999 about the amount of room that was cleared in history education for the Indisch Dutch. This space gradually increased, but it did not happen by itself: 'If Indisch Dutch want to receive (more of) the attention they deserve, they will have to draw more attention to themselves and their past. They must claim that attention.' (*Moesson*, 15-10-1991). This is precisely what happened with the to-do surrounding L. de Jong's writing of history. See also Van der Geugten, 'Het beeld'.

24 De Lange, '*Een spiegelende oppervlakte*', 80-101. For criticism of the 2001 school final exams see Sutherland, 'Een ontmoeting' and of the 2007 exams see Locher-Scholten & Raben, 'Verengd verleden', further Oostindie & Schulte Nordholt, *NRC Handelsblad*, 15-8-2005 and 'Nederland en zijn koloniale verleden'.

25 Bosma & Raben, *De oude Indische wereld*, Meijer, *In Indië geworteld*, passim; cf. also passages in Baudet & Brugmans, *Balans van beleid*, 83-84, 93-98, 109, 116-118, 351.

26 Kraak, Ellemers & Wittermans, *De repatrianten*, 372, Captain, *Achter het kawat*, 333-334, 346-352, Willems, *De uittocht uit Indië*, 57, 239-245.

27 For instance, as revealed in Willems, *De uittocht*, Meijer, *Indische rekening*, Jones, *Tussen onderdanen*, Schuster, *Poortwachters*.

28 Van Amersfoort, 'De Ambonezen', 111, Smeets & Steijlen, *In Nederland gebleven*, 224-225, Steijlen, *RMS*.

29 Van Klinken, 'Nationale helden', Schulte Nordholt, *De-colonising Indonesian Historiography*.

30 Sartono Kartodirdjo, *Indonesian Historiography*, Klooster, *Indonesiërs*, Oostindie,'Squaring the circle', 146-148, Schulte Nordholt, 'A genealogy of violence', 40-42, 52-54. Information on the current situation based on comments by Jaap Erkelens, Henk Schulte Nordholt and Roger Tol.

31 Van Doorn, *De laatste eeuw*, 15.

32 Walraven, Brieven, 882, cf. Haasse, *Krassen op een rots*.

33 Oostindie, *Paradijs overzee*, 11-38.

34 Quoted in Oostindie & Klinkers, *Knellende koninkrijksbanden*, I, 17; cf. Oostindie, *Paradise overseas*, 80-83.

35 Gowricharn, 'Ethnicity', Meel, 'Towards a typology', Oostindie, *Paradise overseas*, 122-25.

36 The following is largely derived from my earlier publications, 'Slavernij, canon en trauma', 'The slippery paths', 'History brought home' and 'Public memories'. More extensive references may be found here.

37 These are rough estimates. Of the c. 335,000 Surinamese, slightly more than half are probably predominantly of African origin, while of the 153,000 Antilleans and Arubans the lion's share are of African origin.

38 This comparative study has recently got under way; see Van Welie, 'Patterns of slave trading'. The Dutch share of the Atlantic slave trade was in the order of more than 550,000 Africans, 5% of the total of 12 million. The abolition of the slave trade was imposed by the British in 1807. With the end of slavery itself in 1863, the Netherlands were late.

39 De Kom, *Wij slaven*; see also Van Kempen, *Geschiedenis*, 599-605, Oostindie, 'Wij slaven'.

40 De Kom, *Wij slaven*, 49-50, 71.

41 Van Kempen, 'Paramaribo', Meel, 'Towards a typology', 271, Oostindie, *De parels en de kroon*, 29-40, Van Stipriaan, 'July 1', Willemsen, *Dagen van gejuich*.

42 Bacilio, 'Ontketend?'.

43 Bosma, *Terug uit de koloniën*, 88-89, cf. Jansen van Galen, *Hetenachtsdroom*, 98.

44 Martinus Arion, 'Een "beau geste"' [*De Groene Amsterdammer*, 11-3-1998], Jones, 'Het belang van een gedenkteken', Kardux, 'Monuments', Oostindie, *Het verleden*, Van Stipriaan, 'The long road'.

45 The LPS and later NiNsee attempt to correct the dominance of the Afro-Surinamese, but this proved not easy to do. Following the death of the first director of the NiNsee, the Surinamese Glenn Willemsen, a successor

was deliberately chosen who came from (partly) Antillean descent, Artwell Cain.

46 An illustration: Biekman was a fellow member of the liberal-democratic party D66 with the minister responsible, Roger van Boxtel, whose director of Minorities Policy was Afro-Surinamese member of the PvdA labour party, Hugo Fernandes Mendes.

47 In 2000 this was 7%, 16% in 2004 and 24% in 2008; in that last year there was no episode that was mentioned more often (*De Geschiedeniskrant*, 26-3-2008). Oostindie, *Paradise overseas*, 158-62.

48 'In the modern relations within the Kingdom feelings of guilt or expectations of special treatment because of the past can – and will – no longer play a part', State Secretary Ank Bijleveld (CDA), responsible for Kingdom relations, speaking at the official commemoration on 1 July, 2009 in Amsterdam.

49 The LPS (*Landelijk Platform Slavernij-verleden*, National Platform Slavery Past) was thus also maneuvered from a distance, including through the appointment of an ethnically mixed, but primarily more moderate Committee of Recommendation. This committee was chaired by the prominent Afro-Curaçaoan engineer Gilbert Wawoe, a former director of Shell and at the time member of the Council of State. I was one of the six members of the committee, which had a difficult relationship with the LPS.

50 Debate Amsterdam, IISG, 3-3-2009.

51 Oostindie, 'Slavernij, canon en trauma', 14-18, Withuis, *Erkenning*, 10, 213-214.

52 Fortuyn, *De puinhopen*, 158. Speech by Rita Verdonk at the launch of her political movement *Trots op Nederland* (Proud of the Netherlands), Amsterdam, 3-4-2008.

53 Van Stipriaan, 'Between Diaspora', 169; cf. my comments in Oostindie, 'History brought home', 314-318. My Leiden colleague P.C. Emmer, *De Nederlandse slavenhandel*, often plays the role of the politically incorrect.

54 For the Netherlands see Van Stipriaan et al., *Op zoek naar de stilte*.

55 Blom, *In de ban*, 9-29, 155-179, Oostindie,

'Slavernij, canon, trauma', 20-21 and 'History brought home', 326-327.

56 This paragraph is for a large part based on 'Slavernij, canon en trauma', 11-14.

57 Grever & Ribbens, 'De historische canon', 4; for highly critical views see also Grever et al., *Controverses*, Davids, *Global history*, Lucassen & Willems, *Gelijkheid en onbehagen*, 73-74 and passim, and Duyvendak, Engelen & De Haan, *Het bange Nederland*, 46, 107-113. The tone and harshness of the criticism of the idea and its execution by these authors are extremely different; what they share is an aversion to narrow (and fundamentally often mythical) nationalistic frameworks for the canon.

58 *entoen.nu* A, 24-27.

59 Byvanck & Schilp, *Het Nationaal Historisch Museum*, 31. However, they too dedicate much space to colonial and postcolonial history (*26, 33, 39, 49*).

60 *entoen.nu en verder*, 28-30. Grever et al., *Controverses*, 107 speak of the 'defining power' of the commission.

61 *Plaatsen van herinnering* (Amsterdam 2005-2006), Grever et al., *Controverses*, 110.

6 TRANSNATIONALISM: A TURNING TIDE?

1 This chapter is partly based on conversations and correspondence with Wim Manuhutu and Yayah Siegers-Samaniri (Moluccas), Hans Breeveld, Ruben Gowricharn, Maurits Hassankhan, Winston Kout, Hans Lim A Po and Marten Schalkwijk (Suriname), Carel de Haseth and Gilbert Wawoe (Netherlands Antilles) in the spring of 2009; furthermore, on a survey held between March and May 2009 among representatives of postcolonial groups and organizations (Oostindie & Steijlen, 'Zestig jaar').

2 Levitt & Jaworsky, 'Transnational migration', 131-133, 146, Bloemraad, Korteweg & Yurdakul, 'Citizenship', 167. Alba & Nee, *Remaking the American mainstream*, is a recent authoritative argument that migration still leads to assimilation and thereby also to a decrease in transnationalism.

3 Basch, Glick Schiller & Szanton-Blanc, *Nations unbound*, 6, Glick Schiller, 'The centrality'; cf. Snel, Engersen & Leerkens, 'Transnational involvement', 286.

4 Koopmans & Statham, 'How national citizenship'; cf. Snel, Engersen & Leerkens, 'Transnational involvement', 287, Nell, *Transnational migrant politics*, 31.

5 There was equally little room for Papuan nationalism, which was kept alive in the Netherlands by a small group around Nicolaas Jouwe.

6 Of course, there were (and are) exceptions. See Van de Loo, *Familie gebleven*, Steijlen, 'Het Gebaar'.

7 For colonial language politics in the Dutch East Indies, see Groeneboer, *Weg tot het westen*.

8 For the policy in Suriname see Gobardhan-Rambocus, *Onderwijs als sleutel*; for the significance of language in Surinamese and Antillean identity see Oostindie, *Paradise overseas*, 128-129.

9 English is the lingua franca on the Windward Islands; in view of the small size of the Windward community in the Netherlands, this language issue is not discussed here. For Papiamentu, see Van Putte, *Dede pikina*.

10 Ridder, *Eindelijk erkenning?*, 61, 92-93, 97, 110.

11 Ridder, *Eindelijk erkenning?*, 78, 99. More than 90 per cent of payments to individuals were issued in the Netherlands (26, 56-57).

12 Oostindie & Steijlen, 'Zestig jaar'.

13 Steijlen, 'Molukkers in Nederland', Van Heelsum, *Migrantenorganisaties*, I, 64; IISG-database on Postcolonial migrants, see Bosma & Alferink, 'Multiculturalism and settlement'; cf. Oostindie & Steijlen, 'Zestig jaar'.

14 Gowricharn, 'Moral capital', 615, Unger & Siegel, *The Netherlands-Suriname corridor*, 21, 118. The proportion of Surinamese households who say they send money to the country of origin (35 per cent) was higher than for Turks, Moroccans and Antilleans and the average amount sent is higher (€225); *CBS Webmagazine*, 20-5-2009. Further, there is still a sizeable, perhaps even larger, monetary circuit attached to

the drugs trade, estimated in 2006 by Unger & Siegel, *The Netherlands-Suriname corridor*, 118, to be worth approx. 150 million euros; we may assume that this is, relatively speaking, less aimed at poorer Surinamese.

15 Oostindie, *Paradijs overzee*, 345-347, Snel, Engersen & Leerkens, 'Transnational involvement', 291-292; Oostindie & Steijlen, 'Zestig jaar'. The number of Antillean households that said they sent money to their country of origin was 16 per cent, the average amount sent was 105 euros; *CBS Webmagazine*, 20-5-2009.

16 *Kambio; Portabos independiente antijano*, 1965-1966.

17 De Kom, *Wij slaven*, 164.

18 Poeze, *In het land van de overheerser*.

19 Lijphart, *The trauma of decolonization*, 285-290.

20 Fasseur, *Indischgasten*, 248-270, Schulte Nordholt, *Indonesië*, 253-257; Koning, *De Pasar Malam*, 180; see also Ch. 4.

21 *NRC Handelsblad*, 9-12-2008, 15-1-2009, 24-2-2009; the force behind the rediscovery of Rawagede is the mixed Indonesian-Dutch foundation Committee of Dutch Debts of Honour, www.kukb.nl/new/.

22 Steijlen, RMS, 226-228, also Smeets & Steijlen, *In Nederland gebleven*, 340.

23 Steijlen, Kerusuhan and 'Molukkers in Nederland'. Wattilete, interviewed in *Nederlands Dagblad*, 17-8-2009. As late as 1990 M.F. Mual, chair of the Moluccan welfare organization *Inspraakorgaan Welzijn Molukkers* declared, 'We were forced to come here. [...] We want to return to the Moluccas. But, the political situation makes this impossible [...] *Badan Pesatuan* is a liberation movement that strives for Moluccan self-determination. Only when this has been achieved can there be peace.' (Moesson, 15-6-1990).

24 A distinctive feature of this was that the Ministry of Foreign Affairs in 2000 commissioned research into the winding up of the handover of New Guinea to Indonesia, but former Foreign Minister, Maxime Verhagen (CDA), refused to accept the report for diplomatic reasons. Drooglever, *Een daad van vrije keuze*, Meijer, 'Geschiedenis is nu eenmaal altijd politiek'.

25 Steijlen, *Kerusuhan*, 27-30, Smeets & Steijlen, *In Nederland gebleven*, 340-354, NOS *Journaal* (national TV news), 25-4-2008. It is typical that it was not the Dutch Minister for Foreign Affairs, but his colleague the minister responsible for Urban and Integration Policy, Roger van Boxtel (D66) who, according to his own report, took part in these vehement discussions (personal statement, 14-10-2006).

26 Oostindie and Maduro, *In het land van de overheerser*, 54-55, 66-76, 80-85, 112-113, Meel, *Tussen autonomie en onafhankelijkheid*, 175-229, Marshall, *Ontstaan en ontwikkeling*.

27 Arron, quoted in *Elsevier*, 1-6-1974; cf. Jansen van Galen, *Kapotte plantage*, 142, Oostindie & Klinkers, *Knellende koninkrijksbanden*, 11, 249. *Elseviers Weekblad*, 21-10-1978 and next in *Famiri*, 2/11 & 12 (1978), 6. Lachmon, quoted in Jones, *Tussen onderdanen*, 248-249.

28 Hence, Corly Verlooghen wrote in 1978 in *Famiri*: 'Compatriots! We must have no illusions about the dream of remigration. We must assume that most Surinamese in the Netherlands will live and die here. [...] All the fine talk, from whichever side it comes, is delusional.' This provoked furious reactions. The editors of *Famiri* distanced themselves from this statement responding, 'If you regard remigration to be a dream it can mean only one thing: that I have to integrate. If you choose that sad fate, go and get yourself converted by the CRM [former Ministry for Culture, Recreation and Welfare]. But, we should not assume this, neither will we assume this! We assume that neocolonialism in our Fatherland will be destroyed and that we will return to Suriname.' *Famiri*, 2/3 (1978) 10, 2/4 (1978), 5. Cf. Aisa Samachar 3/6 (1977) 5-6, 4/2 (1978) 11-13, 6/4 (1980) 3-4, 10/9 (1984) 6-7, Bosma, *Terug uit de koloniën*,164-165.

29 The irony is that the Surinamese exodus even became a significant force behind the increasing indulgence of the Dutch government: the cabinet under Prime Minister Den Uyl was prepared to make many concessions in order to achieve a rapid transfer of sovereignty and thereby bring an end to the migration.

30 Jones, *Tussen onderdanen*, 255-256.

31 Thus, against the wishes of prominent Surinamese in the Netherlands and *Weekkrant Suriname*, the government in Paramaribo rapidly rejected the possibility of a 'Commonwealth' relationship with the Netherlands; see *de Volkskrant* 29-9-1993, Jansen van Galen, 'De PvdA', 91-93, Oostindie & Klinkers, *Knellende koninkrijksrelaties*, 111, 177, *Gemenebest-relatie*; cf. also Nell 132-139.

32 This was well reported in the *Weekkrant Suriname*, in particular around the date of the revolution (25 February 1980) and the December Murders (8 December 1982).

33 Cf. Nell, *Transnational migrant politics*, 91-92.

34 From 16 to 5 per cent; the Afro-Surinamese focus on Suriname was somewhat higher at 24 per cent in 1980 and 10 per cent in 2000; Vermeulen & Van Heelsum, 'Group- or host state-related', table 2. Researcher Liza Nell describes Surinamese transnational politics as weak compared with the political activities of Turkish and Kurdish organizations (Nell, *Transnational migrant politics*, 8, 82-83, 118).

35 Bosma, *Terug uit de koloniën*, 217-218. Based on the annual report on the independence celebrations published in the *Weekkrant Suriname*.

36 Sedney, *De toekomst*, 159; cf. Nell, *Transnational migrant politics*, 92-95, 126-128, 142-143. A recent move by the Surinamese Dutch Romeo Hoost and others to indict the Dutch state for involvement in the 1980 military coup in Suriname was dismissed in Surinamese circles, also because it would compromise Surinamese politicians (NRC *Handelsblad*, 23-3-2009).

37 Bosma, *Terug uit de koloniën*, 116; cf. the interviews with Stanley Brown, Jeanne Henriquez, Harold Hollander and Adriaan Moen in Oostindie, *Curaçao 30 mei 1969*.

38 Oostindie & Steijlen, 'Zestig jaar'.

39 Cohen, 'Cultural diaspora', Koopmans & Statham, 'How national citizenship', 201-202.

40 Willems, *Tjalie Robinson*, 542.

41 Steijlen, 'Molukkers in Nederland', 244, 248-250, in this respect extends the

comparison with the bilateral Surinamese 'hanging over the ocean' (borrowed from Livio Sansone) rather too far.

42 Smeets & Steijlen, *In Nederland gebleven*, 355.

43 Cf. *Aisa Samachar* 3/9 (1977) 16, 4/5 (1978) 13, 5/1 (1979) 19, *Lalla Rookh* 10/5 (1985) 22.

44 Gowricharn, 'Bollywood in diaspora', 'De duurzaamheid' and 'Introduction', 11-12, Nell, *Transnational migrant politics*, 83-90.

45 Snel, Engbersen & Leerkens, 'Transnational involvement', 294-295.

46 Oostindie & Steijlen, 'Zestig jaar'.

47 Cf. Smeets & Steijlen, *In Nederland gebleven*, 365-367 and passim about group pressure around the ideal of the RMS.

7 AN INTERNATIONAL PERSPECTIVE

1 Cf. Bosma, Lucassen & Oostindie, *Postcolonial migrations and identity politics*.

2 Judt, *Postwar*, 8, 826; see also 763, 800.

3 Smith, 'Introduction', 32.

4 For the countries discussed here, the first category was larger than the second, in the order of 3.3 million to 4 million, as opposed to 2.1 to 2.8 million (Smith, 'Introduction',32).

5 The following is based on Bade et al., *Enzyklopädie*, and the literature given paragraph by paragraph. See also Clark Hine, Keaton & Small, *Black Europe*. For France, see Cohen, 'Postcolonial immigration', Favell, *Philosophies of integration*, Hargreaves, *Multi-ethnic France*, and Noiriel, *Immigration*.

6 De Gaulle spoke these words in 1941, but this statement was immortalized not that long ago on his statue on the Champs Élysées.

7 Weil, *Liberté*, 23-90.

8 The total number repatriated from all the French colonies between 1954 and 1964 is estimated to be in the order of 1.8 million (Bade et al., *Enzyklopädie*, 853). Among the pieds noirs were approx. 120,000 Jewish colonists (Cohen, 'Pied-noir memory', 134).

9 Weil, *Liberté*, 92-98.

10 For these debates see Favell, *Philosophies of integration*, Hargreaves, *Multi-ethnic France*, Hargreaves & McKinney, 'Introduction'.

11 Sarkozy was born in France to a Hungarian father and a French mother whose family had a long history of migration.

12 Cf. Blanchard et al., *La fracture coloniale*, Bruckner, *La tyrannie de la penitence*, Coquio, *Retour du colonial?*, Gallo, *Fier d'être français*, Hargreaves, *Multi-ethnic France*, Lefeuvre, *Pour en finir avec la répentence coloniale*, Stora, *Les guerres des mémoires* and *Les guerres sans fin*, Weil, *Liberté*; for a more extensive discussion see Oostindie, 'Koloniën, migranten en Franse *grandeur*'.

13 Hargreaves, *Immigration*, 31.

14 Hargreaves, *Immigration*, as early as in 1995; he also refers to this in Hargreaves, *Multi-ethnic France*, 1; also MacMaster, *Colonial migrants*, 207.

15 There was perhaps a 'playful' element of competition between different neighbourhoods (*cités*): who could provoke the police best, who could create the biggest riot, who could get the most TV coverage? Slooter, 'Cité dreams', 61.

16 Beriss, *Black skins*, p. 31-33, 128; Hargreaves, *Multi-ethnic France*, 111-120.

17 Beriss, *Black skins*; Browne, *Creole economics*, 98-100; Giraud, 'Antilles in France' and 'Colonial racism'; Marie, 'Antillais en France', Tardieu, *Les Antillais à Paris*.

18 See in particular the work of Stora, such as 'Quand une mémoire', *Guerre des mémoires* and *Les guerres sans fin*. Cf. Judt, *Postwar*, 289.

19 Colley, *Britons*, also names Protestantism and the constant struggle with France as crucial elements in the 'invention of Britishness'. Successful colonialism explicitly belonged to this national identity. Cf. Winder, *Bloody foreigners*, 348-356.

20 Commission for Racial Equality, *Citizenship and belonging*, 7-8.

21 Estimate in Smith, *Europe's invisible migrants*, 32. Miège & Dubois, 'Introduction', 18, estimate between 500,000 and 700,000. The literature pays little attention to the possible significance of these repatriations.

22 Paul, *Whitewashing Britain*, 132-133, 178 en passim, argues that the gradually more restrictive laws were an expression of an

elitist racism which created fertile ground for racism in broader layers of the population. Hansen, *Citizenship*, 245-253 argues against this, on good grounds. Spencer, *British immigration policy*, 150-151, stresses the fear of (more) race riots as the motive behind restrictive legislation.

23 Cf. Commission on Integration and Cohesion, *Our shared future*, 106.

24 Up until the mid 1970s, the West Indian population was as large as that from former British India; thereafter the latter group grew more rapidly (Byron & Condon, *Migration*, Spencer, *British immigration policy*, 130, Peach, 'Demographics', 168-169).

25 Bade et al., *Enzyklopädie*, 841, 1110.

26 Too moderate, according to critics, cf. Back et al., 'New Labour's white heart'.

27 Winder, *Bloody foreigners*, 332, Thandi, 'Postcolonial migrants in Britain'.

28 See, for example, Parekh, *Report*.

29 Even Trevor Phillips, of Guyanese heritage and for many years head of the Commission for Racial Equality, expressed views critical of British multiculturalism ('sleepwalking into segregation'). Amartya Sen, *Identity and violence*, 152-165, is more optimistic in his analysis, which is also in part based on personal experience.

30 Judt, *Postwar*, 160-161, 301.

31 Hall, *Het minimale zelf*, Gilroy, *The Black Atlantic* and *After Empire*; Cannadine, *Ornamentalism*, Ferguson, *Empire*.

32 See, for instance, Parekh, *Report*; Runnymede, *Realising*; Commission for Racial Equality, *Citizenship*. These reports again led to a flood of publications in both the British media and academia; cf. Winder, *Bloody foreigners*, 364-366.

33 Kowaleski Wallace, *British slave trade*, Oldfield, 'Chords of freedom' and *Way forward*.

34 'Speech on multiculturalism and integration', Tony Blair, 8-12-2008. Illustrative of the shifting views is that in 2009 the CRE merged with two other commissions to form the Equality and Human Rights Commission. The EHRC has a much broader mandate (gender, disability etc.) and certainly no longer bears a label of postcolonialism.

35 Speech on the first UK Veteran's Day (now Armed Forces' Day), 27-6-2006, quoted in the *The Herald*.

36 'Our relative stability as a nation is reflected in a relative lack of precision about what we mean to be British. [...] There is room to celebrate multiple and different identities, but none of these identities should take precedence over the core democratic values that define what it means to be British.' *Governance*, 53, 57.

37 Gilroy, *After Empire*; Back et al, 'New Labour's white heart', 447, spoke of a 'melancholic desire for an imperial past'.

38 Ali, Kalra & Sayyid, *A postcolonial people*; Fisher, Lahiri & Thandi, *South-Asian history*, 181, 183, 204; Modood, 'Politics'; Thandi, 'Postcolonial migrants in Britain'. See Peach, 'Demographics', for a concise comparison of demographic profiles.

39 Commission, *Our shared future*.

40 *Estatísticas demográficas 2007*.

41 Lubkemann, 'Race'; Ovalle-Bahamón, 'The wrinkles'; *Haagse Post* 46, 15-11-1975.

42 Vale de Almeida, *Earth-colored sea*, 107-114; cf. also Marques, 'Postcolonial migrants in Portugal'.

43 *The way forward*; Walvin, 'Commemorating abolitionism'; Hall, 'Feature'.

44 Kowaleski Wallace, *The British slave trade*; Oldfield, 'Chords of freedom'; cf. Oostindie, 'Public memories'.

45 *Reflecting on the past*, paragraphs 7 and 13.

46 *Codes noires* passed into law in 2001.

47 Official gestures in the *départments d'outre-mer* themselves, considering the delicate postcolonial status, are no less sensitive and always bear the risk, in the words of Richard Price, of 'banalization and tokenism' ('Monuments', 62).

48 Speech by Sarkozy in Dakar, 26-7-2007, quoted in Coquio, *Retour du colonial?*, 16-17. During his time in office President Chirac displayed a perhaps paternalistic engagement with (Francophone) Africa which, although undoubtedly perfectly compatible with France's interests, was nonetheless sincere. This is born out by his *grande oeuvre*, the museum Quai Branly; Sally Price, *Paris primitive*, gives an at times hilarious analysis of the French debate

about 'the house that Jacques built'.

49 Beriss, *Black skins*, 51-54, 63, Hargreaves, *Multi-ethnic France*, 129-131, Vergès, *La mémoire enchaînée*; cf. Oostindie, 'Koloniën' and 'Public memories'.

50 Pétré-Grenouillé, *Les traites négrières* and www.clionautes.org/spip.php?article925. Bruckner, *La tyrannie*, Gallo, *Fier d'être francais*, Lefeuvre, *Pour en finir*.

51 Nora, Pierre & Francoise Chandernagor, *Liberté pour l'histoire*.

52 Stora, *Les guerres des mémoires* 2007: 71-75, Weil, *Liberté*, 17-22, 165-209.

53 The United Kingdom chose 23 August, the date set by UNESCO as the International Day for the Remembrance of the Slave Trade and its Abolition. The Netherlands stuck to 1 July, which has been the Dutch Day of Emancipation since 1863.

54 Oostindie, 'Commemorating the VOC', 156-158 and 'Public memories'.

55 Salmon, 'Les retours'. The study of Belgian Congo, *King Leopold's ghost*, which is as famous as it is controversial, was written by the American Hochschildt. Fifty years after the independence of Congo however, David van Reybroeck's very critical study *Congo* was widely acclaimed.

56 On 1-1-2006 the foreign population of Spain totaled more than 4 million, 2.3 million of whom were from Europe, 1.5 million from (primarily Spanish-) America, and 690,000 from Africa (mainly Morocco) (Bruquetas-Callejo et al., 'Immigration', 5).

57 Fog Olwig, 'Narrating deglobalization'. What remained of a colonial legacy is the relationship with Greenland and the Faroe Islands, which were for centuries colonies, but which became autonomous parts of the Union of Denmark after WWII. Greenland has taken steps towards independence. There is an ethnic dimension to this; Greenlanders are Inuit. The pro-independence parties in Greenland and the Faroe Islands are local and not dependent on the modest migrant communities in Denmark.

58 Rainero, 'Repatriés'; Andall, 'Immigration'; Ben-Ghiat & Fuller, *Italian colonialism*.

59 Ben-Ghiat, *Italian colonialism*, 1-4, Andall & Duncan, *Italian colonialism*, 9-17. In the same year Ethiopia was just given back the Obelisk of Axum which had been stolen under Mussolini.

60 The centuries-old German *Drang nach Osten* (Drive to the East) is described as colonialist, but was different to the colonialism discussed here.

61 Lutz & Gawarecki, *Kolonialismus*.

62 Blakely, 'Postcolonial immigration in Russia'.

63 Cohen, 'Return of the natives?'

64 Duany, 'La nación en la diaspora' and 'The Puerto Rican diaspora', Oostindie & Klinkers, *Decolonising the Caribbean*, 42-56, 212-214.

8 'POSTCOLONIAL' (IN THE) NETHERLANDS

1 Blom, 'Jaren van tucht en ascese', *In de ban*, 155-179; Bossenbroek, *De meelstreep*, 571-576; Vuijsje, *Vermoorde onschuld*, 180-188; Sniderman & Hagendoorn, *When ways of life collide*, 15. Cf. also Buruma, *The wages of guilt* and 'The joys and perils of victimhood'.

2 Bossenbroek, *De meelstreep*, 452, 559, 602, Locher-Scholten, 'Die "Indische generation"', Withuis, *Erkenning*. Jewish colonists played a major role in Dutch-Caribbean history, including in slavery and the local elites. Although this memory has remained alive, there is almost no instance of openly anti-Semitism in Antillean and Surinamese identity politics, rather the opposite; cf. Kerkhof, 'Postkoloniale identiteitspolitiek', 605-606 and the explanation by OCAN chair, Roy Pieters, for the Blok Commission (*Bruggen bouwen*, 511).

3 In chronological order: Tenerife (1977), 583 dead, almost half of whom were onboard the KLM aircraft; Suriname (1989), 176 dead; Bijlmer Disaster (1992), 43 dead; Faro (1992), 56 dead; Eindhoven (1996), 34 dead; Enschede (2000), 22 dead; plane crash on the Surinamese interior (2008), 20 dead.

4 Van Doorn, *Indische lessen*, 106, entoen.nu, 24-27, *entoen.nu en verder*, 28-30. It was recently decided that the official historical canon should be prescriptive for schools and universities, nor for the forthcoming National Museum of History. Cf. also the

qualifying conclusions in *National thought in Europe*, 250-251.

5 Radio Nederland Wereldomroep (Netherlands World Service Radio), 8-10-2007.

6 Quoted in Koning, *De Pasar Malam*, 150.

7 Blakely, *Blacks in the Dutch world*, 291 and passim; Hondius, *Gemengde huwelijken*, 176-179, 315-318, 328.

8 A parallel with the ideals of an earlier, well-intentioned policy of providing education in minority languages which, in terms of effectiveness, was almost impossible to defend empirically, cannot be avoided here; cf. Lucassen & Köbben, *Het partiële gelijk*, 117-118, 129, 150-151.

9 For the United States cf. Lee, 'Race, immigration'.

10 Cf. De Beus, 'God dekoloniseert niet', 307, 310, 312; also Van Doorn, *Indische lessen*, 128-129.

11 Oostindie & Steijlen, 'Zestig jaar'.

12 Oostindie & Steijlen, 'Zestig jaar'. Seriese, 'Wie dit lees', 201, for instance, complains that renowned institutions such as KITLV left the Indisch Dutch out in the cold for too long, a complaint that is all the more striking because from 1963 KITLV employed Rob Nieuwenhuys. The institute gave him all the room he needed to create the image of the Netherlands East Indies of the *tempoe doeloe* ('good old colonial times') era (Kuitenbrouwer, *Tussen wetenschap en oriëntalisme*, 208-212). A similar discontentment with 'white' institutions' was critical to the state-sponsored foundation of NiNsee (National Institute for the Study of Dutch Slavery and its Legacy).

13 Cf. Lilian Ducelle, quoted in Van Leeuwen, *Ons Indisch erfgoed*, 43. The understanding of this inverted exclusion was appositely summarized by Wim Willems, looking back on the aversion he encountered during his first research into the Indisch Dutch with Annemarie Cottaar: 'Those two Dutch faces don't fit the subject matter,' is how they experienced the implicit scepticism (Willems, *De uittocht*, 11). I would like to thank Peter Keppy, Hans Meijer, Fridus Steijlen and Wim Willems for sharing their experiences with me.

14 Van Stipriaan, 'Between diaspora'; Oostindie, 'Slavernij, canon en trauma', 18-21 and 'History brought home', 314-318. I would like to thank Ruben Gowricharn for sharing his experiences on this matter, also as a Hindustani researcher in what was initially a strongly 'Afro' Caribbean realm.

15 Van Doorn, *Indische lessen*, 72.

16 Bosma, 'Sailing through Suez'; Willems, *Tjalie Robinson*, 32.

17 Van Doorn, *De laatste eeuw*, 110-123, *Indische lessen*, 41-56, Van Kaa & De Roo, *De leden*, 182-201, Kuitenbrouwer, *Tussen oriëntalisme en wetenschap*.

18 Wesseling, *Indië verloren*, 305, Baudet & Brugmans, *Balans van beleid*, 6-7, 11, 119, 207, 349-351, 358-359. Bank, 'Lijphart malgré lui', and Schulte Nordholt, *Indonesië na Soeharto*, 254, modify the metaphors of rupture and trauma.

19 Van Doorn, 57-77; Willems, *Tjalie Robinson*, 309-310; 350, 492, 529.

20 Helman & De Roo, *Groot geld tegen klein geld*; Oostindie, 'Cultuurbeleid'; Oostindie & Klinkers, *Knellende koninkrijksbanden*, II, 210-221, and III, 318-326.

21 Sartono, *Indonesian Historiography*, Klooster, *Indonesiërs*, 142 en passim. Interesting is the reification of Indonesian identity in Sartono, 67 ('the peoples of the Indonesian archipelago emerged from the Revolution as an independent nation with an awareness that they did not yet possess a full-fledged national identity [...] being oppressed and underprivileged, they had lost their identity'), cf. 51, 62-63.

22 The editors of the 1995 jubilee publication *Nederland-Indonesia 1945-1995* stated frankly that this book was about 'cultural interweaving' and, therefore, in the first instance aimed at (Indisch) Dutch. And that the amount of interest they had encountered in Indonesia for the shared history was very limited (Wolters, *Nederland-Indonesia*, 6). Ten years later, the exhibition *Indonesia: The discovery of the past* at De Nieuwe Kerk in Amsterdam attracted a large number of visitors, but failed to do so in Jakarta. This probably had nothing to do with objections to the colonial content (cf. Sri Hardiati & Ter Keurs, *Indonesia*); the Dutch component

was limited to the collected institutions and individuals, the 'Indisch' element was very modest, apart from the Dutch-language audio tour which was narrated by Marion Bloem and Willem Nijholt. For a playful approach to colonial exhibitions, see Oostindie, Van der Linden & Raben, 'De koloniale opstelling'.

23 The cultural accord agreed with Suriname in 1976 was badly executed and was suspended under the military dictatorship. After Sticusa closed down, cultural relations with the Antilles as often as not lacked dynamism and mutual enthusiasm, except in relation to colonial architecture.

24 The seventh country is Russia, where the centuries-old relationship is, of course, not marked by colonialism. Russia is, therefore, the odd one out.

25 The following is borrowed from my publications 'Historical memory and national canons', 'Commemorating the VOC' and 'The slippery paths'.

26 Cf. Lowenthal, 'Heritage and history', 30: 'Heritage is not any old past, let alone what objective history tells us was the past; it is the past we glory in or agonize over, the past through whose lens we construct our present identity, the past that defines us to ourselves and presents us to others.' See also Legêne, 'Canon van verschil', on the past and current role of museums in the canonization of colonial history.

27 Recently by Bosma, *Terug uit de koloniën*, 345-346 en passim, 'Why is there no postcolonial debate' and Van Leeuwen, *Ons Indisch erfgoed*, 12-13, 345-346 and passim; cf. Boehmer & Gouda, 'Postcolonial studies'; Gouda, 'Immigration and identity politics'; Legêne, *De bagage*, 13-33; Pattynama, 'Assimilation and masquerade' and '... de baai'; Wekker, *Nesten bouwen*.

28 For an extensive introduction see Young, *Postcolonialism*, especially 57-69; further Hargreaves & McKinney, 'Introduction'.

29 Typically, in his study of Surinamese history published shortly after the war, Suriname-born scholar Rudolf van Lier, together with Harry Hoetink (founder of post-war Caribbean studies in the Netherlands) made only cursory mention of the

life and work of Anton de Kom – inaccurately (he called de Kom a 'teacher') and denigrating (he thought *Wij slaven van Suriname* expressed a 'pathetic resentment and rancour' about slavery) (Van Lier, *Samenleving*, 278-282).

30 Van Doorn, *Indische lessen*.

31 Essed, *Alledaags racisme* and *Inzicht in alledaags racisme*. Ramdas belonged to the collective that introduced Hall's work in translation into the Netherlands (Hall, *Het minimale zelf*); see Ramdas, 'Een noodzakelijke fantasie'.

32 Sniderman & Hagendoorn, *When ways of life collide*, 127-128.

33 Bancel, *Qui a peur*; Coquio, *Retour du colonial*; Grosfoguel, *Colonial subjects*, 180, 197.

34 Said, *Orientalism* and *Culture and imperialism*; Hall, 'New ethnicities'; Gilroy, *There ain't no Black in the Union Jack* and *The Black Atlantic*.

35 For criticism see Favell, 'Multi-ethnic Britain', Howe, 'Internal decolonization?' and, against cultural studies in a wider sense, see Benson & Stangroom, *Why truth matters*.

36 Bernstein, 'Identity politics', 67.

37 Cf. the later work of Paul Gilroy, e.g. *After Empire*.

38 Recently, for example, the exhibition *Black is beautiful*, in the Nieuwe Kerk, Amsterdam (2008) and 'De exotische mens' in het Teylers Museum, Haarlem (2009).

39 Judt, *Postwar Europe*, 829: 'Some measure of neglect and even forgetting is the necessary condition for civic health.' A parallel may be found in Barack Obama's approach to American slavery. In the past, he made very strong statements on the subject, but on the eve of his election, he moved to referring to the honourable tradition of 'our founding fathers' without referring to their involvement in slavery.

40 This phenomenon of a blurring of memory is, of course, not limited to the Netherlands; cf. Young, *The texture of memory*, about the use of ever more monuments in the battle to prevent the Holocaust from being forgotten.

BIBLIOGRAPHY

Alba, Richard & Victor Nee
2003 *Remaking the American mainstream: Assimilation and contemporary immigration*. Cambridge: Harvard University Press.

Alferink, Marga
2011 'Festivals of postcolonial migrants in the Netherlands', in: Ulbe Bosma (ed.), *Postcolonialism in the Netherlands*. Amsterdam: IMISCOE/Amsterdam University Press. [in print]

Ali, N., V.S. Kalra & S. Sayyid (eds)
2006 *A postcolonial people: South Asians in Britain*. London: Hurst.

Alofs, Luc & Leontine Merkies
1990 *Ken ta Arubiano? Sociale integratie en natievorming op Aruba*. Leiden: KITLV Uitgeverij.

Amersfoort, J.M.M. van
1971 'De Ambonezen', in: H. Verwey-Jonker (ed.), *Allochtonen in Nederland: Beschouwingen over de gerepatrieerden, Ambonezen, Surinamers, Antillianen, buitenlandse werknemers, Chinezen, vluchtelingen en buitenlandse studenten in onze samenleving*, pp. 109-42. 's-Gravenhage: Staatsuitgeverij.
1974 *Immigratie en minderheidsvorming: Een analyse van de Nederlandse situatie 1945-1973*. Alphen aan de Rijn: Samson.

Amersfoort, Hans van & Mies van Niekerk
2006 'Immigration as a colonial inheritance: Post-colonial immigrants in the Netherlands, 1945-2002', *Journal of Ethnic and Migration Studies* 32-3:323-46.

Amesz, Ieneke, Fridus Steijlen & Hans Vermeulen
1989 *Andere Antillianen; Carrières van laaggeschoolde Antilliaanse jongeren in een grote stad*. Amsterdam: Het Spinhuis.

Andall, Jacqueline
2005 'Immigration and the legacy of colonialism: the Eritrean diaspora in Italy', in: Jacqueline Andall & Derek Duncan (eds), *Italian colonialism: Legacy and memory*, pp. 191-216. Oxford: Lang.

Anderson, Benedict R.O'G
1983 *Imagined communities: Reflections on the origin and spread of nationalism*. London: Verso.

Andi Lolo, Tandi Roma
2002 *De V.O.C. in de Indonesische archipel: Handeldrijven en koloniseren*. Den Haag/Jakarta: Ambassade van de Republiek Indonesia/P.T. Balai Pustaka.

Aspeslagh, Rob
2000 *Gewenst en niet geliefd: Advies over het monument aan Apollolaan/Olympiaplein*. Den Haag: Clingendael.

Bacilio, Gilbert Felix
1999 'Ontketend? Een droom is werkelijkheid geworden', in: Gert Oostindie (ed.), *Het verleden onder ogen: Herdenking van de slavernij*, pp. 67-76. Amsterdam/Den Haag: Arena/Prins Claus Fonds.

Back, Less et al.
2002 'New Labour's white heart: Politics, multiculturalism and the return of

assimilation', *The Political Quarterly* 73-4:445-54.

Bade, Klaus J., Pieter C. Emmer, Leo Lucassen & Jochen Oltmer (eds)
2007 *Enzyklopädie Migration in Europa: Von 17. Jahrhundert bis zur Gegenwart.* Padernborn/München: Schöningh/ Fink.

Bagley, Christopher
1973 *The Dutch plural society.* London: Oxford University Press.

Bal, Ellen & Kathinka Sinha-Kerkhoff
2004 '"Een Hindostaanse diaspora": India en de moslim-Hindostanen in Nederland en Suriname', *Oso: Tijdschrift voor Surinamistiek* 23-2:236-56.

Bancel, Nicolas et al.
2008 *Qui a peur du postcolonial? Dénis et controverses. Mouvements des idées et des luttes* 51, September/October.

Bank, Jan
1984 'Lijphart malgré lui: The politics of accommodation in the "Indonesian question"', *Acta Politica* 19:73-83.

Basch, Linda, Nina Glick Schiller & Cristina Szanton-Blanc
1994 *Nations unbound: transnationalized projects and the deterritorialized nation-state.* New York: Gordon & Breach.

Baudet, H. & I.J. Brugmans (eds)
1961 *Balans van beleid: Terugblik op de laatste halve eeuw van Nederlandsch-Indië.* Assen: Van Gorcum.

Beets, Gijs et al.
2002 *De demografische geschiedenis van de Indische Nederlanders.* Den Haag: Nederlands Interdisciplinair Demografisch Instituut.

Beets, Gijs, Evert van Imhoff & Corina Huisman
2003 'Demografie van de Indische Nederlanders, 1930-2001', *Bevolkingstrends* 51-1:58-66.

Beijering, Marjan (ed.)
[2003] *Gedeeld verleden, gezamenlijke toekomst: Aspecten van de Nederlandse koloniale geschiedenis: lezingen en discussies in Rotterdam.* Rotterdam: Stichting Gedeeld verleden, gezamenlijke toekomst.

Ben-Ghiat, Ruth & Mia Fuller (eds)
2005 *Italian colonialism.* New York: Palgrave Macmillan.

Benson, Ophelia & Jeremy Stangroom
2006 *Why truth matters.* London: Continuum.

Beriss, David
2004 *Black skins, French voices: Caribbean ethnicity and activism in urban France.* Boulder: Westview.

Bernstein, Mary
2005 'Identity politics', *Annual Review of Sociology* 31:47-74.

Beus, Jos de
2001 'God dekoloniseert niet: Een kritiek op de Nederlandse geschiedschrijving over de neergang van Nederlands-Indië en Nederlands Suriname', *BMGN* 116-3:307-24.

Bijnaar, Aspha
2002 *Kasmoni: Een spaartraditie in Suriname en Nederland.* Amsterdam: Bert Bakker.

Bink, Susan & Giovanni Massaro
2007 'Media en etnische culturele diversiteit', http://media.wereldjournalisten. nl/media

Blakely, Allison
1993 *Blacks in the Dutch world: The evolution of racial imaginary in a modern society.* Bloomington: Indiana University Press.
2012 'Postcolonial immigration and identity formation in Europe since 1945: The Russian variant', in: Ulbe Bosma, Jan Lucassen & Gert Oostindie (eds), *Postcolonial migrations and identity politics.* Oxford: Berghahn. [in print]

Bleich, Anet, Peter Schumacher e.a.
1984 *Nederlands racisme.* Amsterdam: Van Gennep.

Bloem, Marion
1983 *Geen gewoon Indisch meisje.* Haarlem: In de Knipscheer.

Bloemberg, Lucie
1995 *Tussen traditie en verandering: Hindostaanse zelforganisaties in Nederland.* Utrecht/Amsterdam: KNAG/Instituut voor Sociale Geografie UvA.

Bloemraad, Irene, Anna Korteweg & Gökçe Yurdakul

2008 'Citizenship and immigration: Multiculturalism, assimilation, and challenges to the nation-state', *Annual Review of Sociology* 34:153-79.

Blok, S.A.

2004 *Bruggen bouwen: Deel 1 Eindrapport.* 's-Gravenhage: SDU Uitgevers. [Tijdelijke Commissie Onderzoek Integratiebeleid.]

Blom, J.C.H.

1981 'Jaren van tucht en ascese: Enige beschouwingen over de stemming in herrijzend Nederland (1940-1945)', *Bijdragen en Mededelingen betreffende de Geschiedenis der Nederlanden* 96-2:300-33.

2007 *In de ban van goed en fout: Geschiedschrijving over de bezettingstijd in Nederland.* Amsterdam: Boom.

Boedhoe, Naushad

1990 'Hindostaanse moslims', in: Corstiaan van den Burg, Theo Damsteegt & Krishna Autar (eds), *Hindostanen in Nederland*, pp. 107-23. Leuven/Apeldoorn: Garant.

Boehmer, Elleke & Frances Gouda

2009 'Postcolonial studies in the context of the "diasporic" Netherlands', in: Michelle Keown, David Murphy & James Procter (eds), *Comparing postcolonial diasporas*, pp. 37-55. Basingstoke: Palgrave Macmillan.

Boekholt, Ralph

1992 *De staat, dr. L. de Jong en Indië.* Den Haag: Moesson.

Bosma, Ulbe

2007 'Sailing through Suez from the South: The emergence of an Indies-Dutch migration circuit, 1815-1940', *International Migration Review* 41-2:511-36.

2009 *Terug uit de koloniën: Zestig jaar postkoloniale migranten en hun organisaties.* Amsterdam: Bert Bakker.

2011 'Why is there no postcolonial debate in the Netherlands?' in: Ulbe Bosma (ed.), *Postcolonialism in the Netherlands.* Amsterdam: IMISCOE/ Amsterdam University Press. [in print]

Bosma, Ulbe & Marga Alferink

2011 'Multiculturalism and settlement: The case of Dutch postcolonial migrant organisations', *Journal of International Migration and Integration* [in print].

Bosma, Ulbe & Remco Raben

2003 *De oude Indische wereld 1500-1920.* Amsterdam: Bakker.

Bosma, Ulbe, Remco Raben & Wim Willems

2006 *De geschiedenis van Indische Nederlanders.* Amsterdam: Bert Bakker.

Bossenbroek, Martin

2001 *De meelstreep: Terugkeer en opvang na de Tweede Wereldoorlog.* Amsterdam: Bakker.

Brand, Marieke, Henk Schulte Nordholt & Fridus Steijlen

2005 *Indië verteld: Herinneringen, 1930-1950.* Zutphen/Leiden: Walburg/KITLV Uitgeverij.

Breman, Jan

2006 'De sociologie van het polderland', *Sociologie* 2(3).

Broek, Aart G.

2007 *De terreur van de schaamte: Brandstof voor agressie.* Haarlem: In de Knipscheer.

Browne, Katherine E.

2004 *Creole economics: Caribbean cunning under the French flag.* Austin: University of Texas Press.

Bruckner, Pascal

2006 *La tyrannie de la penitence.* Paris: Grasset.

Bruijn, Jaap R. de, et al.,

2002 *Roemrucht verleden. De Staten-Generaal en de VOC.* Den Haag: Staten-Generaal.

Bruquetas-Callejo, María et al.

2008 'Immigration and integration policymaking in Spain'. IMISCOE Working paper no. 21.

Buruma, Ian

1995 *The wages of guilt.* London: Meridian.

1999 'The joys and perils of victimhood', *New York Review of Books*, 8 April.

2006 *Murder in Amsterdam.* New York: Penguin Press.

Byron, Margaret & Stéphanie Condon

2008 *Migration in comparative perspective:*

Caribbean communities in Britain and France. New York: Routledge.

Byvanck, Valentijn & Erik Schilp

2008 Het Nationaal Historisch Museum stimuleert de historische verbeelding. Arnhem: Nationaal Historisch Museum.

Cannadine, David

2001 Ornamentalism: How the British saw their empire. New York: Oxford University Press.

Captain, Esther

2002 Achter het kawat was Nederland: Indische oorlogservaringen en -herinneringen 1942-1995. Kampen: Kok.

Captain, Esther, Maartje de Haan, Fridus Steijlen & Pim Westerkamp (eds)

2005 De Indische zomer in Den Haag: Het cultureel erfgoed van de Indische hoofdstad. Leiden: KITLV Uitgeverij.

Chambon, Laurent

2002 Le sel de la démocratie; L'accès des minorités au pouvoir politique en France et aux Pays-Bas. Amsterdam: Amsterdamse School voor Sociaal Wetenschappelijk Onderzoek.

Choenni, Chan

2004 'Organisatievorming onder Hindoestanen in Nederland: Een historische schets', Oso; Tijdschrift voor Surinamistiek 23-2:305-21.

2009 Madad Sahára Saháyta: Analyse en aanpak sociale problematiek onder Hindostanen in Suriname. Den Haag/ Haarlem: Seva Network Foundation/ BOX Press.

Choenni, Chan & Kanta Sh. Adhin (eds)

2003 Hindostanen: Van Brits-Indische emigranten via Suriname tot burgers van Nederland. Den Haag: Sampreshan.

Choenni, Chan & Carel Harmsen

2007 'Geboorteplaats en etnische samenstelling van Surinamers in Nederland', Bevolkingstrends 55-1:74-8.

Clark Hine, Darlene, Trica Danielle Keaton & Stephen Small (eds)

2009 Black Europe and the African Diaspora. Urbana: University of Illinois Press.

Codes noirs

2006 Codes noirs de l'esclavage aux abolitions.

Paris: Dalloz. [Inleiding van Christiane Taubira.]

Coenders, Marcel, Marcel Lubbers & Peer Scheepers

2006 '"Het tolerante land" in historisch en landenvergelijkend perspectief', in: Frank van Tubergen & Ineke Maas (eds), Allochtonen in Nederland in internationaal perspectief, pp. 89-110. Amsterdam: Amsterdam University Press.

Cohen, James

2012 'Postcolonial immigrants in France and their descendants: the meanings of France's "postcolonial moment"', in: Ulbe Bosma, Jan Lucassen & Gert Oostindie (eds), Postcolonial migrations and identity politics. Oxford: Berghahn. [in print]

Cohen, Nicole Leah

2012 'Return of the natives? Children of empire in postcolonial Japan', in: Ulbe Bosma, Jan Lucassen & Gert Oostindie (eds), Postcolonial migrations and identity politics. Oxford: Berghahn. [in print]

Cohen, Robin

1998 'Cultural diaspora: The Caribbean case', in: Mary Chamberlain (ed.), Caribbean migration: Globalised identities, pp. 21-35. London: Routledge.

Cohen, William B.

2003 'Pied-noir memory, history, and the Algerian war', in: Andre L. Smith (ed.), Europe's invisible migrants, pp. 129-45. Amsterdam: Amsterdam University Press.

Colley, Linda

1992 Britons: Forging the nation 1707-1837. New Haven: Yale University Press.

Commission on Integration & Cohesion

2007 Our shared future. London: Commission on Integration & Cohesion 2007.

Commission for Racial Equality

2005 Citizenship and belonging: What is Britishness? London: Commission for Racial Equality.

Cooper, Frederick & Rogers Brubaker

2005 'Identity', in: Frederick Cooper, Colonialism in question: Theory, knowledge, history, pp. 59-90. Berkeley: University of California Press.

Coquio, Catherine (ed.)
2008 Retours du colonial? Disculpation et rehabilitation de l'histoire coloniale. Nantes: l'Atalante.

Davids, C.A.
2005 Global history en de 'canon' van de Nederlandse geschiedenis. Amsterdam: KNAW.

Deventer, C. Th. van
1899 'Een ereschuld', De Gids 63-3:215-28, 249-52.

Dis, Adriaan van
1994 Indische duinen. Amsterdam: Meulenhof.
1983 Nathan Sid. Amsterdam: Meulenhof.
2007 Leeftocht: Veertig jaar onderweg. Amsterdam: Augustus.

Doel, H.W. van den
2000 Afscheid van Indië: De val van het Nederlandse imperium in Azië. Amsterdam: Prometheus.

Doorn, J.A.A. van
1995 Indische lessen: Nederland en de koloniale ervaring. Amsterdam: Bert Bakker.
1995 De laatste eeuw van Indië: Ontwikkeling en ondergang van een koloniaal project. Amsterdam: Bert Bakker.
2002 Gevangen in de tijd: Over generaties en hun geschiedenis. Amsterdam: Boom.
2009 Nederlandse democratie: Historische en sociologische waarnemingen. Samengesteld en ingeleid door Jos de Beus en Piet de Rooy. Amsterdam: Mets & Schilt.

Doorn, J.A.A. van & W.J. Hendrix
1970 Ontsporing van geweld: Over het Nederlands-Indisch-Indonesisch conflict. Rotterdam: Universitaire Pers Rotterdam.

Drooglever, P.J.
2005 Een daad van vrije keuze: De Papoea's van westelijk Nieuw-Guinea en de grenzen van het zelfbeschikkingsrecht. Den Haag/Amsterdam: Instituut voor Nederlandse Geschiedenis/Boom.

Duany, Jorge
2007 'La nación en la diaspora: Las multiples repercusiones de la émigración puertorriqeña a Estados Unidos', Revista de Ciencias Sociales 17:118-53.
2012 'The Puerto Rican diaspora to the United Status: A postcolonial migration?', in: Ulbe Bosma, Jan Lucassen & Gert Oostindie (eds), Postcolonial migrations and identity politics. Oxford: Berghahn. [in print]

Duyvendak, Jan Willem, Ewald Engelen & Ido de Haan
2008 Het bange Nederland: Pleidooi voor een open samenleving. Amsterdam: Bert Bakker.

Emmer, P.C.
2003 De Nederlandse slavenhandel 1500-1850. Amsterdam: Arbeiderspers. [2000]

Endang Sri Hardiati & Pieter ter Keurs
2005 Indonesia: De ontdekking van het verleden. Amsterdam: KIT Publishers.

Ensel, Remco
2003 'Multiculturalisme in de politieke partij: Migrantennetwerken in de PvdA en het CDA', Migrantenstudies: Driemaandelijks tijdschrift voor onderzoek naar etnische minderheden en de Nederlandse samenleving 19:156-72.

entoen.nu
2006 entoen.nu: De canon van Nederland; Rapport van de Commissie Ontwikkeling Nederlandse Canon. delen A en B. Den Haag: Ministerie van OCW.

entoen.nu en verder
2007 entoen.nu en verder: De canon van Nederland; Rapport van de Commissie Ontwikkeling Nederlandse Canon. deel C. Amsterdam: Amsterdam University Press.

Entzinger, Han
1990 'Overheidsbeleid', in: H.B. Entzinger & P.J.J. Stijnen (eds), Etnische minderheden in Nederland, pp. 244-64. Meppel: Boom.
2002 Voorbij de multiculturele samenleving. Assen: Van Gorcum.
2003 'The rise and fall of multiculturalism: the case of the Netherlands', in: Christian Joppke & Ewa Morawska (eds), Toward assimilation and citizenship: Immigrants in liberal nation-states, pp. 59-86. Basingstoke: Palgrave Macmillan.

Entzinger, Han & Alfons Fermin

2006 'Gidsland achter de Waterlinie: Het recente Nederlandse immigratie- en integratiebeleid in Europees perspectief', in: Frank van Tubergen & Ineke Maas (eds), *Allochtonen in Nederland in internationaal perspectief*, pp. 37-62. Amsterdam: Amsterdam University Press.

Essed, Philomena

1984 *Alledaags racisme*. Amsterdam: Feministische Uitgeverij Sara.

1991 *Inzicht in alledaags racisme*. Utrecht: Spectrum.

Estatísticas demográficas

2008 *Estatísticas demográficas 2007*. Lissabon: Instituto Nacional de Estatística.

Fabricius, Johan

1997 *De scheepsjongens van Bontekoe*. Amsterdam: Leopold. [eerste druk 1923.]

Fasseur, C.

1985 'Het verleden tot last: Nederland, de Tweede Wereldoorlog en de dekolonisatie van Indonesië', in: David Barnauw, Madelon de Keizer & Gerrold van der Stroom (eds), *1940-1945: Onverwerkt verleden?: Lezingen van het symposium georganiseerd door het Rijksinstituut voor Oorlogsdocumentatie, 7 en 8 mei 1985*, pp. 133-55. Utrecht: Hes Uitgevers.

1995 *De weg naar het paradijs en andere Indische geschiedenissen*. Amsterdam: Bert Bakker.

1996 *Indischgasten: Indische levensgeschiedenissen*. Amsterdam: Bert Bakker.

Favell, Adrian

2001 'Multi-ethnic Britain: An exception in Europe?', *Patterns of Prejudice* 35-1:35-57.

Fennema, Meindert et al.

2000 *Sociaal kapitaal en politieke participatie van etnische minderheden*. Amsterdam: IMES.

2001 'De politieke integratie van etnische minderheden in Nederland', *Migrantenstudies; Driemaandelijks tijdschrift voor onderzoek naar etnische minderheden en de Nederlandse samenleving* 17:142-57.

Fennema, Meindert & Wouter van der Brug

2006 'Nederlandse anti-immigratiepartijen in Europees perspectief', in: Frank van Tubergen & Ineke Maas (eds), *Allochtonen in Nederland in internationaal perspectief*, pp. 37-62. Amsterdam: Amsterdam University Press.

Fennema, Meindert & Jean Tillie

2001 'Civic communities, political participation and political trust of ethnic groups', *Connections* 24-1:26-41.

Ferguson, Niall

2004 *Empire: How Britain made the modern world*. London: Penguin.

Fermin, Alfons

1997 *Nederlandse politieke partijen over minderhedenbeleid, 1977-1995*. Amsterdam: Thesis Publishers.

Fisher, Michael H., Shompa Lahiri & Shinder Thandi

2007 *A South-Asian history of Britain*. Oxford: Greenwood.

Fog Olwig, Karen

2003 'Narrating deglobalization: Danish perceptions of a lost empire', *Global Networks* 3-3:207-22.

Fortuyn, Pim

2002 *De puinhopen van acht jaar Paars: De wachtlijsten in de gezondheidszorg; Een genadeloze analyse van de collectieve sector en aanbevelingen voor een krachtig herstelprogramma*. Uithoorn/Rotterdam: Karakter/Speakers Academy.

Gaastra, Femme S.

2002 *De geschiedenis van de VOC*. Zutphen: Walburg Pers.

Gallo, Max

2006 *Fier d'être français*. Paris: Fayard.

Gans, Herbert

1979 'Symbolic ethnicity: The future of ethnic groups and cultures in America', *Ethnic and Racial Studies* 2:1-20.

Geemert, Ko van

2007 *Monument Indië Nederland*. Amsterdam: Stadsdeelraad Zuid, gemeente Amsterdam.

Gemenebest-relatie

1991 *Gemenebest-relatie Nederland en Suriname: Een opinie-onderzoek onder de*

Surinaamse bevolking in opdracht van Weekkrant Suriname. Voorburg: s.n.

Geugten, Tom van der

2000 'Droombeeld of werkelijkheid: Het beeld van tempo doeloe', *Kleio: Tijdschrift van de Vereniging van Docenten in Geschiedenis en Staatsinrichting in Nederland* 41-8:28-36.

Gilroy, Paul

1987 *There ain't no Black in the Union Jack*. London: Unwin Hyman.

1993 *The Black Atlantic: Modernity and double consciousness*. Cambridge: Harvard University Press.

2004 *After Empire: Melancholia or convivial culture?* Abingdon: Routledge.

Giraud, Michel

2004 'The Antilles in France: Trends and prospects', *Ethnic and Racial Studies* 27:622-40.

2009 'Colonial racism, ethnicity, and citizenship: The lessons of the migration experiences of French-speaking Caribbean populations', in: Margarita Cervantes-Rodríguez, Ramón Grosfoguel & Eric Mielants (eds), *Caribbean migration to Western Europe and the United States*, pp. 43-57. Philadelphia: Temple University Press.

Glick Schiller, Nina

2003 'The centrality of ethnography in the study of transnational migration', in: Nancy Foner (ed.), *American arrivals; Anthropology engages the new immigration*, pp. 99-128. Santa Fe: School for Advanced Research Press.

Gobardhan-Rambocus, Lila

2001 *Onderwijs als sleutel tot maatschappelijke vooruitgang: Een taal- en onderwijsgeschiedenis van Suriname, 1651-1975*. Zutphen: Walburg Pers.

Gouda, Frances

2008 'Immigration and identity politics in a postcolonial world: Review of *Recalling the Indies; Colonial culture & postcolonial identities*', *The Asia Pacific Journal of Anthropology* 9-4:293-301.

Goudt, Mieke (ed.)

1989 *In de Gemeenteraad! Gesprekken met de eerste zwarte en migrantenraadsvrouw-en in Nederland*. Leiden: Stichting Burgerschapskunde Nederlands Centrum voor Politieke Vorming.

Governance

2007 *The Governance of Britain*. Norwich: The Licensing Division, HMSO.

Gowricharn, Ruben

2003 'De emancipatie van Hindostanen', in: Chan E.S. Choenni & Kanta Sh. Adhin (eds), *Hindostanen: Van Brits-Indische emigranten via Suriname tot burgers van Nederland*, pp. 90-105. Den Haag: Sampreshan.

2003 'Bollywood in de diaspora', *Agora* 19-4:21-5.

2006 'Ethnicity and political stability in plural societies', in: Ruben Gowricharn (ed.), *Caribbean transnationalism: Migration, pluralization, and social cohesion*, pp. 223-37. Lanham: Lexington Books.

Grasveld, Fons & Klaas Breunissen

1990 *'Ik ben een Javaan uit Suriname'*. Hilversum/Amsterdam: Stichting Ideële Filmproducties/Jan Mets.

Grever, Maria & Kees Ribbens

2004 'De historische canon onder de loep', *Kleio; Tijdschrift van de Vereniging van Docenten in Geschiedenis en Staatsinrichting in Nederland* 45-7:2-7.

Grever, Maria, Ed Jonker, Kees Ribbens & Siep Stuurman

2006 *Controverses rond de canon*. Assen: Van Gorcum.

Groeneboer, Kees

1995 *Weg tot het Westen: Het Nederlands voor Indië 1600-1950*. Leiden: KITLV Uitgeverij.

Grosfoguel, Ramón

1996 'Colonial Caribbean migrations to the metropoles in comparative perspective', *Journal of Social Sciences* 2-1/2:20-39.

2003 *Colonial subjects: Puerto Ricans in a global perspective*. Berkeley: University of California Press.

Haan, Ido de

1995 'Over de grenzen van de politiek: De integratie van allochtonen in de sfeer van de politiek', in: Godfried Engbersen & René Gabriëls (eds),

Sferen van integratie; Naar een gedifferentieerd allochtonenbeleid,
pp. 157-79. Amsterdam: Boom.

1997 *Na de ondergang: De herinnering aan de jodenvervolging in Nederland 1945-1995.* Den Haag: SDU Uitgevers.

Haasse, Hella S.

1973 *Krassen op een rots: Notities bij een reis op Java.* Amsterdam: Querido.

Hall, Catherine

2008 'Feature; Remembering 1807: Histories of the slave trade, slavery and abolition', *History Workshop Journal* 64-1:1-5.

Hall, Stuart

1991 *Het minimale zelf en andere opstellen.* Amsterdam: Sua Amsterdam.

1992 'New ethnicities', in: J. Donald & A. Rattansi (eds), *Race, culture and difference,* pp. 252-9. London: Sage.

Hannerz, Ulf

1992 *Cultural complexity.* New York: Columbia University Press.

Hansen, Randall

2000 *Citizenship and immigration in post-war Britain: The institutional origins of a multicultural nation.* Oxford: Oxford University Press.

Hargreaves, Alec G.

2007 *Multi-ethnic France: Immigration, politics, culture and society.* New York: Routledge.

Hargreaves, Alec G. & Mark McKinney

1997 'Introduction: The post-colonial problematic in contemporary France', in: Alec G. Hargreaves & Mark McKinney (eds), *Post-colonial cultures in France,* pp. 3-25. London: Routledge.

Heelsum, Anja van

2004 *Migrantenorganisaties in Nederland.* Utrecht: Forum.

2005 'Political participation and civic community of ethnic minorities in four cities in the Netherlands', *Politics* 25-1:19-30.

2007 *De etnisch-culturele positie van de tweede generatie Surinamers.* Amsterdam: Het Spinhuis.

Heelsum, Anja van & Eske Voorthuysen

2002 *Surinaamse organisaties in Nederland: Een netwerkanalyse.* Amsterdam: Aksant.

Heijer, Henk, den

2002 *De geschiedenis van de WIC.* Zutphen: Walburg Pers. [1994.]

Helder, Lulu & Scotty Gravenberch (eds)

1998 *Sinterklaasje, kom maar binnen zonder knecht.* Berchem: EPO.

Helman, Albert & Jos de Roo

1988 *Groot geld tegen klein geld: De voorgeschiedenis van Sticusa.* Amsterdam: Sticusa.

Helsdingen, W.H. van (ed.)

1941 *Daar wèrd wat grootsch verricht...: Nederlandsch-Indië in de XXste eeuw.* Amsterdam: Elsevier.

Helsloot, John

2005 'Het feest; De strijd om Zwarte Piet', in: Isabel Hoving, Hester Dibbits & Marlou Schrover (eds), *Cultuur en migratie in Nederland: Veranderingen van het alledaagse, 1950-2000,* pp. 249-71. Den Haag: SDU Uitgevers.

Hermans, W.F.

1969 *De laatste resten tropisch Nederland.* Amsterdam: De Bezige Bij.

H.M. Government

2007 *The way forward: Bicentenary of the abolition of the Slave Trade Act 1807-2007.* London: HM Government.

Hochschildt, Adam

1998 *King Leopold's ghost: A story of greed, terror and heroism in colonial Africa.* New York: Houghton Mifflin.

Hondius, Dienke

1999 *Gemengde huwelijken, gemengde gevoelens: Aanvaarding en ontwijking van etnisch en religieus verschil sinds 1945.* Den Haag: SDU Uitgevers.

Horst, Liesbeth van der

2004 *Wereldoorlog in de West: Suriname, de Nederlandse Antillen en Aruba 1940-1945.* Hilversum: Verloren.

Houben, Vincent

2002 'Koloniale geschiedenis van Indonesië in de twintigste eeuw: Meerzijdig en dubbelzinnig', in: J. Thomas Lindblad & Willem van der Molen (eds), *Macht en majesteit; Opstellen voor Cees Fasseur bij zijn afscheid als hoogleraar in de geschiedenis van Indonesië aan de Universiteit Leiden,* pp. 293-303. Leiden: TCZOA, Universiteit Leiden.

Hoving, Isabel
2004 'Nat hout: Astrid Roemers postkoloniale verbeelding', in: Rosemarie
Buikema & Maaijke Meijer (eds),
*Cultuur en migratie in Nederland:
Kunsten in beweging 1980-2000*, pp.
323-42. Den Haag: SDU Uitgevers.

Howe, Stephen
2003 'Internal decolonization? British
politics since Thatcher as post-colonial trauma', *Twentieth Century British
History* 14-3:286-304.

Hulst, Hans van
1997 *Morgen bloeit het diabaas: De Antilliaanse volksklasse in de Nederlandse
samenleving.* Amsterdam: Het
Spinhuis.

Integratiebeleid
1994 *Integratiebeleid etnische minderheden:
Contourennota.* 's-Gravenhage: SDU
Uitgevers.

Jansen van Galen, John
1995 *Kapotte plantage: Suriname, een
Hollandse erfenis.* Amsterdam: Balans.
2000 *Hetenachtsdroom: Suriname, erfenis van
de slavernij.* Amsterdam: Contact.

Jones, Guno
2001 'Het belang van een gedenkteken',
*Kleio; Tijdschrift van de Vereniging van
Docenten in Geschiedenis en Staatsinrichting in Nederland* 42-5:9-13.
2007 *Tussen onderdanen, rijksgenoten en
Nederlanders: Nederlandse politici over
burgers uit Oost & West en Nederland
1945-2005.* Amsterdam: Rozenberg
Publishers.

Jong, L. de
2002 *The collapse of a colonial society: The
Dutch in Indonesia during the Second
World War.* Leiden: KITLV Press.

Jong, Sjoerd de
2008 *Een wereld van verschil: Wat is er mis
met cultuurrelativisme?* Amsterdam:
De Bezige Bij.

Judt, Tony
2005 *Postwar: A history of Europe since 1945.*
New York: Penguin Press.

Kaa, D.J. van de & Y. de Roo
2008 *De leden van de Koninklijke Nederlandse
Akademie van Wetenschappen: Een
demografisch perspectief: 1808 tot 2008.*
Amsterdam: KNAW Press.

Kardux, Johanna
2004 'Monuments of the black Atlantic:
Slavery memorials in the United
States and the Netherlands', in: Heike
Raphael-Hernandez (ed.), *Blackening
Europe: The African American presence*,
pp. 87-105. New York: Routledge.

Kempen, Michiel van
2003 *Een geschiedenis van de Surinaamse
literatuur.* Breda: De Geus.
2004 'De Nederlandse taal als onderdruk-
ker en bevrijder', in: Rosemarie
Buikema & Maaijke Meijer (eds),
*Cultuur en migratie in Nederland:
Kunsten in beweging 1980-2000,*
pp. 19-36. Den Haag: SDU Uitgevers.
2006 'Paramaribo: slavernijmonument
Kwakoe', in: Jan Bank & Marita
Mathijsen (eds), *Plaatsen van
herinnering: Nederland in de negen-
tiende eeuw,* pp. 238-51. Amsterdam:
Bert Bakker.

Keppy, Peter
2006 *Sporen van vernieling: Oorlogsschade,
roof en rechtsherstel in Indonesië
1940-1957.* Amsterdam: Boom.

Kerkhof, Erna
2007 'Postkoloniale identiteitspolitiek van
Caraïbische Nederlanders in drie
hedendaagse herdenkingen', *Tijdschrift voor Geschiedenis* 120-4: 592-607.

Klinken, Gerry van
2009 'Nationale helden in Indonesië', in:
Rosemarijn Hoefte, Peter Meel &
Hans Renders (eds), *Tropenlevens:
De [post]koloniale biografie,* pp. 216-35.
Amsterdam/Leiden: Boom/ KITLV
Uitgeverij.

Klooster, H.A.J.
1985 *Indonesiërs schrijven hun geschiedenis:
De ontwikkeling van de Indonesische
geschiedboefening in theorie en praktijk,
1900-1980.* Dordrecht: Foris.

Koch, Koen & Paul Scheffer (eds)
1996 *Het nut van Nederland: Opstellen over
soevereiniteit en identiteit.* Amsterdam: Bert Bakker.

Kom, Anton de
1999 *Wij slaven van Suriname.* Amsterdam:
Contact. [1934]

Koning, Florine

2009 *De Pasar Malam van Tong Tong: Een Indische onderneming.* Den Haag: Stichting Tong Tong.

Koopmans, Ruud

2006 'De politieke mobilisatie van allochtonen: Een vergelijking van Nederland, Duitsland, Frankrijk, Groot-Brittannië en Zwitserland', in: Frank van Tubergen & Ineke Maas (eds), *Allochtonen in Nederland in internationaal perspectief*, pp. 111-35. Amsterdam: Amsterdam University Press.

Koopmans, Ruud & Paul Statham

2003 'How national citizenship shapes transnationalism: A comparative analysis of migrant and minority claims-making in Germany, Great Britain and the Netherlands', in: Christian Joppke & Ewa Morawska (eds), *Toward assimilation and citizenship: Immigrants in liberal nation-states*, pp. 195-238. London: Palgrave.

Kossmann, E.H.

1996 'Verdwijnt de Nederlandse identiteit?: Beschouwingen over natie en cultuur', in: Koen Koch & Paul Scheffer (eds), *Het nut van Nederland: Opstellen over soevereiniteit en identiteit*, pp. 56-68. Amsterdam: Bert Bakker.

Kowaleski Wallace, Elizabeth

2006 *The British slave trade and public memory.* New York: Columbia University Press.

Kraak, J.H., J.E. Ellemers & E. Wittermans

1958 *De repatriëring uit Indonesië: Een onderzoek naar de integratie van de gerepatrieerden uit Indonesië in de Nederlandse samenleving.* 's-Gravenhage: Staatsdrukkerij- en Uitgeverijbedrijf.

Kuitenbrouwer, Maarten

2001 *Tussen oriëntalisme en wetenschap: Het Koninklijk Instituut voor Taal-, Land- en Volkenkunde in historisch verband, 1851-2001.* Leiden: KITLV Uitgeverij.

Lammers, C.J.

2005 *Vreemde overheersing: Bezetten en bezetting in sociologisch perspectief.* Amsterdam: Bert Bakker.

Lange, Daan de

2009 'Een spiegelende oppervlakte': Een onderzoek naar de herinneringscultuur rond Nederlands-Indië. [MA-scriptie Geschiedenis, Vrije Universiteit Amsterdam.].

Lechner, Frank J.

2008 *The Netherlands: Globalization and national identity.* London: Routledge.

Lee, Taeku

2008 'Race, immigration, and the identity-to-politics link', *Annual Review of Political Sciences* 11:457-78.

Leerssen, Joep van

2007 *National thought in Europe: A cultural history.* Amsterdam: Amsterdam University Press.

Leeuwen, Lizzy van

2008 *Ons Indisch erfgoed: Zestig jaar strijd om cultuur en identiteit.* Amsterdam: Bakker.

Lefeuvre, Daniel

2006 *Pour en finir avec la répentence coloniale.* Paris: Flammarion.

Legêne, Susan

1998 *De bagage van Blomhoff en Van Breugel: Japan, Java, Tripoli en Suriname in de negentiende-eeuwse Nederlandse cultuur van het imperialisme.* Amsterdam: KIT.

2005 'Canon van verschil: Musea en koloniale cultuur in Nederland', in: Rob van der Laarse (ed.), *Bezeten van vroeger: Erfgoed, identiteit en musealisering*, pp. 124-52. Amsterdam: Het Spinhuis.

Levitt, Peggy & B. Nadya Jaworsky

2007 'Transnational migration studies: Past developments and future trends', *Annual Review of Sociology* 33:129-56.

Liem, Pretty

2000 *Stapvoets voorwaarts: Maatschappelijke status van Surinamers in Nederland.* Amsterdam: Thela Thesis.

Lier, Rudolf A.J. van

1977 *Samenleving in een grensgebied: Een sociaal-historische studie van Suriname.* Amsterdam: Emmering. [1949]

Lijphart, Arend

1966 *The trauma of decolonization: The Dutch and West New Guinea*. New Haven/London: Yale University Press.

1975 *The politics of accommodation: Pluralism and democracy in the Netherlands*. Berkeley: University of California Press.

Locher-Scholten, Elsbeth

2003 'From urn to monument: Dutch memories of World War II in the Pacific, 1945-1995.' In: Andrea L. Smith (ed.), *Europe's invisible migrants*, pp. 105-28. Amsterdam: Amsterdam University Press.

2006 'Die "Indische Generation" in den Niederlanden: Koloniales Erbe als innen- wie außenpolitisches Problem (1950-2005)', *Werkstattgeschichte* 43:63-83.

Locher-Scholten, Elsbeth & Remco Raben

2006 Verengd verleden: Kanttekeningen bij het eindexamen geschiedenis voor havo en vwo 2007 en 2008. *Kleio: Tijdschrift van de Vereniging van Docenten in Geschiedenis en Staatsinrichting in Nederland* 47-8:4-9.

Loo, Vilan van de

2009 *Familie gebleven: Hulp aan landgenoten in Indonesië*. De Rijp: Orange House.

Lowenthal, David

2005 'Heritage and history: Rivals and partners in Europe', in: Rob van der Laarse (ed.), *Bezeten van vroeger: Erfgoed, identiteit en musealisering*, pp. 29-39. Amsterdam: Het Spinhuis.

Lubkemann, Stephen C.

2003 'Race, class, and kin in the negotiation of 'internal strangerhood' among Portuguese retornados, 1975-2000', in: Andre L. Smith (ed.), *Europe's invisible migrants*, pp. 75-94. Amsterdam: Amsterdam University Press.

Lucassen, Jan & Leo Lucassen (eds)

1997 *Migrants, migration history, history: Old paradigms and new perspectives*. Bern: Lang.

Lucassen, Jan & Rinus Penninx

1994 *Nieuwkomers, nakomelingen, Nederlanders: Immigranten in Nederland 1550-1993*. Amsterdam: Het Spinhuis.

Lucassen, Leo

2003 'Appendix; Een kort overzicht van de immigratie naar Nederland in de twintigste eeuw', in: Rosemarie Buikema & Maaike Meijer (eds), *Cultuur en migratie in Nederland: Kunsten in beweging 1900-1980*, pp. 421-35. Den Haag: SDU Uitgevers.

2005 *The immigrant threat: The integration of old and migrants in Western Europe since 1850*. Urbana: Illinois University Press.

Lucassen, Leo, David Feldman & Jochen Oltmer (eds)

2006 *Paths of integration: Migrants in Western Europe (1880-2004)*. Amsterdam: Amsterdam University Press.

Lucassen, Leo & André J.F. Köbben

1992 *Het partiële gelijk: Controverses over het onderwijs in de eigen taal en cultuur en de rol daarbij van beleid en wetenschap (1951-1991)*. Amsterdam: Swets & Zeitlinger.

Lucassen, Leo & Wim Willems

2006 *Gelijkheid en onbehagen: Over steden, nieuwkomers en nationaal geheugenverlies*. Amsterdam: Bert Bakker.

Lucassen, Leo & Charlotte Laarman

2009 'Immigration, intermarriage and the changing face of Europe in the post war period', *History of the Family* 14-1:52-68.

Lutz, Helma & Kathrin Gawarecki (eds)

2005 *Kolonialgeschichte und Erinnerungskultur: Die Kolonialvergangenheit im kollektiven Gedächtnis der deutschen und niederländischen Einwanderungsgesellschaft*. Münster: Waxmann.

MacMaster, Neil

1997 *Colonial migrants and racism: Algerians in France, 1900-62*. Basingstoke: Macmillan.

Mahawat Khan, M.A.

2003 'Hindostaanse moslims en hun organisatievorming', in: Chan E.S. Choenni & Kanta Sh. Adhin (eds), *Hindostanen: Van Brits-Indische emigranten via Suriname tot burgers van Nederland*, pp. 122-36. Den Haag: Sampreshan.

Marie, Claude-Valentin

2002 'Les Antillais en France: une nouvelle donne', *Hommes et Migrations* 1237:26-39.

Marques, Margarida

2012 'Postcolonial Portugal: Between Scylla and Charybdis?', in: Ulbe Bosma, Jan Lucassen & Gert Oostindie (eds), *Postcolonial migrations and identity politics*. Oxford: Berghahn. [in print]

Marshall, Edwin

2003 *Ontstaan en ontwikkeling van het Surinaamse nationalisme: Natievorming als opgave*. Delft: Eburon.

Martinus Arion, Frank

1999 'Een "beau geste"', in: Gert Oostindie (ed.), *Het verleden onder ogen: Herdenking van de slavernij*, pp. 19-23. Amsterdam/Den Haag: Arena/Prins Claus Fonds. [1998.]

Mee, Tonny van der & Domingo Tomasouw

2005 *Andere verhalen: Molukkers in Nederland met een andere aankomstgeschiedenis of beroepsachtergrond dan de KNIL-groep van 1951*. Utrecht: Moluks Historisch Museum.

Meel, Peter

1998 'Towards a typology of Suriname nationalism', *New West Indian Guide* 72-3/4:257-81.

1999 *Tussen autonomie en onafhankelijkheid: Nederlands-Surinaamse betrekkingen 1954-1961*. Leiden: KITLV Uitgeverij.

Meijer, Hans

2004 *In Indië geworteld*. Amsterdam: Bakker.

2005 *Indische rekening: Indië, Nederland en de backpay-kwestie 1945-2005*. Amsterdam: Boom.

2007 '"Geschiedenis is nu eenmaal altijd politiek": De studie-Drooglever als symptoom van de moeizame omgang van Nederland met het koloniale verleden en de complexe relatie met Indonesië', *Bijdragen en Mededelingen betreffende de Geschiedenis der Nederlanden* 122-1:72-90.

Meijer, Maaike et al. (eds)

2003-5 *Cultuur en migratie in Nederland*. Den Haag: SDU Uitgevers [5 delen]

Meijer, Remco

1995 *Oostindisch doof: Het Nederlandse debat over de dekolonisatie van Indonesië.* Amsterdam: Bert Bakker

Michon, Laure, Jean Tillie & Anja van Heelsum

2007 *Political participation of migrants in the Netherlands since 1986.* Amsterdam: Instituut voor Migratie en Etnische Studies.

Miège, Jean-Louis & Colette Dubois (eds)

1994 'Introduction', in: Jean-Louis Miège & Colette Dubois (eds), *L'Europe retrouvée; Les migrations de la décolonisation*, pp. 9-22. Paris: L'Harmattan.

Mochtar Lubis

1979 *Het land onder de regenboog: De geschiedenis van Indonesië*. Alphen: Sijthoff.

Modood, Tariq

2006 'Politics of blackness and Asian identity', in: N. Ali, V.S. Kalra & S. Sayyid (eds), *A postcolonial people: South Asians in Britain*, pp. 64-71. London: Hurst.

Molleman, Henk

2003 'Het minderhedenbeleid in retrospectief', *Socialisme en Democratie* 1/2: 62-66.

Niekerk, Mies van

2000 *'De krekel en de mier': Fabels en feiten over maatschappelijke stijging van Creoolse en Hindoestaanse Surinamers in Nederland*. Amsterdam: Het Spinhuis.

2004 'Afro-Caribbeans and Indo-Caribbeans in the Netherlands: Premigration legacies and social mobility', *International Migration Review* 38:158-83.

Noiriel, Gérard

2007 *Immigration, antisémitisme et racisme en France (XIXe - XXe Siècle); Discours publics, humiliations privées.* Paris: Fayard.

Nora, Pierre & Françoise Chandernagor

2008 *Liberté pour l'histoire.* Paris: CNRS Editions.

Obdeijn, Herman & Marlou Schrover

2008 *Komen en gaan: Immigratie en emigratie in Nederland vanaf 1550.* Amsterdam: Bakker.

Oldfield, J.R.

2007 *'Chords of freedom': Commemoration, ritual and British transatlantic slavery.* Manchester: Manchester University Press.

Oord, Ad van den

2004 *Allochtonen van nu & de oorlog van toen: Marokko, de Nederlandse Antillen, Suriname en Turkije in de Tweede Wereldoorlog.* Den Haag/Utrecht: SDU Uitgevers/Forum.

Oostindie, Gert J.

1989 'Cultuurbeleid en de loden last van een koloniaal verleden: Sticusa, 1948-1989', *Sticusa Jaarverslag*: 60-88.

1997 *Het paradijs overzee: De 'Nederlandse' Caraïben en Nederland.* Amsterdam: Bert Bakker.

2003 'Squaring the circle: Commemorating the VOC after 400 years', *Bijdragen tot de Taal-, Land- en Volkenkunde* 159:135-61.

2004 'Wij slaven van Suriname en het intellectuele eigendom van het koloniale verleden', in: Michiel van Kempen et al. (eds), *Wandelaar onder de palmen; Opstellen over koloniale en postkoloniale literatuur opgedragen aan Bert Paasman*, pp. 495-504. Leiden: KITLV Uitgeverij.

2005 *Paradise overseas: The Dutch Caribbean: colonialism and its transatlantic legacies.* Oxford: Macmillan.

2005 'The slippery paths of commemoration and heritage tourism: The Netherlands, Ghana, and the rediscovery of Atlantic slavery', *New West Indian Guide* 79:55-77.

2006 *De parels en de kroon: Het koningshuis en de koloniën.* Amsterdam: De Bezige Bij.

2008 'Slavernij, canon en trauma: debatten en dilemma's', *Tijdschrift voor Geschiedenis* 121-1:4-21.

2008 'Historical memory and national canons', in: Gert Oostindie (ed.), *Dutch colonialism, migration and cultural heritage*, pp. 63-93. Leiden: KITLV Press.

2009 'History brought home: Postcolonial migrations and the Dutch rediscov-

ery of slavery', in: Wim Klooster (ed.), *Migration, trade, and slavery in an expanding world: Essays in honor of Pieter Emmer*, pp. 305-27. Leiden: Brill.

2009 'Koloniën, migranten en Franse grandeur: Scheuren in het beeld van de voorbeeldnatie', *Academische Boekengids* 73:34-9.

2009 'Migration paradoxes of non-sovereignty: A comparative perspective on the Dutch Caribbean', in: Peter Clegg & Antonio Pantojas-García, *Governance in the non-independent Caribbean: Challenges and opportunities in the 21st century*, pp. 163-81. Kingston: Ian Randle.

2009 'Public memories of the Atlantic slave trade and slavery in contemporary Europe', *European Review* 17(3&4): 611-27.

2012 'Postcolonial migrants in the Netherlands', in: Ulbe Bosma, Jan Lucassen & Gert Oostindie (eds), *Postcolonial migrations and identity politics.* Oxford: Berghahn. [in print]

Oostindie, Gert (ed.)

1999 *Het verleden onder ogen: Herdenking van de slavernij.* Amsterdam/Den Haag: Arena/Prins Claus Fonds.

1999 *Curaçao 30 mei 1969: Verhalen over de revolte.* Amsterdam: Amsterdam University Press.

2001 *Facing up to the past: Perspectives on the commemoration of slavery from Africa, the Americas and Europe.* Kingston/ The Hague: Ian Randle/Prince Claus Fund.

Oostindie, Gert & Inge Klinkers

2001 *Knellende koninkrijksbanden: Het Nederlandse dekolonisatiebeleid in de Caraïben, 1940-2000.* Amsterdam: Amsterdam University Press.

2003 *Decolonising the Caribbean: Dutch policies in comparative perspective.* Amsterdam: Amsterdam University Press.

Oostindie, Gert, Liane van der Linden & Remco Raben

2002 'De koloniale opstelling', *De Gids* 165:415-45.

Oostindie, Gert & Emy Maduro

1986 *In het land van de overheerser: II. Antillianen en Surinamers in Nederland 1634/1667-1954.* Dordrecht: Foris.

Oostindie, Gert & Henk Schulte Nordholt

2006 'Nederland en zijn koloniale verleden: Moeizame overgang van dekolonisatie naar buitenlands beleid', *Internationale Spectator* 60-11:573-77.

Oostindie, Gert, Henk Schulte Nordholt & Fridus Steijlen

2011 *Postkoloniale monumenten in Nederland/Post-colonial monuments in the Netherlands.* Leiden: KITLV Press.

Oostindie, Gert & Fridus Steijlen

2009 'Zestig jaar na de eerste "kille" ontvangst: Onderzoek legt onvrede onder "postkoloniale" migranten bloot', *Contrast* 16 (November):24-9.

Ovalle-Bahamón, Ricardo E.

2003 'The wrinkles of decolonization and nationness: White Angolans as *retornados* in Portugal', in: Andre L. Smith (ed.), *Europe's invisible migrants*, pp. 147-68. Amsterdam: Amsterdam University Press.

Parekh, Bhikhu

2000 *Report of the Commission on the future of multi-ethnic Britain.* London: Profile Books. [The Parekh Report.]

Pattynama, Pamela

2000 'Assimilation and masquerade: Self-constructions of Indo-Dutch women', *European Journal of Women's Studies* 7:281-99.

2007 '... de baai ... de binnenbaai...': Indië herinnerd.* Amsterdam: Vossiuspers.

Paul, Kathleen

1997 *Whitewashing Britain: Race and citizenship in the postwar era.* Ithaca: Cornell University Press.

Peach, Ceri

2006 'Demographics of BrAsian settlement, 1951-2001', in: N. Ali, V.S. Kalra & S. Sayyid (eds), *A postcolonial people: South Asians in Britain*, pp. 168-81. London: Hurst.

Penninx, R., J. Schoorl & C. van Praag

1994 *The impact of international migration on receiving countries: The case of the Netherlands.* Den Haag: NIDI.

Pétré-Grenouillé, Olivier

2004 *Les traites négrières: Essai d'histoire globale.* Paris: Gallimard.

Petronilia, Saron (ed.)

2000 *Raadsleden met dubbele antenne: Ervaringen van allochtone politici.* Amsterdam: Instituut voor Publiek en Politiek.

Plaatsen van herinnering

2005-6 *Plaatsen van herinnering.* Amsterdam: Bert Bakker. [4 volumes]

Poeze, Harry A., Cees van Dijk & Inge van der Meulen

1986 *In het land van de overheerser: I. Indonesiërs in Nederland 1600-1950.* Dordrecht: Foris.

Polletta, Francesca & James M. Jasper

2001 'Collective identity and social movements', *Annual Review of Sociology* 27:283-305.

Portes, Alejandro & Rubén G. Rumbaut

1996 *Immigrant America: A portrait.* Berkeley: University of California Press.

Praag, C.S. van

1971 'Het overheidsbeleid inzake allochtone groepen', in: H. Verwey-Jonker (ed.), *Allochtonen in Nederland: Beschouwingen over de gerepatrieerden, Ambonezen, Surinamers, Antillianen, buitenlandse werknemers, Chinezen, vluchtelingen en buitenlandse studenten in onze samenleving*, pp. 19-44. s'-Gravenhage: Staatsuitgeverij.

Price, Richard

2001 'The miracle of creolization: A retrospective', *New West Indian Guide* 75:35-64.

2001 'Monuments and silent screamings: A view from Martinique', in: Gert Oostindie (ed.), *Facing up to the past: Perspectives on the commemoration of slavery from Africa, the Americas and Europe*, pp. 58-62. Kingston/The Hague: Ian Randle/Prince Claus Fund.

Price, Sally

2007 *Paris primitive: Jacques Chirac's museum on the Quai Branly.* Chicago: University of Chicago Press.

Put, Roos van
2005 'Den Haag: eigentijdse beeldende kunst van Indische kunstenaars', in: Esther Captain et al. (eds), *De Indische zomer in Den Haag: Het cultureel erfgoed van de Indische hoofdstad*, pp.159-92. Leiden: KITLV Uitgeverij.

Putte, Florimon van
1999 *Dede pikiña ku su bisiña: Papiamentu – Nederlands en de overwerk verleden tijd*. Zutphen: Walburg Pers.

Putnam, Robert
2000 *Bowling alone: The collapse and revival of American community*. New York: Simon & Schuster.

Raben, Remco
2000 'Postkoloniaal Nederland', *Internationale Spectator* 54-7/8:359-64.
2002 'De VOC: Het geheim achter succesvol modern leven', *Historisch Nieuwsblad*, December, pp. 26-30.

Raben, Remco (ed.)
1999 *Beelden van de Japanse bezetting van Indonesië: Persoonlijke getuigenissen en publieke beeldvorming in Indonesië, Japan en Nederland*. Zwolle/Amsterdam: Waanders/Nederlands Instituut voor Oorlogsdocumentatie.

Rainero, Romain
1994 'Repatriés et réfugiés italiens; Un grand problème méconnu', in: Jean-Louis Miège & Colette Dubois (eds), *L'Europe retrouvée: Les migrations de la decolonization*, pp. 23-33. Paris: L'Harmattan.

Ramdas, Anil
2008 'Een noodzakelijke fantasie', *Vrij Nederland*, 12 January: 36-41.
2009 *Paramaribo: De vrolijkste stad in de jungle*. Amsterdam: De Bezige Bij.

Ramlal, D.
2003 'Politieke participatie van Hindostanen', in: Chan E.S. Choenni & Kanta Sh. Adhin (eds), *Hindostanen: Van Brits-Indische emigranten via Suriname tot burgers van Nederland*, pp. 204-13. Den Haag: Sampreshan.

Ramos, Aarón Gamaliel & Angel Israel Rivera (eds)
2001 *Islands at the crossroads: Politics in the non-independent Caribbean*. Kingston/ Boulder: Randle Publishers/Rienner Publishers.

Ramsoedh, Hans
2002 'Surinaamse hindoes en moslims in Nederland', *Oso; Tijdschrift voor Surinaamse Taalkunde, Letterkunde, Cultuur en Geschiedenis* 21-1:135-53.
2003 'Religieuze organisatievorming bij Hindoes', in: Chan E.S. Choenni & Kanta Sh. Adhin (eds), *Hindostanen: Van Brits-Indische emigranten via Suriname tot burgers van Nederland*, pp. 106-20. Den Haag: Sampreshan.

Rath, J.
1985 'Immigrant candidates in the Netherlands', *Cahiers d'études sur la Méditerranée orientale et le monde turco-iranien* 1:46-62.

Reflecting
2006 *Reflecting on the past and looking to the future*. London: Department for Culture, Media and Sport.

Reybroeck, David van
2010 *Congo: Een geschiedenis*. Amsterdam: De Bezige Bij.

Ribbens, Kees, Joep Schenk & Martijn Eickhoff
2008 *Oorlog op vijf continenten: Nieuwe Nederlanders & de geschiedenissen van de Tweede Wereldoorlog*. Amsterdam: Boom.

Ridder, Ilonka M. de (ed.)
2007 *Eindelijk erkenning? Het Gebaar: de tegemoetkoming aan de Indische gemeenschap*. Den Haag: Stichting Het Gebaar.

Rietbergen, Peter,
2002 'De VOC herdenken?', *Tijdschrift voor Geschiedenis* 115:504-24.

Rijkschroeff, B.R., G.T. The & S.M. Wu
1993 *Bij leven en welzijn: De positie van oudere Chinezen en oudere Indische Nederlanders vergeleken*. Capelle: Labyrinth Publication.

Robinson, Tjalie
1976 *Piekerans van een straatslijper: Zoveelste druk*. Den Haag: Moesson/ Tong Tong.

Roemer, Astrid
1974 *Neem mij terug, Suriname*. Den Haag: Pressag.

Runnymede Trust
2004 *Realising the vision: Progress and further challenges.* London: Runnymede Trust.

Said, Edward
1978 *Orientalism.* London: Routledge.
1993 *Culture and imperialism.* New York: Knopf.

Salmon, Pierre
1994 'Les retours en Belgique induits par la décolonisation', in: Jean-Louis Miège & Colette Dubois (eds), *L'Europe retrouvée; Les migrations de la decolonization,* pp. 191-212. Paris: L'Harmattan.

San, Marion van
1998 *Stelen en slikken: Delinquent gedrag van Curaçaose jongens in Nederland.* [Dissertatie, Universiteit Utrecht]

Sansone, Livio
1992 *Schitteren in de schaduw: Overlevings-strategieën, subcultuur en etniciteit van Creoolse jongeren uit de lagere klasse in Amsterdam 1981-1990.* Amsterdam: Het Spinhuis.
2000 'The internalization of black culture: A comparison of lower-class youth in Brazil and the Netherlands', in: Hans Vermeulen & Joel Perlmann, *Does culture make a difference?,* pp. 150-83. Basingstoke/New York: Macmillan/St. Martin's Press.
2009 'The making of Suriland: The binational development of a Black community between the tropics and the North Sea', in: Margarita Cervantes-Rodríguez, Ramón Grosfoguel & Eric Mielants (eds), *Caribbean migration to Western Europe and the United States,* pp. 169-88. Philadelphia: Temple University Press.

Sartono Kartodirdjo
2001 *Indonesian historiography.* Yogyakarta: Kanisius.

Sayyid, S.
2006 'Introduction: BrAsians: Postcolonial people, ironic citizens', in: N. Ali, V.S. Kalra & S. Sayyid (eds), *A postcolonial people: South Asians in Britain,* pp. 1-10. London: Hurst.

Scagliola, Stef
2002 *Last van de oorlog: De Nederlandse oorlogsmisdaden in Indonesië en hun verwerking.* Amsterdam: Balans.

Schama, Simon
1988 *The embarrassment of riches: An interpretation of Dutch culture in the Golden Age.* New York: Fontana.

Scheffer, Paul
1996 'Land zonder spiegel: Over de politieke cultuur in Nederland', in: Koen Koch & Paul Scheffer (eds), *Het nut van Nederland: Opstellen over soevereiniteit en identiteit,* pp. 10-39. Amsterdam: Bert Bakker.
2000 'Het multiculturele drama', NRC *Handelsblad,* 29 January.
2006 *Het land van aankomst.* Amsterdam: De Bezige Bij.
2011 *The land of arrival: Immigrant nations.* Cambridge: Polity.

Schnabel, Paul et al.
2000 *De multiculturele illusie: Een pleidooi voor aanpassing en assimilatie. Met replieken van Ruben Gowricharn en Ineke Mok.* Utrecht: Forum.

Schulte Nordholt, Henk
2002 'A geneology of violence', in: Freek Columbijn & J. Thomas Lindblad (eds), *Roots of violence in Indonesia,* pp. 33-63. Leiden: KITLV Press.
2004 *De-colonising Indonesian historiography.* Lund: Lund University, Centre for East and South-East Asian Studies.
2008 *Indonesië na Soeharto: Reformasi en restauratie.* Amsterdam: Bert Bakker.

Schumacher, Peter
1980 *De minderheden: 600.000 vreemdelingen in Nederland.* Amsterdam: Van Gennep.

Schuster, John
1999 *Poortwachters over immigranten: Het debat over immigratie in het naoorlogse Groot-Brittannië en Nederland.* Amsterdam: Het Spinhuis.

Sedney, Jules
1997 *De toekomst van ons verleden: Democratie, etniciteit en politieke machtsvorming in Suriname.* Paramaribo: VACO.

Sen, Amartya
2006 *Identity and violence: The illusion of destiny.* New York: Norton.

Seriese, Edy

1997 'Wie dit lees is gek: Het Indische na Indië', in: Wim Willems, *Uit Indië geboren: Vier eeuwen familiegeschiedenis*, pp. 198-212. Zwolle: Waanders.

Sharpe, Michael

2005 'Globalization and migration: Post-colonial Dutch Antillean and Aruban immigrant political incorporation in the Netherlands', *Dialetical Anthropology* 29-3/4:291-314.

Smeets, Henk & Fridus Steijlen

2006 *In Nederland gebleven: De geschiedenis van Molukkers 1951-2006*. Amsterdam/Utrecht: Bert Bakker/Moluks Historisch Museum.

Smith, Andrea L.

2003 *Europe's invisible migrants*. Amsterdam: Amsterdam University Press.

Snel, Erik, Godfried Engbersen & Arjen Leerkes

2006 'Transnational involvement and social integration', *Global Networks* 6-3:265-84.

Sniderman, Paul M. & Louk Hagendoorn

2007 *When ways of life collide*. Princeton: Princeton University Press.

Soekarno

1931 Soekarno, *Indonesië klaagt aan! Pleirede voor den landraad te Bandoeng op 2 December 1930 gehouden*. Amsterdam: Arbeiderspers.

Somers, Erik & Stance Rijpma (eds),

2002 *Nederlanders Japanners Indonesiërs: Een opmerkelijke tentoonstelling*. Zwolle: Waanders, Amsterdam: NIOD.

Steijlen, Fridus

1996 *RMS; Moluks nationalisme in Nederland 1951-1994*. Amsterdam: Het Spinhuis.

2001 *Kerusuhan: Het misverstand over de Molukse onrust*. Utrecht: Forum.

2004 'Molukkers in Nederland: geschiedenis van een transnationale relatie', *Migrantenstudies* 4:238-51.

2010 'Het Gebaar', in: Madelon de Keijzer & Marije Plomp, *Het blijft gevoelig: Hoe wij ons de Tweede Wereldoorlog herinneren*. Amsterdam: Prometheus [in print].

Stipriaan, Alex van

2001 'The long road to a monument', in:

Gert Oostindie (ed.), *Facing up to the past: Perspectives on the commemoration of slavery from Africa, the Americas and Europe*, pp. 118-22. Kingston/The Hague: Ian Randle/Prince Claus Fund.

2004 'July 1; Emancipation Day in Suriname: A contested *lieu de mémoire*, 1863-2003', *New West Indian Guide* 78:269-304.

2006 'Between diaspora, (trans)nationalism, and American globalization: A history of Afro-Surinamese Emancipation Day', in: Ruben Gowricharn (ed.), *Caribbean transnationalism: Migration, pluralization, and social cohesion*, pp. 155-78. Lanham: Lexington Books.

Stipriaan, Alex van & Ellen Bal

2002 'De VOC is een geloof: Kanttekeningen bij een populair Nederlands imago', in: Manon van der Heijden & Paul van de Laar (eds), *Rotterdammers en de VOC: Handelscompagnie, stad en burgers (1600-1800)*, pp. 213-43. Amsterdam: Bakker.

Stipriaan, Alex van, Waldo Heilbron, Aspha Bijnaar & Valika Smeulders

2007 *Op zoek naar de stilte: Sporen van het slavernijverleden in Nederland*. Leiden/Amsterdam: KITLV Uitgeverij/NiNsee.

Spencer, Ian R.G.

1997 *British immigration policy since 1939: The making of multi-racial Britain*. London: Routledge.

Stora, Benjamin

2005 'Quand une mémoire (de guerre) peut en cacher une autre (coloniale)', in: Pascal Blanchard, Nicolas Bancel & Sandrine Lemaire (eds), *La fracture coloniale: La société française au prisme de l'héritage coloniale*, pp. 59-68. Paris: La Découverte.

2007 *Les guerres des mémoires: La France face à son passé colonial; Entretiens avec Thierry Leclère*. Paris: l' Aube.

2008 *Les guerres sans fin: Un historien, La France et l'Algérie*. Paris: Stock.

Surie, H.G.

1971 'De gerepatrieerden', in: H. Verwey-

Jonker (ed.), *Allochtonen in Nederland: Beschouwingen over de gerepatrieerden, Ambonezen, Surinamers, Antillianen, buitenlandse werknemers, Chinezen, vluchtelingen en buitenlandse studenten in onze samenleving*, pp. 45-108. 's-Gravenhage: Staatsuitgeverij.

Sutherland, Heather
2000 '"Een ontmoeting tussen twee culturen"? Eindexamenonderwerp geeft misleiden perspectief op Indonesische geschiedenis', *Spieghel Historiael* 35-11/12:455-60.

Tardieu, Marc
2005 *Les Antillais à Paris: D'hier à aujourd'hui*. Monaco: Editions du Rocher.

Thandi, Shinder
2012 'Postcolonial migrants in Britain: From unwelcome guests to partial and segmented assimilation', in: Ulbe Bosma, Jan Lucassen & Gert Oostindie (eds), *Postcolonial migrations and identity politics*. Oxford: Berghahn. [in print]

Thio, May Ling
2007 *Genoegens van wederzijds ((h)er) kennen: Identiteitsbeleving van peranakan Chinezen bij de vereniging De Vriendschap*. Amsterdam: Rozenberg.

Tillie, Jean
2000 *De etnische stem: Opkomst en stemgedrag van migranten tijdens gemeenteraadsverkiezingen, 1986-1998*. Utrecht: Forum.

Trouillot, Michel-Rolph
1995 *Silencing the past: Power and the production of history*. Boston: Beacon Press.

Unger, Brigitte & Melissa Siegel
2006 *The Netherlands-Suriname corridor for worker's remittances: Study prepared for the World Bank and the Dutch Ministry of Finance*. Utrecht: s.n.

Vale de Almeida, Miguel
2004 *An earth-colored sea: 'Race', culture and the politics of identity in the post-colonial Portuguese-speaking world*. New York: Berghahn.

Vanvugt, Ewald
1998 *De maagd en de soldaat: Koloniale monumenten in Amsterdam en elders*. Amsterdam: Mets.

Vergès, Françoise
2006 *La mémoire enchaînée: Questions sur l'esclavage*. Paris: Hachette.

Vermeulen, Floris & Anja van Heelsum
2011 'Group- or host state-related? Understanding the historical development of Suriname organizations in Amsterdam, 1965-2000', in: Ulbe Bosma (ed.), *Postcolonialism in the Netherlands* [in print].

Vermeulen, Hans en Rinus Penninx (eds)
1994 *Het democratisch ongeduld: De emancipatie en integratie van zes doelgroepen in het minderhedenbeleid*. Amsterdam: Het Spinhuis.

Verwey-Jonker, H.
1971 *Allochtonen in Nederland: Beschouwingen over de gerepatrieerden, Ambonezen, Surinamers, Antillianen, buitenlandse werknemers, Chinezen, vluchtelingen, buitenlandse studenten in onze samenleving*. 's-Gravenhage: Staatsuitgeverij.

Vianen, Bea
1973 *Het paradijs van Oranje*. Amsterdam: Querido.

Vlasblom, Dirk
2004 *Papoea: Een geschiedenis*. Amsterdam: Mets & Schilt.

Vogel, Jaap
2005 *Nabije vreemden: Een eeuw wonen en samenleven*. Den Haag: SDU Uitgevers.

Vogels, Ria, Paul Geense & Edwin Martens
1999 *De maatschappelijke positie van Chinezen in Nederland*. Assen: Van Gorcum.

Vree, Frank van
1995 *In de schaduw van Auschwitz: Herinneringen, beelden, geschiedenis*. Groningen: Historische Uitgeverij.

Vries, Marlene de
2009 'Indisch is een gevoel': De tweede en derde generatie Indische Nederlanders. Amsterdam: Amsterdam University Press.

Vuijsje, Herman
1986 *Vermoorde onschuld: Etnisch verschil als Hollands taboe*. Amsterdam: Bert Bakker.

2008 *Correct: Weldenkend Nederland sinds de jaren zestig.* Amsterdam: Contact. [1997]

Wal, Jessika ter
2005 'Active civic participation of immigrants in the Netherlands', *Politis; Building Europe with new citizens?: An inquiry into the civic participation of naturalized citizens and foreign residents in 25 countries.* http://www.uni-oldenburg.de/politis-europe/download/Netherlands.pdf.

Wallace, Elizabeth Kowaleski
2006 *The British slave trade and public memory.* New York: Columbia University Press.

Walraven, W.
1966 *Brieven aan familie en vrienden 1919-1941.* Amsterdam: Van Oorschot.

Walvin, James
2008 'Commemorating abolition 1807-2007'. [Paper presented at an international workshop 'The abolition of slavery: Long-term consequences' at the IISG/ International Institute for Social History, Amsterdam, 2 July.]

Weil, Patrick
2008 *Liberté, égalité, discriminations; L'identité nationale au regard de l'histoire.* Paris: Grasset.

Wekker, Gloria
2002 *Nesten bouwen op een winderige plek: Denken over gender en etniciteit in Nederland.* Inaugural address, Universiteit Utrecht.

Welie, Rik van
2008 'Patterns of slave trading and slavery in the Dutch colonial world, 1596-1863', in: Gert Oostindie (ed.), *Dutch colonialism, migration and cultural heritage*, pp. 155-259. Leiden: KITLV Press.

esseling, H.L.
1988 *Indië verloren, rampspoed geboren en andere opstellen over de geschiedenis van de Europese expansie.* Amsterdam: Bert Bakker.

Wetenschappelijke Raad voor het Regeringsbeleid
1979 *Etnische minderheden.* 's-Gravenhage: Staatsuitgeverij.

1989 *Allochtonenbeleid.* 's-Gravenhage: SDU Uitgevers.
2007 *Identificatie met Nederland.* Amsterdam: Amsterdam University Press.

Willems, Wim
2001 *De uittocht uit Indië 1945-1995.* Amsterdam: Bert Bakker.
2008 *Tjalie Robinson: Biografie van een Indo-schrijver.* Amsterdam: Bert Bakker.

Willemsen, Glenn
2006 *Dagen van gejuich en gejubel.* Den Haag/Amsterdam: Amrit/NiNsee.

Winckelman, Frank von & Wim Willems
1997 'Zwijgend inburgeren: Indisch in Nederland', in: Wim Willems, *Uit Indië geboren: Vier eeuwen familiegeschiedenis*, pp. 166-81. Zwolle: Waanders.

Winder, Robert
2004 *Bloody foreigners: The story of immigration to Britain.* London: Little, Brown.

Withuis, Jolande
2002 *Erkenning: Van oorlogstrauma naar klaagcultuur.* Amsterdam: De Bezige Bij.

Wolters, Hester et al. (eds)
1995 *Nederland-Indonesia 1945-1995: Een culturele vervlechting/Suatu pertalian budaya.* Den Haag: [Z]oo producties.

Yap Kie Hien
1987 'Het Peranakan-gezin in Nederland: Bestaat het?', in: Vriendenkring Lian Yi Hui, *Het Peranakan-gezin in Nederland: Tweede minisymposium Vriendenkring Lian Yi Hui*, pp. 32-44. [S.l.]: Vriendenkring Lian Yi Hui.

Young, J.E.
1993 *The texture of memory: Holocaust memorials and meaning.* New Haven: Yale University Press.

Young, Robert J.C.
2001 *Postcolonialism: An historical introduction.* Oxford: Blackwell.

Zijl, Annejet van der
2004 *Sonny Boy.* Amsterdam: Nijgh & Van Ditmar.

ACKNOWLEDGEMENTS

This book is a slightly revised translation of my book published in early 2010, *Postkoloniaal Nederland; Vijfenzestig jaar vergeten, herdenken, verdringen* (Amsterdam: Bert Bakker). *Postkoloniaal Nederland* was the culmination of a research programme carried out under my supervision between 2005 and 2009 by three institutions of the Royal Netherlands Academy of Arts and Sciences (KNAW): the International Institute of Social History (IISH), the Meertens Institute (MI) in Amsterdam, and my own Royal Netherlands Institute of Southeast Asian and Caribbean Studies (KITLV) in Leiden. The research was funded by the Netherlands Organisation for Scientific Research (NWO) and the KNAW.

A research sabbatical in the academic year 2008-2009 gave me the opportunity to write this book and a number of related articles, and also to edit, with Ulbe Bosma and Jan Lucassen, the volume *Postcolonial migrations and identity politics* (Berghahn, 2012). I would like to thank the KITLV and KNAW for granting me this freedom and the Fondation Maison des Sciences de l'Homme (Paris), the Eric Remarque Institute for European Studies at New York University, and the Netherlands Institute for Advanced Study in the Humanities and Social Sciences (NIAS-KNAW) in Wassenaar for their hospitality. The NWO provided some of the funding for the translation and publication by Amsterdam University Press (AUP), both in book form and open access.

Apart from the funders, my gratitude above all goes to the readers of early versions or parts of this book, to the researchers on the programme, and to all those who joined us for a time – whether short or long – during the course of the project. Marga Alferink, Ulbe Bosma, Ingrid Koulen, Jan Lucassen, Henk Schulte Nordholt and Fridus Steijlen commented on the entire manuscript, Ruben Gowricharn, Carel de Haseth, Wim Manuhutu, Yayah Siegers-Samaniri and Gilbert Wawoe on one or more chapters. Annika Ockhorst stood by me as an exemplary research assistant. Jan Breman made some useful suggestions for adjustments to the translation. Annabel Howland was a professional and cheerful translator, much appreciated, and the staff at AUP was as professional as ever.

Finally, for innumerable instructive contacts and conversations, many thanks go to my conversation partners from the world of postcolonial organizations, not least to all those who cherish their postcolonial backgrounds in no other way than as just one of their roots or benchmarks.

INDEX OF PEOPLE, ORGANIZATIONS AND MEMORIAL SITES

Aboutaleb, Ahmed 68-69, 246n.
Achter het Nieuws 89
Adhin, Kanta 120
Aisa Samachar 65, 177, 256-257n.
Alba, Richard 243n., 254n.
Albayrak, Nebahat 68
Alferink, Marga 56, 65, 245n.-246n., 251n., 255n.
Amersfoort, J.M.M. van 30, 243n.-244n., 249n., 251n., 253n.
Amsterdam, official residence of the Mayor 153
Amsterdam, city council of
Anderson, Benedict 103, 248n.-249n.
Antilliaans Netwerk 64, 182
Antillean Summer Carnival 123-124
Archipel 169
Arion, Frank Martinus 123, 151, 181, 253n.
Arron, Henck 32, 34, 54, 177, 256n.
Aspeslagh, Rob 252n.

Baay, Reggie 111
Badan Persatuan 59, 255n.
Bagley, Christopher 10, 30, 43, 243n.-244n.
Balie, De 252n.
Balkenende, Jan Peter 130, 132, 152, 225, 252n.
Baudet, H. 250n., 253n., 260n.
Beatrix, Queen 13, 86, 90, 93, 112, 152
Beek, Relus ter 90
Belliot, Hannah 68
Berlusconi, Silvio 210
Bernhard, Prince 90
Biekman, Barryl 151, 254n.
Bijleveld, Ank 254n.
Bijlhout, Philomena 68, 70, 246n.
Birney, Alfred 111
Black Panthers 141

Blair, Tony 199-201, 203, 258n.
Bleich, Anet 245n.
Bloem, Marion 111, 261n.
Blok, commissie-S. 31, 65, 244n.-246n., 248n., 259n.
Blom, Hans 125, 251n., 254n., 259n.
Blue Diamonds 110
Boehmer, Elleke 261n.
Boekholt, Ralph 109, 136-137, 248n.-250n., 252n.
Boekholt, Rudy 84
Boon, Jan zie Tjalie Robinson
Boon, Rogier 108
Boon, Siem 108, 111-112
Borst-Eilers, Els 85, 94
Bosma, Ulbe 26, 56-57, 65, 78, 244n.-250n., 253n., 255n.-257n., 260n.-261n.
Bossenbroek, Martin 82, 87, 247-249n., 252n., 259n.
Bot, Ben 58, 138
Bouterse, Desi 68, 147, 178-179, 246n.
Boxtel, Roger van 254n., 256n.
Brinkman, Elco 63
Bronbeek zie Indisch Herinneringscentrum (IHC)
Brouwers, Jeroen 77
Brown, Gordon 201
Brubaker, Rogers 249n., 251n.
Brückel-Beiten, Mary 112
Brug, De 108
Brugmans, I.J. 250n., 253n., 260n.
Buruma, Ian 10, 43, 259n.
Bussemaker, Herman 95
Bussemaker, Jet 77
Buyne, Hannah 68
Byvanck, Valentijn 160, 254n.

Cain, Artwell 254n.
Cairo, Edgar 118
Campbell, Eddy 154
Captain, Esther 77, 93, 112-113, 247n.,
    249n.-250n., 253n.
CDA 10, 67, 246n., 254n.-255n.
*Centraal Comité van Kerkelijk en Particulier
    Initiatief voor Sociale Zorg ten behoeve
    van Gerepatrieerden* (CCKP) 57
Chandernagor, Françoise 205-206, 259n.
Chirac, Jacques 196, 204-205, 258n.
Choenni, Chan 120, 244n., 246n., 251n.
Christen Unie 246n.
Cleintuar, Guus 109, 250n.
Clingendael 252n.
Coen, Jan Pietersz 136
Coenradi, Herman 246n.
Cohen, Job 152
Colijn, Hendrik 146, 229
Colonies, Ministry for the 145
Columbus, Christoffel 133, 208
Comité 2004 182
*Comité Geschiedkundig Eerherstel Nederlands-
    Indië* 136, 249n.
*Comité Herdenking Gevallenen in Nederlands-
    Indië* 139
Commission for Racial Equality (CRE) 198,
    257-258n.
Commission on Integration & Cohe-
    sion 201, 258n.
Committee of Dutch Depts of Honour 255n.
Committee of Recommendatation (Slavery
    Past) 254n.
Cooper, Frederick 249n., 251n.
Cottaar, Annemarie 260n.
Couperus, Louis 144, 229
Croes, Betico 183
Culture, Recreation and Social Welfare
    (CRM), Ministry of 30, 59

D66 67, 246n., 254n., 256n.
Deetman, Huub 113
Derksen, Ellen 91, 108, 112, 218
De stem van Ambon 59
Deventer, C.Th. van 135, 252n.
Dis, Adriaan van 74, 111
Door de Eeuwen Trouw (DDET) 59
Doorn, J.A.A. van 76, 89-90, 96, 131, 144, 228,
    235, 246n., 248n., 252-253n., 259-261n.
Dort, Wieteke van 111
Drees, Willem 29, 79

Drooglever, P.J. 255n.
Ducelle, Lilian 107-108, 137, 250n., 252n.,
    260n.
Dutch World service (RNWO) 171
Duyvendak, Jan Willem 245n., 249n., 254n.

Ecury, Boy 97, 181
Eickhoff, Martijn 249n.
Ellemers, J.E. 75, 243n., 245n., 247n., 253n.
Elsevier 34, 244n., 256n.
Emmer, P.C. 254n.
Engelen, Ewald 245n., 249n., 254n.
Entzinger, Han 243-245n.
Equality and Human Rights Commis-
    sion 199, 258n.
Essed, Philomena 236
Evangelical (Moravian) Brotherhood 11

Fabricius, Johan 134
Famiri 65, 177, 256n.
Fasseur, Cees 91, 247-248n., 255n.
Fennema, Meindert 245-246n., 251n.
Fermin, Alfons 244-245n.
Fermina, Hubert-Geronimo 67
Fernandes Mendes, Hugo 254n.
Ferrol-Macintosh, Elfriede 98
Finance, Ministry of 92
Foreign Affairs, Ministry for 58, 132, 179,
    255n.
Fortuyn, Pim 10, 41, 43, 68, 127, 156, 244n.,
    254n.
Forsa 64
Franco, Francisco 100

Gama, Vasco da 133
Gans, Herbert 243n.
Gaulle, Charles de 193, 257n.
Gebaar, Het 81, 83-85, 88, 91, 94, 169,
    247n.-248n., 255n.
Geugten, Tom van der 253n.
Gilroy, Paul 200-201, 237, 258n., 261n.
Giscard d'Estaing, Valérie 194
Gouda, Frances 236, 261n.
Governance of Britain, the 201
Gowricharn, Ruben 120, 253n.-255n., 257n.,
    260n.
Grever, Maria 254n.
Groenberg, Roy 251n.
Groene Amsterdammer, De 151, 253n.
GroenLinks 246n.
Grönloh, Anneke 107, 110

Haan, Ido de 245n.-246n., 249n., 254n.
Haasse, Hella 85, 253n.
Hagendoorn, Louk 245n., 259n., 261n.
Hall, Stuart 200, 236-237, 258n., 261n.
Hardiati, Endang Sri 260n.
Hatta, Mohammad 76
Hazes, André 216
Health, Welfare and Sports (vws),
    Ministry of 85, 99, 249n.
Hein, Piet 131-132
Helberg, Glenn 246n.
Helman, Albert 176, 260n.
Helsdingen, W.H. van 136, 252n.
Hendrix, W.J. 89, 248n.
Hermans, W.F. 146
Hessing, Enrique 133
Heutsz, J.B.van 139
Heutsz-monument, Van 139
Hindom, Saul 29
Hirohito, keizer 84, 142
Historisch Nieuwsblad 153, 225
Hochschildt, Adam 259n.
Hoetink, Harry 261n.
Hoost, Romeo 256n.
Horst, Liesbeth van der 249n.
Ho Ten Soeng, Roy 68
Hueting, J.E. 89

Indische Kunst Kring 108
Indische Pensioenbond 78
Indische Zomer 249n.-250n.
Indisch Gebaar 67, 248n.
Indisch Genootschap 229
Indisch House 95, 102, 127, 224, 249n.
Indisch Memorial Centre (ihc) 67, 81, 95,
    102, 111, 249n.
Indisch Monument 84, 90, 93-95, 142
Indisch Netwerk 114
Indisch Platform 57, 81, 84, 95, 248n.
Indisch Wetenschappelijk Instituut 109
Indo4life 114
Indo-European Alliance (iev) 79
Inspraakorgaan Welzijn Molukkers 59, 255n.
Interior, Ministry of the 41, 86

Janmaat, Hans 41
Jaworsky, B.N. 251n., 254n.
Jere 65
Jesurun, E.A.V. 182
Johannes Post primary school 11-12, 21
Jones, Guno 51-52, 245n., 253n., 256n.

Jong, Lou de 84, 95, 136-138, 253n.
Jong, Piet de 175
Jong, Sjoerd de 244n.-245n.
Jouwe, Nicolaas 29, 255n.
Judt, Tony 190, 257n.-258n., 261n.
Juliana, Queen 90, 92-93
Junior Dutch football team 185

Kaifu, Toshiki 84, 142
Kaisiepo, Marcus 29
Kaisiepo, Victor 29
Kambio; Portabos independiente antijano 172,
    255n.
Keppy, Peter 77-78, 247n., 249n., 260n.
Keurs, Pieter ter 260n.
Khaddafi, Muammar 210
Klompé, Marga A.M. 92
Kluveld, Amanda 85, 248n.
Koerier, de 171
Kok, Wim 13, 81-84, 94, 132, 151-152, 248n.
Koloniaal Instituut 229
Kom, Anton de 97, 119, 147, 149, 172, 176, 186,
    251n., 253n., 255n., 261n.
Koning, Florine 112, 245n., 247n., 250n.,
    255n., 260n.
Koninklijk Nederlands Aardrijkskundig
    Genootschap (knag) 229
Kontakto Antiyano 181
Koopmans, Ruud 164, 245n., 251n.-252n.,
    255n.-256n.
Kossmann, E.H. 251n.
Kousbroek, Rudy 77, 111
Kraak, J.H. 75, 243n., 245n., 247n., 253n.
Kwakoe Festival 119, 151

Lachmon, Jagernath 177, 256n.
Lalla Rookh 61, 120
Lalla Rookh 65, 251n., 257n.
Lammers, C.J. 243n.
Landelijk Overlegorgaan Welzijn Moluk-
    kers (lowm) 42
Landelijk Platform Slavernijverleden
    (lps) 151, 254n.
Landelijke Federatie van Welzijnsorganisat-
    ies 61
Leeuwen, Boeli van 123
Leeuwen, Lizzy van 32, 109-111, 218, 236,
    243n., 249n.-250n., 260n.-261n.
Legêne, Susan 236, 261n.
Levitt, P. 251n., 254n.
Liem, Pretty 244n.

Lier, Rudolf van 261n.
Lijphart, Arend 9, 173, 249n., 255n., 260n.
Lilipaly, John 67, 69
Loon, Jikke van 251n.
Lowenthal, David 261n.
LPF 68, 246n.
Lubbers, Ruud 86
Lubis, Mochtar 144
Lucassen, Jan 43, 244n.
Lucassen, Leo 244n.

Maarseveen, J.H. van 136
Madjoe 78
Maduro, George 97, 181, 244n.-245n., 256
Madurodam 97, 248n.
Mahieu, Vincent zie Tjalie Robinson
Manuhutu, Wim 116, 250n., 254n.
Manusama, J.A. 175
Marinjo 170, 250n., 252n.
Marugg, Tip 123
Massada 115
Mataheru, Giovanni 116
Máxima, Princess 103, 217
Major, John 199
Meijer, Hans 26, 77-78, 80, 85, 245n.,
    247n.-250n., 252n.-253n., 255n., 260n.
Melatti van Java 229
Metiarij, S. 86
Metselaar, Charles 250n.
Milan Festival 120
Moesson 65, 68, 108, 169, 246n., 250n.,
    252n.-253n., 255n.
Molleman, Henk 245n.
Moluccan Historical Museum 87, 101, 127
Monument Indië Nederland zie Van
    Heutsz-monument
Movimentu Antiano i Arubano pa Promové
    Partisipashon (MAAPP) 65
Mual, M.F. 250n., 255n.
Multatuli 144, 229
Museum Maluku zie Moluks Historisch
    Museum
Mussolini, Benito 209-210, 259n.

Nassau-Siegen, Johan Maurits van 232
Nationaal Monument Kamp Amers-
    foort 249n.
Nationaal Monument Kamp Vught 249n.
Nationaal Monument Westerbork 249n.
Nationale Actie Steunt Spijtoptanten in
    Indonesië (NASSI) 58

National Historical Museum 238, 254n.
National institute for the Study of Dutch
    Slavery and its Legacy (NiNsee) 102, 153,
    228, 260n.
National minorities consultation platform
    (LOM) 42
National Monument on the Dam square 91-
    92, 249n.
National Monument to Dutch Slavery 13,
    148, 151-152, 157
National UNESCO Commission, Dutch 111
Nederlands-Indische Bond van ex-Krijgsgevan-
    genen en -Geïnterneerden (NIBEG) 57, 66,
    78-79
Nee, Victor 243n., 254n.
Netherlands Institute for War Documenta-
    tion (NIOD) 100, 248n.
Netherlands Organisation for Scientific
    Research (NWO) 248n.
Niekerk, Mies van 243n.-244n.
Nieuwe Kerk 260n.-261n.
Nieuwenhuys, Rob 260n.
Nijholt, Willem 261n.
Nora, Pierre 205-206, 259n.

Obama, Barack 261n.
Obdeijn, Herman 43, 244n.
Oedayraj Singh Varma, Tara 68, 70, 246n.
Ons Suriname 61, 98, 181
Onze Stem 79
Oord, Ad van den 249n.
Oostindie, Gert 11-13, 19-21, 151, 248n., 252n.,
    254n.
Oostrom, Frits van 160, 217
Oso 171
Oud-Zuid, Amsterdam Borough of 139
Oudkerk Pool, Lucky 250n.
Overlegorgaan Caraïbische Nederlanders
    (OCaN) 42, 64-65, 182, 246n., 259n.

Paradiso 115
Pasar Malam Besar 57, 91, 107-108, 110-112,
    114, 174, 218
Pattynama, Pamela 74, 247n., 261n.
Paul, Kathleen 257n.
Pelita, foundation 57, 91, 95
Penninx, Rinus 31, 43, 244n.-245n.
Peters, L.A.H. 79
Pétré-Grenouillé, Olivier 205, 259n.
Phillips, Trevor 258n.
Phoa, Khee Liang 68

Pieters, Roy 259n.
Pormes, Sam 70, 246n.
Portes, Samuel 68, 243n.
Pramoedya Ananta Toer 144
Price, Richard 249n., 258n.
Price, Sally 258n.
Prince Claus Fund 151
Princen, Poncke 89
Putnam, Robert 245n.
PvdA 13, 29, 67-69, 79, 246n., 254n., 256n.

Raben, Remco 26, 244n., 247n., 249,
    252n.-253n., 261n.
Ramdas, Anil 120, 236, 261n.
Ramlal, Dowlatram 67, 246n.
Raymann, Jörgen 119
Republik Maluku Selatan (RMS) 28, 53, 115
Resistance Museum 249n.
Ribbens, Kees 249n., 254n.
Rietkerk, Koos 86
Rijksmuseum 231, 238, 252n.
Robinson, Tjalie 32, 48, 91, 93, 101, 104-108,
    110-114, 126, 169, 185, 218, 228, 244n.,
    248n.-250n., 256n., 260n.
Roemer, Astrid 118
Royal Dutch East-Indian Army (KNIL) 28,
    52, 76, 78, 85-86, 88, 92, 114-116, 141, 170,
    243n., 247n.
Royal Netherlands Academy of Arts en
    Sciences (KNAW) 229
Royal Netherlands Institute of Southeast
    Asian and Caribbean Studies
    (KITLV) 229
Ruyter, Michiel de 132

Said, Edward 237
Sansone, Livio 244n., 251n., 257n.
Santi, Usman 67
Sarkozy, Nicolas 195-196, 205, 257n.-258n.
Sarnami Institute 249n.
Sartono Kartodirdjo 253n., 260n.
Saueressig, Poldi 250n.
Scagliola, Stef 89, 248n.
Scheffer, Paul 16, 43, 126-127, 243n.-245n.,
    251n.
Schenk, Joep 249n.
Schilp, Erik 160, 254n.
Schnabel, Paul 243n.
Schrover, Marlou 43, 244n.
Schulte Nordholt, Henk 243n., 246n., 248n.,
    253n., 255n., 260n.

Schumacher, Peter 244n.-245n.
Schuster, John 51, 244n.-245n., 253n.
Scientific Council for Government Policy
    (WRR) 41, 103, 244n., 249n.
Sedney, Jules 179, 256n.
Sen, Amartya 258n.
Seriese, Edy 109, 250n., 260n.
Sharpe, Michael 251n.
Slavery Monument Middelburg 152
Smeets, Henk 26, 87, 116, 244n.-246n.,
    248n.-250n., 253n., 255n.-257n.
Sniderman, Paul M. 245n., 259n., 261n.
Soeharto, Haji Muhammad 260n.
Sophiedela 151
Sorgdrager, Winnie 67
Spencer, Ian 258n.
Sranan Krioro Suriname 151
Statham, Paul 161, 251n.-252n., 255n.-256n.
Steijlen, Fridus 26, 87-88, 116, 175, 243n.-
    251n., 253n.-257n., 260n.
Stichting Herdenking 15 augustus
    1945 249n.
Stichting abc Advies 182
Stichting Eer en Herstel Betalingen
    Slachtoffers van Slavernij in Surina-
    me 151, 252n.
Stichting Japanse Ereschulden 78
Stichting Nederlandse Ereschulden (SNE) 80
Stichting Onderzoek Terugkeer en Opvang
    Oorlogsslachtoffers (SOTO) 83, 248n.
Stichting Viering 400 jaar voc 133-134
Stichting Vriendschap voor de Nederlandse
    Antillen en Aruba 182
Sticusa 231, 261n.
Stipriaan, Alex van 156, 252n.-254n., 260n.
Stokhuyzen, Kick 247n.
Stoové, Erry 95, 249n.
Stora, Benjamin 73-74, 206, 247n., 257n.,
    259n.
Subrahmanyan, Sanjay 133, 252n.
Sukarno, Ahmed 27, 76, 88, 133, 173, 252n.
Surinaams Inspraak Orgaan (SIO) 42, 61
Surinameplein, 30 juni/1 juli herdenk-
    ing 151
Sweet, Elvira 68
Sylvester, Joyce 68
Szekely-Lulofs, Madelon 229

Taubira, Christiane 204-206
Teylersmuseum 261n.
Thandi, Shinder 251n., 258n.

Thatcher, Margaret 199
Thiel, F.J. van 51-52
Thio, May Ling 244n.
Tielman Brothers 110
Tillie, Jean 246n., 251n.
Tjarda van Starkenborgh Stachouwer,
     A.W.L. 92-93
Tong Tong 57, 65, 93, 107-108, 112, 169
Tong Tong Fair 112
Trefassi 118
Tromp, Maarten 132
Tropenmuseum 231, 239

UNESCO 111, 259n.
Union Affairs and Overseas Territories,
     Ministry of 79
Urban and Integration Policy, Ministry
     for 256n.
Uyl, Joop den 54, 98, 256n.

VARA 89
Verdier, Jos 69
Verdonk, Ad 251n.
Verdonk, Rita 127, 156, 254n.
Verenigde Oost-Indische Compagnie
     (VOC) 12-13, 73, 130-135, 143, 148, 157-158, 160,
     225-226, 232, 252n., 259n., 261n.
Verhagen, Maxime 255n.
Verheem, Rudy 81
Verlooghen, Corly 256n.
Vermeulen, Hans 244n., 246n., 251n., 256n.
Verwey-Jonker, H. 30, 244n.
Veterans' Platform 90
Veteranenmonument Roermond 90
Vianen, Bea 118
Volkskrant, de 118, 251n., 256n.
Vollenhoven, Pieter van 182
Vries, Marlene de 113, 152, 250n.
Vrijburg, G.S. 93

Vrije Indische Partij 246n.
Vuijsje, Herman 71, 244n.-246n., 259n.
VVD 10, 67, 91, 246n.

Walraven, Willem 144, 253n.
Wattilete, John 175, 255n.
Wawoe, Gilbert 254n.
Weekkrant Suriname 171, 256n.
Weil, Patrick 206, 257n., 259n.
Wekker, Gloria 236, 261n.
Welfare, Health and culture, Ministry
     of 63
Wesseling, Henk 33, 230, 244n., 260n.
West-Indiër, de 171
West India Company (WIC) 13, 130-132,
     134-135, 145, 153, 225-226, 232, 252n.
Wie Eegie Sanie 61, 117, 176, 181, 186
Wiebenga, Jan Kees 67, 85, 91
Wilders, Geert 10, 127, 217, 251n.
Wilhelmina, Queen 58, 76, 139
Willem I, King 160
Willem III, King 149
Willems, Wim 26, 32, 106-107, 141, 185,
     244n., 246n.-250n., 252n.-254m., 256n.,
     260n.
Willemsen, Glenn 253n.
Winckelman, Frank 252n.
Wit, Augusta de 229
With, Witte de 132
Wittermans, E. 75, 243n., 245n., 247n., 253n.
Witteveen, H.J. 92
Woiski, Max 118
Wolters, Hester 260n.

Young, J.E. 261n.

Zele, Lilian van zie Lilian Ducelle
Zijl, Annejet van der 249n.
Zwarte Piet 119, 251n.